T0333029

Embroidery Stitches

STEP BY STEP

Embroidery Stitches

STEP BY STEP

Lucinda Ganderton

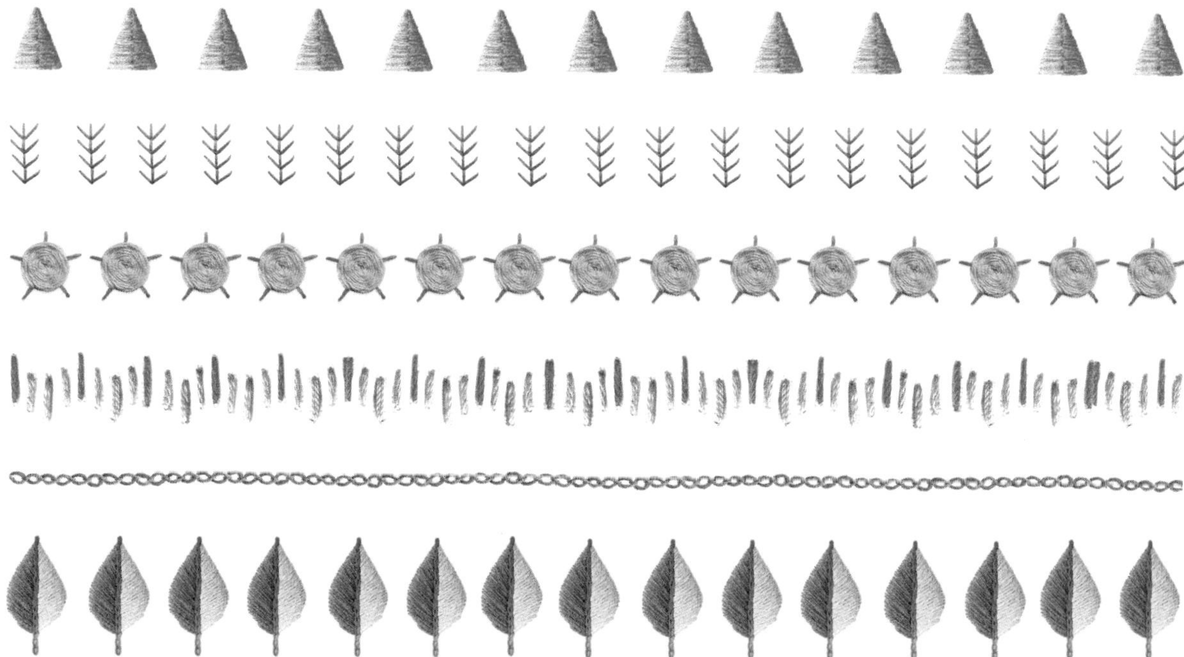

Contents

Introduction

The art of embroidery has been defined simply as "the ornamentation of textiles with decorative stitchery". It is an ancient craft which encompasses a wealth of history, and the same stitches are used throughout the world. They provide an international vocabulary that crosses the boundaries of land and time. Local patterns, design, and ways of working may vary from place to place, but the actual stitch techniques remain the same. The language of stitches is infinitely adaptable. It is being constantly reinterpreted by contemporary textile artists, who produce their new work as part of a continuing tradition.

INTERNATIONAL HERITAGE

Sewing was once an essential part of daily life. Before mass production, clothing and domestic furnishings had to be made at home and embroidery evolved as a means of decorating and personalizing the plain needlework used for household linen and garments. Creative concepts have always been interchanged; patterns and ideas have travelled and developed throughout the world, reflected in names such as Bokhara couching, Antwerp edging, Portuguese border, and Algerian eye.

TYPES OF STITCH

Embroidery stitches are worked on fabric, while needlepoint stitches are sewn onto canvas. The hundreds of individual stitches used for both techniques can be classified into just four groups, according to the way they are constructed: flat stitches, which lie on the surface of the fabric; looped stitches, where one stitch is anchored by another; knotted stitches, in which the thread is twisted back on itself to form a raised stitch; and openwork stitches, which create a regular pattern of spaces, integrating the thread with the background fabric.

Floral border
Long decorative bands, like this Victorian tent stitch pattern of flowers and berries in bright Berlin wools, were used to adorn soft furnishings and accessories.

USING STITCHES

The various stitches within these four groups are endlessly adaptable and can be used in many ways, depending on the effect required. They can outline a design or fill in a shape, be repeated in rows, used singly, or stitched in a solid line.

Certain techniques have developed for practical reasons. Gold thread is costly and too fragile to pass through fabric, so couching is used to anchor it down with small tie stitches in fine thread. Turkey stitch evolved in imitation of a rug's cut pile, and insertion stitches as a means of joining two pieces of fabric. One single stitch may be repeated throughout a piece of work. Rows of tent and cross stitches are used to create both samplers and embroidered pictures, while straight stitch can be used randomly to build up a textured, three-dimensional surface. It is when the patterns and shapes of the various stitches are combined, however, that their full potential is realized.

STITCH NAMES

For many centuries, knowledge of embroidery stitches was handed down as part of a wider folk tradition. It was not until 1631, with the publication of *The Needle's Excellency*, that their names were first recorded. This was a book of patterns, not a practical manual, and there were no working diagrams or stitch illustrations. Many of the stitches listed – Fern-stitch, Chain-stitch, Back-stitch, and The Crosse-stitch – are still familiar. Various other names were adopted over time. Some described the way in which the actual stitches were made; for example, twisted insertion and back stitch trellis. Cushion, ladder, window, and rope were named after the objects of daily life that they resembled, while others were inspired by the surroundings of the natural world: star, wave, cloud, feather, coral, leaf, petal, and wheatear.

Needlework was not valued as a separate area of academic study until the late 19th century. Under the influence of the Arts and Crafts Movement, designers interested in the evolution of stitching set about examining and unpicking old embroidered textiles to discover how they had been worked. New historical texts and instruction books were written, and the format and names of stitches were standardized for the first time.

Portrait of a lady
Fine silk threads in a subtle range of natural dyes were used to embroider this 18th century picture. Layers of straight stitches have been worked in many directions to build up the image.

Country garden
This characteristic transfer design from the 1930s features plants worked with French knots, link, fly, and buttonhole stitches, and outlines in stem stitch.

Inspiration from nature
Animals, birds, and insects jostle for space amongst flowers and foliage in this vibrant Tenango embroidery from Mexico, which is worked in a variation of herringbone stitch.

Blue and white
Japanese Sashiko, which translates as "little stabs" in reference to the simple straight stitches that make up its intricate geometric patterns, is traditionally worked in a matte cotton thread on a background of indigo linen.

CURRENT TRENDS

Recent years have seen a new appreciation for all aspects of fibre art, especially embroidery and needlepoint. The simple physical process of hand sewing is now recognized as promoting a sense of inner calmness, in addition to being creatively fulfilling, as stitchers work completely in the moment when concentrating on needle and thread. Intricate techniques including silk shading, laid gold threadwork, and monogramming have been rediscovered and revived, alongside innovative new ideas like sewing over printed images, stitching with fine wire, and playing with scale to make oversized stitches, all of which challenge convention.

MINDFUL STITCHING

The slow stitching movement, meanwhile, focuses on the meditative nature of making repeated rows of basic stitches instead of creating a pictorial image, and takes its inspiration from Japanese boro and sashiko techniques. Like all patchwork and quilting, these were originally thrift crafts, born of necessity when threads and fabric were scarce. There is a current shift back to this mindset, and embellishing, upcycling, and darning old or worn garments is once again popular as part of a wider textile craft movement

Contour quilting
Spirals and concentric rows of running stitches, alongside finely embroidered motifs, give a three-dimensional texture to this 19th-Century Indian Kantha cloth.

Mirror, mirror
Shisha stitch, using tiny mirrors, highlights the traditional chain stitch design of a contemporary Indian embroidery in silk rayon.

HOW TO USE THIS BOOK

The book is divided into six chapters. The first one covers the equipment, threads, and fabrics used for stitchery, and the various techniques involved. This is followed by the Gallery of Stitches on pp.22–35, which provides a photographic overview of all 234 stitches, including Stitch Variations, listed in the order in which they appear.

The step-by-step instructions are grouped into four chapters – Lines and Borders, Filling Stitches, Openwork, and Needlepoint – each of which has several sub-sections showing the different types of stitches within the category.

STITCH INSTRUCTIONS

The individual step-by-step instructions include notes on the skill level, usage, and construction method for each stitch, along with information about the type of needle, thread, fabric, and any other equipment needed to create it. The Technique Variations, meanwhile, suggest different ways of working the stitch or an alternative colour scheme.

The embroidery and openwork instructions on pp.39–115 are annotated with letters which show you the points at which the needle enters and exits the fabric, in alphabetical order. For needlepoint stitches, which appear from p.119 onwards, the instructions feature a grid system, which indicates the position of every hole on the canvas. The horizontal rows are labelled with numbers down one side and the vertical rows with letters across the top or bottom edge. The start and end points for each stitch are given as a number (from the horizontal row) followed by a letter (from the vertical row), e.g. 4A to 1A.

Materials, Tools, and Techniques

Tools, Fabrics, Threads, and Frames

The basic equipment required for embroidery is minimal; as with many other sewing crafts, all that you really need is a needle, a length of thread, a piece of cloth and a pair of scissors. Much time and skill goes into creating a finished piece of needlework, so the choice of materials at the outset is important. To achieve a professional and long-lasting result it is worth investing in the best quality tools, threads, and fabric.

SEWING KIT

You will need two pairs of sharp scissors: large shears for fabric and pointed embroidery scissors for thread. Use a thread unpicker to take out unwanted stitches and remove tacking. A needle threader and a thimble will prove helpful, along with a ruler and tape measure. Store your pins in a pincushion and needles in a needle book.

MARKING TOOLS

Chalk pencils or heat-erasable and washable marker pens are ideal for tracing a design onto fabric via a light box. Use an iron-on pencil to transfer a pattern from paper or trace it over a sheet of dressmaker's carbon. For detailed designs, print or draw directly onto water-soluble stabilizer, then fix it to the fabric and mount in a frame or hoop.

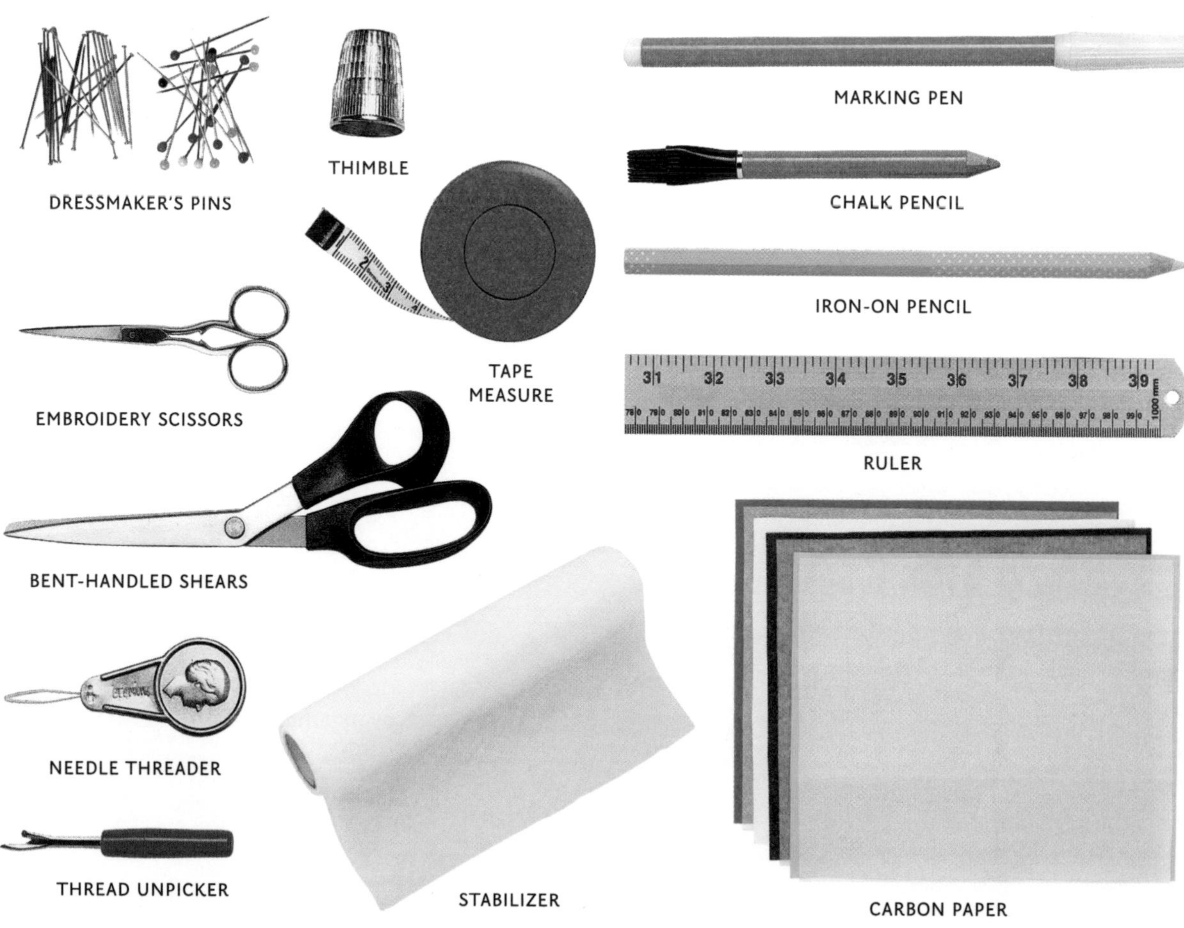
DRESSMAKER'S PINS
THIMBLE
TAPE MEASURE
EMBROIDERY SCISSORS
BENT-HANDLED SHEARS
NEEDLE THREADER
THREAD UNPICKER
STABILIZER
MARKING PEN
CHALK PENCIL
IRON-ON PENCIL
RULER
CARBON PAPER

FABRIC AND CANVAS

Stitches can be worked onto any fabric, but there is a wide range designed especially for embroidery. Woven from cotton or linen, they all have a square mesh that produces regular, even stitches. This is gauged by the count or number of threads to every 2.5cm (1in): the more threads, the finer the fabric. Use soft, single thread evenweave for counted thread, pulled fabric, and drawn thread work; double thread (Aida, Binca, or Hardanger) for geometric patterns and cross stitch, and canvas for needlepoint.

Canvas
Both single and double weaves come in a variety of counts, as does rigid plastic.

SINGLE CANVAS (INTERLOCK)

SINGLE CANVAS (MONO WEAVE)

PLASTIC CANVAS

DOUBLE CANVAS

Evenweave fabric
Manufactured in gauges from 8- to 36-count, this is available in many colours and textures.

HARDANGER FABRIC

SINGLE THREAD EVENWEAVE

BINCA

AIDA CLOTH

Plain and non-woven fabric
Decorative silk, felt, cotton stripes, and checks are all used for freestyle stitching.

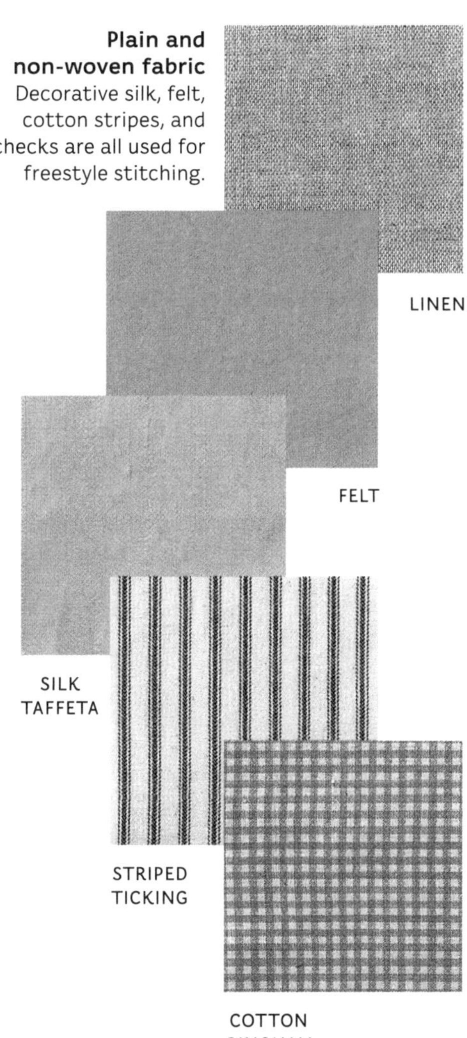

LINEN

FELT

SILK TAFFETA

STRIPED TICKING

COTTON GINGHAM

Woven bands
Narrow strips of fabric with decorative woven edges such as this natural linen band, are available in various widths.

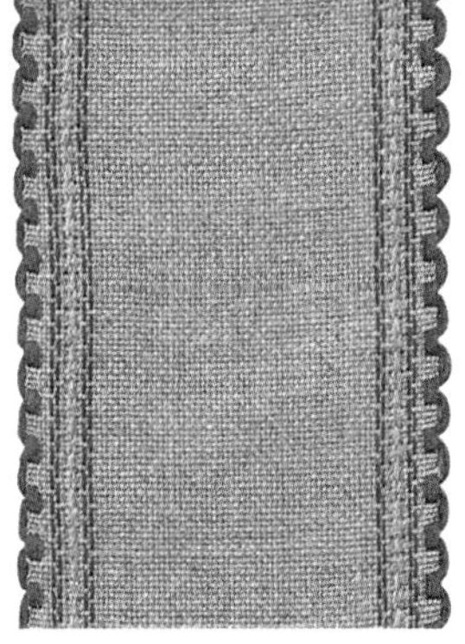

THREADS

Embroidery threads come in myriad colours and a broad spectrum of textures and weights. The thickness of the thread dictates the size and shape of the stitch, which will have a very different appearance if worked in a fine matt yarn or a lustrous pearl cotton. Certain wools and threads are spun in a single strand, whilst others consist of up to six individual strands or plys which are loosely twisted together. These can be separated out and re-combined, depending on the line width required: use strands of two or more colours to create subtle shaded effects. Manufacturer's sample books and shade cards show the full range of different threads that are available and can be a good source of inspiration when planning a new project.

SOFT COTTON

SILK RAYON

STRANDED COTTON

SILK RIBBON

SILK THREAD

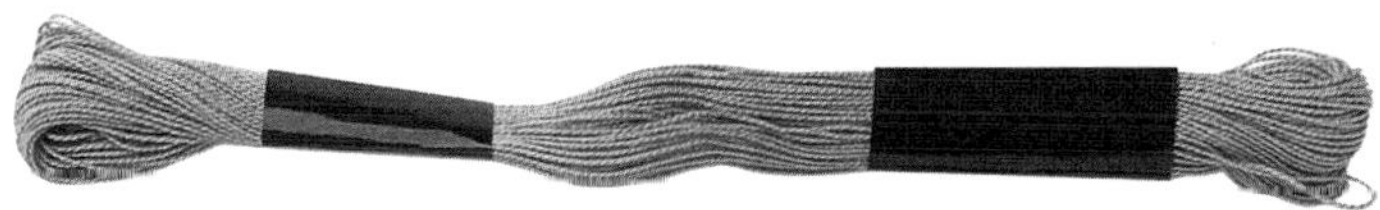
PEARL COTTON

SILK THREAD

FLOWER THREAD

Silks and cottons

Silks and cottons are made in both single and stranded skeins. Silk, rayon, and twisted pearl cotton all have a high sheen, whilst mercerized 6-ply stranded cotton gives a smooth finish. Use fine flower thread or the thicker soft cotton for a more matt appearance. Metallic threads add texture, and silk ribbon is used for embroidering naturalistic flowers.

METALLIC THREAD

STRANDED SILK

TAPESTRY WOOL

PERSIAN WOOL

Wools

The thickest wool is 4-ply tapestry, used on 10- to 14-count canvas. Use several strands of fine 2-ply crewel on canvas or a single strand on fabric. Persian has three easily separated medium-weight strands: use two or three for needlepoint and one to stitch on fabric.

CREWEL WOOL

NEEDLES

There are five different kinds of needle used for decorative stitching, each with a particular purpose. All come in a range of thicknesses and lengths, so select one that can be threaded easily and that passes smoothly through the fabric without snagging the thread.

TYPES OF NEEDLE

Chenille needles have long eyes and sharp points, designed for working on heavy plainweave fabrics with thick threads. Tapestry needles are similar but with blunt tips. Choose them for evenweave or canvas, interlacing and openwork. Versatile crewel needles are used for most embroidery stitches. They are long with easily-threaded eyes which take up to six strands. Small-eyed sharps are mainly for hand-sewing but, like betweens, they are good for fine stitching and French knots.

PREPARING THE THREAD

It is easy to unwind thread from a reel, but take care when working with yarn or cotton that comes in individual skeins. Twisted skeins have to be undone before use, but the paper bands should not be removed from looped skeins or they will tangle. To prevent the thread fraying as it passes repeatedly through the fabric, cut off a working length of no more than 50cm (20in). Use a needle threader with fine cotton and silk, or the loop method (see below) for stranded and pearl cottons, or wool.

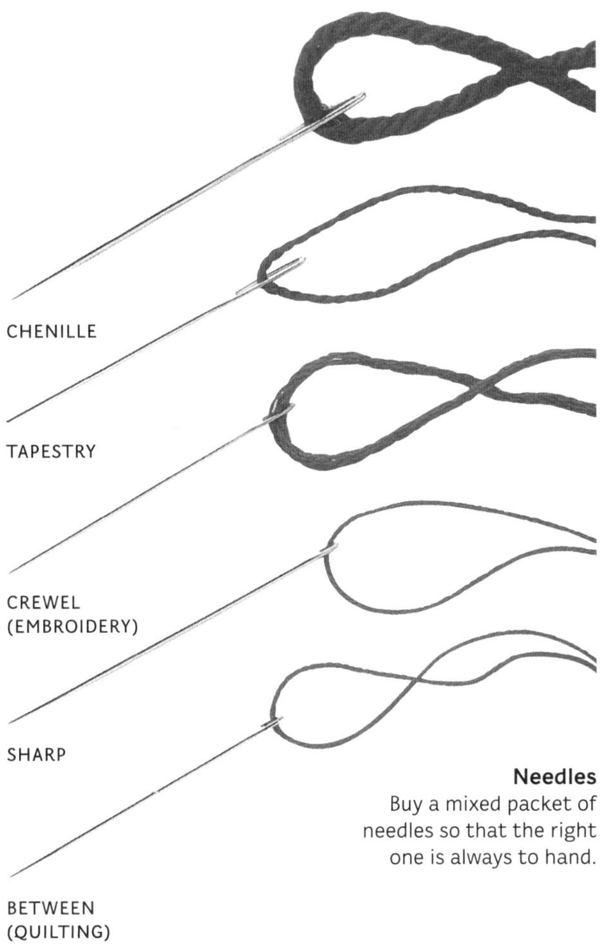
CHENILLE
TAPESTRY
CREWEL
(EMBROIDERY)
SHARP
BETWEEN
(QUILTING)

Needles
Buy a mixed packet of needles so that the right one is always to hand.

Keep slip knot loose

Untying a twisted skein
Remove the paper bands. Untwist the skein and cut through the threads, then tie them together with a loose slip knot.

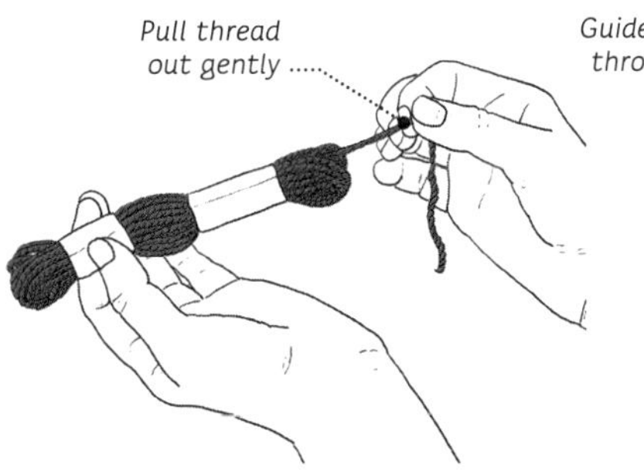
Pull thread out gently

Using a looped skein
Leave the bands in place. Hold the top of the skein firmly and draw out the loose thread at the bottom end to the required length.

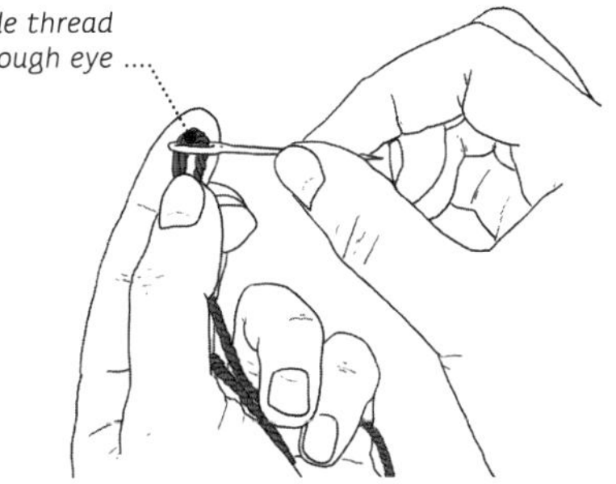
Guide thread through eye

Threading a needle
Fold thread over needle and hold between finger and thumb. Slide the needle out, then push the eye down over the loop.

FRAMES

Smaller pieces, garments, and some needlepoint can be stitched in the hand, but working on a frame will always give the best result. It maintains fabric at an even tension and holds the grain straight, keeping the stitches even and protecting the work by reducing the amount of handling it undergoes. The choice of frame depends on both the size of a project and the background fabric, but is very often a personal preference. There are three types: fixed stretchers and adjustable scroll frames, which are used for all types of fabric and canvas, and wooden hoops for cotton and linen. All are available with stand attachments which free up both hands for stitching.

SQUARE AND RECTANGULAR FRAMES

These can be used for canvas or embroidery fabric. Stretcher frames are sold as two pairs of struts which can be chosen and assembled to fit a particular piece of work. Scroll frames come in several widths, depending on the roller length.

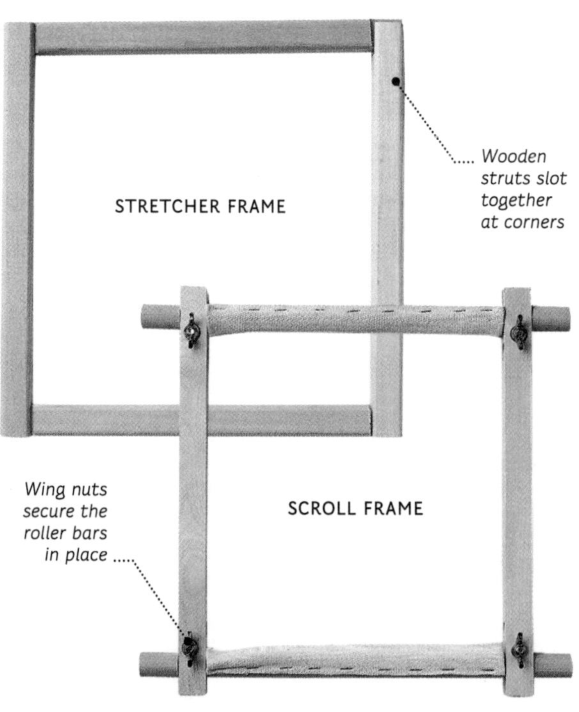
Wooden struts slot together at corners
STRETCHER FRAME
Wing nuts secure the roller bars in place
SCROLL FRAME

ROUND FRAMES

Wooden hoops range in diameter from 8 to 40cm (3¹/₈ to 15¾in). They are light, portable, and easily held in one hand. Ideally a hoop should be large enough to contain the whole design, but if this is not possible, remove the fabric at the end of each sewing session to protect the stitches.

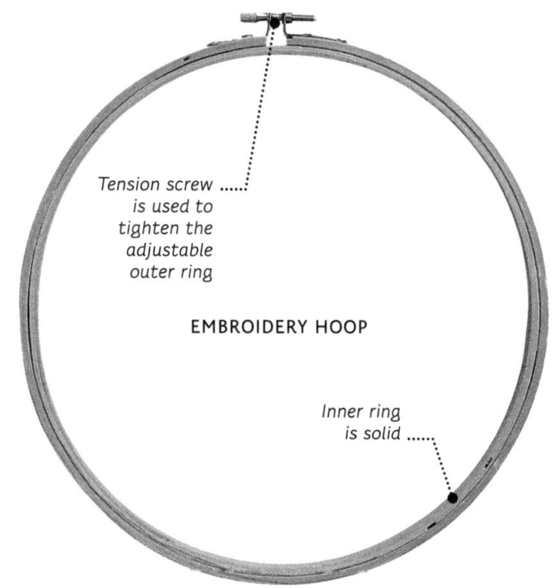
Tension screw is used to tighten the adjustable outer ring
EMBROIDERY HOOP
Inner ring is solid

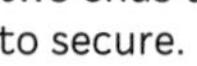

Preparing the inner ring

To prevent delicate fabrics from becoming damaged and to stop them slipping within the hoop, bind the inner ring tightly with narrow cotton tape or bias binding. Stitch the two ends together to secure.

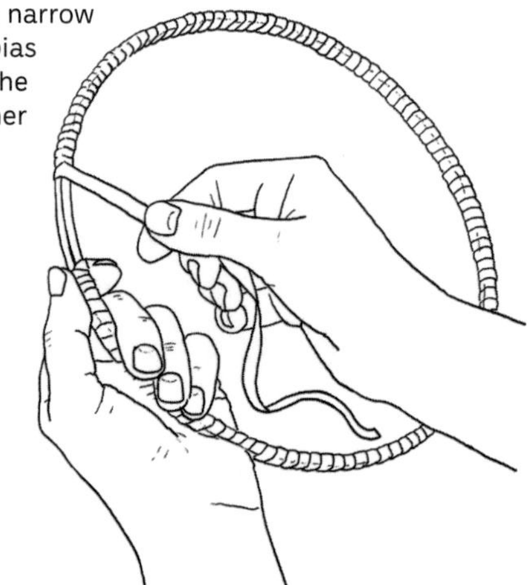

Mounting Techniques

Prepare the fabric by neatening the raw edges to prevent any fraying or snagging: hem linen and cotton, or bind canvas with masking tape. Press lightly, then fold into quarters and tack along each crease with a contrasting thread, following the weave. Keep these two lines straight to make sure that the grain doesn't distort when stretched. A tear-off stabilizer at the back adds extra support to finer fabrics.

USING AN EMBROIDERY HOOP

The fabric should be at least 8cm (3⅛in) larger all round than the diameter of the hoop. Loosen the screw and separate the rings.

Mounting the fabric
Centre the fabric over the inner ring, then push the outer ring in place. Gently pull the edges of the fabric until it is taut and tighten the screw.

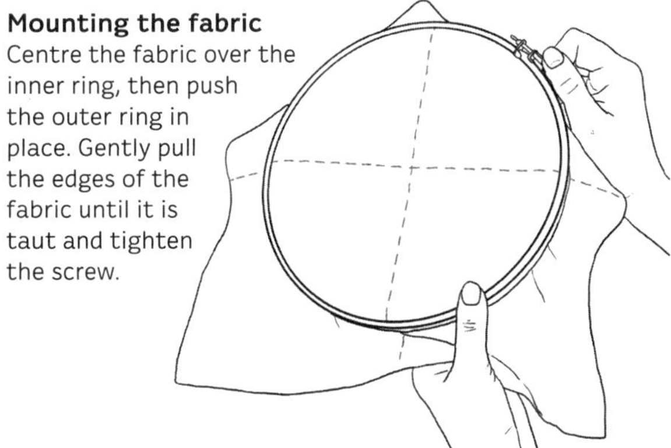

PREPARING A STRETCHER FRAME

The neatened fabric or canvas should be the same size as the frame. Use drawing pins or a staple gun to fix the fabric in place.

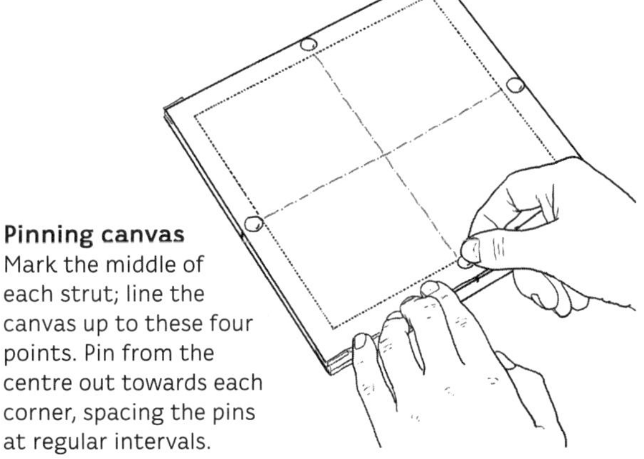

Pinning canvas
Mark the middle of each strut; line the canvas up to these four points. Pin from the centre out towards each corner, spacing the pins at regular intervals.

SETTING UP A SCROLL FRAME

Cut the fabric or canvas to the same width as the webbing. If it is longer than the struts, any surplus can be wrapped round the bottom roller and adjusted as work progresses.

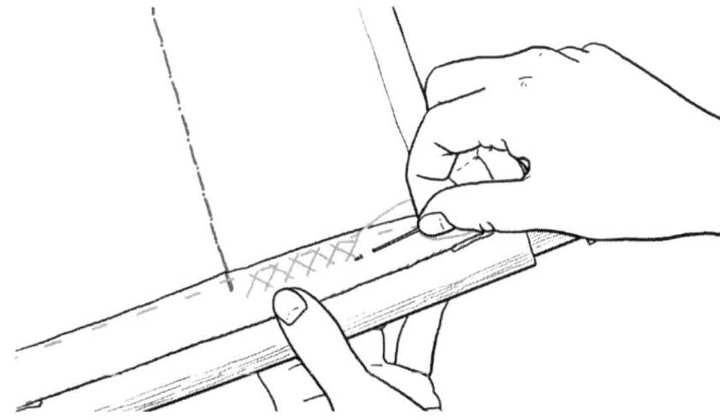

1 Neaten the side edges. Match the midpoints of the canvas and webbing, then tack together. Sewing outwards from the centre, work herringbone stitch (see p.52) over the join.

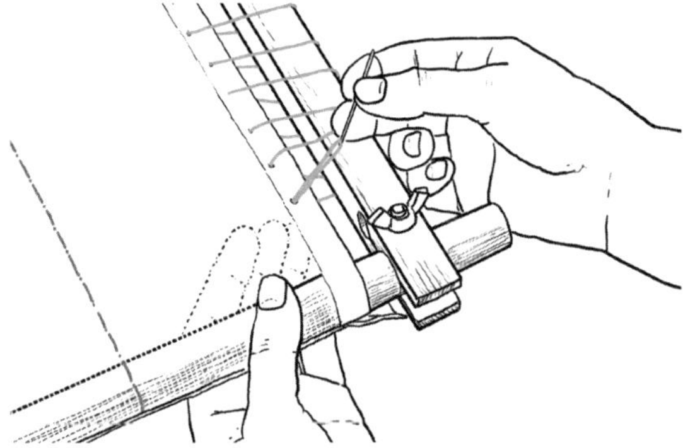

2 Slot the rollers into the spaces in the struts. Tighten the two top screws, then turn the bottom roller to stretch the fabric. Secure the other screws, then lace the fabric tightly over the edges using thin string and a tapestry needle.

Stitching Techniques

The key to a perfect finish for any piece of needlework is to keep the stitch length regular and to maintain an even tension throughout, whether or not the fabric is mounted on a frame. Take time to sew a small sample piece before embarking on any new project, to become familiar with the stitches and to establish a rhythmic pattern of working. Embroidery stitches are constructed either vertically, usually from top to bottom, or horizontally towards the left or right, although they may appear at any angle in the finished piece. Needlepoint fillings, which form all-over patterns, are worked in diagonal, horizontal, or vertical rows.

BEGINNING TO STITCH

Follow one of the two techniques shown below to start off or to join a new length of thread. Both will help to ensure that the reverse side of the stitching is as neat as the front.

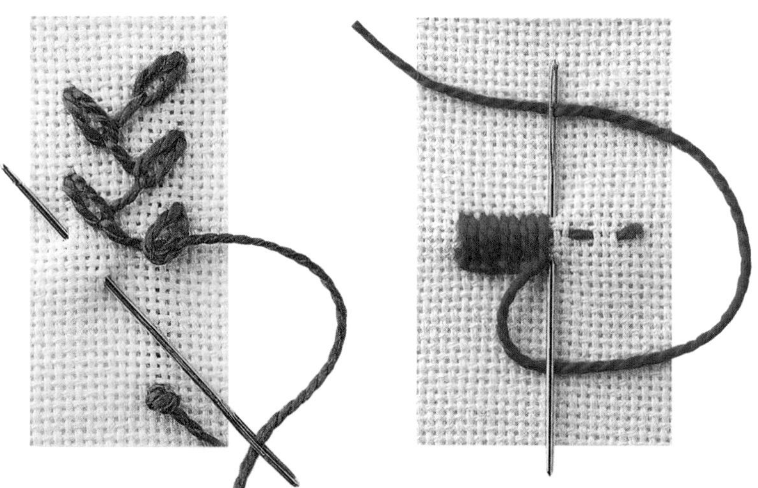

Lost knot method
Use this for needlepoint and open embroidery stitches. Knot one end of the thread and insert the needle from the front, 2–3cm (¾–1¼in) behind your start point. As the stitches progress, the end of the thread will be held down at the back. Cut off the knot.

Running stitch method
This is ideal for closely-spaced stitches and needlepoint. Leaving a loose tail of thread at the back, sew a few small running stitches along the stitch line, then work back over them. The end is darned through the reverse of the stitches.

FASTENING OFF

Finish a thread when there is about 10cm (4in) left, or before it gets worn. Try not to end too many threads in the same area as this can create an uneven surface, especially in needlepoint.

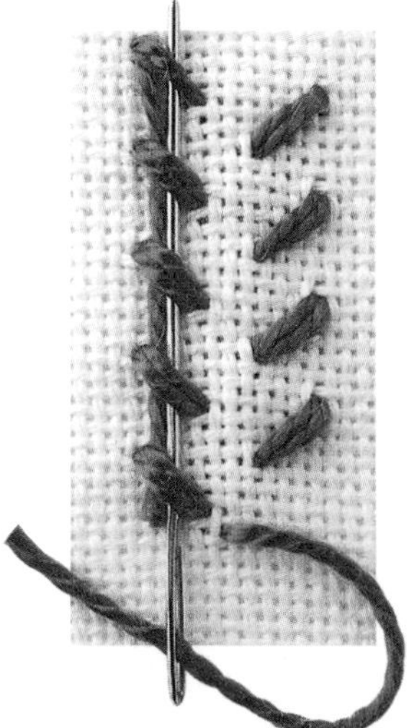

Securing the thread
Take the needle through to the wrong side of the fabric and turn the work over. Pass the needle under the loops at the back of the final few stitches for a distance of about 2.5cm (1in), then clip the end of the thread close to the fabric surface.

WAYS OF WORKING

Holding fabric in the hand is a familiar sewing technique, and is the best way to stitch on to finished garments. Stabilize the back of knitted and delicate fabrics with a tear-off interfacing to keep the stitches even. Some embroidery stitches, especially looped ones, can be worked like this.

EMBROIDERING IN THE HAND

Support the area being worked over the forefinger. Hold the needle in the other hand and slide it in and out in a single movement.

Looped stitches
Loop the thread from one side to the other and use the free thumb to hold it down. Pull the needle through over the working thread.

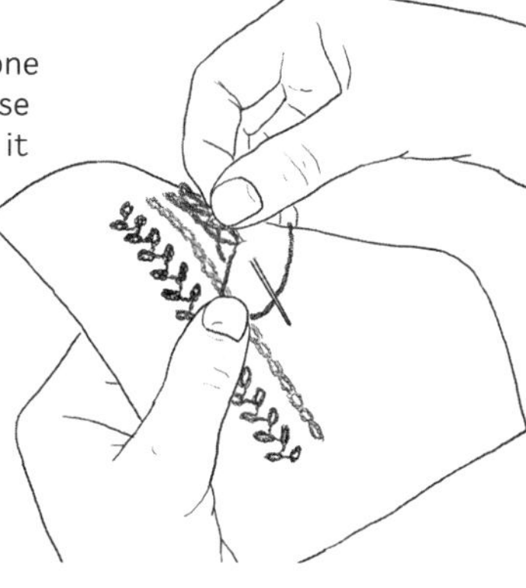

USING BOTH HANDS

A free-standing frame may seem awkward to begin with but, with a little practice, working with one hand on each side of the fabric can prove the quickest way to stitch.

Stabbing technique
Push the needle down into the fabric from the top and pull it through from below. Pass it back up with this hand, and draw it through from above.

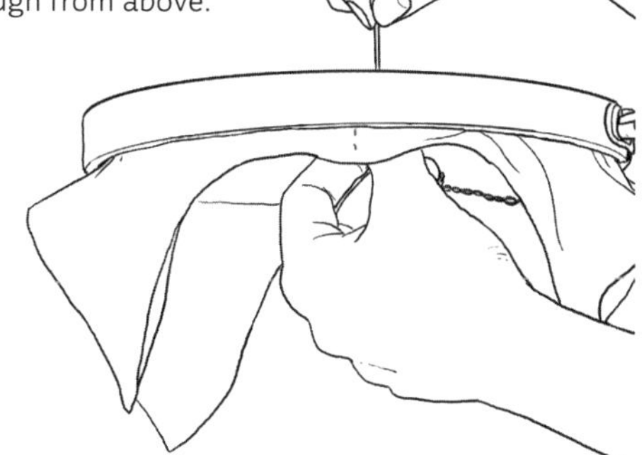

COUNTED THREAD AND FREESTYLE

Embroidery stitches can be worked on either evenweave or plainweave. Space stitches evenly by counting the visible threads on evenweave, and mark guidelines on other fabrics to keep freestyle stitching regular.

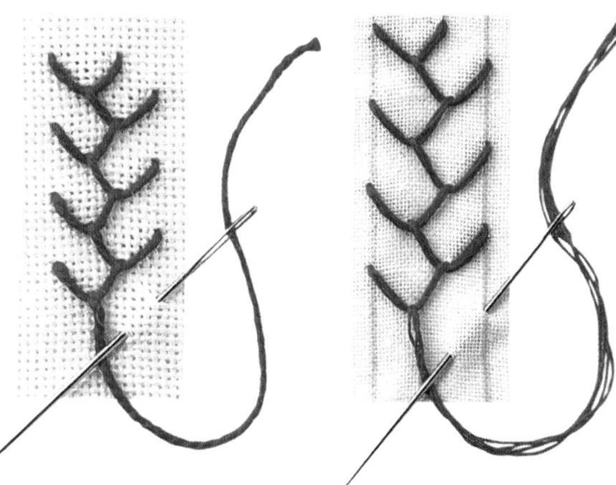

Evenweave fabric
Make each stitch over the same number of threads or thread intersections.

Plainweave fabric
Draw temporary parallel guidelines onto the fabric with an erasable marker pen.

WORKING NEEDLEPOINT STITCHES

Stitches on canvas are worked into the square holes between the woven threads. To avoid splitting the stitches, always bring the needle up through an unworked hole and take it back down into a worked one. Use a frame for diagonal needlepoint stitches to minimize distortion.

Needlepoint fillings
Start each stitch from the unworked side and insert the needle at the base of the previous stitch. When filling in a shape, count the intersections carefully and make short stitches to square off the edges.

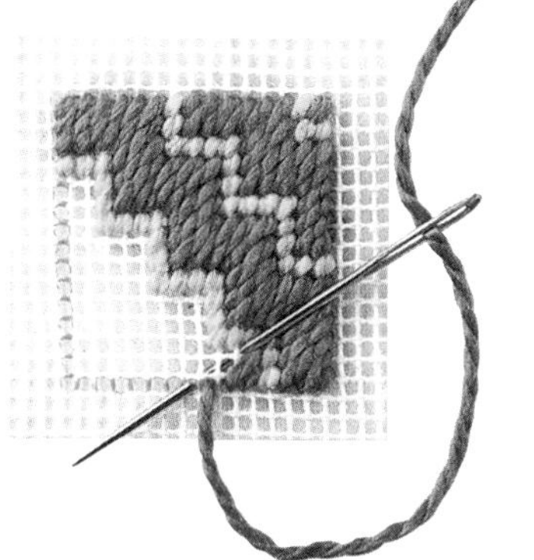

FILLING STITCHES

Embroidered fillings are worked within a defined area, so sometimes the length of the individual stitches has to be altered to fill the shape. For open and solid fillings, this means you will work different length stitches to fit within a curved outline, like a leaf or petal. Powdered fillings are sewn singly in rows or randomly.

Open and solid fillings

Start a leaf at the top with a short straight stitch to fill in the point, then work downwards, first increasing, then reducing the length of the stitches. Insert the needle just beyond the edge of the shape so the stitches hide the line.

Powdered fillings

Work a fine outline stitch over the guideline to define the motif, then fill the shape with individual stitches. These can be scattered randomly or arranged in a regular pattern.

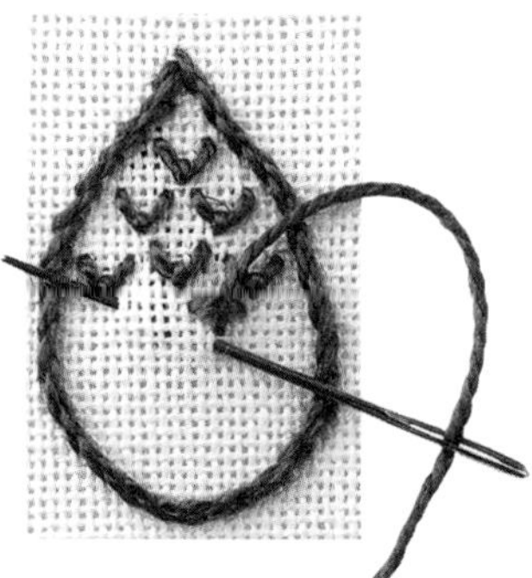

TIE STITCHES

These short stitches are used to anchor looped stitches such as chain stitch, in couching, and to bunch together groups of straight stitches.

Making a tie stitch

Bring the needle up above the long stitch or inside the loop and insert it just below the thread.

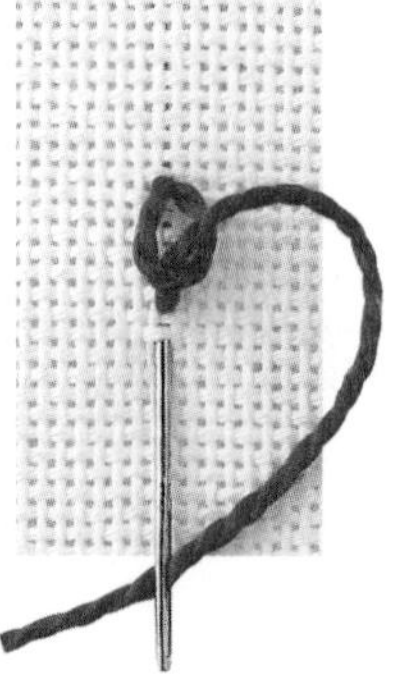

WORKING OPENWORK STITCHES

In all types of openwork the background fabric is as important as the stitches themselves, and forms an integral part of the finished piece. It has to be carefully prepared for drawn thread work and for insertion stitches.

DRAWN THREAD STITCHES

The open spaces that give drawn thread work its characteristic lacy appearance are formed by removing some of the woven threads that make up the fabric.

Pulling out the threads

Evenweave cotton or linen are the best fabrics to work with. Use the point of a needle to lift up the threads and pull out enough to make an open band or bands of the required width.

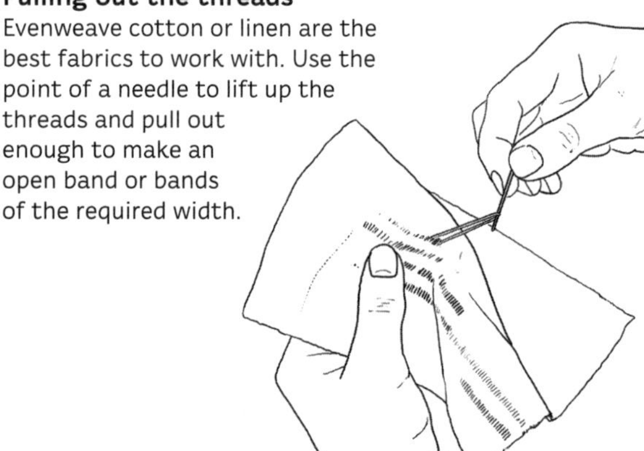

INSERTION STITCHES

To ensure that the space between the two hems remains constant and the stitches are worked regularly, the fabric being joined has to be stitched onto paper before starting.

Mounting the fabric

Stitch a narrow hem along each long edge. Draw two parallel lines, 6mm (¼in) apart onto a strip of heavy paper. With the right sides facing, tack one piece of fabric along each line.

FINISHING OFF

When the final stitches have been completed, take the work off the frame. Press embroidery lightly on the wrong side, cushioned by a clean cloth.

BLOCKING

A piece of needlepoint which incorporates diagonal stitches will inevitably become pulled out of shape as it is worked. Any distortion can be remedied by blocking the canvas.

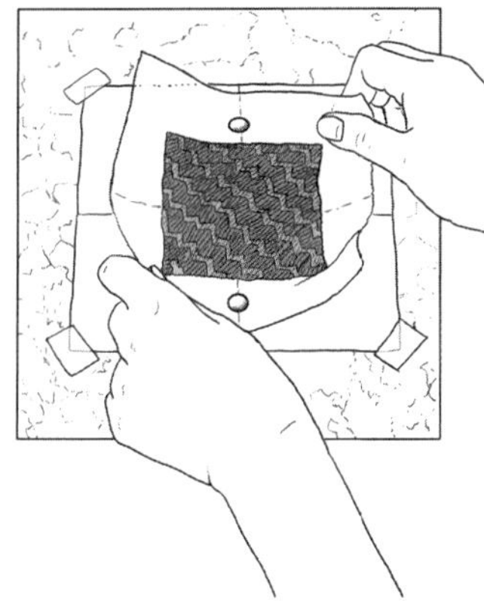

How to block
Make a template of the finished piece and mark into quarters. Tape to a board and cover with polythene. Place the dampened work face down. Match the centre top edge to the template and pin. Stretch and pin the bottom edge and two sides. Insert more pins at 2.5cm (1in) intervals. Allow to dry.

MOUNTING

If a project is to be framed it should first be mounted onto acid-free board to keep it in shape, whether it is worked on fabric or canvas.

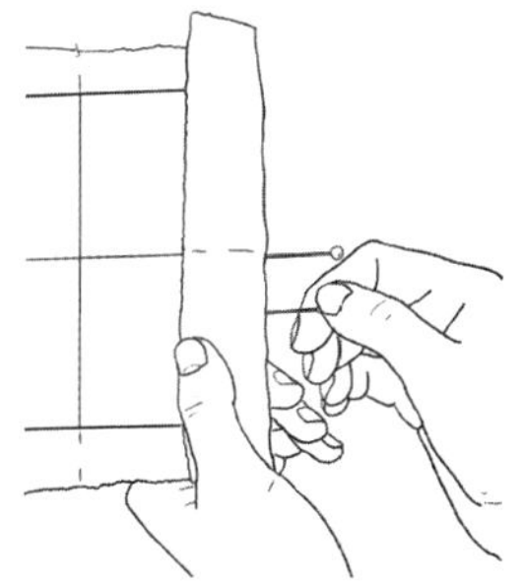

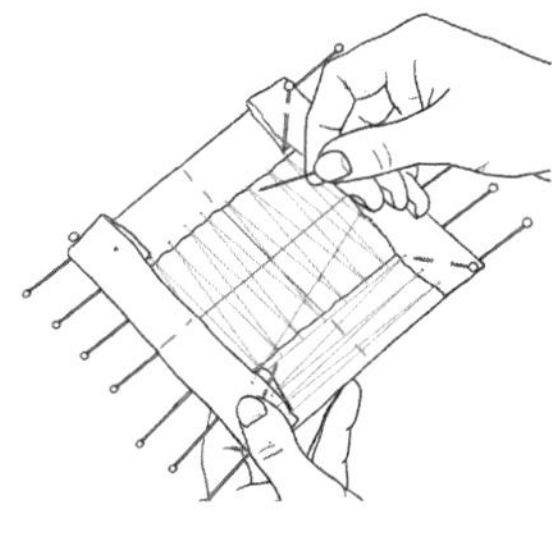

1 Cut the board to size and mark into quarters. Centre it on the wrong side of the fabric and fold back long edges. Pin them to the card from the centre out.

2 Using strong thread, lace the edges together. Do the same with the other two sides. Check the fabric is centred, then tighten up and secure the threads.

DISPLAY HOOPS

An embroidery hoop provides a ready-made frame for a completed project. Use a wooden or bamboo hoop with an adjustable screw, or a clip-together flexible circle or oval frame produced specially for display, which comes complete with a metal hanger.

PREPARATION

To make the backing, draw round the inside of the inner ring onto toning felt and cut out. Slipping a piece of white felt (the same size as the background fabric) under the embroidery before mounting will add a smooth, padded look.

HOW TO FINISH A HOOP

1 Trim the fabric back to a 3cm (1¼in) margin all round. Leaving a tail at the start, use a strong thread to work a line of long running stitches 1cm (½in) from the trimmed edge, then remove the needle.

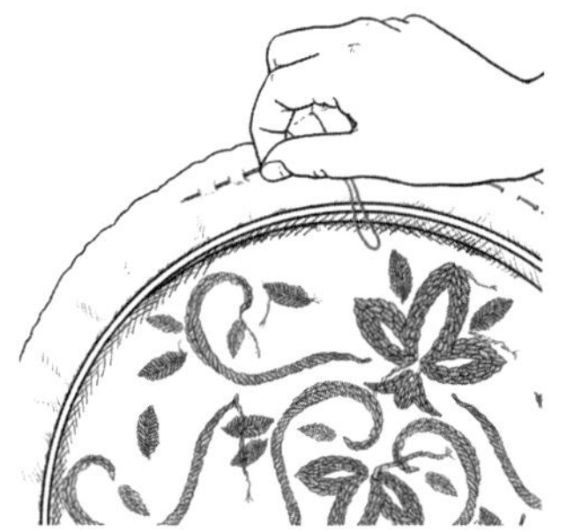

2 Draw both ends of the thread up tightly to gather the fabric and tie them together with a secure knot.

3 Pin the backing felt in place and sew the outside edge to the gathers. A strip of felt or ribbon can be added at this stage to make a hidden hanger.

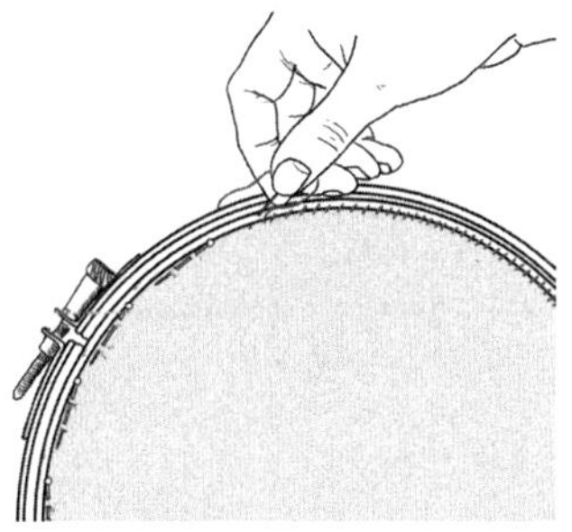

Gallery of Stitches

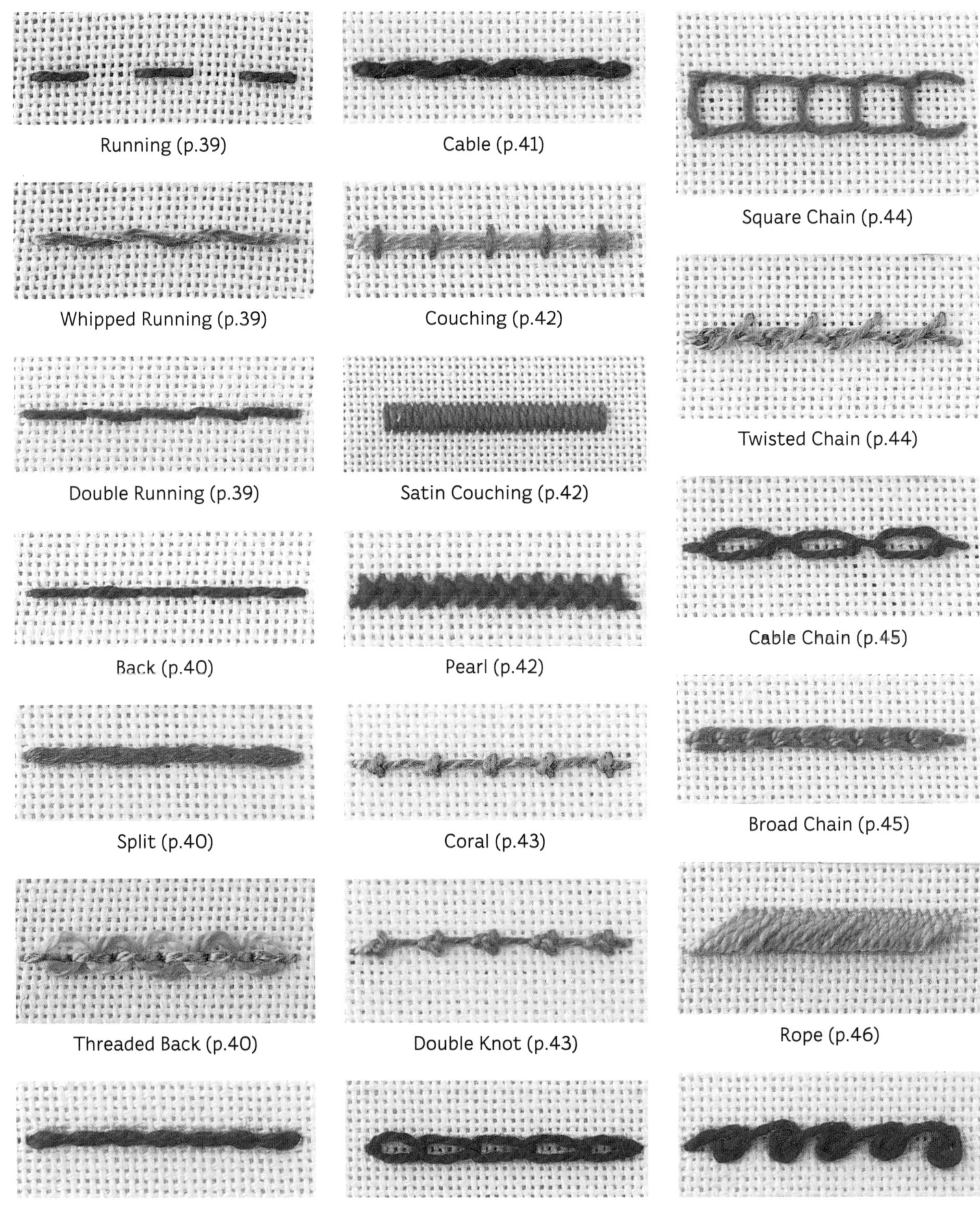

Running (p.39)

Whipped Running (p.39)

Double Running (p.39)

Back (p.40)

Split (p.40)

Threaded Back (p.40)

Stem (p.41)

Cable (p.41)

Couching (p.42)

Satin Couching (p.42)

Pearl (p.42)

Coral (p.43)

Double Knot (p.43)

Chain (p.44)

Square Chain (p.44)

Twisted Chain (p.44)

Cable Chain (p.45)

Broad Chain (p.45)

Rope (p.46)

Scroll (p.46)

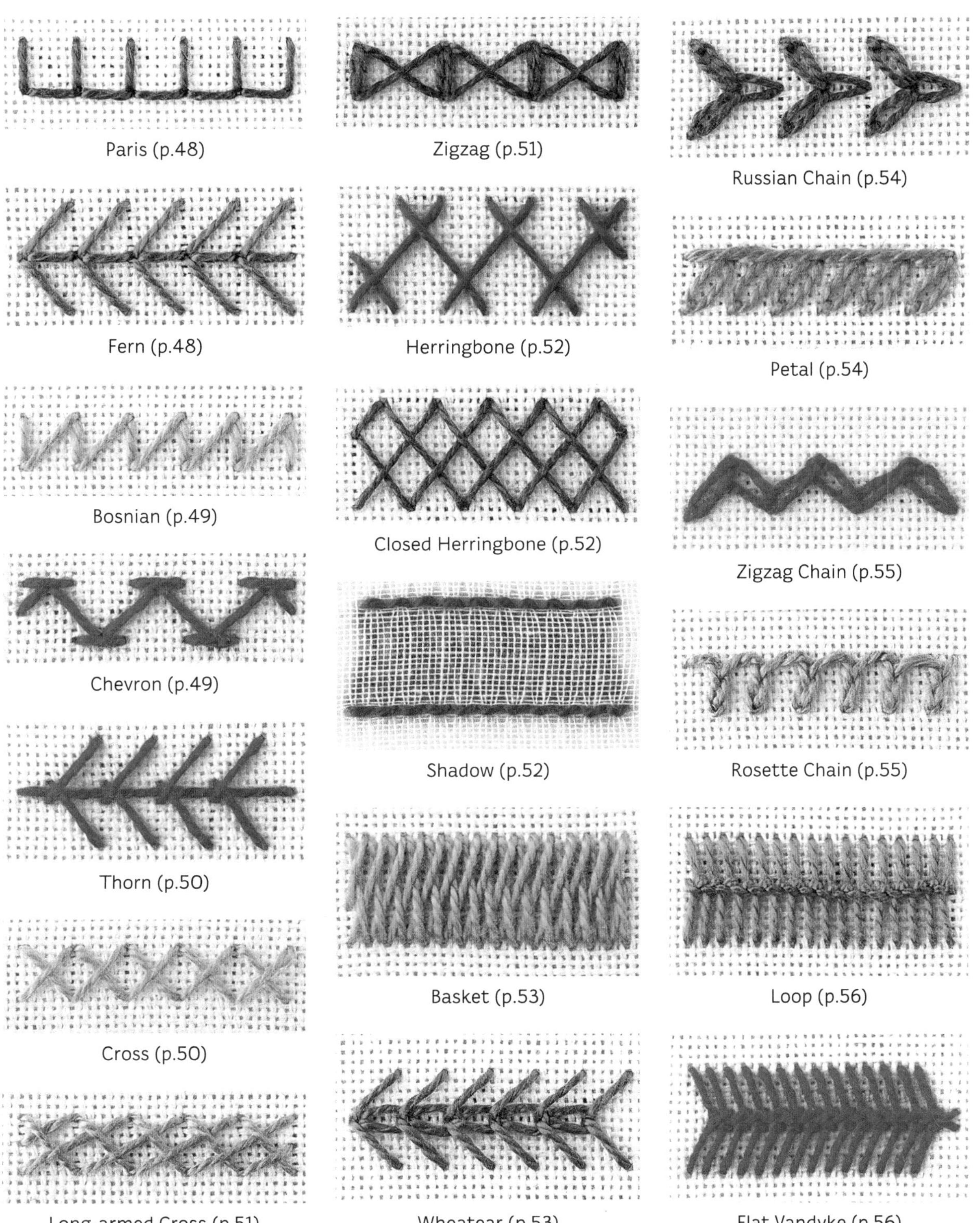

Paris (p.48)

Fern (p.48)

Bosnian (p.49)

Chevron (p.49)

Thorn (p.50)

Cross (p.50)

Long-armed Cross (p.51)

Zigzag (p.51)

Herringbone (p.52)

Closed Herringbone (p.52)

Shadow (p.52)

Basket (p.53)

Wheatear (p.53)

Russian Chain (p.54)

Petal (p.54)

Zigzag Chain (p.55)

Rosette Chain (p.55)

Loop (p.56)

Flat Vandyke (p.56)

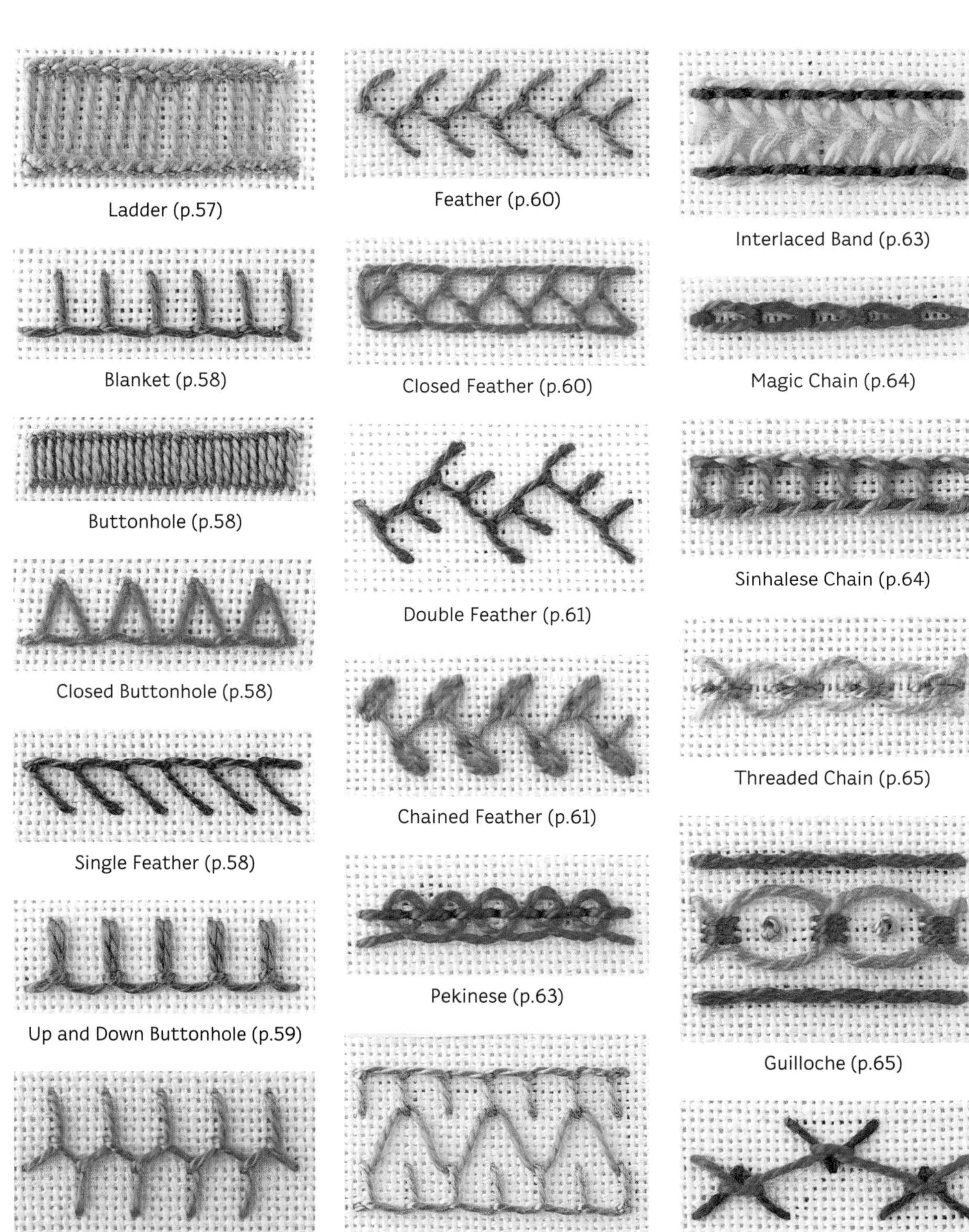

Ladder (p.57)

Blanket (p.58)

Buttonhole (p.58)

Closed Buttonhole (p.58)

Single Feather (p.58)

Up and Down Buttonhole (p.59)

Open Cretan (p.59)

Feather (p.60)

Closed Feather (p.60)

Double Feather (p.61)

Chained Feather (p.61)

Pekinese (p.63)

Laced Buttonhole (p.63)

Interlaced Band (p.63)

Magic Chain (p.64)

Sinhalese Chain (p.64)

Threaded Chain (p.65)

Guilloche (p.65)

Raised Chevron (p.66)

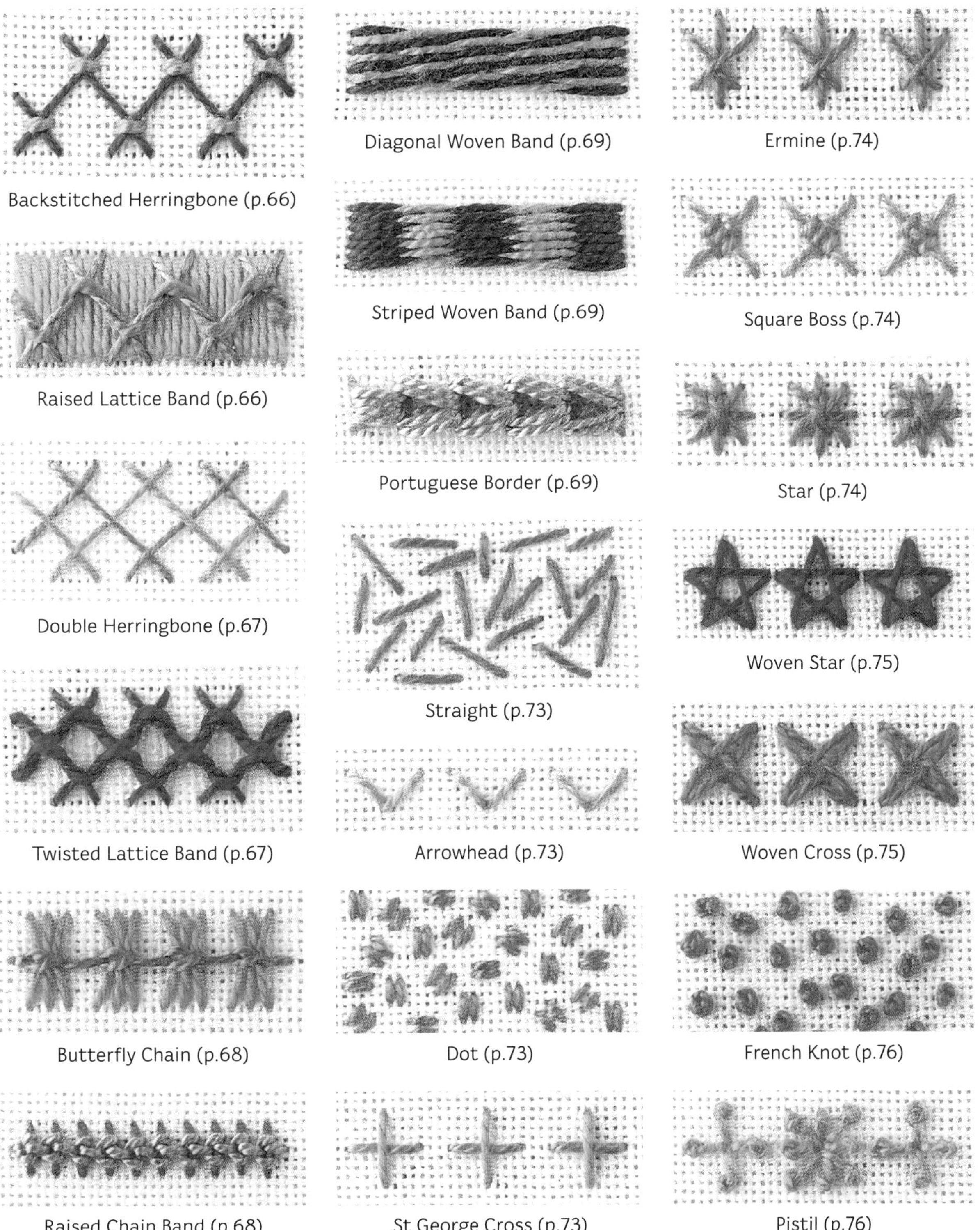

Backstitched Herringbone (p.66)

Raised Lattice Band (p.66)

Double Herringbone (p.67)

Twisted Lattice Band (p.67)

Butterfly Chain (p.68)

Raised Chain Band (p.68)

Diagonal Woven Band (p.69)

Striped Woven Band (p.69)

Portuguese Border (p.69)

Straight (p.73)

Arrowhead (p.73)

Dot (p.73)

St George Cross (p.73)

Ermine (p.74)

Square Boss (p.74)

Star (p.74)

Woven Star (p.75)

Woven Cross (p.75)

French Knot (p.76)

Pistil (p.76)

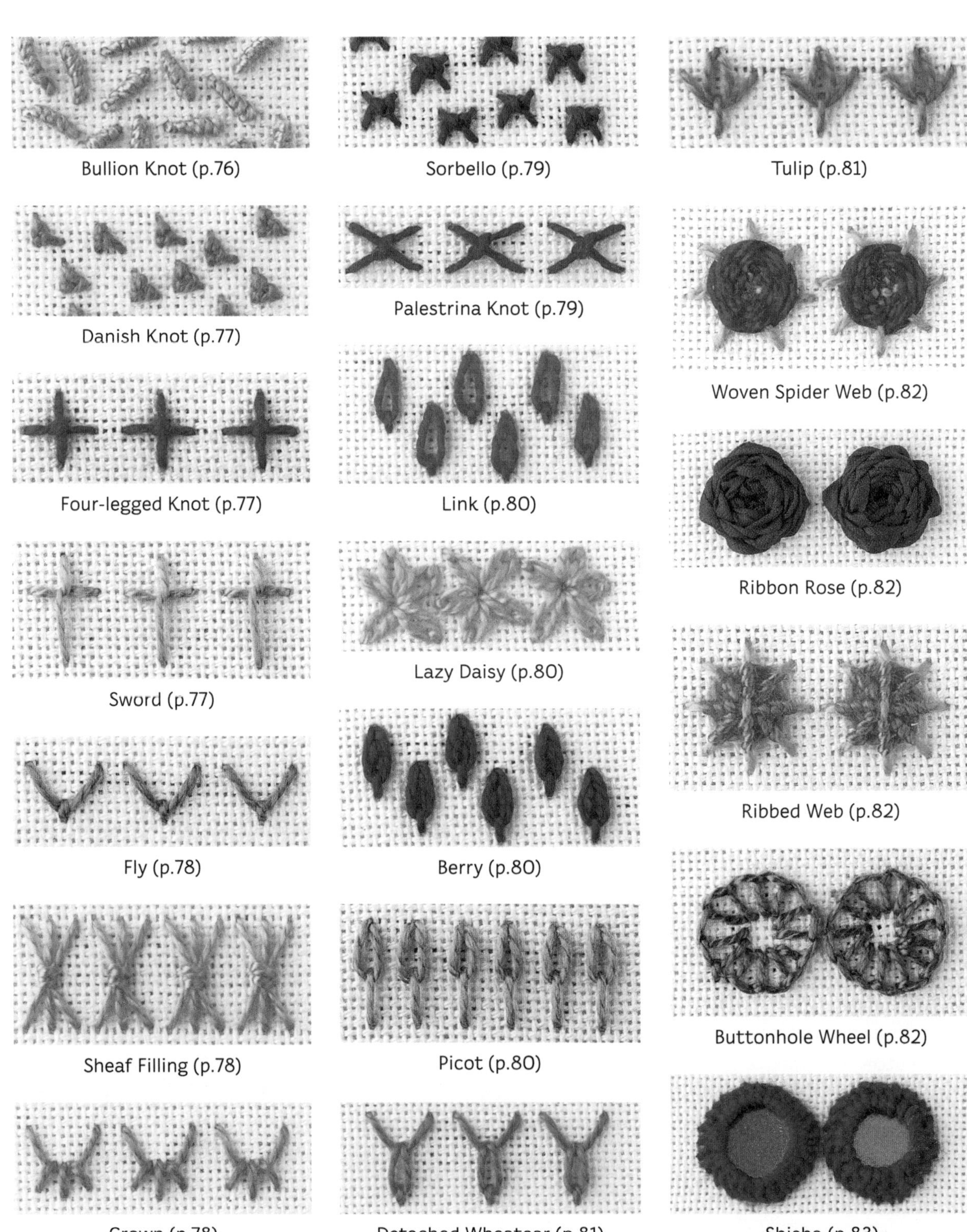

Bullion Knot (p.76)

Danish Knot (p.77)

Four-legged Knot (p.77)

Sword (p.77)

Fly (p.78)

Sheaf Filling (p.78)

Crown (p.78)

Sorbello (p.79)

Palestrina Knot (p.79)

Link (p.80)

Lazy Daisy (p.80)

Berry (p.80)

Picot (p.80)

Detached Wheatear (p.81)

Tulip (p.81)

Woven Spider Web (p.82)

Ribbon Rose (p.82)

Ribbed Web (p.82)

Buttonhole Wheel (p.82)

Shisha (p.83)

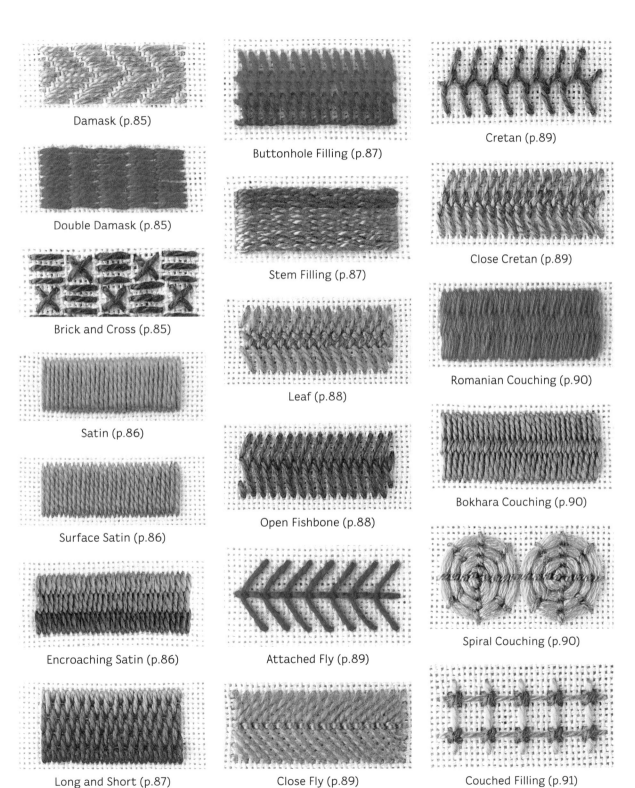

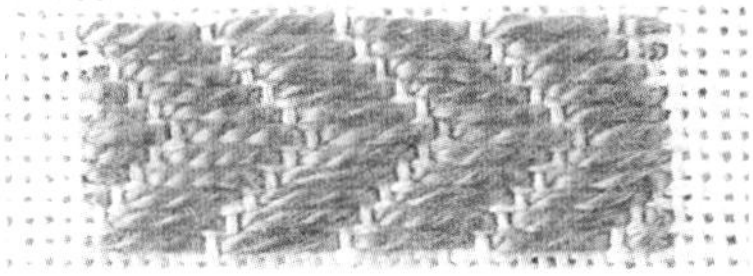

Damask (p.85)

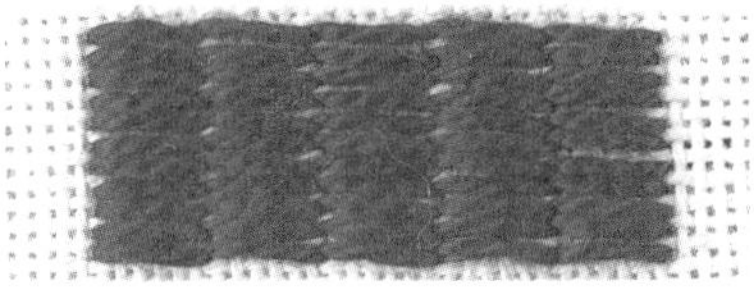

Double Damask (p.85)

Brick and Cross (p.85)

Satin (p.86)

Surface Satin (p.86)

Encroaching Satin (p.86)

Long and Short (p.87)

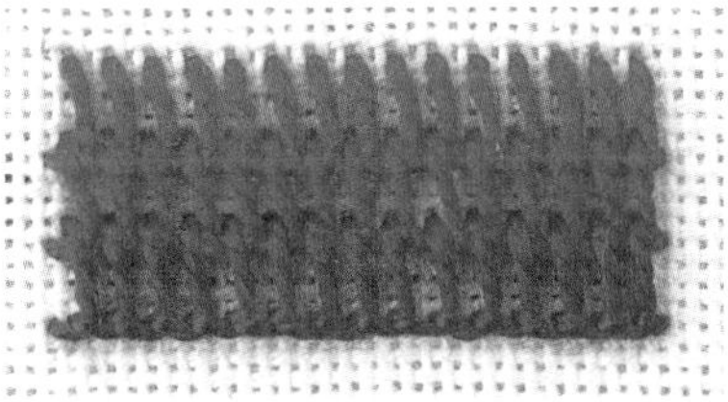

Buttonhole Filling (p.87)

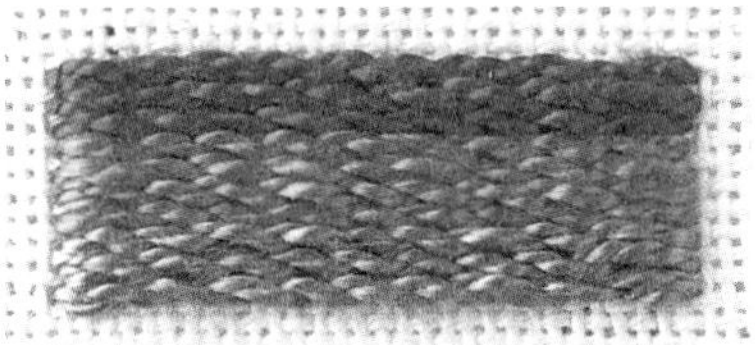

Stem Filling (p.87)

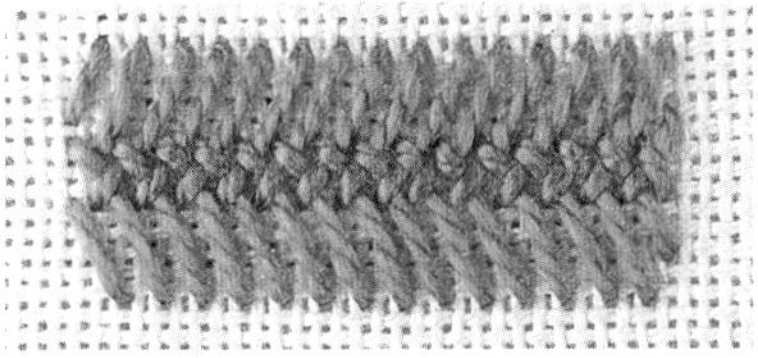

Leaf (p.88)

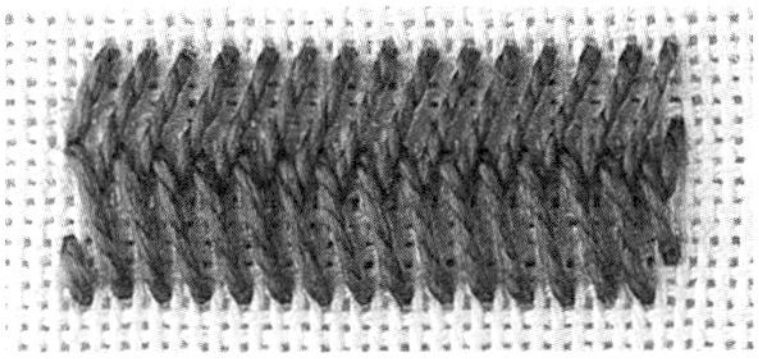

Open Fishbone (p.88)

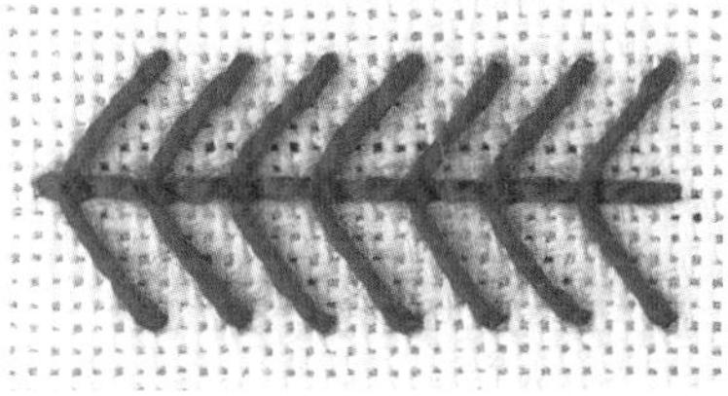

Attached Fly (p.89)

Close Fly (p.89)

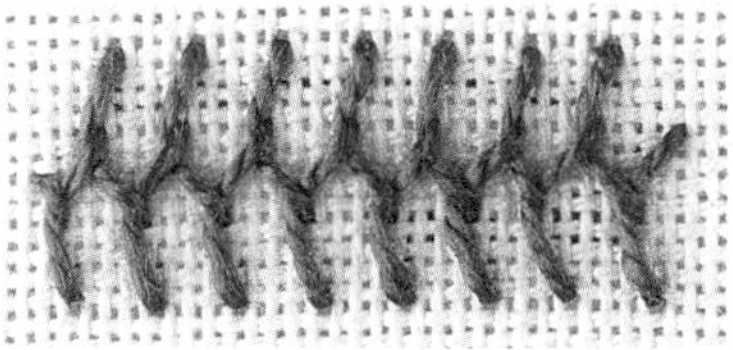

Cretan (p.89)

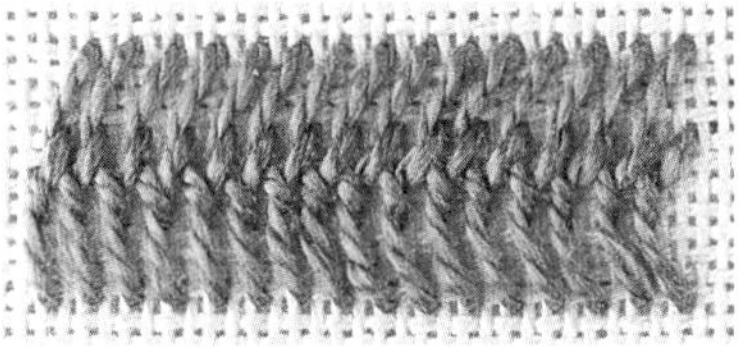

Close Cretan (p.89)

Romanian Couching (p.90)

Bokhara Couching (p.90)

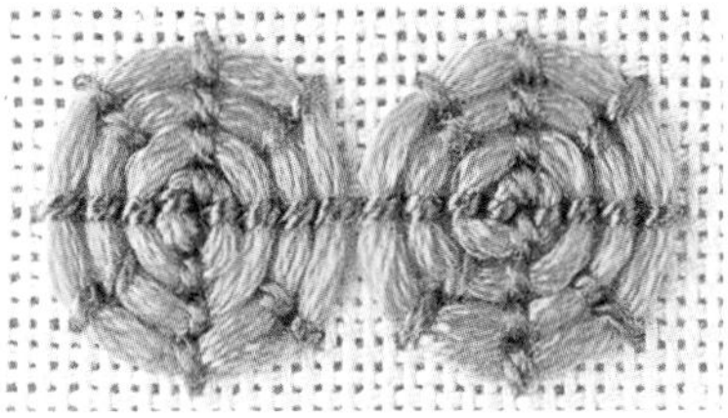

Spiral Couching (p.90)

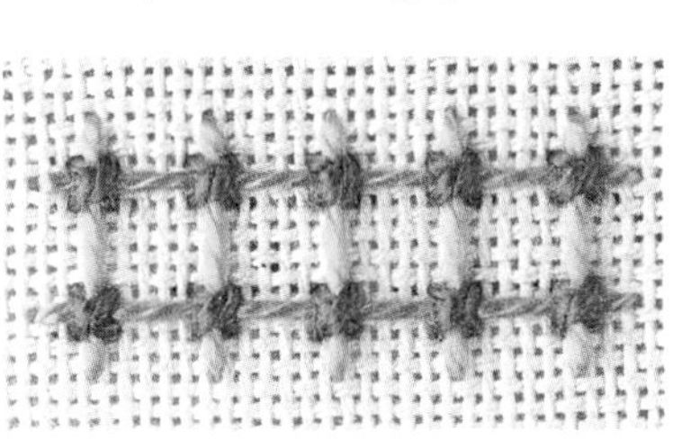

Couched Filling (p.91)

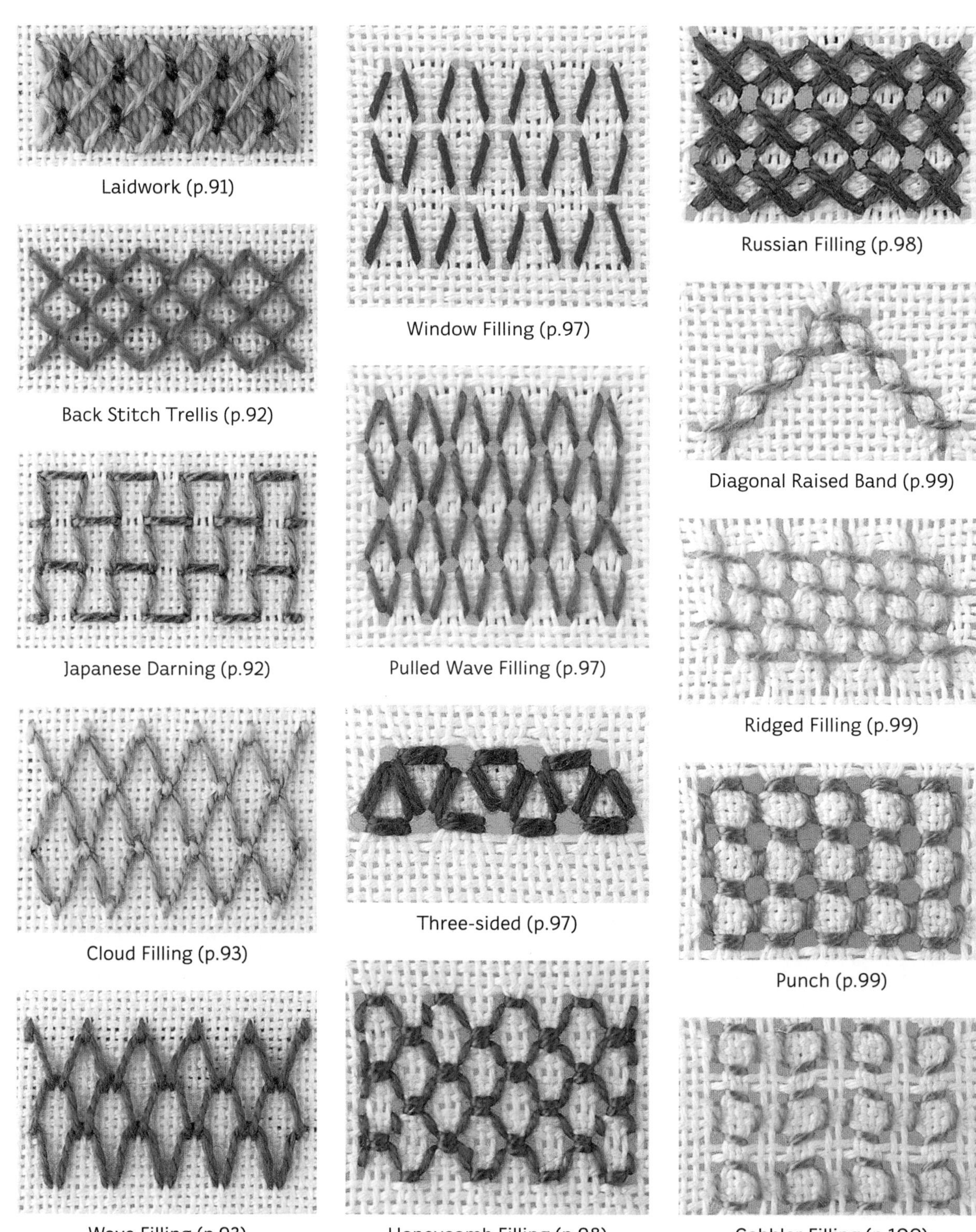

Laidwork (p.91)

Back Stitch Trellis (p.92)

Japanese Darning (p.92)

Cloud Filling (p.93)

Wave Filling (p.93)

Window Filling (p.97)

Pulled Wave Filling (p.97)

Three-sided (p.97)

Honeycomb Filling (p.98)

Russian Filling (p.98)

Diagonal Raised Band (p.99)

Ridged Filling (p.99)

Punch (p.99)

Cobbler Filling (p.100)

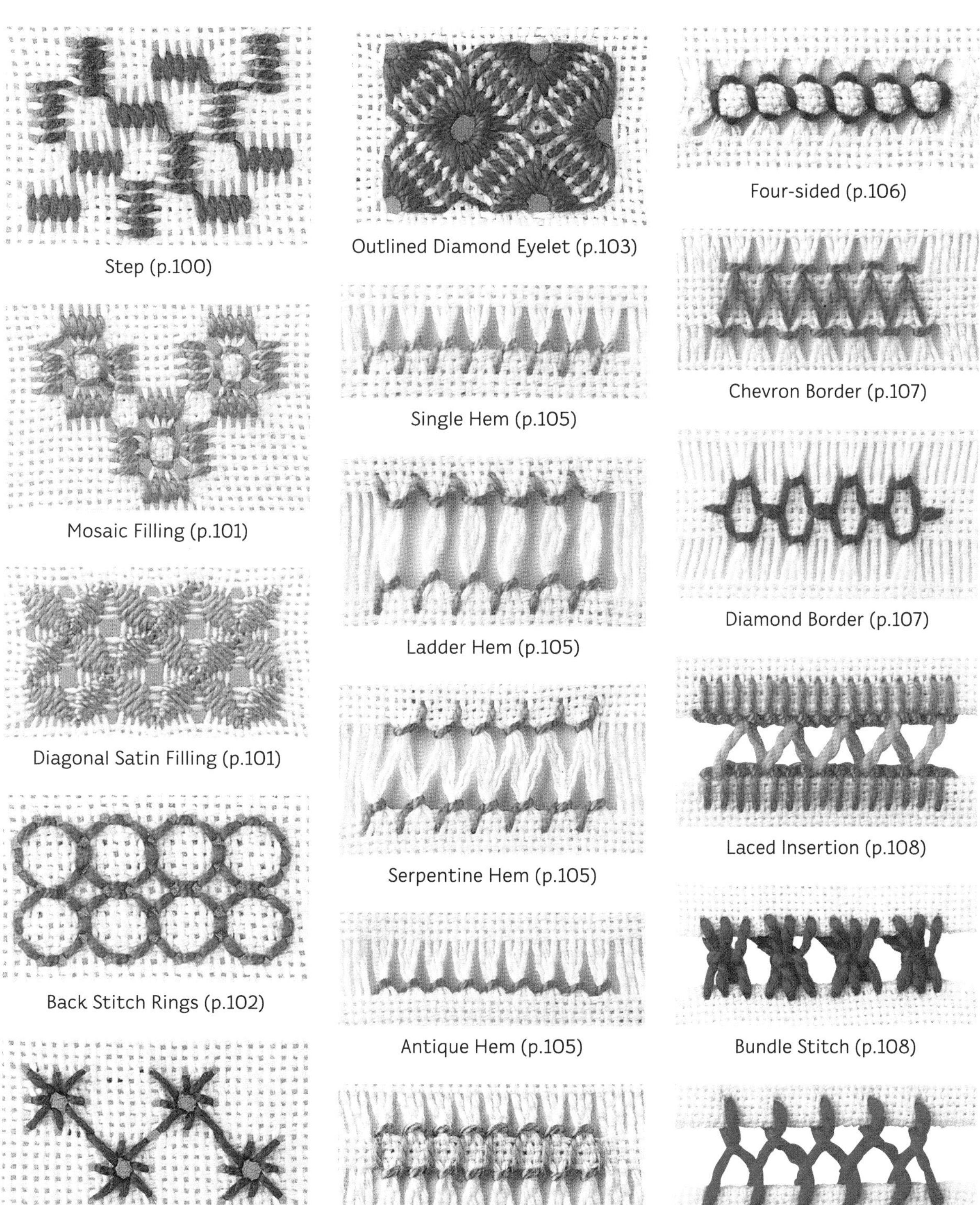

Step (p.100)

Mosaic Filling (p.101)

Diagonal Satin Filling (p.101)

Back Stitch Rings (p.102)

Algerian Eye (p.102)

Outlined Diamond Eyelet (p.103)

Single Hem (p.105)

Ladder Hem (p.105)

Serpentine Hem (p.105)

Antique Hem (p.105)

Italian Border (p.106)

Four-sided (p.106)

Chevron Border (p.107)

Diamond Border (p.107)

Laced Insertion (p.108)

Bundle Stitch (p.108)

Cretan Insertion (p.108)

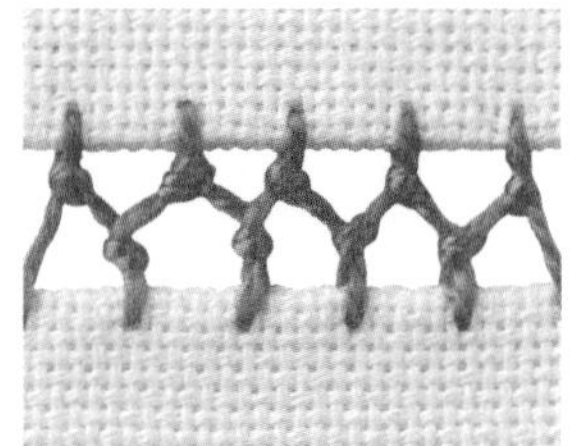
Knotted Insertion (p.109)

Buttonhole Insertion (p.109)

Needleweaving Bars (p.110)

Zigzag Clusters (p.110)

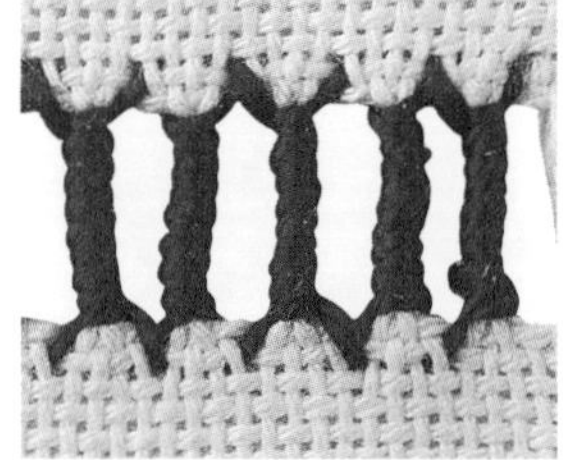
Corded Clusters (p.110)

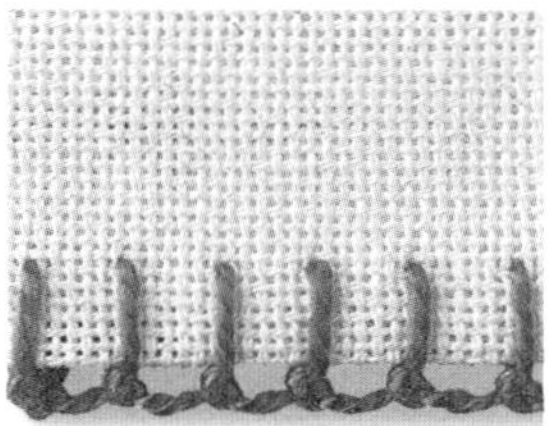
Antwerp Edging (p.112)

Sailor Edging (p.112)

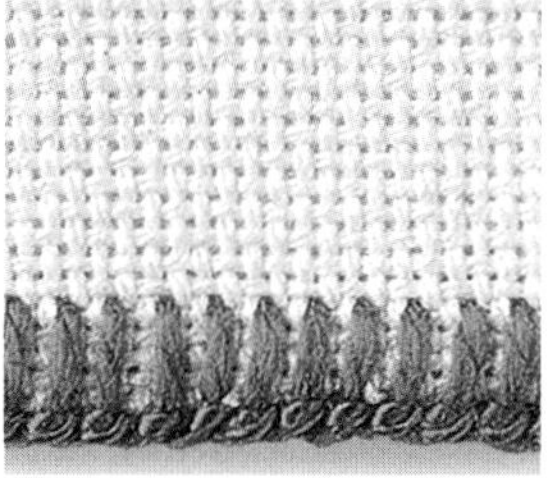
Looped Edge (p.113)

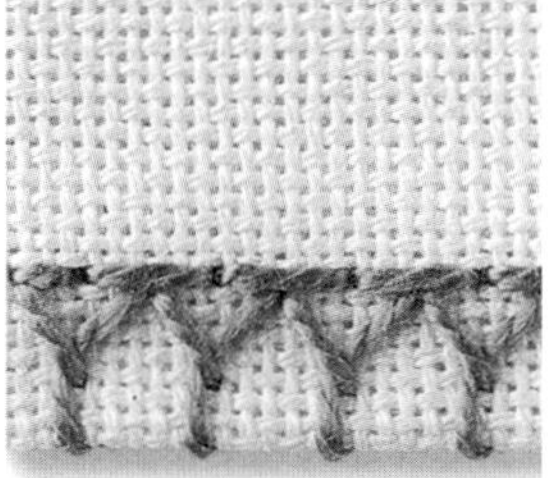
Half Chevron (p.113)

Scalloped Edge (p.114)

Ring Picot Edge (p.114)

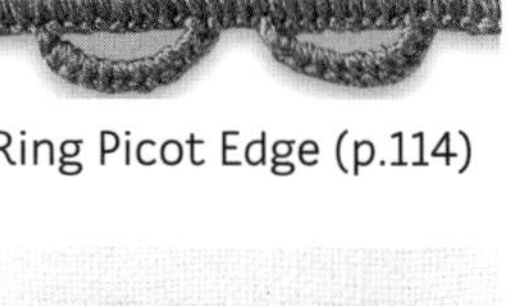

Buttonhole Eyelet (p.115)

Overcast Eyelet (p.115)

Square Eyelet (p.115)

Upright Gobelin (p.119)

Gobelin Filling (p.119)

Parisian (p.119)

Hungarian (p.120)

Hungarian Diamond (p.120)

Single Twill (p.121)

Double Twill (p.121)

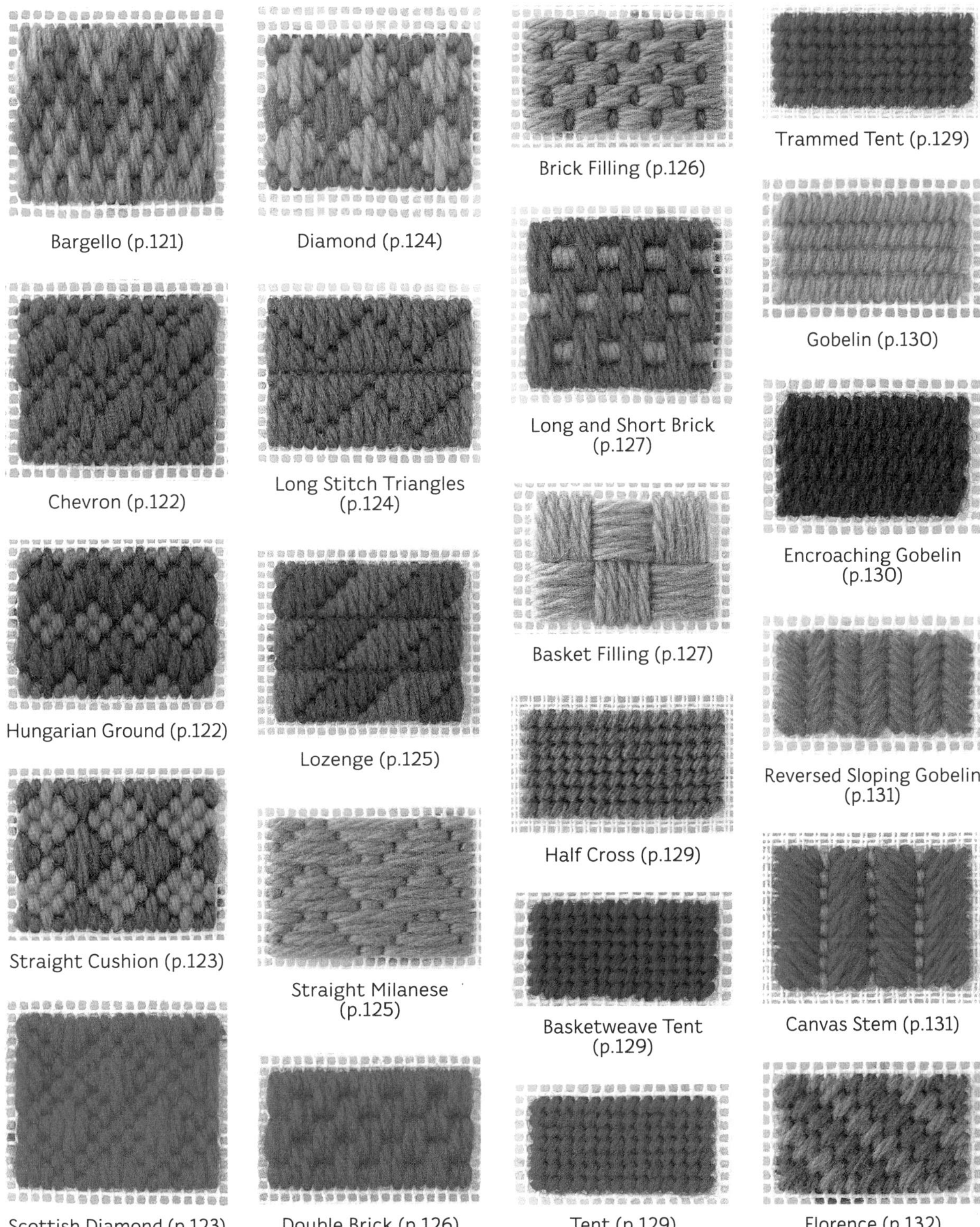

Bargello (p.121)

Chevron (p.122)

Hungarian Ground (p.122)

Straight Cushion (p.123)

Scottish Diamond (p.123)

Diamond (p.124)

Long Stitch Triangles (p.124)

Lozenge (p.125)

Straight Milanese (p.125)

Double Brick (p.126)

Brick Filling (p.126)

Long and Short Brick (p.127)

Basket Filling (p.127)

Half Cross (p.129)

Basketweave Tent (p.129)

Tent (p.129)

Trammed Tent (p.129)

Gobelin (p.130)

Encroaching Gobelin (p.130)

Reversed Sloping Gobelin (p.131)

Canvas Stem (p.131)

Florence (p.132)

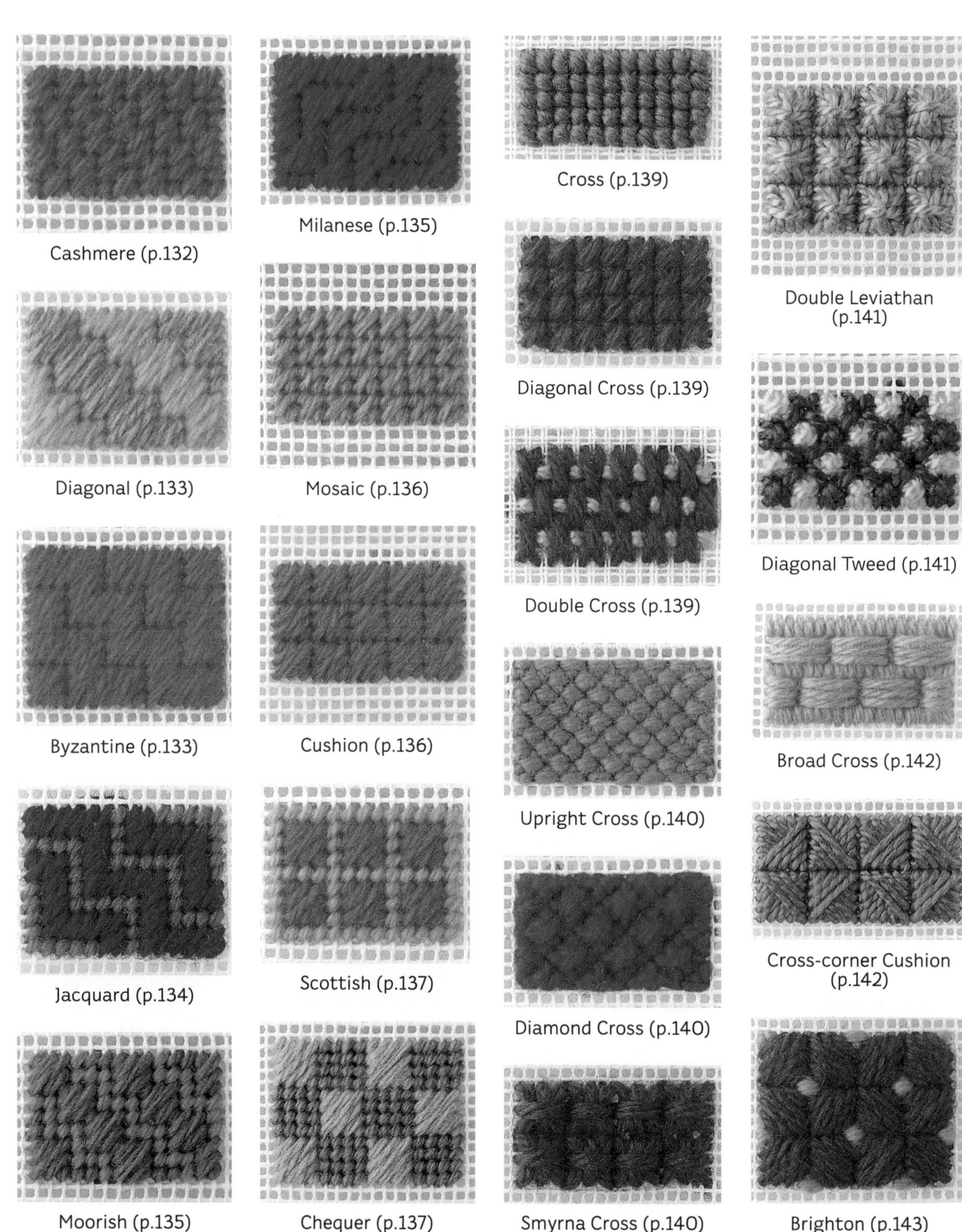

Cashmere (p.132)

Diagonal (p.133)

Byzantine (p.133)

Jacquard (p.134)

Moorish (p.135)

Milanese (p.135)

Mosaic (p.136)

Cushion (p.136)

Scottish (p.137)

Chequer (p.137)

Cross (p.139)

Diagonal Cross (p.139)

Double Cross (p.139)

Upright Cross (p.140)

Diamond Cross (p.140)

Smyrna Cross (p.140)

Double Leviathan (p.141)

Diagonal Tweed (p.141)

Broad Cross (p.142)

Cross-corner Cushion (p.142)

Brighton (p.143)

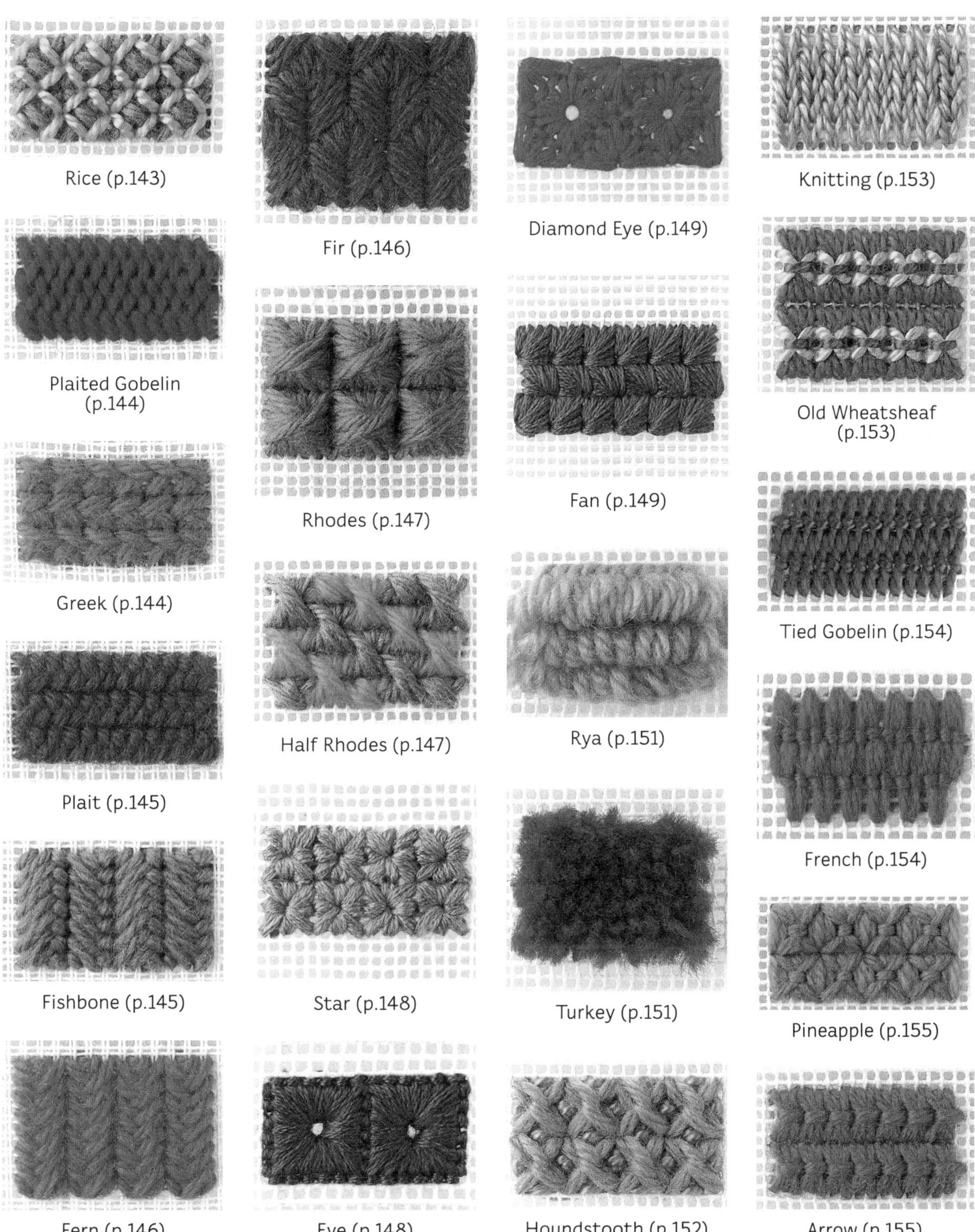

Rice (p.143)

Plaited Gobelin (p.144)

Greek (p.144)

Plait (p.145)

Fishbone (p.145)

Fern (p.146)

Fir (p.146)

Rhodes (p.147)

Half Rhodes (p.147)

Star (p.148)

Eye (p.148)

Diamond Eye (p.149)

Fan (p.149)

Rya (p.151)

Turkey (p.151)

Houndstooth (p.152)

Knitting (p.153)

Old Wheatsheaf (p.153)

Tied Gobelin (p.154)

French (p.154)

Pineapple (p.155)

Arrow (p.155)

Line and Border Stitches

Outline Stitches

This group covers both basic and intricate stitches, all of which are worked in a continuous line. They can be sewn in any thread, on any type of fabric, to create fine details as well as strong graphic outlines, depending on the effect required. Use them to draw motifs, to write monograms and messages, or to define a shape that will be filled in with another stitch.

The first and simplest of these – running stitch – is the foundation for many needlework techniques from across the world, including darning, appliqué, Indian kantha and Welsh wholecloth quilting, as well as Japanese sashiko embroidery and boro patching.

Running

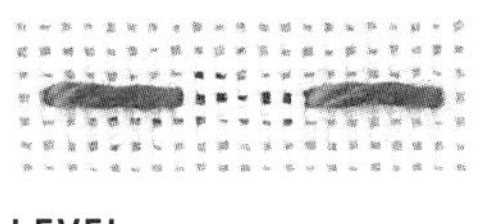

LEVEL
Easy

USES
Simple lines and outlines; basis for other stitches; hand sewing and quilting; reinforcement for cutwork

METHOD
Regularly spaced straight stitches of equal length

MATERIALS
Any fabric; any thread

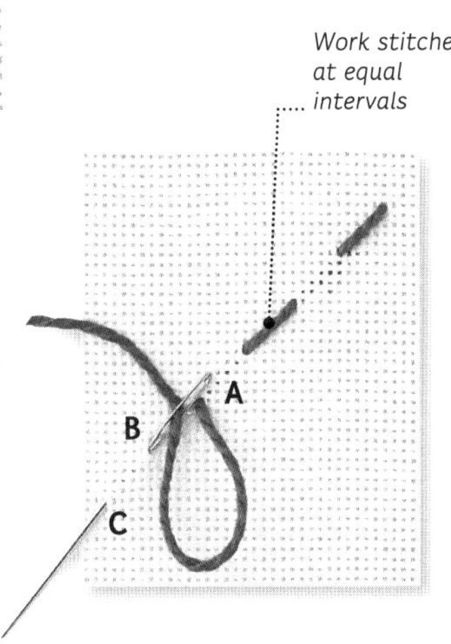

Work stitches at equal intervals
A
B
C

Come up at **A**, then insert the needle at **B**. Bring it out again at **C**. Continue, spacing the stitches evenly and making them all the same length.

Whipped Running

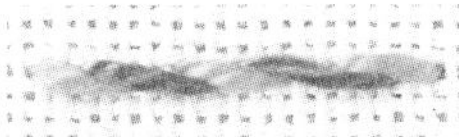

OTHER NAME
Cordonnet stitch

LEVEL
Easy

USES
Straight or curved outlines

METHOD
Laced running stitch

MATERIALS
Any fabric; any two threads – contrasting colours and thicknesses for greater effect; blunt needle for whipping

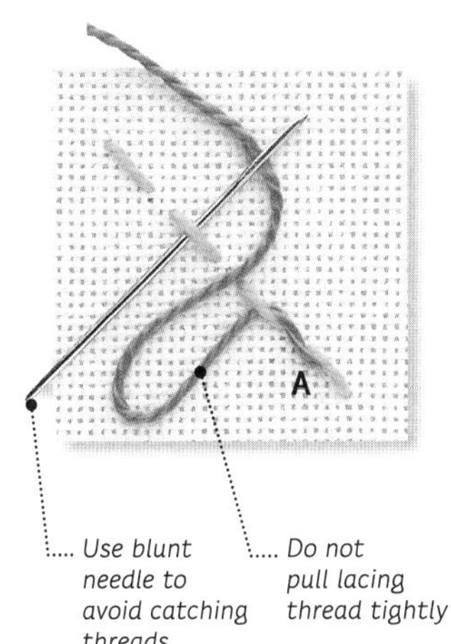

A
Use blunt needle to avoid catching threads
Do not pull lacing thread tightly

Work a foundation of closely spaced running stitch (see left). Using a blunt needle, bring the second thread up at **A**. Slide the needle under the next stitch from right to left and pull through gently. Continue whipping to the end of the line.

Double Running

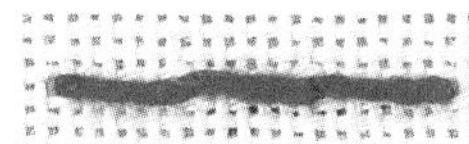

OTHER NAMES
Holbein stitch;
Chiara stitch

LEVEL
Easy

USES
With cross stitch; in Assisi embroidery and blackwork

METHOD
Counted thread stitch worked with two rows of running stitch

MATERIALS
Evenweave fabric; any embroidery thread

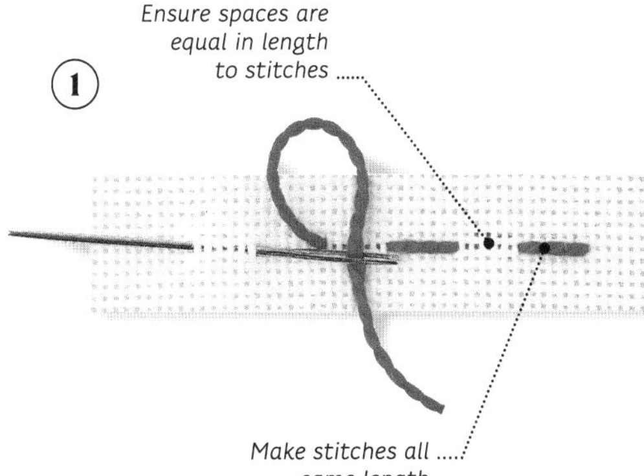

1
Ensure spaces are equal in length to stitches
Make stitches all same length

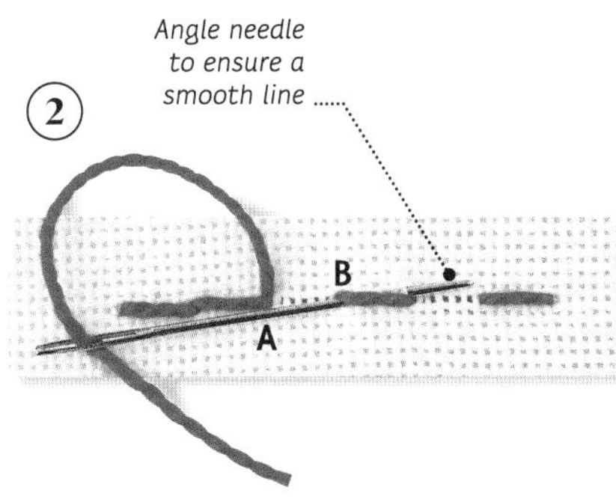

2
Angle needle to ensure a smooth line
B
A

1 Work a line of running stitch (see above). Make sure the stitches are all the same length and equal in length to the spaces.

2 Fill in the spaces on the return journey. Come out at the top of the previous stitch, at **A**. Insert the needle just below the start of the next stitch at **B**. Repeat to the end of the row.

Technique Variation

Double running stitch can be used to create intricate geometric bands and filling patterns. Chart the design on squared paper. Stitch along the line, working every other stitch. On the return journey, fill in the spaces with a second row of running stitch worked in the opposite direction.

Back

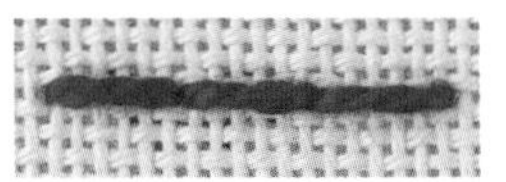

LEVEL
Easy

USES
Details and fine outlines, lettering, basis for other composite stitches

MATERIALS
Any fabric; any thread – untwisted threads give smooth effect

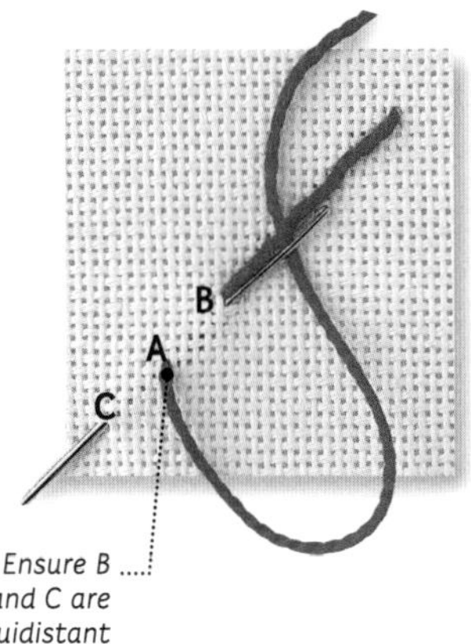
B
A
C
Ensure B and C are equidistant from A

Come up at **A**. Insert the needle at **B**, then bring it out again one stitch length ahead of **A** at **C**. Insert the needle again at A and continue making regular backward stitches in the same way.

Split

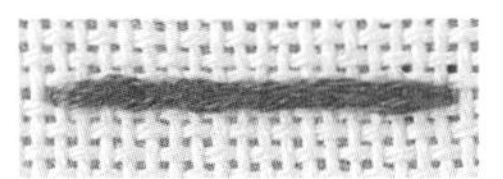

OTHER NAME
Threaded buttonhole stitch

LEVEL
Easy

USES
Accurate outlines; in close rows as filling; padded edge for solid filling stitches

MATERIALS
Any fabric; soft, untwisted thread such as stranded cotton or silk floss; sharp needle

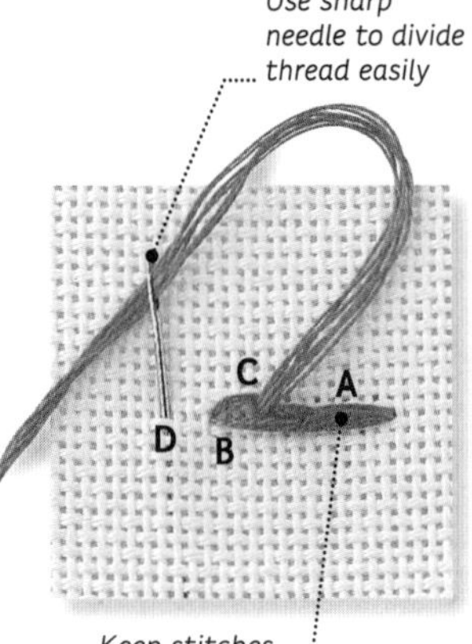
Use sharp needle to divide thread easily
C
A
D
B
Keep stitches regular to create smooth surface

Come up at **A** and work a straight stitch across to **B**. Bring the needle up at **C**, halfway along the stitch, so that it splits the thread. Pull through. Insert the needle at **D** and repeat to continue.

Threaded Back

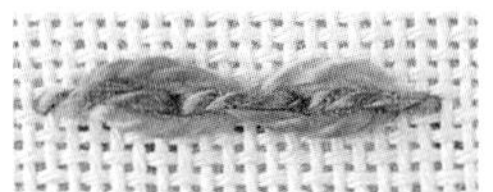

LEVEL
Easy

USES
Flexible, decorative outlines and borders

METHOD
Row of back stitch interlaced with one or two threads

MATERIALS
Any fabric; two or three colours of any thick embroidery thread; blunt needle

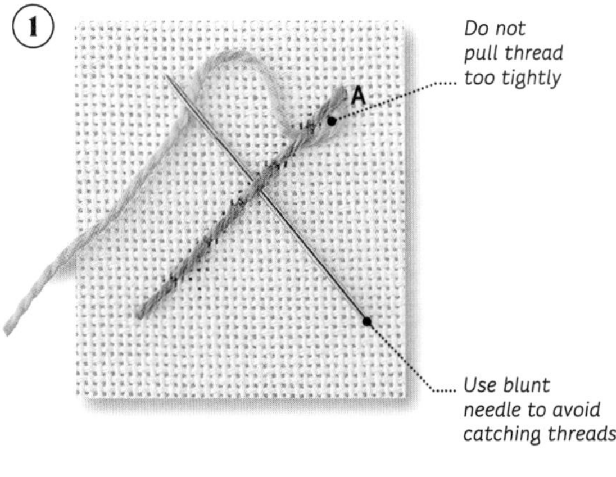
1
A
Do not pull thread too tightly
Use blunt needle to avoid catching threads

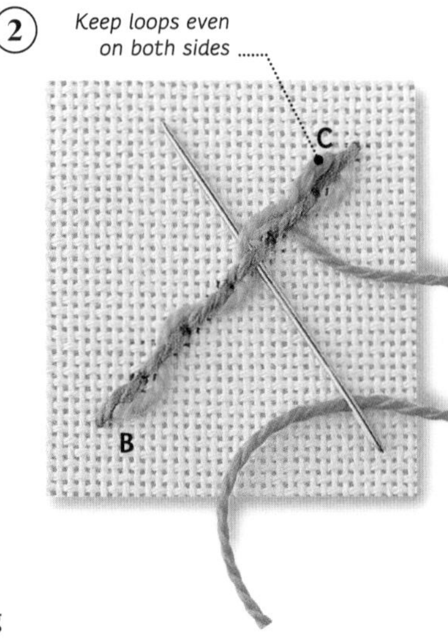
2
Keep loops even on both sides
C
B

1 Work a foundation of back stitch (see above). Bring the second thread up at **A**. Slide the needle under the next stitch, then pass it back under the following stitch. Continue weaving from side to side.

2 Take the thread down at **B** and finish off. For a double-threaded variation bring another thread up at **C** and weave in the same way as before, filling in the gaps.

Stem

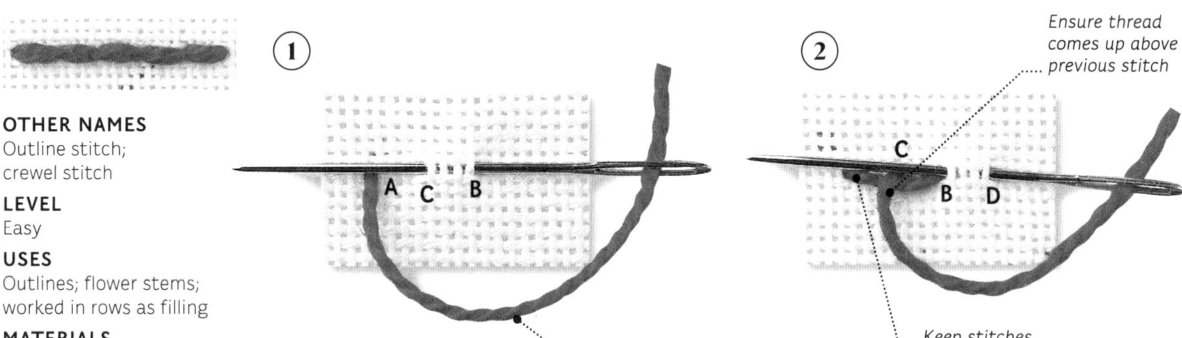
1
A
C
B
Keep loop below needle
2
Ensure thread comes up above previous stitch
C
B
D
Keep stitches all same length

OTHER NAMES
Outline stitch; crewel stitch

LEVEL
Easy

USES
Outlines; flower stems; worked in rows as filling

MATERIALS
Any fabric; any embroidery thread or crewel wool

1 Start at **A**, then insert the needle at **B**. Bring the needle up in the centre at **C**.

2 Insert the needle at **D** and bring it out at the end of the previous stitch, at **B**. Continue making a row of overlapping stitches.

Technique Variation

For a more solid, rope-like effect, work the stitches at an angle.

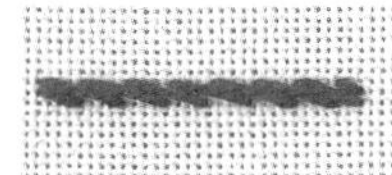

Cable

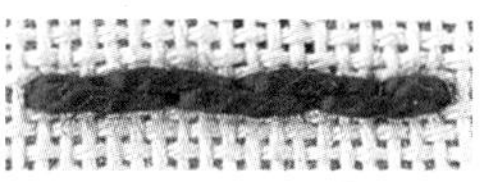

OTHER NAMES
Alternating stem stitch; side-to-side stem stitch

LEVEL
Easy

USES
Straight and curved outlines; narrow border

MATERIALS
Any fabric; any embroidery thread

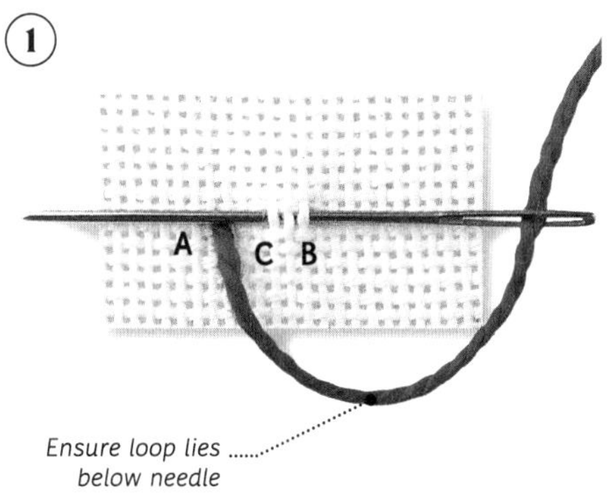
1
A
C
B
Ensure loop lies below needle

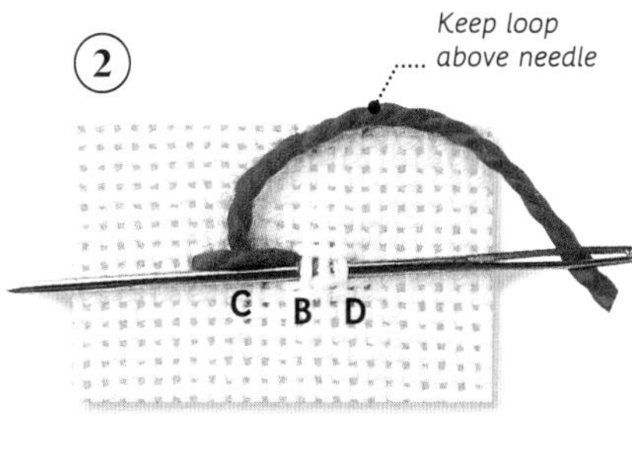
2
Keep loop above needle
C
B
D

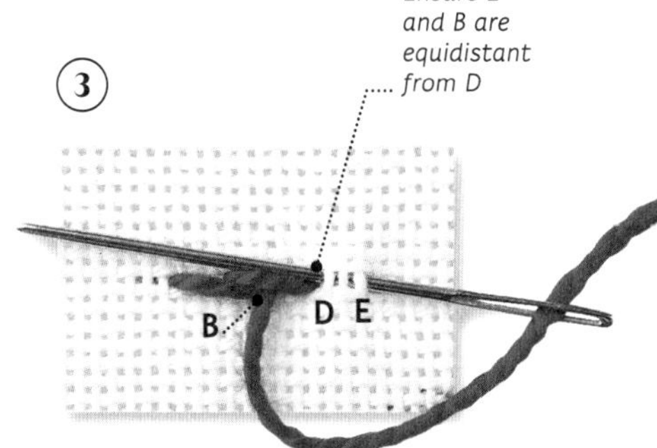
3
Ensure E and B are equidistant from D
B
D
E

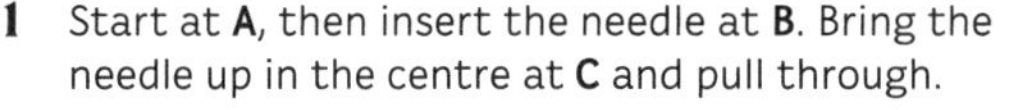

1 Start at **A**, then insert the needle at **B**. Bring the needle up in the centre at **C** and pull through.

2 Insert the needle at **D** and bring it back up at **B**.

3 Keeping the loop below the needle, insert at **E** and come up again at **D**. Repeat steps 2 and 3 to continue stitching.

Couching

LEVEL
Easy

USES
Straight and curved outlines; metal thread work; in rows as filling

METHOD
Laid threads held down with small tie stitches

MATERIALS
Any closely woven fabric; thick or delicate embroidery threads; finer thread for couching; frame

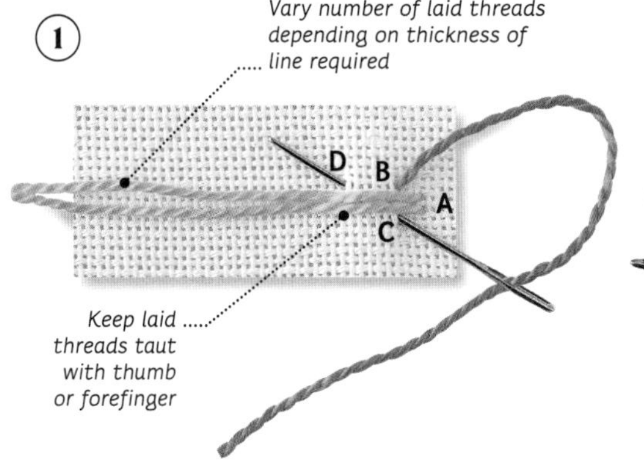
1
Vary number of laid threads depending on thickness of line required
D
B
A
C
Keep laid threads taut with thumb or forefinger

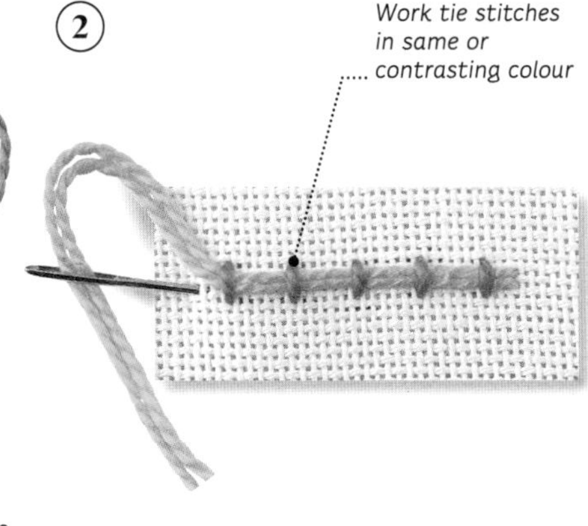
2
Work tie stitches in same or contrasting colour

1 Bring the main threads out at **A** and lay them along the line to be worked. To make the tie stitches (see p.20), come up at **B** using the couching thread. Insert the needle at **C**, over the laid threads, and bring it out at **D** to start the next stitch.

2 Continue working evenly spaced tie stitches over the laid thread to the end of the line. Finish off all threads at the back.

Stitch Variation

Satin couching, known also as trailing stitch, is a variation of couching, in which the tie stitches are worked very closely together so that the laid thread is completely covered.

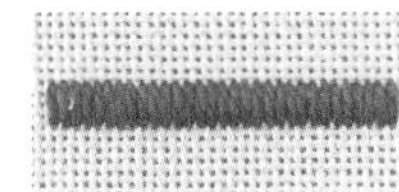

Pearl

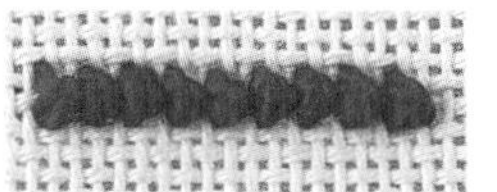

LEVEL
Intermediate

USES
Intricate or straight outlines; monograms

METHOD
Knotted stitch, worked in continuous line

MATERIALS
Any fabric; thick, non-stranded embroidery thread

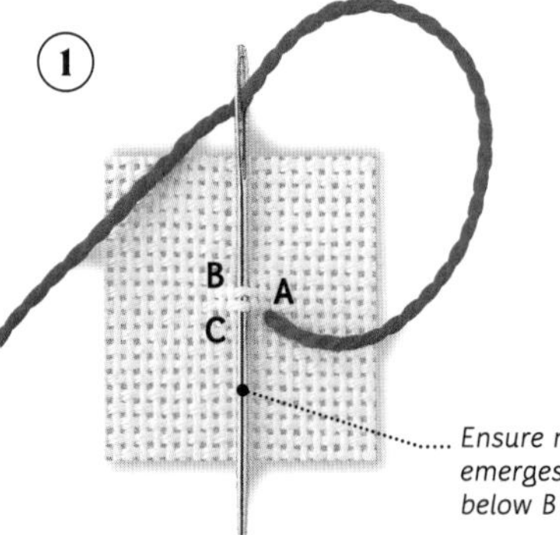
1
B
A
C
Ensure needle emerges directly below B

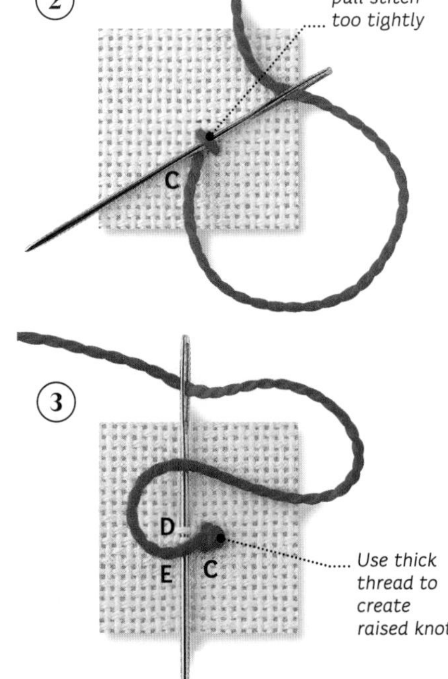
2
Do not pull stitch too tightly
C
3
D
E
C
Use thick thread to create raised knot

1 Start at **A** and make a diagonal stitch up to **B**. Bring the needle out at **C**.

2 Pull the thread to form a loop. Slide the needle under the stitch from right to left.

3 Tighten the knot by pulling the thread gently downwards. Take the needle up to the left and insert at **D** to form the loop for the next stitch. Come out at **E**. Repeat steps 2 and 3 to continue along the row.

Coral

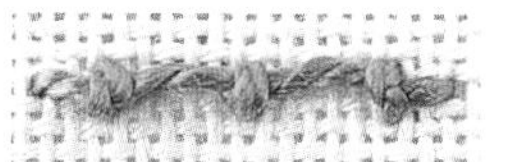

OTHER NAMES
Knotted stitch; snail trail; beaded stitch

LEVEL
Easy

USES
Straight and curved outlines; in rows as textured filling

METHOD
Series of closely or widely spaced single knots

MATERIALS
Any fabric; thick, non-stranded thread

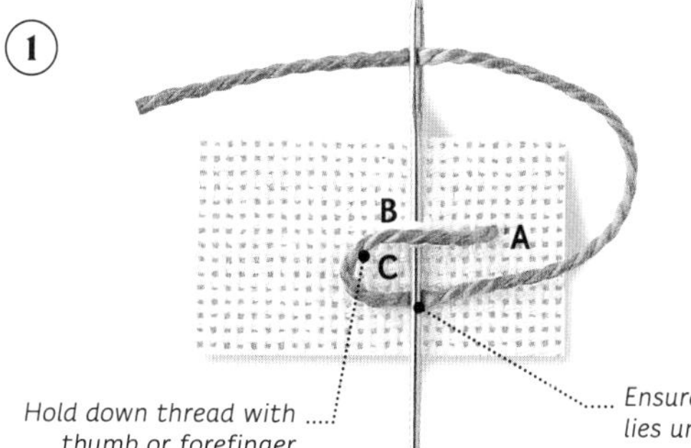
1
B
C
A
Hold down thread with thumb or forefinger
Ensure thread loop lies under needle

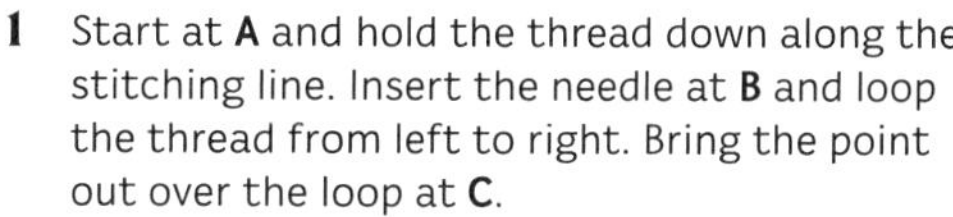

1 Start at **A** and hold the thread down along the stitching line. Insert the needle at **B** and loop the thread from left to right. Bring the point out over the loop at **C**.

2 Pull the needle gently through the loop so that the thread tightens into a knot.

3 Take the needle across to the left and insert it at **D**. Bring it out at **E**, ready for the next knot. Repeat steps 1 and 2 to continue.

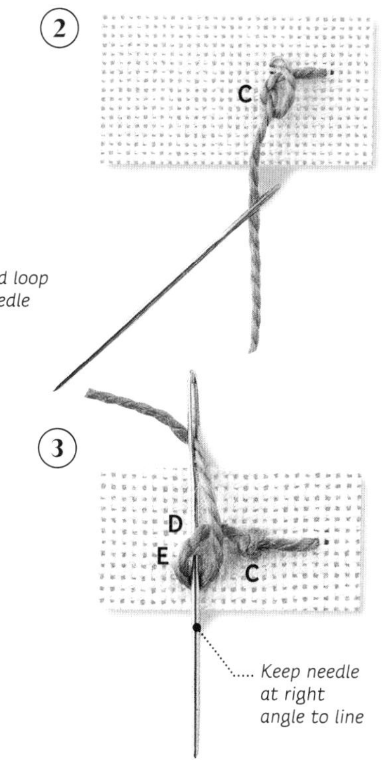
2
C
3
D
E
C
Keep needle at right angle to line

Double Knot

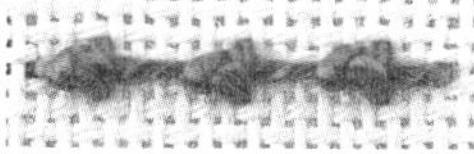

OTHER NAMES
Old English knot stitch; Palestrina stitch; Smyrna stitch

LEVEL
Intermediate

USES
Outlines and borders

METHOD
Knotted stitch, worked in continuous line

MATERIALS
Any fabric; thick, non-stranded embroidery thread

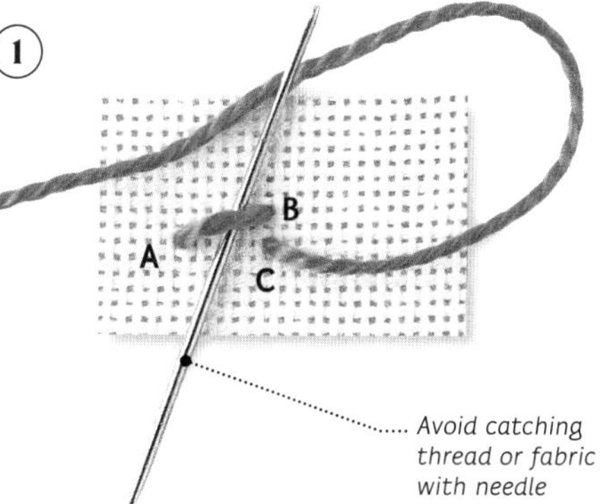
1
B
A
C
Avoid catching thread or fabric with needle

1 Start at **A** and make a diagonal stitch across to **B**. Bring the needle out at **C**, then slide it under the stitch from top to bottom.

2 Take the needle to the right of the loop and pass it under the diagonal stitch again. Bring it through over the working thread.

3 Pull the thread up to form a knot. Insert the needle at **D** and bring it out in line with **C** at **E**, ready to work the next stitch.

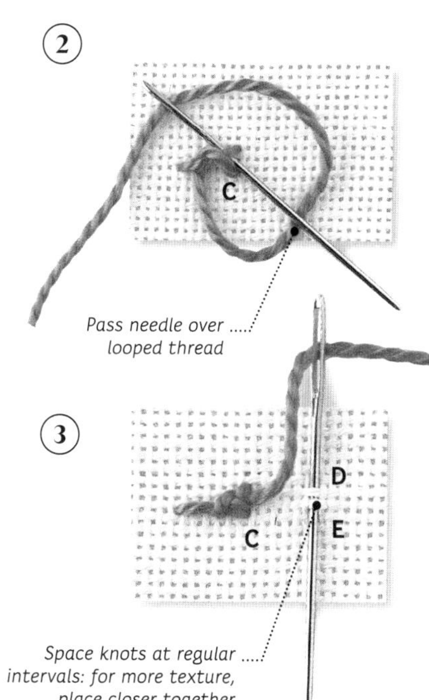
2
C
Pass needle over looped thread
3
D
C
E
Space knots at regular intervals: for more texture, place closer together

Chain

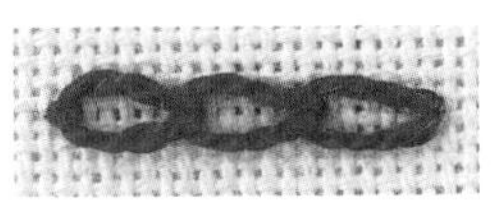

OTHER NAME
Point de chainette; tambour stitch

LEVEL
Easy

USES
Straight lines and curves; lettering; in rows or spiral as filling

METHOD
Looped stitch, worked from top to bottom

MATERIALS
Any fabric; any thread

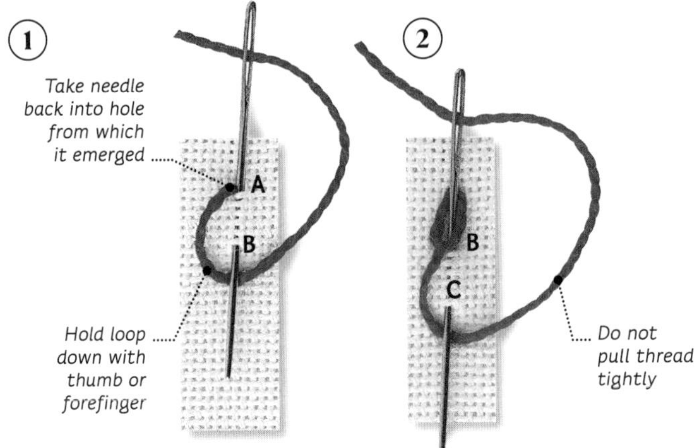
1
Take needle back into hole from which it emerged
A
B
Hold loop down with thumb or forefinger
2
B
C
Do not pull thread tightly

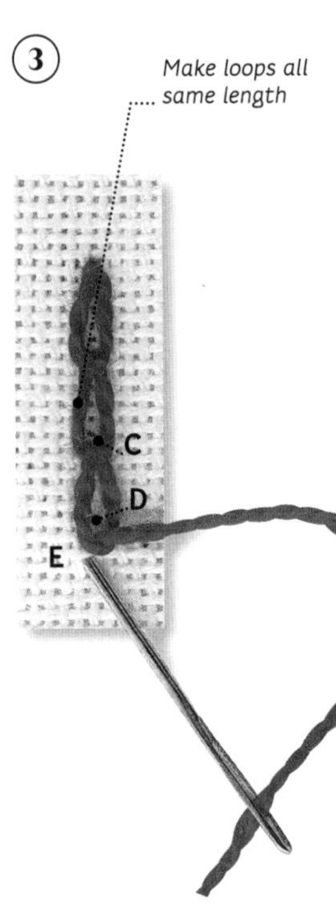
3
Make loops all same length
C
D
E

1 Start at **A**. Loop the thread from left to right and insert the needle again at **A**. Bring it through over the working thread at **B**.

2 Repeat step 1 to make the second stitch. Insert the needle inside the first loop at **B** and bring it out at **C**.

3 When the final stitch has been made, finish off by anchoring the last loop down with a small tie stitch (see p.20) from **D** to **E**.

Square Chain

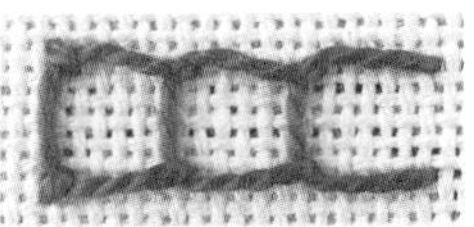

OTHER NAMES
Ladder stitch; Roman chain; open chain stitch

LEVEL
Easy

USES
Broad outlines; couching stitch; foundation for ribbon decoration; traditional Indian embroidery

METHOD
Looped stitch, worked from top to bottom

MATERIALS
Any fabric; any thread

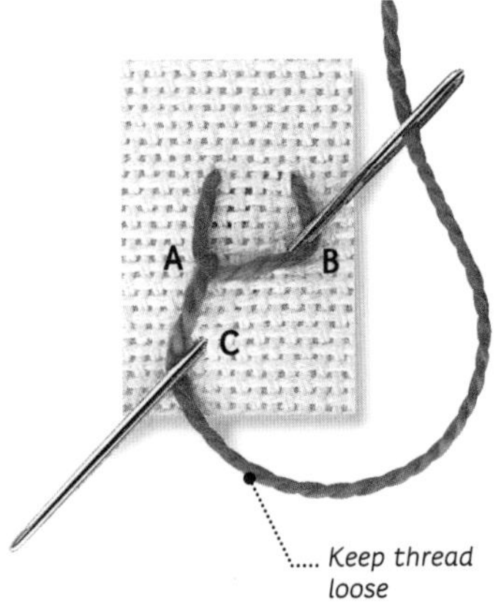
A
B
C
Keep thread loose

Come out at **A**. Insert the needle inside the previous loop at **B**. Bring it through over the working thread at **C**, leaving an open loop. Repeat to continue. Anchor the final loop with a tie stitch (see p.20) at each corner.

Twisted Chain

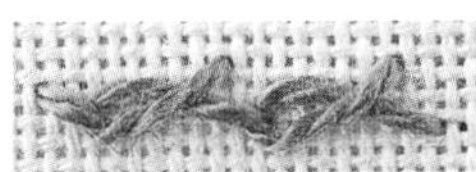

LEVEL
Easy

USES
Curved and textured outlines

METHOD
Chain stitch variation with crossed loop

MATERIALS
Any fabric; any thread – non-stranded threads give best effect

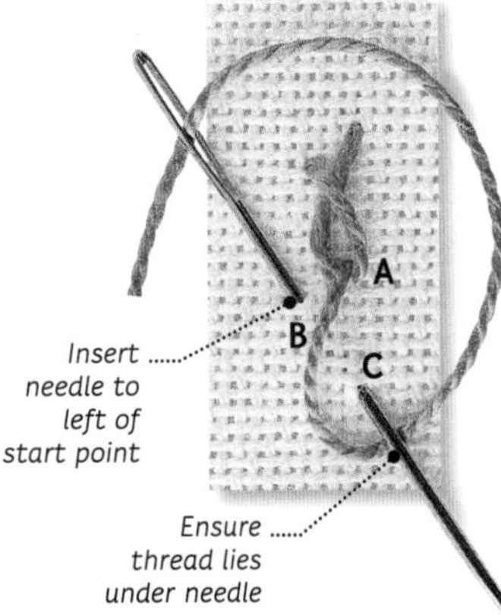
A
B
C
Insert needle to left of start point
Ensure thread lies under needle

Come up at **A**. Loop thread from left to right, insert the needle at **B**. Come up at **C**, pull through over the working thread. Repeat to continue. Finish with a tie stitch (see p.20) over the final loop.

Cable Chain

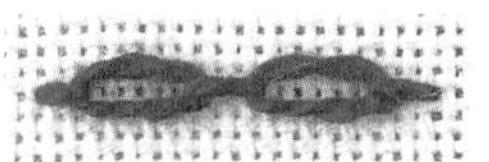

LEVEL
Intermediate

USES
Decorative straight or curved outlines

METHOD
Looped and twisted stitch, worked from top to bottom

MATERIALS
Any fabric; any thick embroidery thread

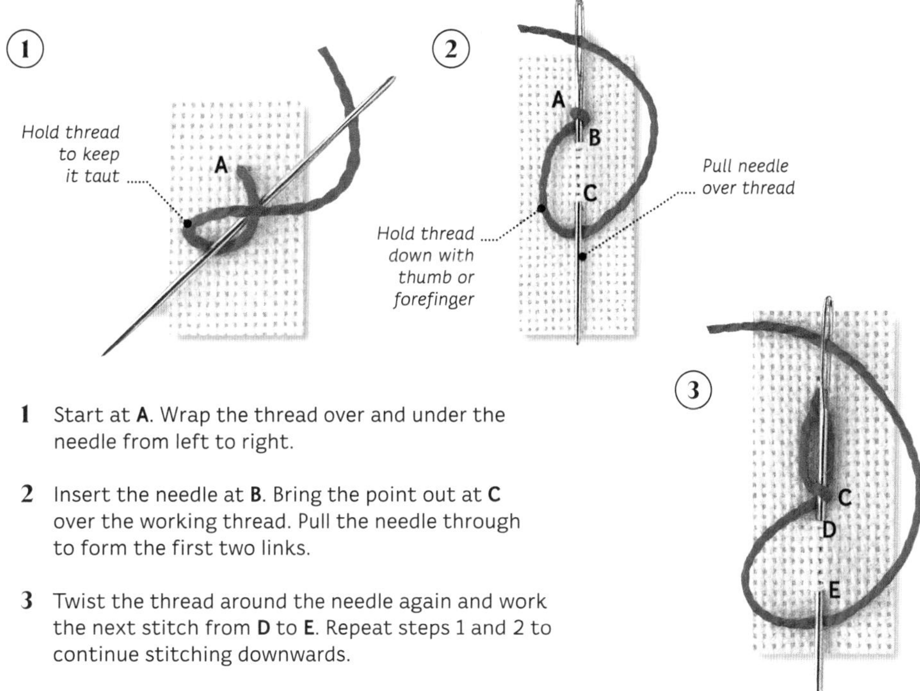
1
Hold thread to keep it taut
A
2
A
B
C
Hold thread down with thumb or forefinger
Pull needle over thread
3
C
D
E

1 Start at **A**. Wrap the thread over and under the needle from left to right.

2 Insert the needle at **B**. Bring the point out at **C** over the working thread. Pull the needle through to form the first two links.

3 Twist the thread around the needle again and work the next stitch from **D** to **E**. Repeat steps 1 and 2 to continue stitching downwards.

Broad Chain

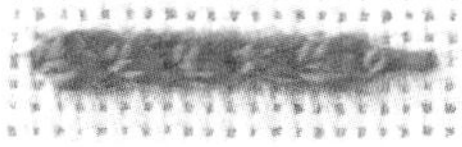

OTHER NAME
Reversed chain stitch

LEVEL
Intermediate

USES
Solid, flexible outline

METHOD
Looped stitch, worked from top to bottom

MATERIALS
Any fabric; firm embroidery thread

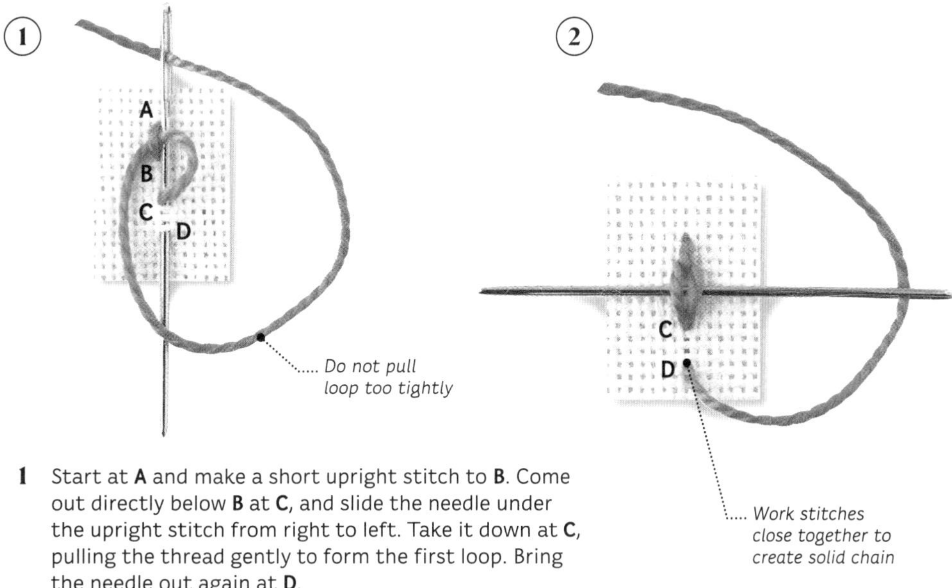
1
A
B
C
D
Do not pull loop too tightly
2
C
D
Work stitches close together to create solid chain

1 Start at **A** and make a short upright stitch to **B**. Come out directly below **B** at **C**, and slide the needle under the upright stitch from right to left. Take it down at **C**, pulling the thread gently to form the first loop. Bring the needle out again at **D**.

2 Pass the needle under both sides of the loop, then take it down at **D**. Repeat from **C** to continue.

Rope

LEVEL
Advanced

USES
Straight, curved or spiral outlines

MATERIALS
Any fabric; any thick thread - stranded cotton gives a smooth effect

TIP
Vary the angle of the stitches to work around a curve

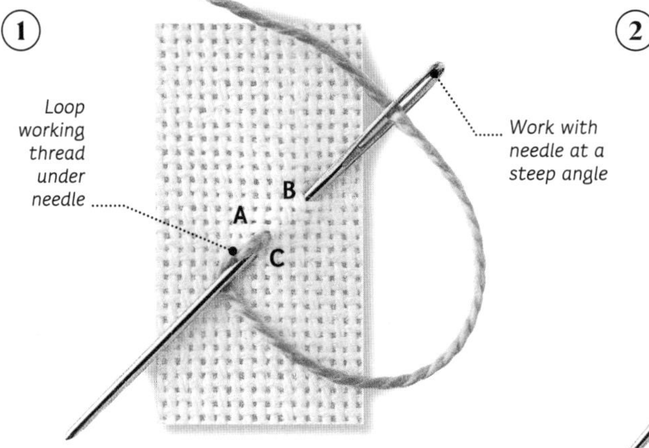
1
Loop working thread under needle
A
B
C
Work with needle at a steep angle

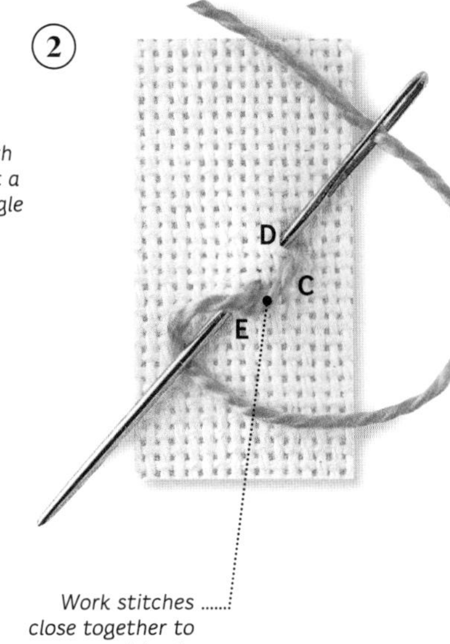
2
D
C
E
Work stitches close together to conceal knots

1 Start at **A**. Take the needle diagonally across and insert at **B**, then bring it up below and to the left of **A**, at **C**.

2 Pull the needle over the working thread to form a small knot at the base of the stitch. Insert the needle at **D** and bring it up at **E** to make the next stitch. Repeat this step to continue.

Scroll

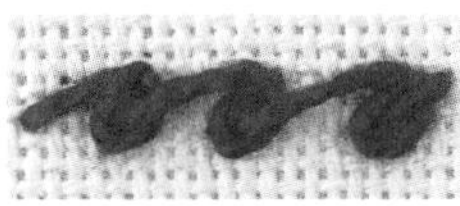

OTHER NAME
Single knotted line stitch

LEVEL
Intermediate

USES
Decorative outlines

METHOD
Looped knot stitch

MATERIALS
Any fabric; firm, non-stranded embroidery thread; frame

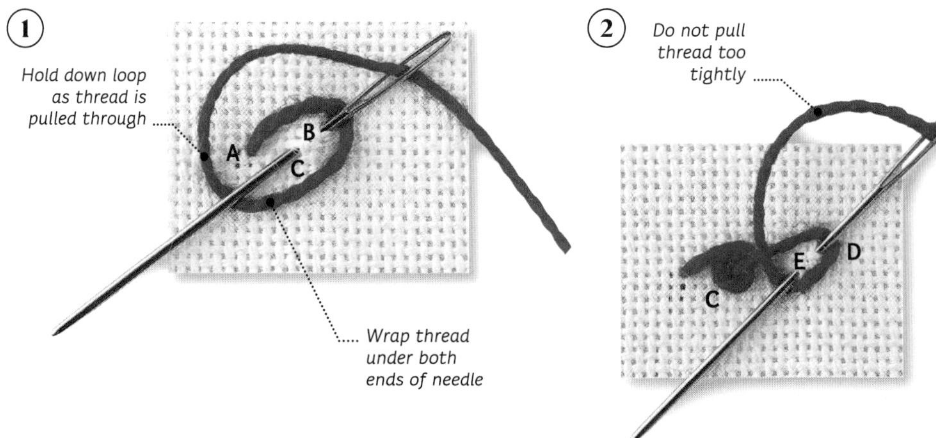
1
Hold down loop as thread is pulled through
A
B
C
Wrap thread under both ends of needle
2
Do not pull thread too tightly
D
E
C

1 Start at **A**. Take the needle diagonally across and insert at **B**. Bring the point out at **C**, so that it lies at an angle. Wrap the working thread clockwise under the needle.

2 Pull the needle through gently, keeping the loop in shape. Insert at **D** and bring the point through at **E**, so that the needle lies at the same angle used for the previous stitch. Repeat the sequence to continue.

Border Stitches

This is the largest, most widely used family of stitches, some of which involve looping and knotting the thread to create interesting visual effects. Use them for broad, decorative straight lines, frames and edgings, or repeat them in straight or curved rows to cover a larger area. Work with plainweave fabric for freestyle embroidery or evenweave to produce the more geometric look of counted thread work.

Border stitches can be adapted in many ways. Blanket stitch gives a decorative finish to a fabric edge, feather stitch and its variations, along with chevron are traditional smocking stitches, and counted cross stitch, which is worked from a chart onto aida cloth, is an enduringly popular type of embroidery.

Paris

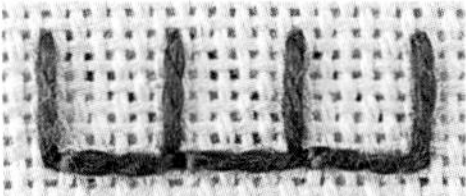

OTHER NAME
Open square stitch

LEVEL
Easy

USES
Light border; in rows as filling

METHOD
Back stitch variation with upright branches

MATERIALS
Evenweave fabric; any thread

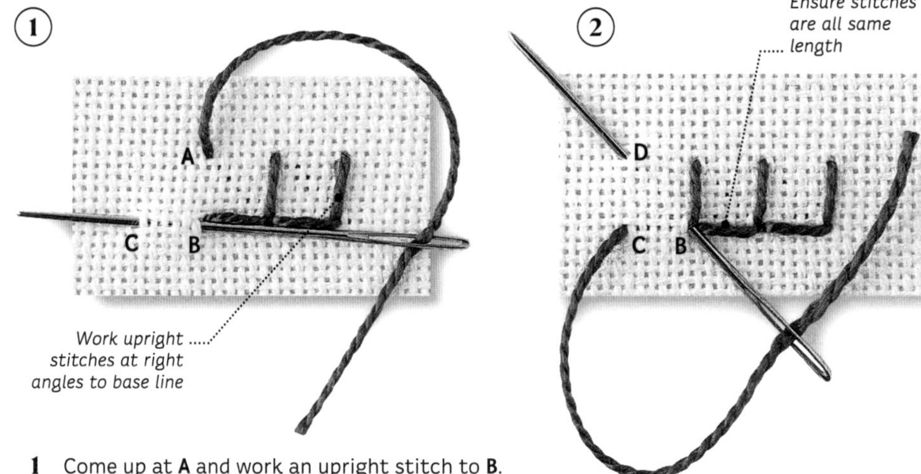

1
A
C
B
Work upright stitches at right angles to base line
2
Ensure stitches are all same length
D
C
B

1 Come up at **A** and work an upright stitch to **B**. Bring the needle out to the left of **B** at **C**.

2 Re-insert the needle at **B** to make a back stitch. Bring it out again above **C**, at **D**. Continue working pairs of stitches at right angles in the same way.

Fern

OTHER NAME
Fern leaf stitch

LEVEL
Easy

USES
Leaf veins and delicate foliage sprays

METERIALS
Any fabric; any thread

TIP
Vary length of stitches when working on a curve

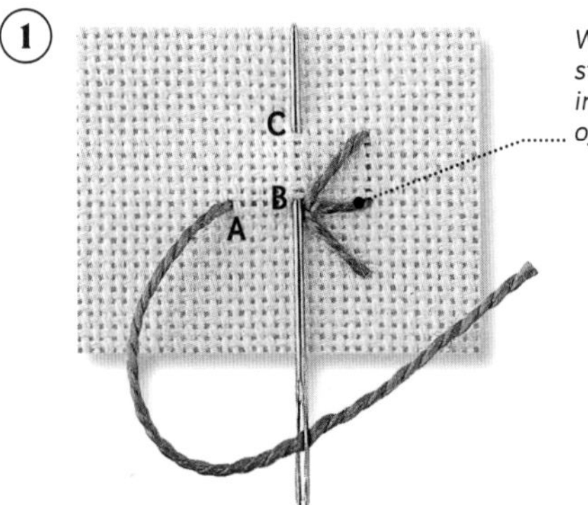

1
C
B
A
Work stitches in groups of three

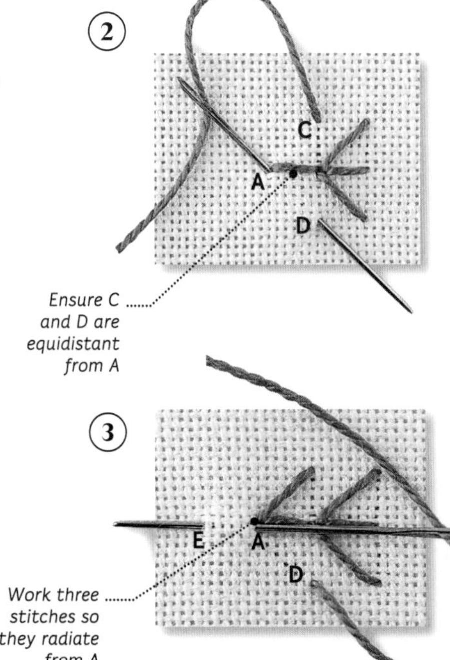

2
C
A
D
Ensure C and D are equidistant from A
3
E
A
D
Work three stitches so they radiate from A

1 Come out at **A**. Insert the needle at **B** to make a horizontal stitch. Come out directly above **B**, at **C**.

2 Re-insert the needle at **A** and bring it out below **C**, at **D**.

3 Insert the needle again at **A** and come out at **E**, ready to start the next group of stitches.

Bosnian

OTHER NAME
Fence stitch

LEVEL
Easy

USES
Straight borders or outlines; in rows as filling

METHOD
Worked horizontally in two journeys

MATERIALS
Any fabric; any thread

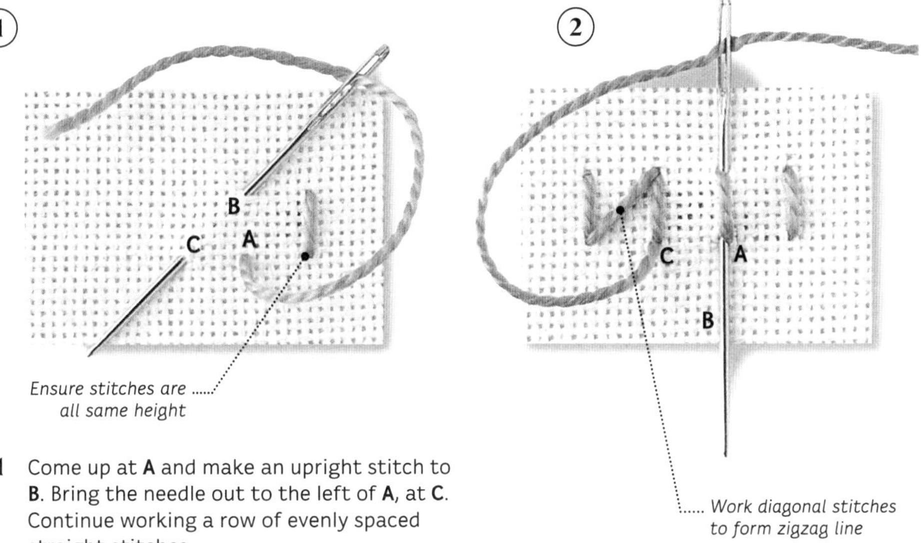
1
B
C
A
Ensure stitches are all same height
2
C
A
B
Work diagonal stitches to form zigzag line

1 Come up at **A** and make an upright stitch to **B**. Bring the needle out to the left of **A**, at **C**. Continue working a row of evenly spaced straight stitches.

2 Fill the spaces with slanting stitches. Come up at **C**, insert the needle at **B**, then bring it out at **A**. Repeat to the end of the row.

Chevron

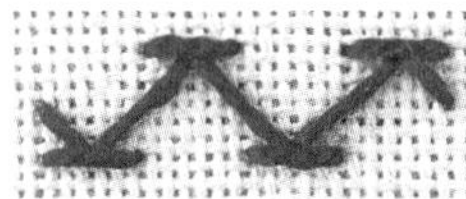

LEVEL
Easy

USES
Straight border; in close rows as light filling; in smocking as surface honeycomb stitch

METHOD
Worked horizontally between parallel lines

MATERIALS
Any fabric; any thread

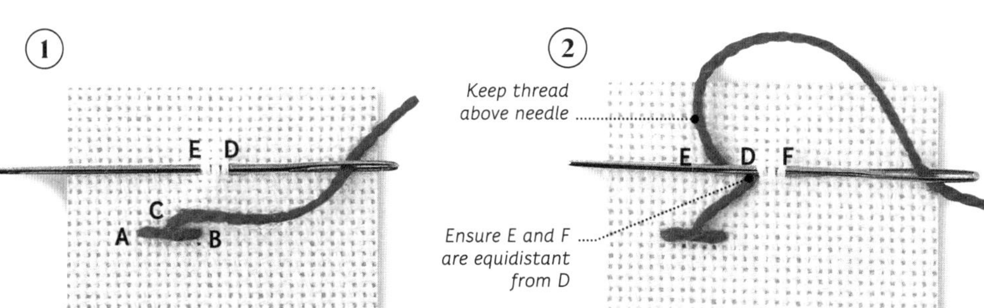
1
E D
C
A
B
2
Keep thread above needle
E
D
F
Ensure E and F are equidistant from D

1 Start at **A** and make a horizontal straight stitch to **B**. Bring the needle out at the centre of the stitch, at **C**. Take the needle up to the right and insert it at **D**, then bring it out in line with **D**, at **E**.

2 Take the needle to the right and insert it at **F**. Come out again at **D**.

3 Take the needle down and insert at **G**, then come out at **H**. Insert the needle to the right, at **J**, and bring it out again at **G**. Repeat the sequence to continue.

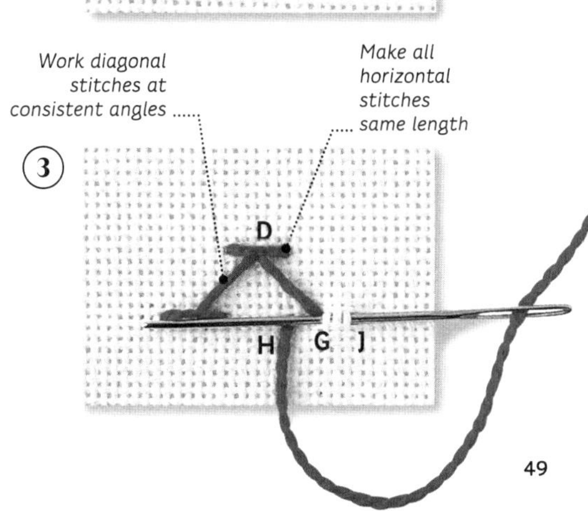
Work diagonal stitches at consistent angles
Make all horizontal stitches same length
3
D
H
G
J

Thorn

LEVEL
Easy

USES
Curved floral sprays and foliage; straight borders

METHOD
Laid thread couched down (see p.42) with pairs of crossed stitches

MATERIALS
Any fabric; any embroidery thread - fine threads give a feathery appearance; frame

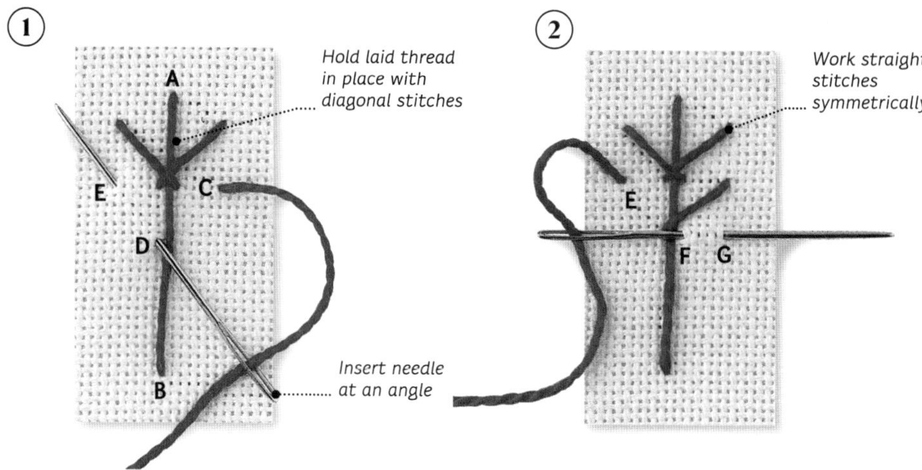
1
A
E
C
D
B
Hold laid thread in place with diagonal stitches
Insert needle at an angle
2
E
F
G
Work straight stitches symmetrically

1 Start at **A** and, following the line to be worked, make a long stitch to **B**. Use a second thread to work the couching stitches. Come up at **C** and take the needle across the laid thread to insert at **D**. Bring the needle out at **E**.

2 Insert the needle at **F** and bring it out at **G**, ready to make the next diagonal stitch. Make further pairs of stitches in the same way along the laid thread.

Cross

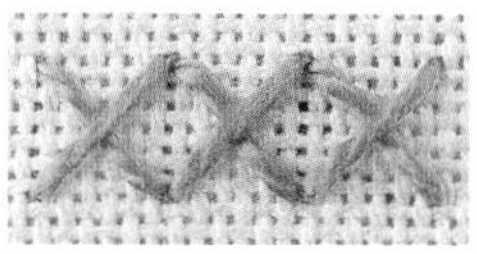

OTHER NAMES
Berlin stitch; sampler stitch

LEVEL
Easy

USES
Geometric designs; charted patterns; lettering

METHOD
Worked over equal number of horizontal and vertical threads

MATERIALS
Evenweave fabric; any embroidery thread

To work in rows:

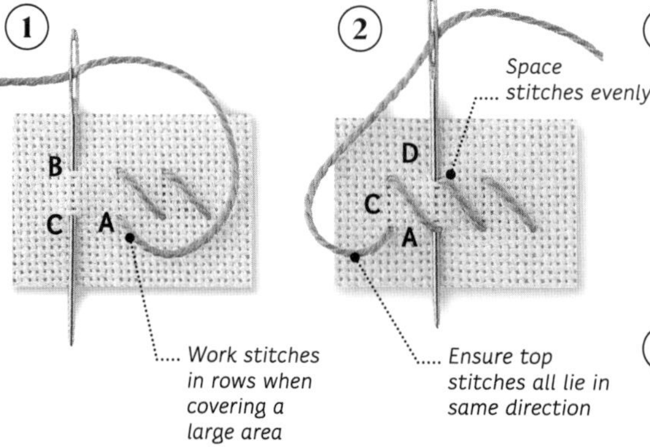
1
B
C
A
Work stitches in rows when covering a large area
2
D
C
A
Space stitches evenly
Ensure top stitches all lie in same direction

1 Come up at **A**, insert the needle at **B** and come out at **C**. Repeat to make a series of evenly spaced diagonal stitches.

2 Work the top stitches in the opposite direction. Take the needle across from **C** and insert at **D**. Come out again at **A**. Repeat to complete the row.

To work stitches singly:

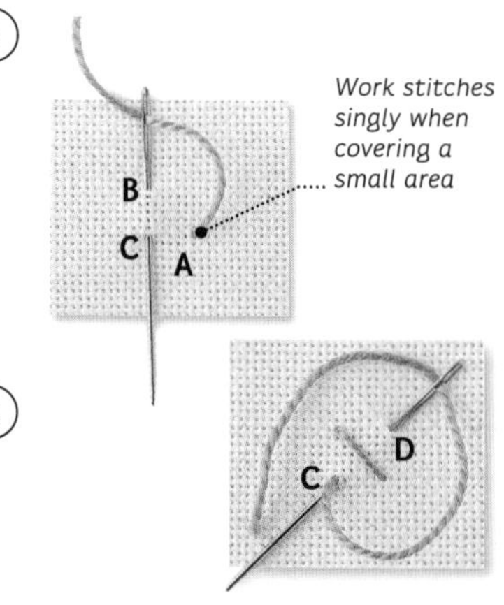
1
B
C
A
Work stitches singly when covering a small area
2
C
D

1 Start at **A**. Take the needle diagonally left and insert at **B**, then bring it out at **C**.

2 Insert the needle at **D** to complete the cross. Bring the needle out at **C** to work the next stitch.

Long-armed Cross

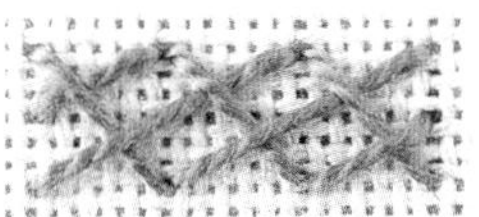

OTHER NAMES
Plaited Slav stitch; Portuguese stitch

LEVEL
Intermediate

USES
Straight frame or border; in rows as filling

METHOD
Cross stitch variation worked horizontally

MATERIALS
Evenweave fabric; thick embroidery threads – heavier threads give a more raised appearance

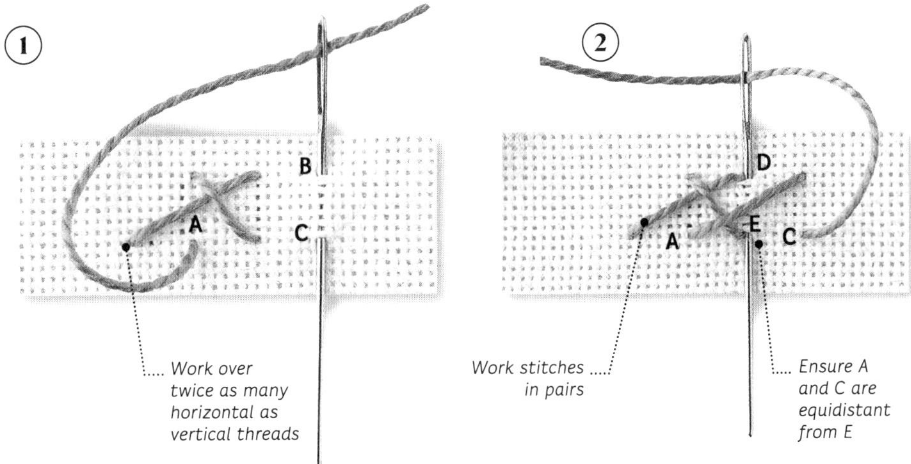
1
B
A
C
Work over twice as many horizontal as vertical threads
2
D
E
A
C
Work stitches in pairs
Ensure A and C are equidistant from E

1 Come up at **A** and make a long diagonal stitch to **B**. Come out directly below **B**, at **C**.

2 Take the needle back and insert at **D**, then bring it out directly below, at **E**. Repeat these two steps to the end of the row.

Zigzag

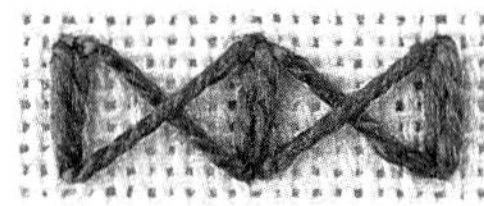

LEVEL
Easy

USES
Open outline; in close rows as open filling

METHOD
Alternate upright and diagonal stitches, worked horizontally in two journeys

MATERIALS
Any fabric; any thread – fine twisted threads give a more open effect

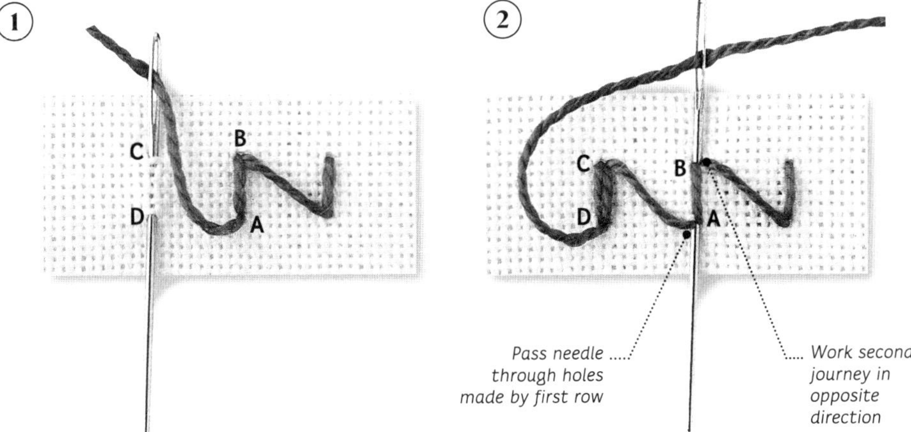
1
C
B
D
A
2
C
B
D
A
Pass needle through holes made by first row
Work second journey in opposite direction

1 Come up at **A** and insert the needle directly above, at **B**. Bring it out again at **A** and make a diagonal stitch to **C**. Come up below **C**, at **D**. Continue to the end of the row, finishing with an upright stitch.

2 Take the needle down again at **C** and bring it up at **D** to make a second upright stitch. Insert at **B** to make a diagonal stitch, then come up at **A**. Repeat this step until all the crosses are complete.

Herringbone

OTHER NAMES
Russian cross stitch; fishnet stitch

LEVEL
Easy

USES
Decorative straight edging; base for composite stitches; in rows as open filling

MATERIALS
Evenweave fabric; any embroidery thread

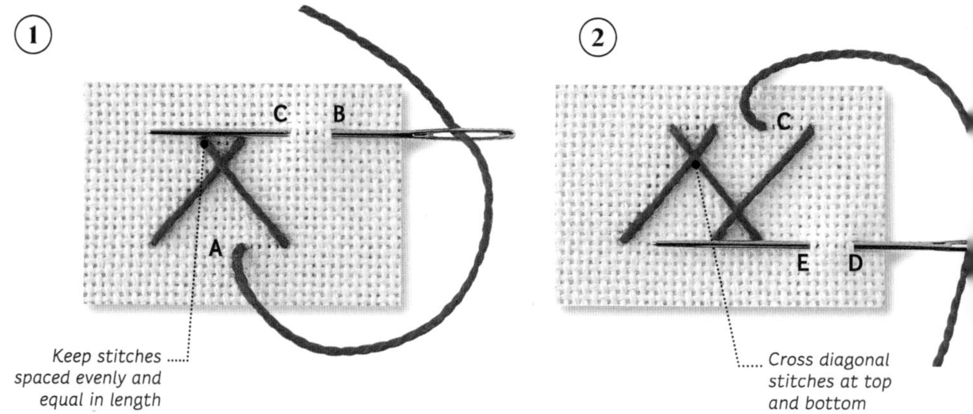
1
C
B
A
Keep stitches spaced evenly and equal in length
2
C
E
D
Cross diagonal stitches at top and bottom

1 Come up at **A**, take the needle diagonally up to **B** and insert. Bring it out at **C**.

2 Take the needle down and insert at **D**, then bring it through at **E**. Repeat these two steps to the end of the row.

Closed Herringbone

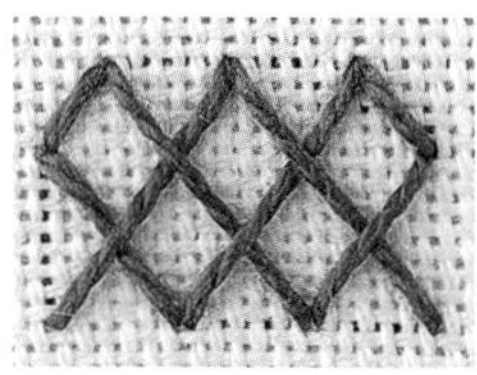

OTHER NAMES
Double back stitch

LEVEL
Intermediate

USES
Open border; in rows as lattice filling

METHOD
Herringbone variation

MATERIALS
Evenweave fabric; any thread; frame

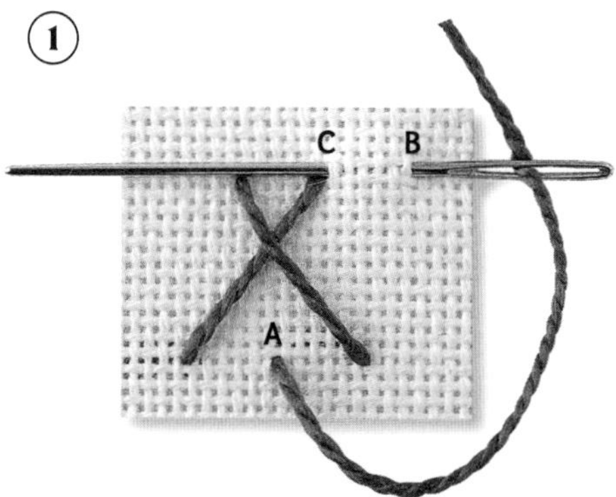
1
C
B
A

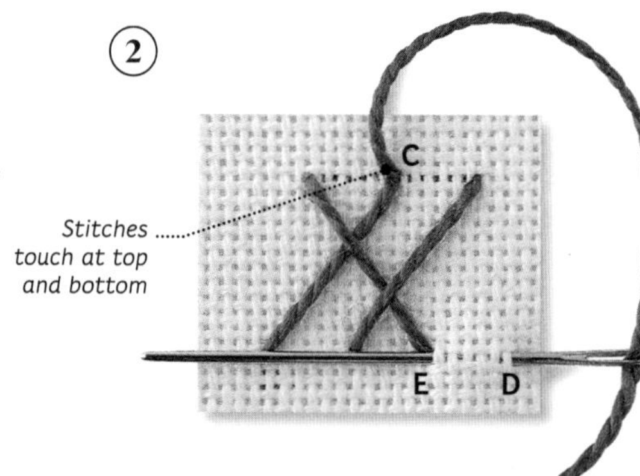
2
C
Stitches touch at top and bottom
E
D

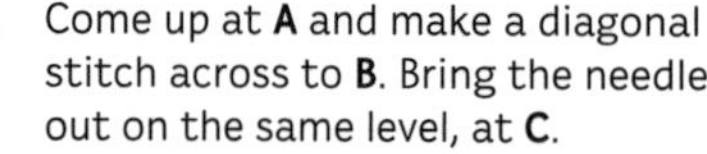

1 Come up at **A** and make a diagonal stitch across to **B**. Bring the needle out on the same level, at **C**.

2 Take the needle down to **D** and insert, then come through at **E**. Repeat these two steps to continue.

Stitch Variation

Shadow stitch is formed when closed herringbone stitch is worked on the reverse side of a semi-transparent material. The design is outlined with back stitch and the crossed threads form a dense band of colour, which shows through the fabric. Mount fabric in a frame.

Basket

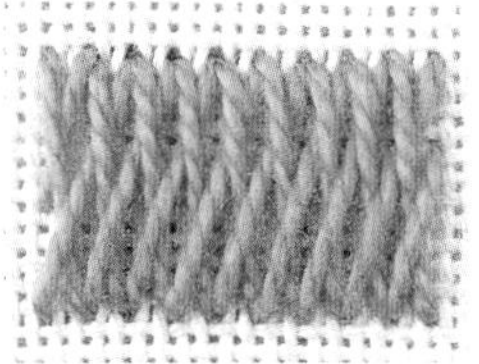

LEVEL
Advanced

USES
Straight bands and borders; in rows as a filling

METHOD
Alternate forward and backward stitches, worked downwards between two parallel lines

MATERIALS
Any fabric; stranded thread gives a smoother finish

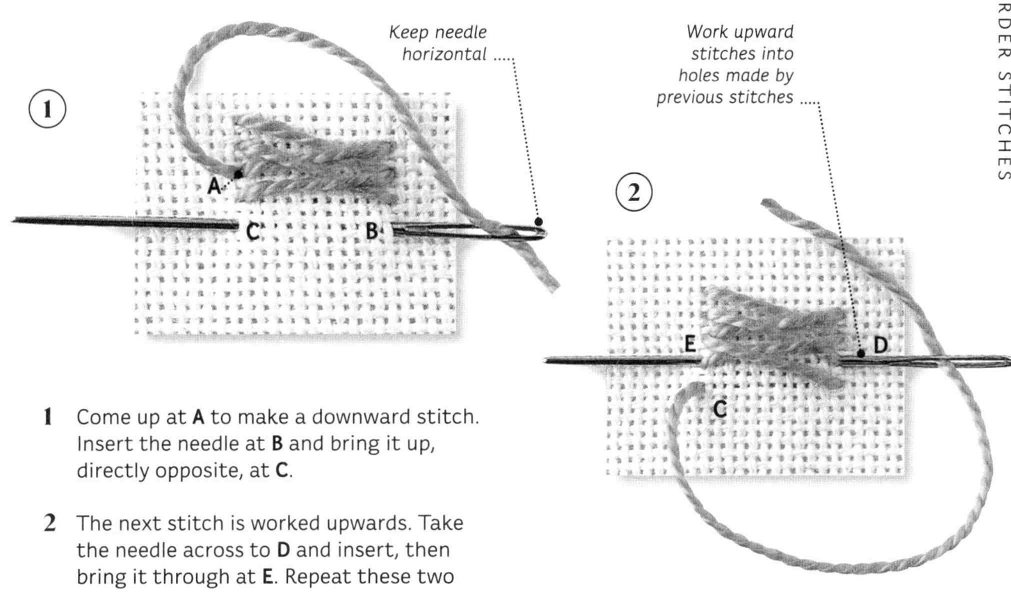
1
Keep needle horizontal
A
C
B
2
Work upward stitches into holes made by previous stitches
E
D
C

1 Come up at **A** to make a downward stitch. Insert the needle at **B** and bring it up, directly opposite, at **C**.

2 The next stitch is worked upwards. Take the needle across to **D** and insert, then bring it through at **E**. Repeat these two steps to continue.

Wheatear

LEVEL
Intermediate

USES
Straight or gently curved outlines; traditionally worked on smocks and childrens' clothes; used singly as filling (see p.81)

METHOD
Looped stitch, worked from top to bottom

MATERIALS
Any fabric; non-stranded threads give raised effect

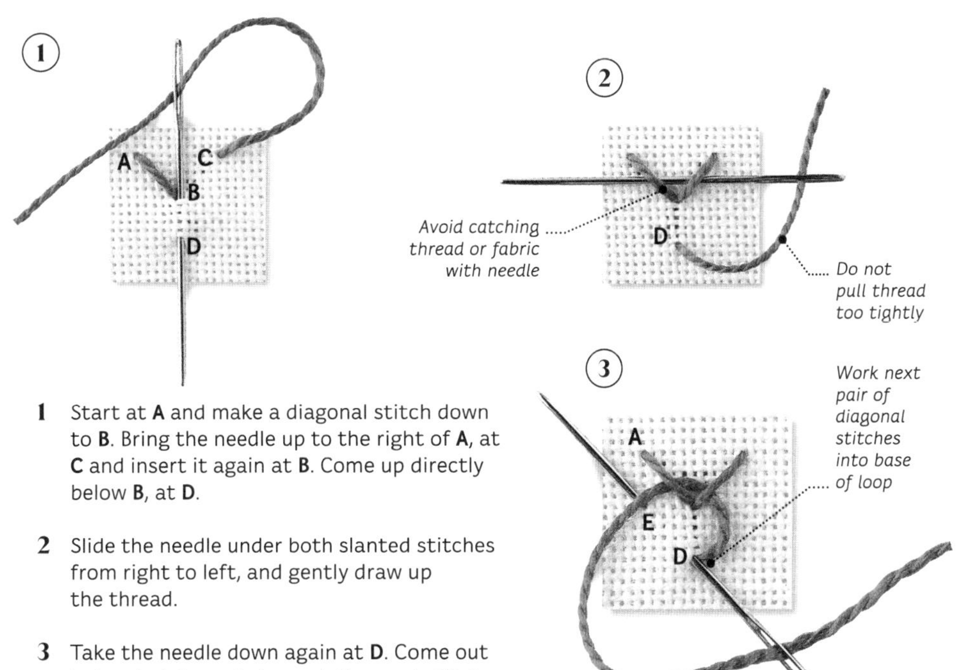
1
A
C
B
D
2
Avoid catching thread or fabric with needle
D
Do not pull thread too tightly
3
A
E
D
Work next pair of diagonal stitches into base of loop

1 Start at **A** and make a diagonal stitch down to **B**. Bring the needle up to the right of **A**, at **C** and insert it again at **B**. Come up directly below **B**, at **D**.

2 Slide the needle under both slanted stitches from right to left, and gently draw up the thread.

3 Take the needle down again at **D**. Come out below **A** at **E**, ready to work the next stitch.

Russian Chain

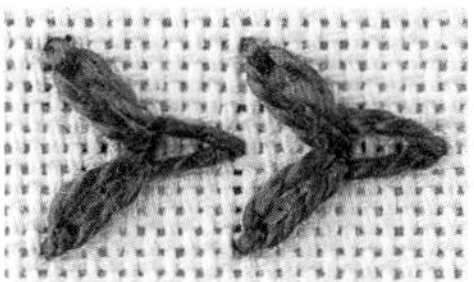

LEVEL
Easy

USES
Straight or curved border; individually as powdered filling

METHOD
Worked in detached groups of three chain stitches

MATERIALS
Any fabric; thick thread

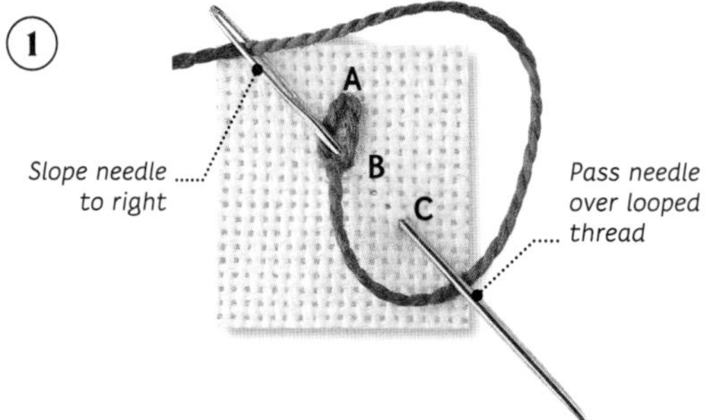

1
A
B
C
Slope needle to right
Pass needle over looped thread

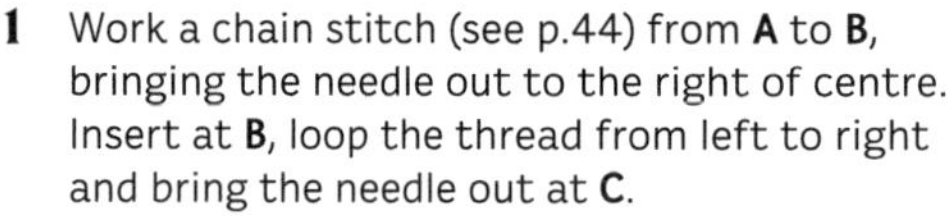

1 Work a chain stitch (see p.44) from **A** to **B**, bringing the needle out to the right of centre. Insert at **B**, loop the thread from left to right and bring the needle out at **C**.

2 Insert the needle at **D** to make a tie stitch (see p.20), then bring the needle up inside the first loop, at **E**.

3 Make the third chain stitch at an angle from **E** to **F** in the same way. Finish with a tie stitch. Work the next and subsequent groups of stitches directly below the first.

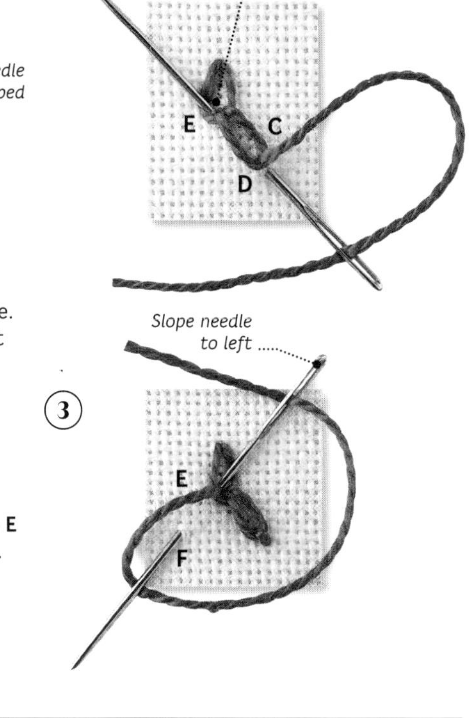

2
Needle emerges to left of previous stitch
E
C
D
Slope needle to left
3
E
F

Petal

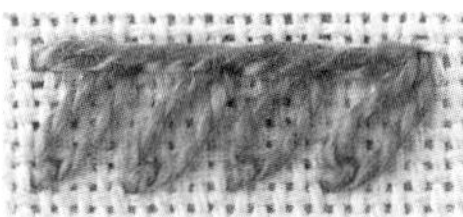

OTHER NAME
Pendant chain stitch

LEVEL
Intermediate

USES
Curved and straight lines; in rows as filling

METHOD
Angled link stitches combined with a row of stem stitches

MATERIALS
Any fabric; any thick thread

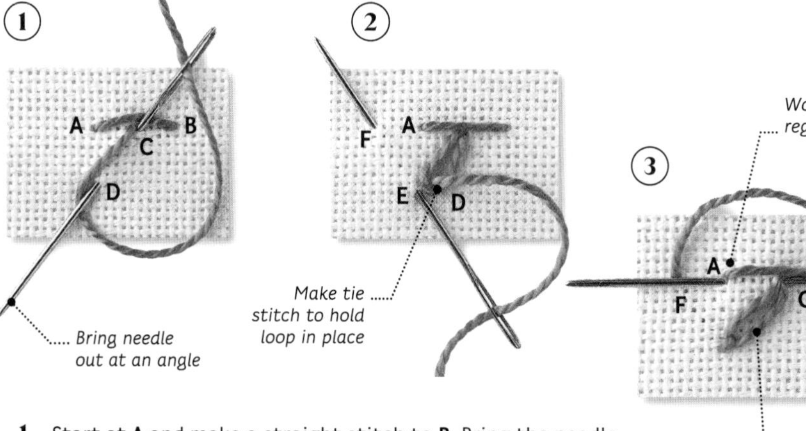

1
A
B
C
D
Bring needle out at an angle
2
F
A
E
D
Make tie stitch to hold loop in place
3
Work stitches at regular intervals
A
F
C
Ensure loops are same length

1 Start at **A** and make a straight stitch to **B**. Bring the needle up at the centre of the stitch at **C**. Work a chain stitch (see p.44) from **C** to **D**.

2 Insert the needle at **E** to make a tie stitch (see p.20). Come out to the left of **A** at **F**.

3 Insert the needle again at the top of the loop, at **C**, and come out at **A**, ready to make the next pair of stitches.

Zigzag Chain

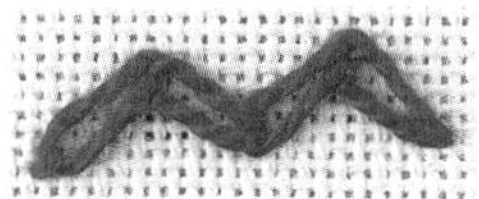

OTHER NAME
Vandyke chain

LEVEL
Intermediate

USES
Straight and gently curved lines and outlines

METHOD
Chain stitches worked at alternate angles

MATERIALS
Any fabric; twisted thread; sharp needle

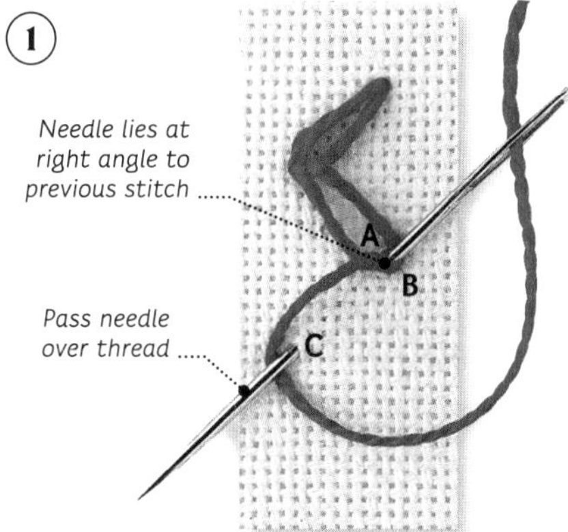
1
Needle lies at right angle to previous stitch
A
B
Pass needle over thread
C

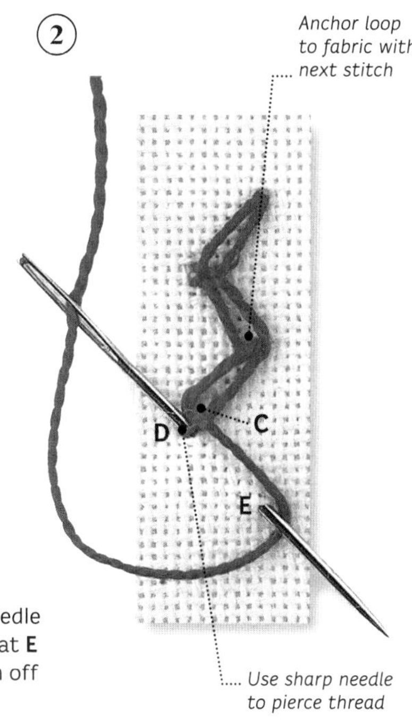
2
Anchor loop to fabric with next stitch
D
C
E
Use sharp needle to pierce thread

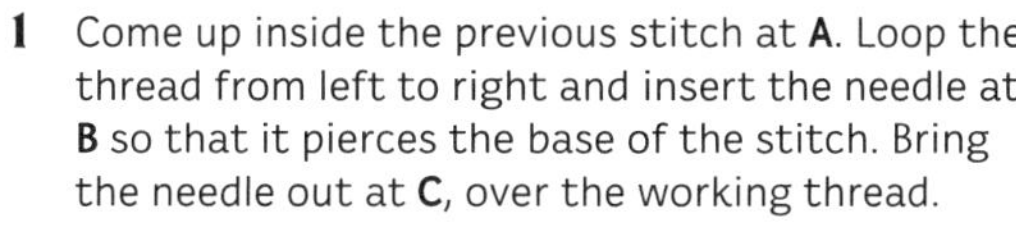

1 Come up inside the previous stitch at **A**. Loop the thread from left to right and insert the needle at **B** so that it pierces the base of the stitch. Bring the needle out at **C**, over the working thread.

2 Loop the thread from right to left and insert the needle at **D**, through the base of the last stitch. Come out at **E** and continue making stitches at right angles. Finish off with a tie stitch (see p.20) over the final loop.

Rosette Chain

OTHER NAME
Bead edging stitch

LEVEL
Advanced

USES
Straight or curved borders

METHOD
Twisted chain variation, worked horizontally

MATERIALS
Any fabric; thick non-stranded thread

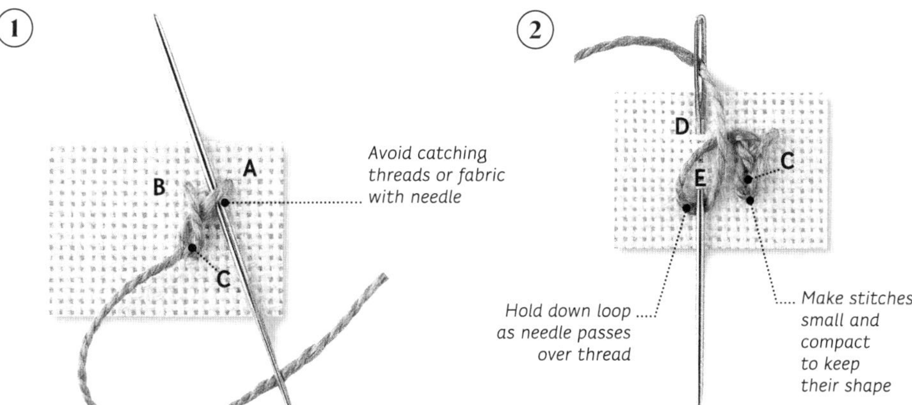
1
A
B
C
Avoid catching threads or fabric with needle
2
D
E
C
Hold down loop as needle passes over thread
Make stitches small and compact to keep their shape

1 Start at **A**. Loop the thread from left to right and insert the needle at **B**. Come up at **C** and pull the needle through the loop. Slide the needle under the thread to the left of **A** from bottom to top, and pull through gently.

2 Insert the needle at **D** and come up through the loop at **E**, as before. Repeat to continue.

Technique Variation

Work rosette chain in a circle to create a petalled flower motif. The stitches radiate from a central point and should be evenly spaced.

Loop

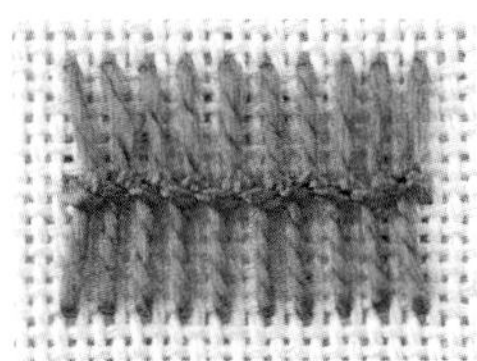

OTHER NAME
Centipede stitch

LEVEL
Intermediate

USES
Straight and curved lines; filling for leaf shapes

METHOD
Looped stitch worked horizontally

MATERIALS
Any fabric; any thread

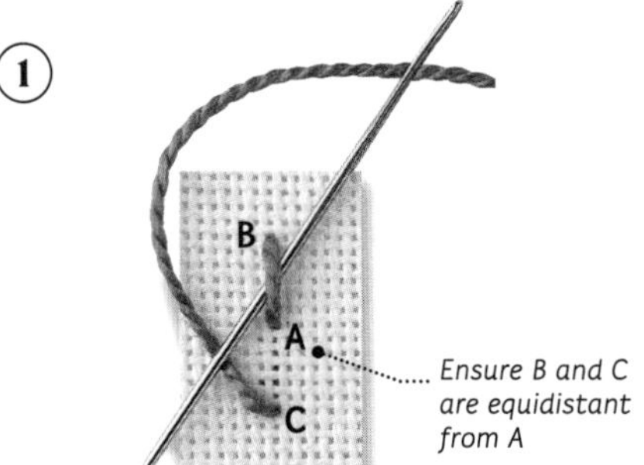

1
B
A
C
Ensure B and C are equidistant from A

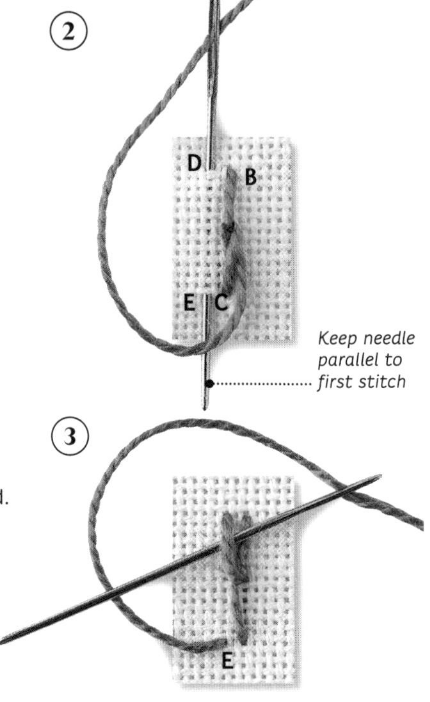

2
D
B
E
C
Keep needle parallel to first stitch
3
E

1 Start at **A**. Make an upright stitch to **B**, then come out directly below **A**, at **C**. Slide the needle under the stitch from right to left, over the working thread.

2 Insert the needle level with **B** at **D**. Come up at **E**, keeping the needle below the working thread.

3 Pass the needle under the previous stitch from right to left, over the working thread. Repeat steps 2 and 3 to continue. Finish off by taking the thread through to the back at the centre of the final stitch.

Flat Vandyke

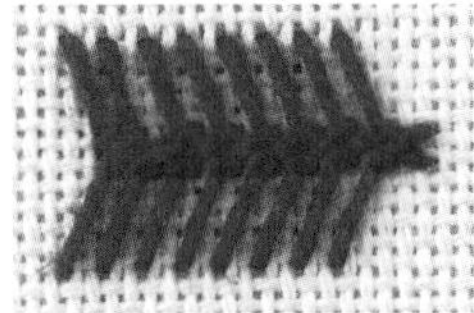

LEVEL
Intermediate

USES
Straight borders; gently curved outlines

METHOD
Overlapping pairs of extended cross stitches worked downwards

MATERIALS
Any fabric; any thick embroidery thread

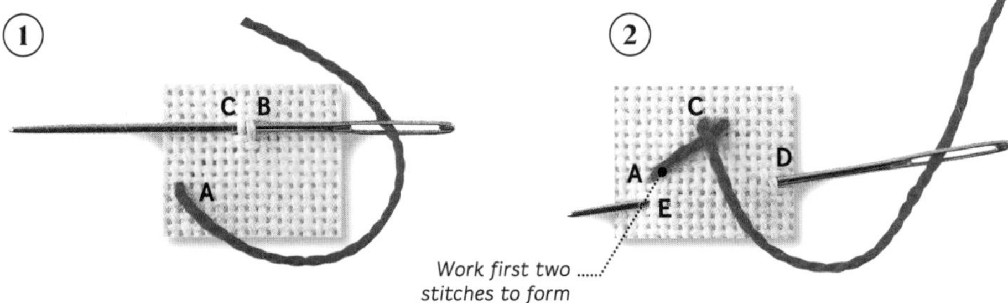

1
C B
A
2
C
A
D
E
Work first two stitches to form broad cross

1 Start at **A**. Make a diagonal stitch up to **B** and bring the needle out to the left of **B**, at **C**.

2 Take the needle down and insert level with **A**, at **D**. Come up below **A**, at **E**.

3 Pass the needle under the crossed stitches from **F** to **G**, picking up two threads of background fabric. Repeat steps 2 and 3 to continue.

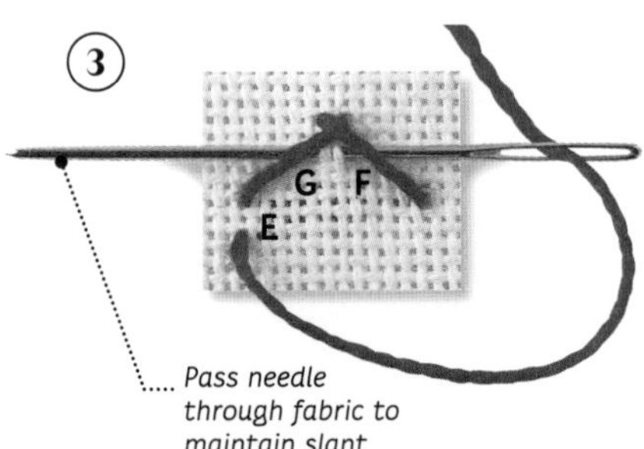

3
G
F
E
Pass needle through fabric to maintain slant

Ladder

OTHER NAME
Step stitch

LEVEL
Advanced

USES
Broad straight lines

METHOD
Worked downwards between parallel lines

MATERIALS
Any fabric; any thread; frame

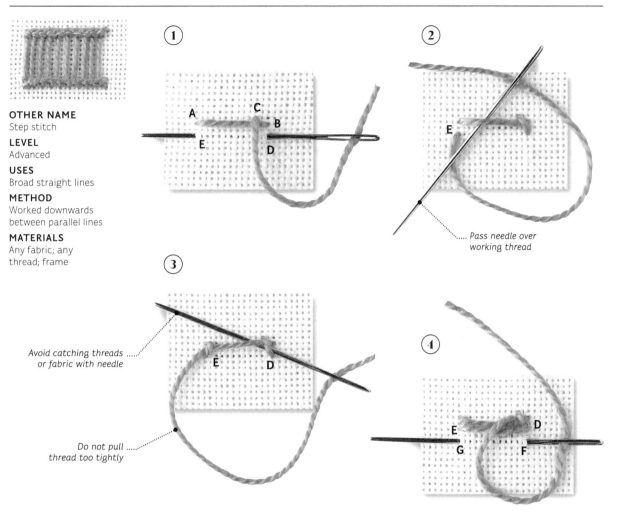

1

A C B E D

2

E

Pass needle over working thread

3

Avoid catching threads or fabric with needle

E D

Do not pull thread too tightly

4

E D G F

5

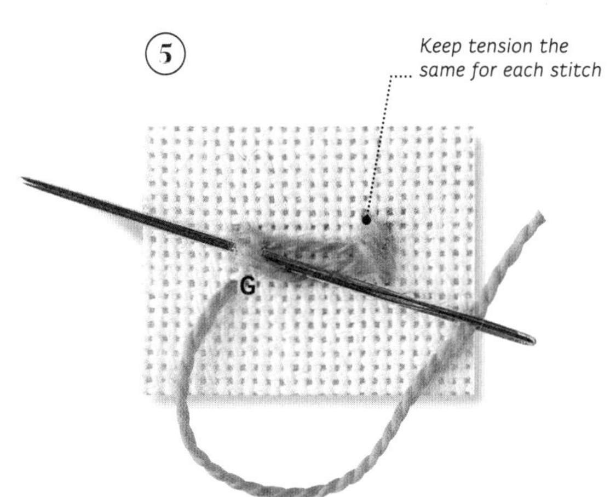

Keep tension the same for each stitch
G

1 Start at **A**. Make a horizontal straight stitch to **B**. Bring the needle out at **C**, then insert it at **D**. Come out below **A**, at **E**.

2 Slide the needle under the long stitch from top to bottom. Gently pull the thread through to the left, to form a knot.

3 Take the needle across to the right and slide it from right to left, diagonally under the first two stitches.

4 Insert the needle below **D**, at **F**. Come up level with **F**, at **G**.

5 Pass the needle up behind the centre of the left knot from right to left. Repeat from step 3 to continue.

Blanket

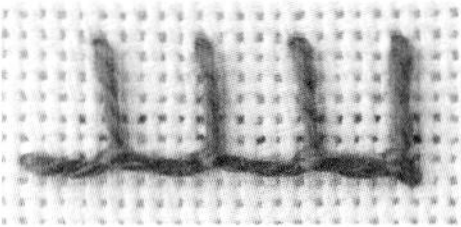

OTHER NAME
Open buttonhole stitch

LEVEL
Easy

USES
Straight or curved borders and outlines; finishing edges; securing appliqué shapes; filling (see p.87)

METHOD
Looped stitch, worked horizontally

MATERIALS
Woven fabrics or felt; any wool or thread

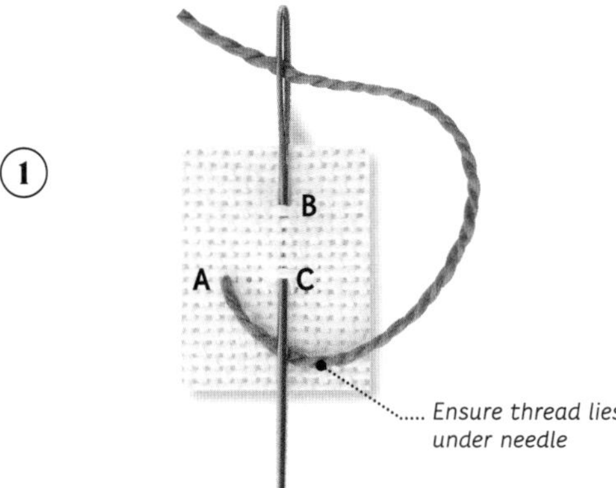

1
B
A
C
Ensure thread lies under needle

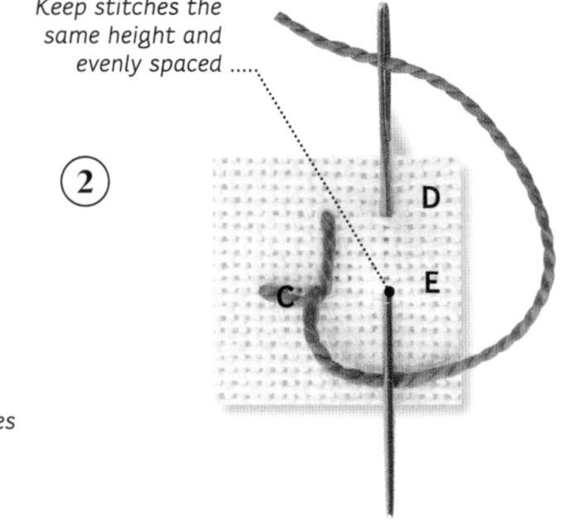

Keep stitches the same height and evenly spaced
2
D
C
E

1 Start at **A**. Take the needle up and insert at **B**, then bring it out directly below and level with **A**, at **C**.

2 Pull the needle down over the working thread. Insert the needle at **D** then bring it out at **E** to make the next stitch. Repeat this step to continue. Finish off with a tie stitch (see p.20) over the final loop.

Stitch Variation

Buttonhole stitch is worked in the same way but the stitches lie next to each other to create a solid line. The background fabric is completely covered and will not fray, so it is ideal for cutwork (see pp.112-113), and neatening hems and buttonholes.

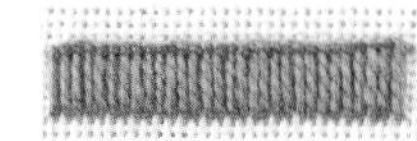

Closed Buttonhole

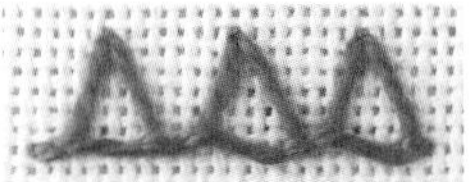

LEVEL
Easy

USES
Decorative edgings and borders; in rows as filling

METHOD
Triangular blanket stitch variation, worked horizontally

MATERIALS
Any fabric; any thread

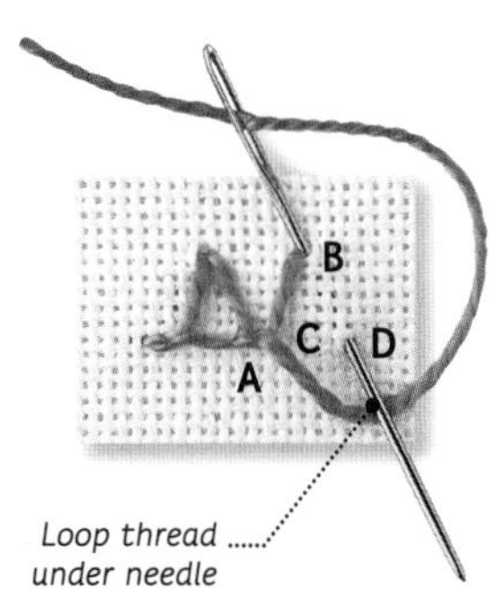

B
C
D
A
Loop thread under needle

Come up at **A** and insert the needle at **B**. Bring it up close to **A**, at **C**. Pull the needle over the working thread. Re-insert at **B** and come up to the right at **D**. Pull the needle over the loop. Repeat to continue.

Single Feather

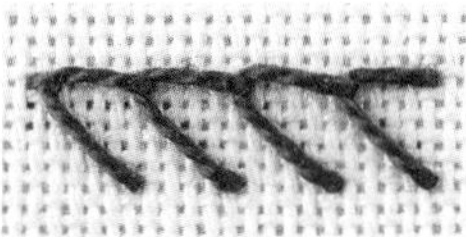

LEVEL
Easy

USES
Decorative edging; outlines and borders; in smocking; in rows as open filling

METHOD
Blanket stitch variation, worked downwards

MATERIALS
Any fabric; any embroidery thread

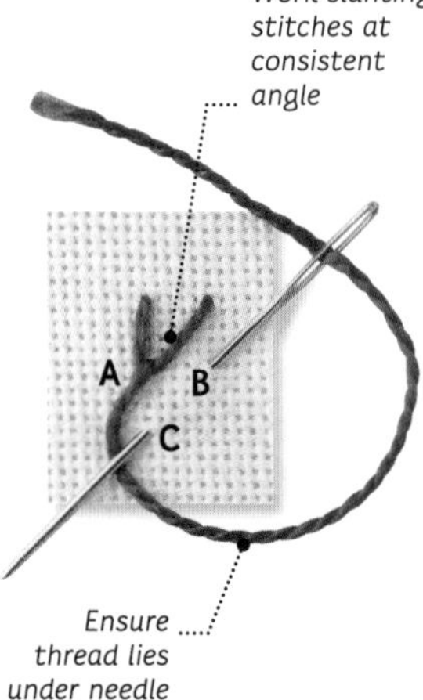

Work slanting stitches at consistent angle
A
B
C
Ensure thread lies under needle

Come up at **A**. Take the needle across to the right and insert it at **B**. Come out below **A**, at **C**. Pull the needle over the working thread. Repeat to continue.

Up and Down Buttonhole

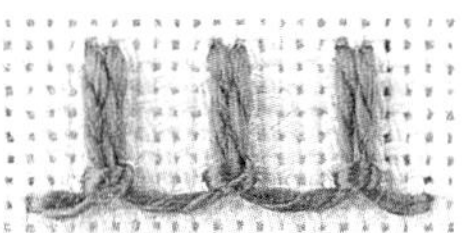

LEVEL
Intermediate

USES
Straight or curved lines and edgings; in rows as filling

METHOD
Buttonhole stitch variation, worked alternately upwards and downwards

MATERIALS
Any fabric; any embroidery thread

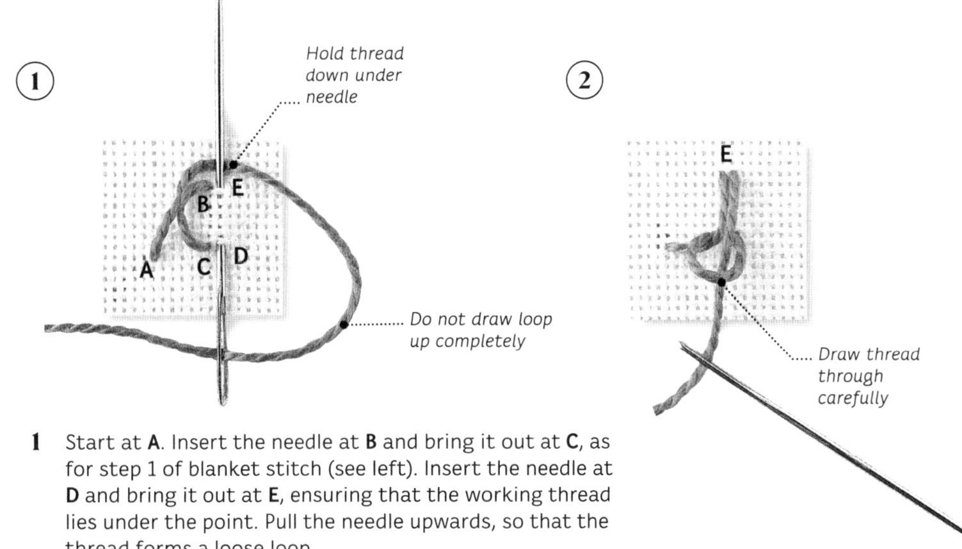
1
Hold thread down under needle
B
E
A
C
D
Do not draw loop up completely
2
E
Draw thread through carefully

1 Start at **A**. Insert the needle at **B** and bring it out at **C**, as for step 1 of blanket stitch (see left). Insert the needle at **D** and bring it out at **E**, ensuring that the working thread lies under the point. Pull the needle upwards, so that the thread forms a loose loop.

2 Take the needle downwards, pulling gently until the loop tightens around the base of the two upright stitches. Repeat these two steps to continue.

Open Cretan

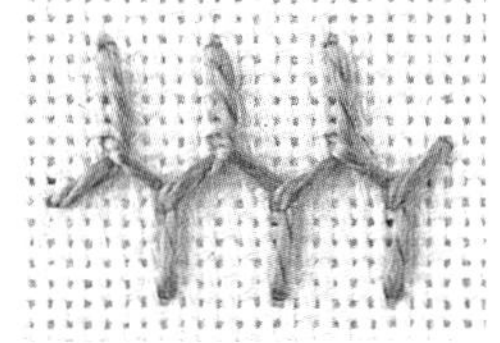

LEVEL
Easy

USES
Curved or straight lines; open filling

METHOD
Looped stitch worked from top to bottom

MATERIALS
Any fabric; any thread – finer threads give a lacy appearance; frame

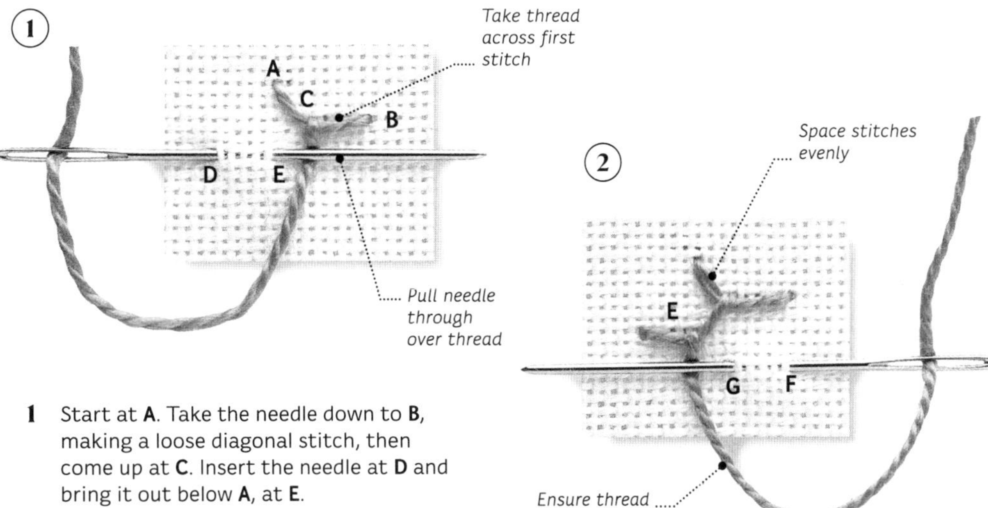
1
Take thread across first stitch
A
C
B
D
E
Pull needle through over thread
2
Space stitches evenly
E
G
F
Ensure thread lies below needle

1 Start at **A**. Take the needle down to **B**, making a loose diagonal stitch, then come up at **C**. Insert the needle at **D** and bring it out below **A**, at **E**.

2 Take the needle down and insert at **F**, then come out at **G**. Repeat these two steps to continue, working the stitches alternately from left to right.

Feather

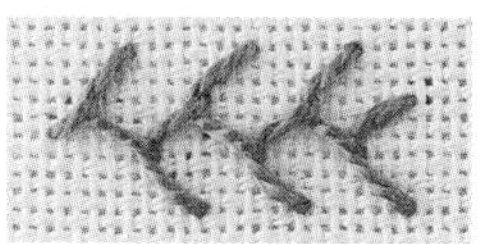

OTHER NAMES
Briar stitch;
single coral stitch

LEVEL
Easy

USES
Smocking; hems; crazy patchwork; with ribbon embroidery

METHOD
Looped stitch, worked alternately from left to right in straight or curved lines

MATERIALS
Any fabric; any thread

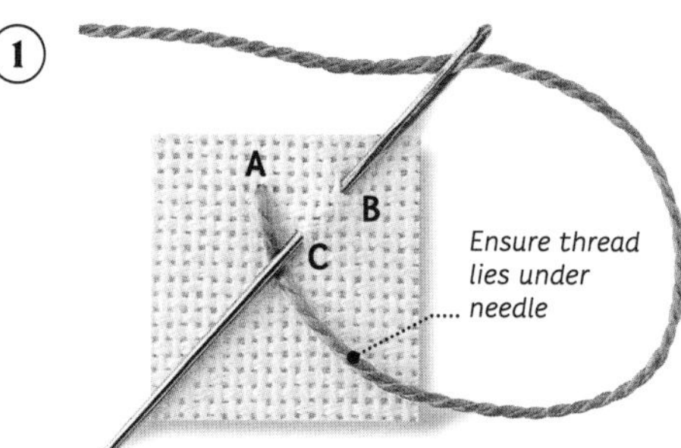
1
A
B
C
Ensure thread lies under needle

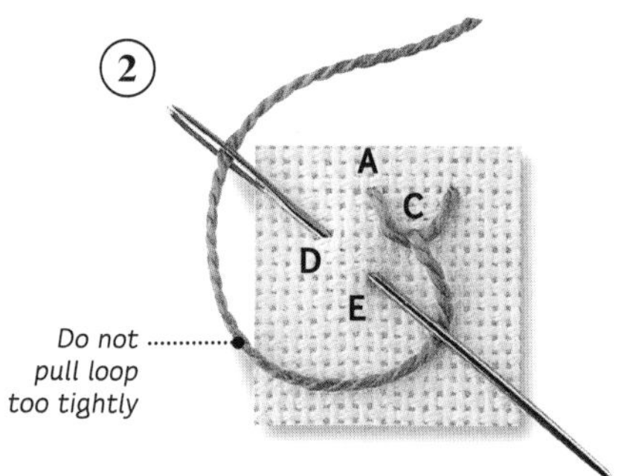
2
A
C
D
E
Do not pull loop too tightly

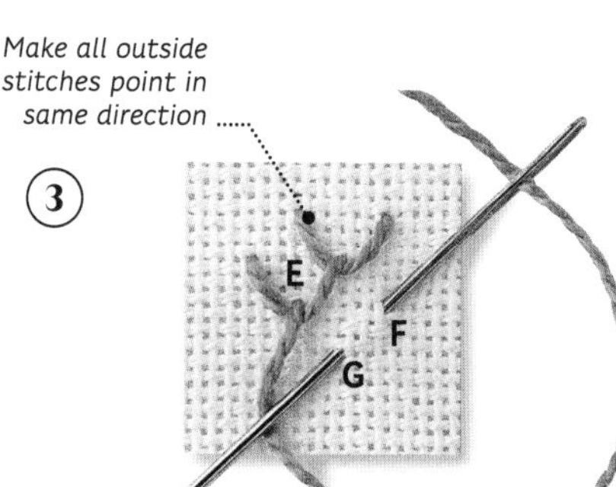
Make all outside stitches point in same direction
3
E
F
G

1 Start at **A** and insert the needle to the right, at **B**, leaving a thread loop. Bring the point out over the thread at **C** and pull through.

2 Insert the needle to the left of **C**, at **D**. Come out directly below **A**, at **E**, and pull through over the loop.

3 Insert the needle at **F** and bring it out at **G**, over the loop. Repeat steps 2 and 3 to continue. Finish off with a tie stitch (see p.20) over the final loop.

Closed Feather

LEVEL
Easy

USES
Straight lines and borders; in rows as open filling

METHOD
Feather variation worked downwards

MATERIALS
Any fabric; thick threads will give a textured effect

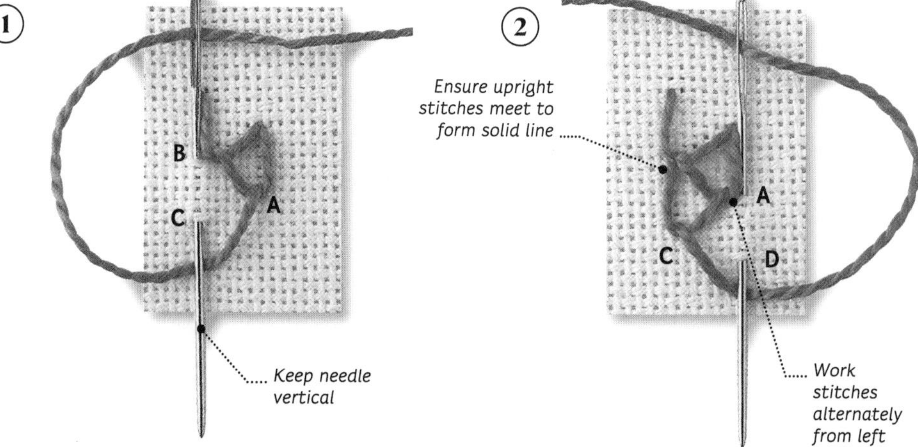
1
B
C
A
Keep needle vertical
2
Ensure upright stitches meet to form solid line
A
C
D
Work stitches alternately from left to right

1 Come up at **A**. Take the needle diagonally up to the left and insert at **B**. Bring the point out over the working thread at **C** and pull through.

2 Re-insert the needle at **A**, bring it out at **D** and pull through over the working thread. Repeat these two steps to continue. Finish off with a tie stitch (see p.20) over the last loop.

Double Feather

OTHER NAME
Thorn and briar stitch

LEVEL
Easy

USES
Foliage and branches; decorating children's garments

METHOD
Looped stitch, worked alternately from left to right

MATERIALS
Any fabric; fine thread will give a lacy effect

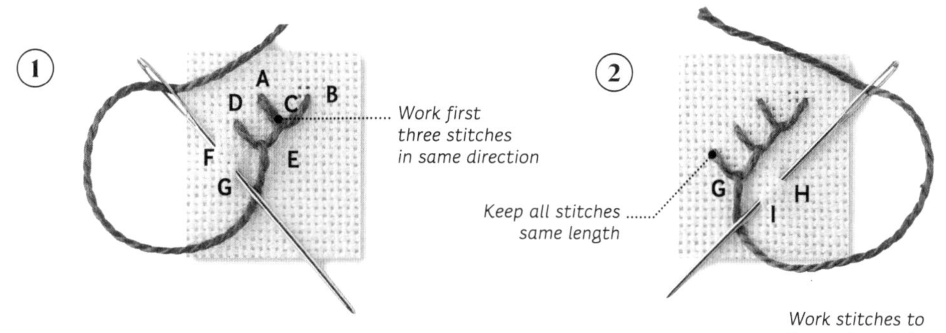
1
A
B
C
D
E
F
G
Work first three stitches in same direction
2
Keep all stitches same length
G
H
I

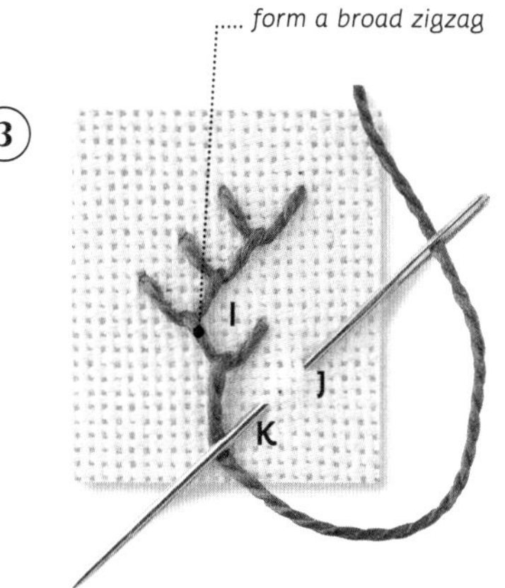
Work stitches to form a broad zigzag
3
I
J
K

1 Work the first two stitches as for feather stitch (see left), then make a second stitch to the left. Insert the needle level with **E** at **F**, and come out at **G**. Pull the needle through over the loop.

2 Take the needle across to the right and insert at **H**. Come out at **I** and pull through over the loop.

3 Make a second stitch to the right; take the needle down at **J**, bring it out at **K** and pull through over the loop. Continue working downwards, making two stitches one side, then the other.

Chained Feather

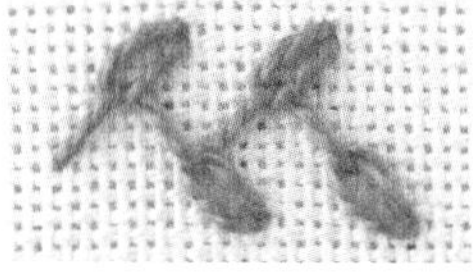

OTHER NAME
Feathered chain stitch

LEVEL
Intermediate

USES
Decorative borders; foliage

METHOD
Row of slanting picot stitches set at alternate angles

MATERIALS
Any fabric; any thread

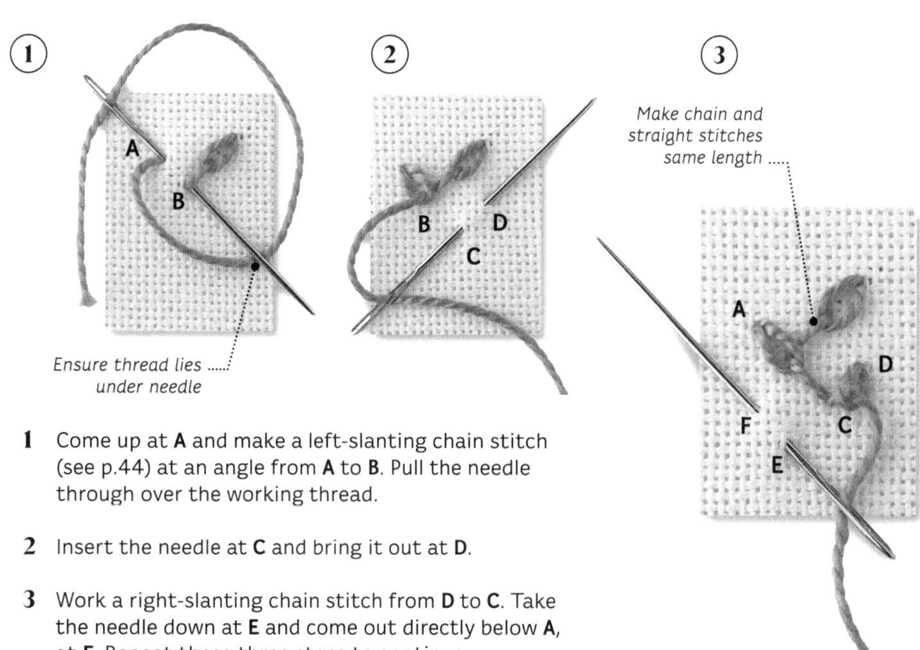
1
A
B
Ensure thread lies under needle
2
B
C
D
3
Make chain and straight stitches same length
A
C
D
E
F

1 Come up at **A** and make a left-slanting chain stitch (see p.44) at an angle from **A** to **B**. Pull the needle through over the working thread.

2 Insert the needle at **C** and bring it out at **D**.

3 Work a right-slanting chain stitch from **D** to **C**. Take the needle down at **E** and come out directly below **A**, at **F**. Repeat these three steps to continue

Composite Border Stitches

Here are the brightest and most detailed of all embroidery stitches. Some are made by interlacing basic outlines and borders with a contrasting thread, while the more complex are a combination of two or even three stitches. Magic chain and Sinhalese chain are flexible and can be sewn along a curved line, but the others are usually worked in straight rows. Repeat these to make textured patterns or get creative by alternating different stitches.

Crazy quilting, an elaborate form of patchwork, developed in the 1800s as a showcase for these elaborate stitches, but they are equally useful for embellishing repairs and patches on a favourite item of clothing, and there are endless ways to give them a new spin by adding isolated stitches and beading.

Pekinese

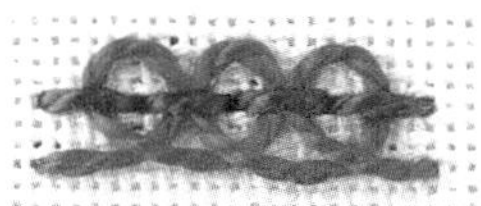

OTHER NAMES
Chinese stitch; forbidden stitch

LEVEL
Easy

USES
Decorative curved and straight outlines; in rows as filling

METHOD
Laced back stitch, worked horizontally

MATERIALS
Any fabric; lacing can be worked in thicker thread; blunt needles

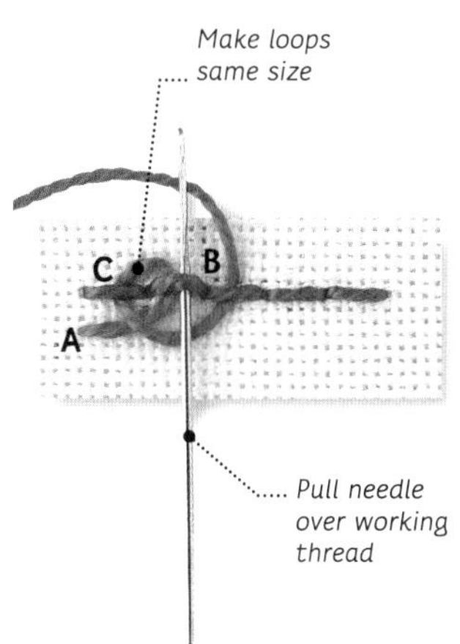
Make loops same size
C
B
A
Pull needle over working thread

Work a row of back stitch (see p.40). Bring the lacing thread out at **A**. Slide the needle upwards beneath **B**, then pass it downwards under **C**. Draw the thread up gently and continue lacing to the end of the row.

Laced Buttonhole

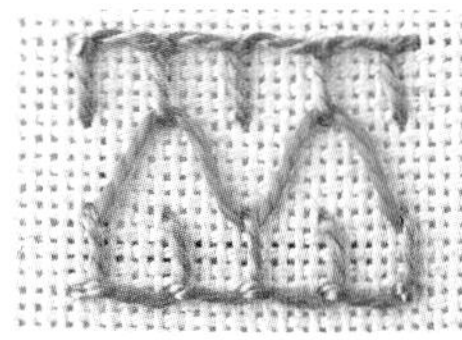

OTHER NAME
Threaded buttonhole stitch

LEVEL
Easy

USES
Decorative straight edgings and borders

METHOD
Two rows of blanket stitch with interlacing

MATERIALS
Any fabric; any thread in two colours; frame; blunt needle

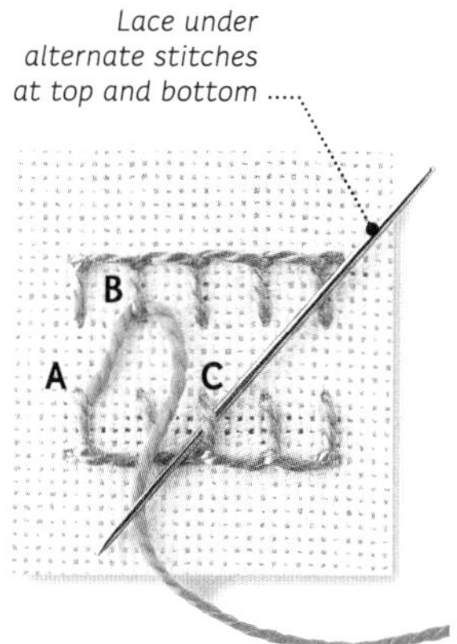
Lace under alternate stitches at top and bottom
B
A
C

Work two parallel rows of blanket stitch (see p.58) with the upright stitches pointing inwards. Bring the lacing thread out at **A**. Slide the needle under **B**, then beneath **C**. Continue lacing to the end of the row.

Interlaced Band

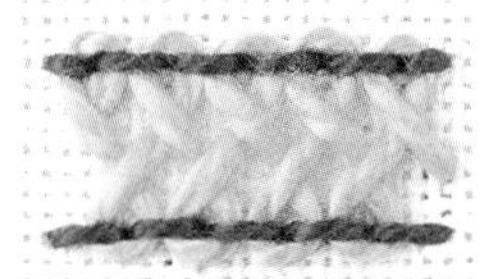

OTHER NAMES
Double Pekinese stitch; herringbone ladder stitch

LEVEL
Intermediate

USES
Braided straight lines

METHOD
Two rows of back stitch with looped interlacing

MATERIALS
Any fabric; any two threads in the same or different thicknesses; frame; blunt needle

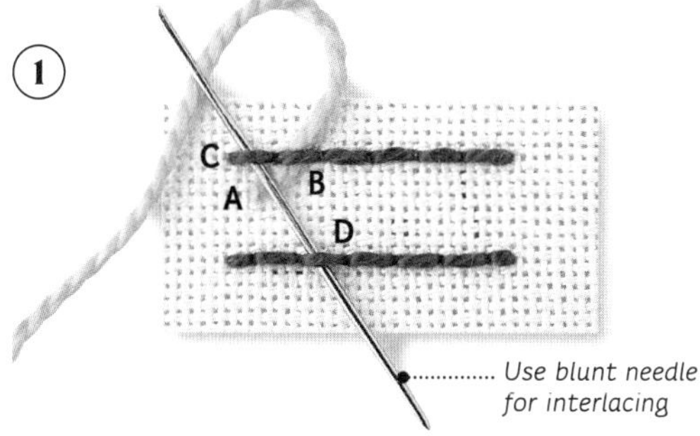
1
C
A
B
D
Use blunt needle for interlacing

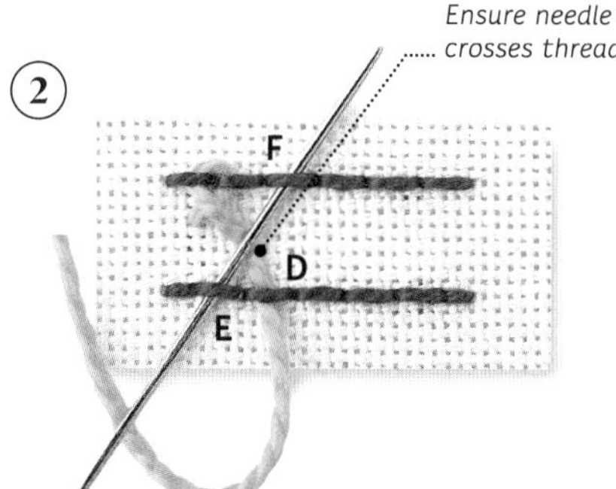
2
Ensure needle crosses thread
F
D
E

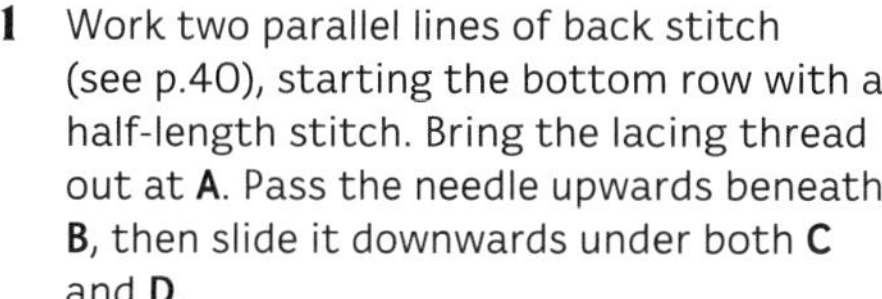

1 Work two parallel lines of back stitch (see p.40), starting the bottom row with a half-length stitch. Bring the lacing thread out at **A**. Pass the needle upwards beneath **B**, then slide it downwards under both **C** and **D**.

2 Take the needle to the left and slide it under **E** and **F**, then pull through. Continue lacing up and down to the end of the row.

Technique Variation

To create a wider, more open border, work the twisted interlacing over two rows of blanket stitch (see p.58), again using two colours.

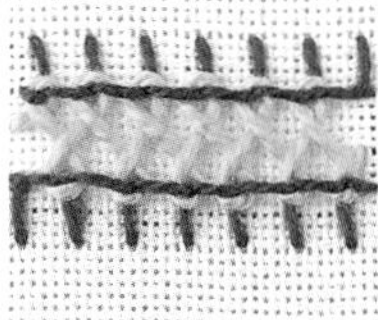

Magic Chain

OTHER NAMES
Chequered chain stitch; two-coloured chain stitch

LEVEL
Intermediate

USES
Straight or curved outlines

METHOD
Chain stitch variation worked with two threads

MATERIALS
Any fabric; two contrasting threads in the same weight; long-eyed needle

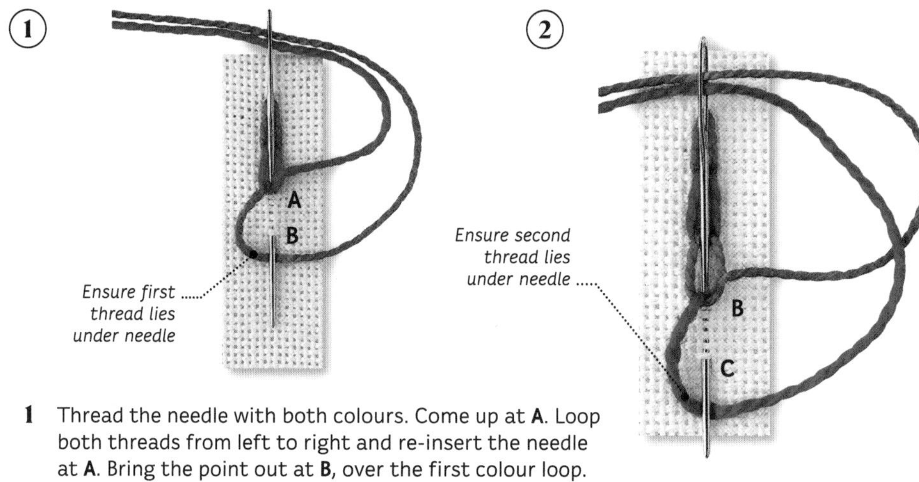
1
A
B
Ensure first thread lies under needle
2
Ensure second thread lies under needle
B
C

1 Thread the needle with both colours. Come up at **A**. Loop both threads from left to right and re-insert the needle at **A**. Bring the point out at **B**, over the first colour loop. Pull through gently; the second thread will slip to the back.

2 Loop the threads from left to right and re-insert the needle at **B**. Bring the point out at **C**, over the second colour loop: pull through. Repeat the steps to the end of the row. Finish with a tie stitch (see p.20) over the last loop.

Sinhalese Chain

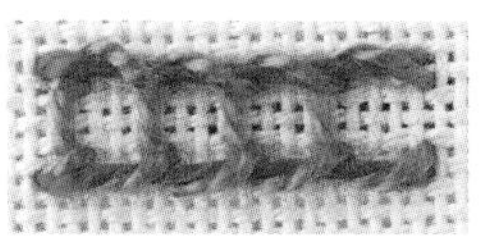

LEVEL
Advanced

USES
Decorative borders; curved or straight outlines; casing for narrow ribbon

METHOD
Square chain stitch worked downwards over contrasting threads

MATERIALS
Any fabric; any two different coloured threads of equal weight

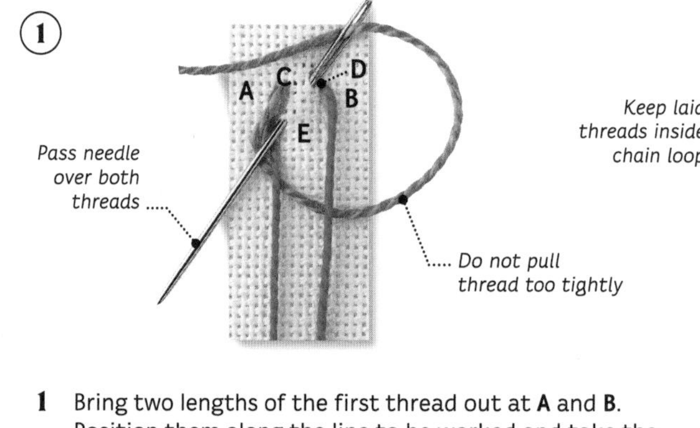
1
A
C
D
B
E
Pass needle over both threads
Do not pull thread too tightly

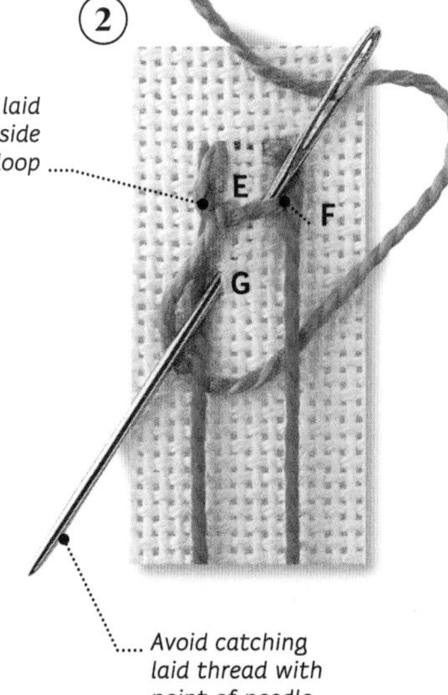
2
Keep laid threads inside chain loop
E
F
G
Avoid catching laid thread with point of needle

1 Bring two lengths of the first thread out at **A** and **B**. Position them along the line to be worked and take the ends through to the back without fastening off. Bring the second thread out at **C**. Pass the needle under the laid threads from left to right and insert it at **D**. Bring the point out over the thread loop at **E**.

2 Pull the needle through and insert to the right of **E**, at **F**, then bring it out at **G**, ready to work the next stitch. Repeat this step to continue, easing the laid threads into position. Fasten down the final loop with two tie stitches (see p.20) and finish off the laid threads on the reverse side.

Threaded Chain

LEVEL
Intermediate

USES
Light borders or outlines

METHOD
Row of link stitches with double interlacing

MATERIALS
Any fabric; any three threads in the same or different colours and weights; blunt needle

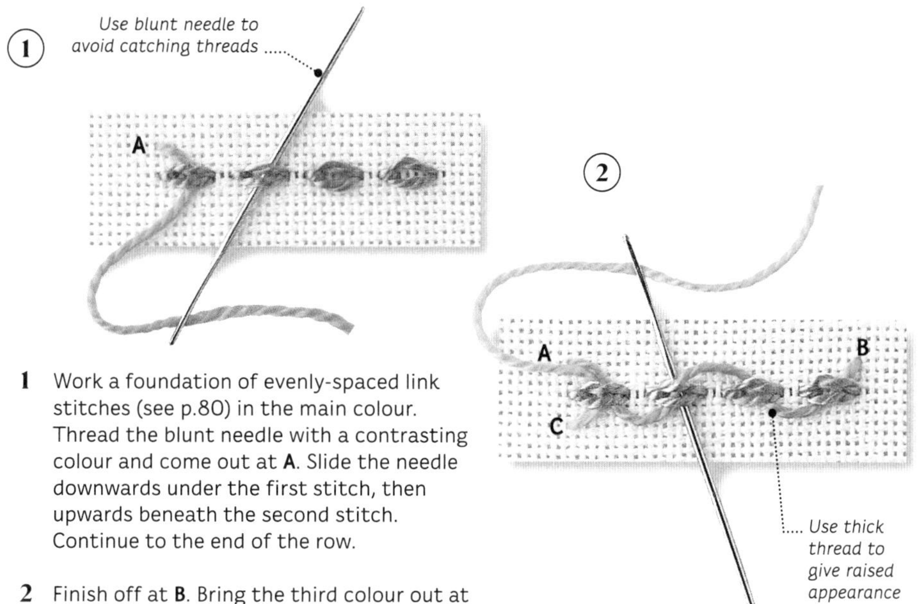
1
Use blunt needle to avoid catching threads
A
2
A
B
C
Use thick thread to give raised appearance to interlacing

1 Work a foundation of evenly-spaced link stitches (see p.80) in the main colour. Thread the blunt needle with a contrasting colour and come out at **A**. Slide the needle downwards under the first stitch, then upwards beneath the second stitch. Continue to the end of the row.

2 Finish off at **B**. Bring the third colour out at **C** and lace it alternately up and down under the link stitches, filling in the spaces.

Guilloche

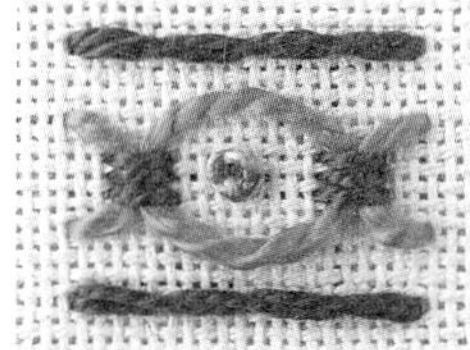

LEVEL
Advanced

USES
Multi-coloured straight borders and edgings

METHOD
Combination of stem and satin stitches with French knots and interlacing

MATERIALS
Evenweave fabric; thick thread in three colours; blunt needle

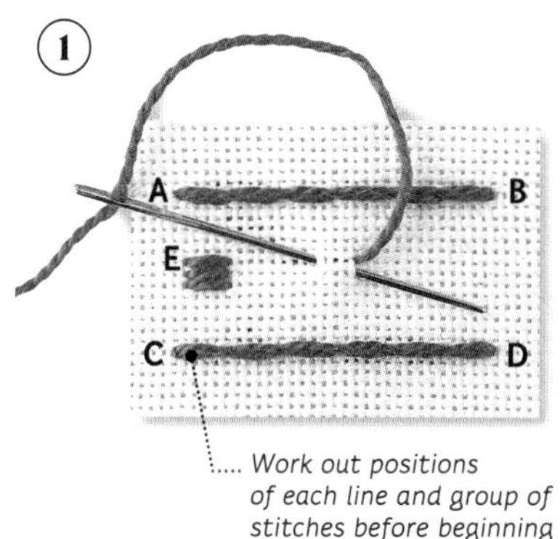
1
A
B
E
C
D

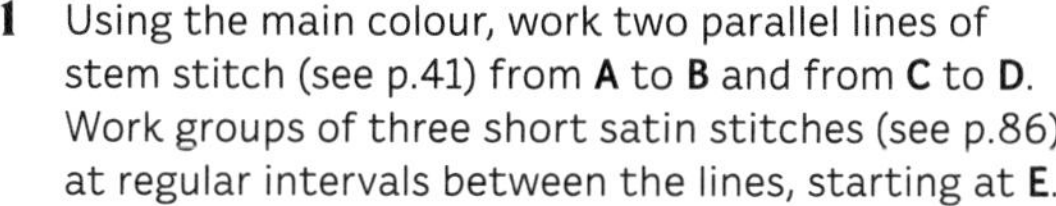
Work out positions of each line and group of stitches before beginning

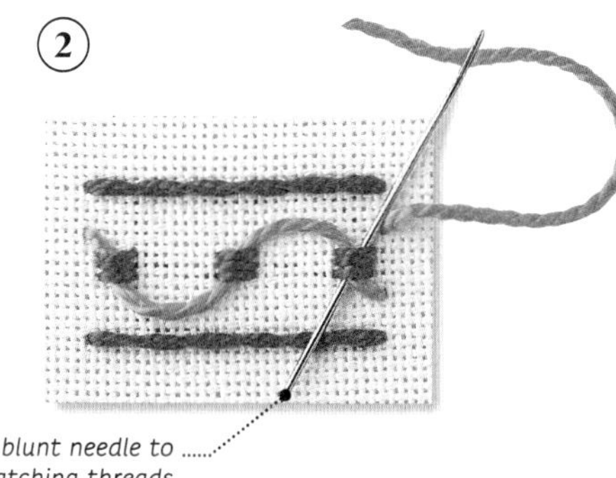
2
Use blunt needle to avoid catching threads

1 Using the main colour, work two parallel lines of stem stitch (see p.41) from **A** to **B** and from **C** to **D**. Work groups of three short satin stitches (see p.86) at regular intervals between the lines, starting at **E**.

2 Interlace the satin stitches with contrasting threads as for threaded chain stitch (see above).

3 Finish off by working a French knot (see p.76) in the centre of each loop, using the third thread.

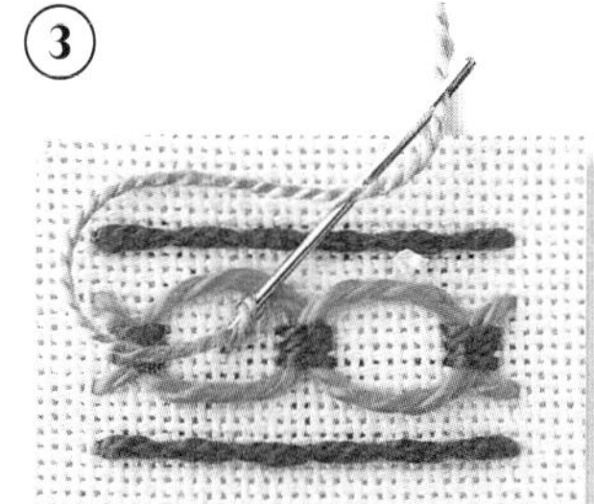
3

Raised Chevron

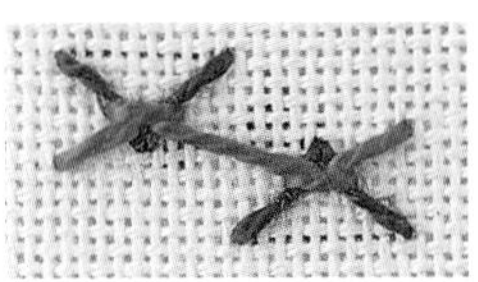

LEVEL
Intermediate

USES
Straight outlines and light borders

METHOD
Chevron stitch worked over two lines of arrowhead stitches

MATERIALS
Any fabric; thicker thread gives more texture – choose two contrasting colours

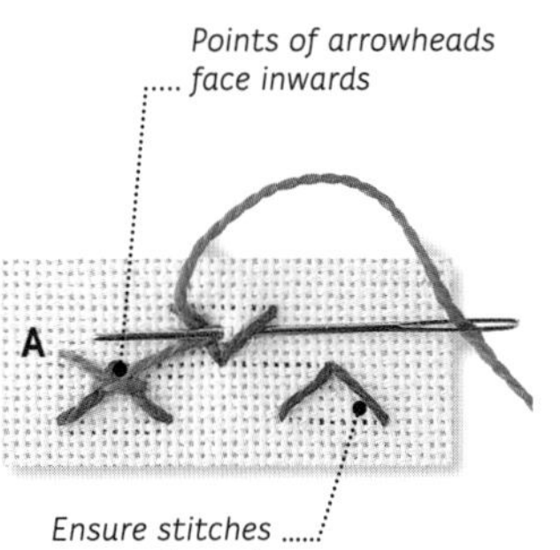
Points of arrowheads face inwards
A
Ensure stitches are spaced evenly

Stitch two parallel rows of arrowheads (see p.73) in the first colour. Bring the second thread out at **A** and work a band of chevron stitch (see p.49) from left to right, so that the horizontal stitches lie across the points of the arrowhead stitches.

Backstitched Herringbone

LEVEL
Easy

USES
Open borders; in rows as a lattice filling

METHOD
Herringbone stitch with back stitch detail

MATERIALS
Any fabric; two contrasting threads in the same or different weights

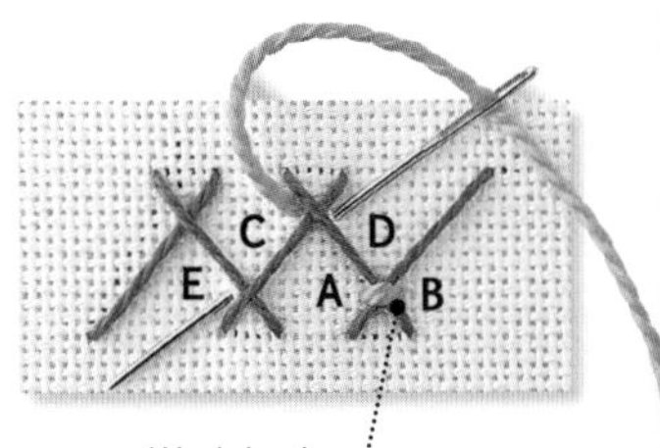
C
D
E
A
B
Work back stitches over crossed threads

Work a line of herringbone stitch (see p.52). Using the second thread, make a back stitch from **A** to **B**. Bring the needle up at **C**, insert at **D**, and come out at **E**. Continue to the end of the row.

Raised Lattice Band

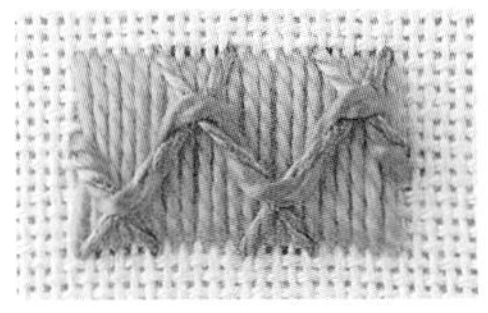

LEVEL
Advanced

USES
Decorative borders

METHOD
Interlaced herringbone stitch worked over padded satin stitch

MATERIALS
Any fabric; lustrous thread in three colours; blunt needle; frame

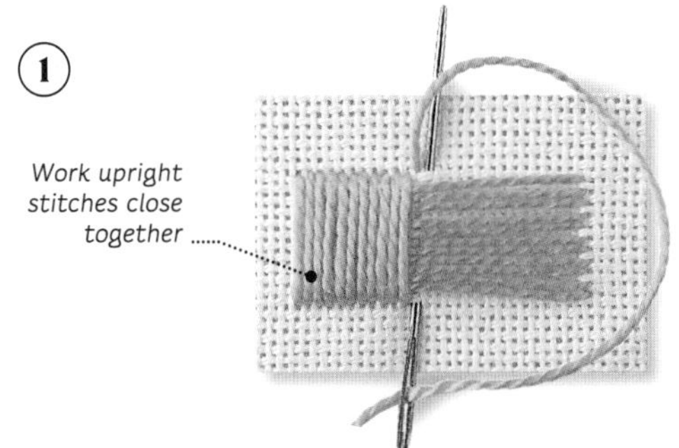
1
Work upright stitches close together

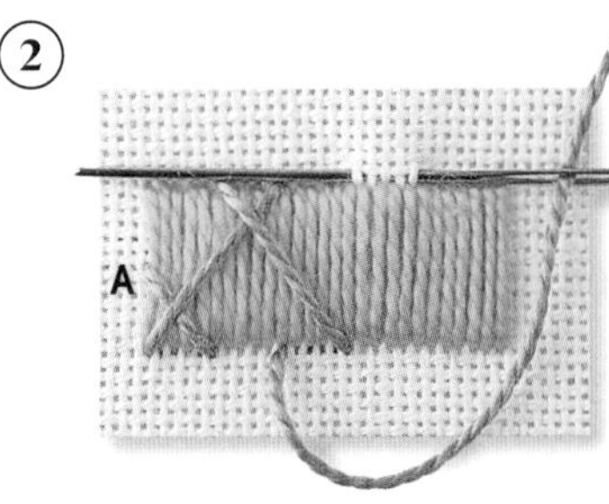
2
A

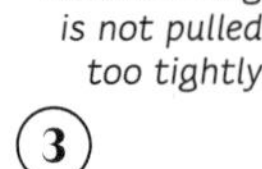
Ensure lacing is not pulled too tightly

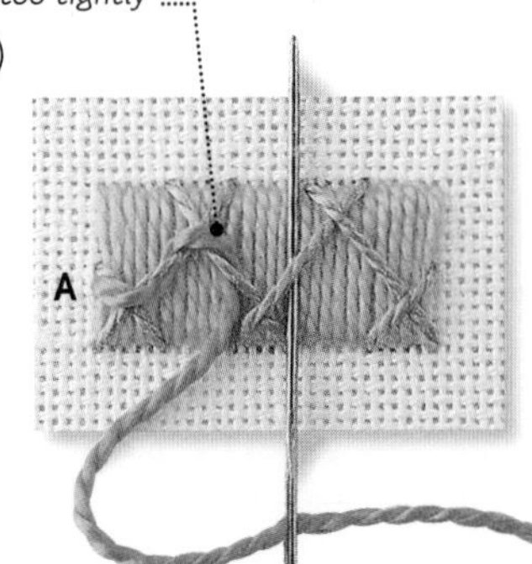
3
A

1 Work a foundation of long horizontal surface satin stitch (see p.86). Work a row of upright satin stitch (see p.86) from left to right over the base stitches.

2 Bring the second thread up at **A** and work a row of herringbone stitch (see p.52).

3 Thread the blunt needle with the third colour thread. Come up at **A** and slide the needle upwards, under the centre of the first long diagonal stitch. Take it back down under the second stitch from top to bottom. Continue lacing to the end of the band.

Double Herringbone

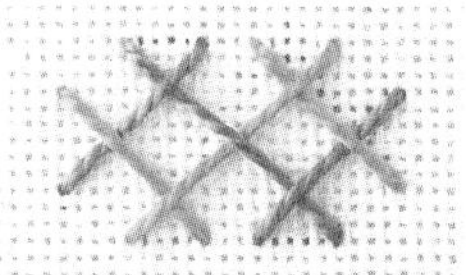

OTHER NAME
Indian herringbone stitch

LEVEL
Advanced

USES
Geometric border; in rows as open filling

METHOD
Two interlaced rows of herringbone stitch

MATERIALS
Any fabric; any thick thread in two colours

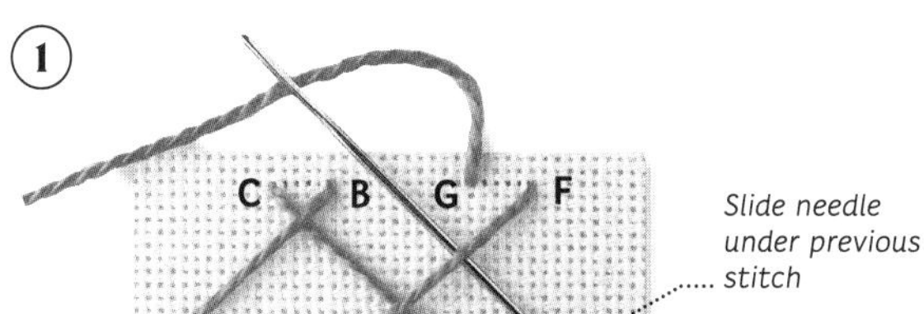

1
C
B
G
F
A
E
D
Slide needle under previous stitch

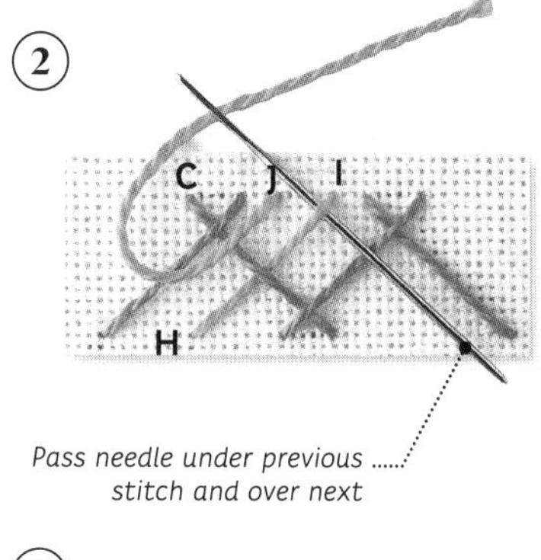

2
C
J
I
H
Pass needle under previous stitch and over next

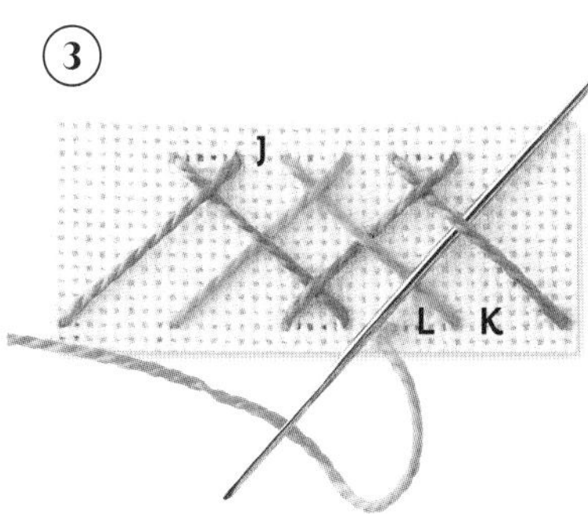

3
J
L
K

1 Start at **A** and make a diagonal stitch to **B**. Bring the needle out at **C**, pass it under the stitch and take it down at **D**. Come out at **E** and insert at **F**. Bring the needle out at **G** and slide it under the last stitch. Continue to the end of the row.

2 Bring the contrast thread up directly below **C**, at **H**. Slide the needle under the second stitch and insert at **I**. Come out at **J** and pass the needle under the previous stitch.

3 Insert the needle at **K** and come out at **L**. Take it over the first thread and under the second. Repeat steps 2 and 3 to continue.

Twisted Lattice Band

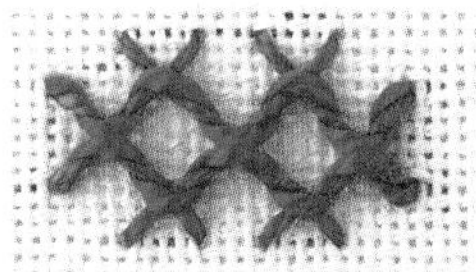

LEVEL
Advanced

USES
Ornamental border; in rows as filling

METHOD
Double herringbone stitch with two rows of interlacing

MATERIALS
Any fabric; any thick thread in two colours

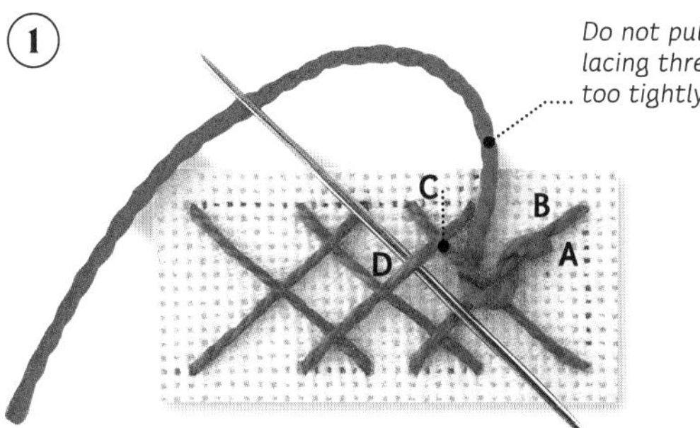

1
Do not pull lacing thread too tightly
C
B
A
D

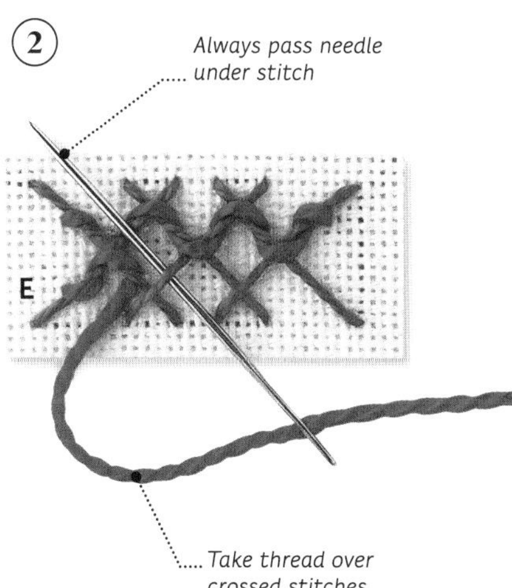

2
Always pass needle under stitch
E
Take thread over crossed stitches

1 Work a foundation of double herringbone stitch (see above) in the first colour. Bring the lacing thread out at **A**. Pass the needle downwards under **B**, then upwards under **C**. Slide it beneath the next stitch, at **D**, from top to bottom.

2 Continue weaving the thread under and over the top stitches to the end of the row. Bring the thread out at **E** and interlace the bottom stitches in the same way to complete.

Butterfly Chain

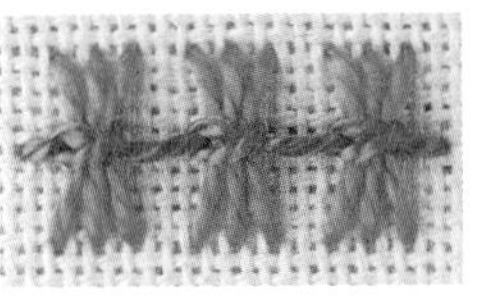

LEVEL
Intermediate

USES
Light frames or borders

METHOD
Twisted chain stitch worked over groups of three straight stitches, without piercing fabric

MATERIALS
Any fabric; thick thread in two colours; blunt needle

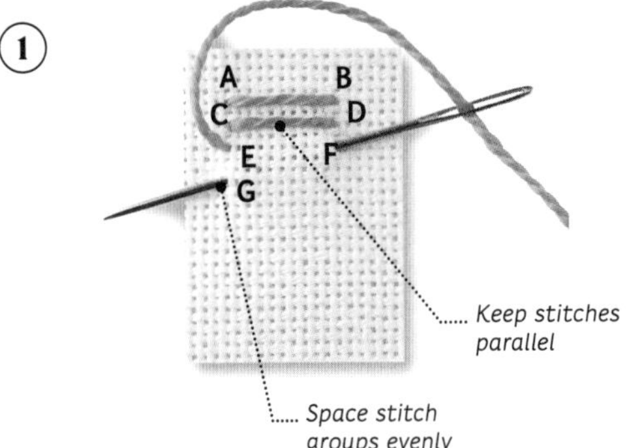
1
A
B
C
D
E
F
G
Keep stitches parallel
Space stitch groups evenly

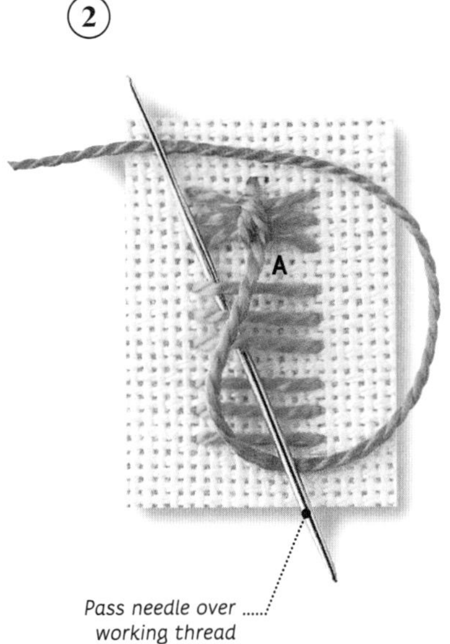
2
A
Pass needle over working thread

1 Start at **A**, and make a horizontal stitch across to **B**. Work two more stitches directly below, from **C** to **D** and **E** to **F**, then bring the needle out at **G** to work the next group of three stitches.

2 Using the contrast thread, work a twisted chain stitch (see p.44) over each group of horizontal stitches. Come through at **A** and loop the thread to the right. Slide the needle under all three stitches and pull it through. Tighten the thread to draw the stitches together.

Raised Chain Band

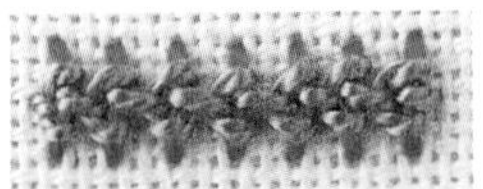

OTHER NAME
Raised chain stitch

LEVEL
Intermediate

USES
Heavy borders

METHOD
Chain stitch worked over straight stitch foundation, without piercing fabric

MATERIALS
Any fabric; any thick thread in two colours; blunt needle

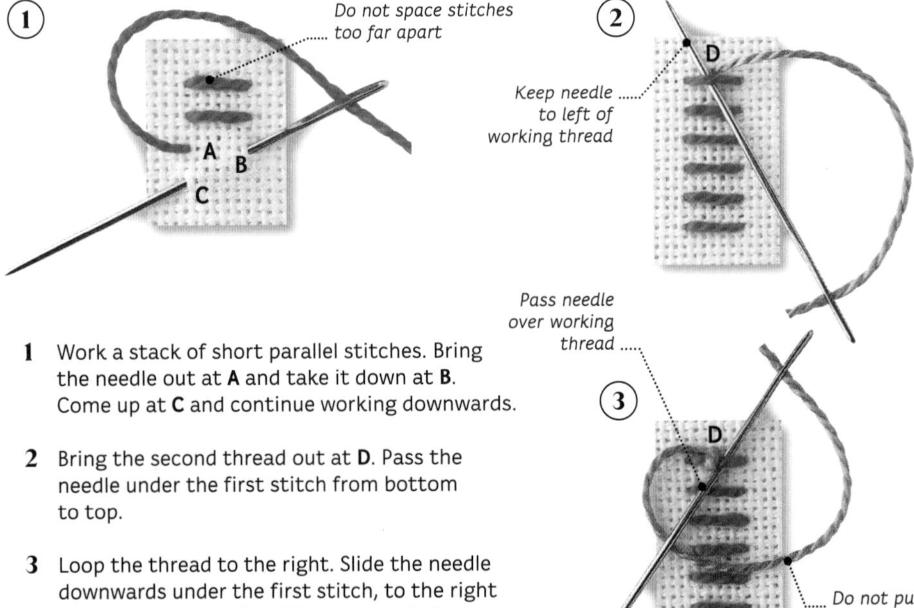
1
Do not space stitches too far apart
A
B
C
2
D
Keep needle to left of working thread
Pass needle over working thread
3
D
Do not pull thread up too tightly

1 Work a stack of short parallel stitches. Bring the needle out at **A** and take it down at **B**. Come up at **C** and continue working downwards.

2 Bring the second thread out at **D**. Pass the needle under the first stitch from bottom to top.

3 Loop the thread to the right. Slide the needle downwards under the first stitch, to the right of **D**. Repeat steps 2 and 3 to the end of the stack.

Diagonal Woven Band

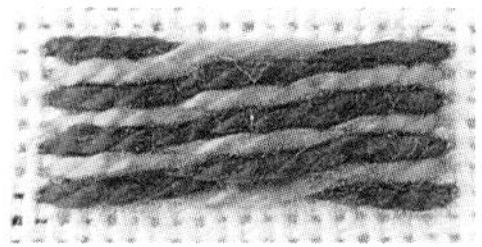

LEVEL
Advanced

USES
Dense striped border or frame

METHOD
Two contrasting threads woven through row of straight stitches

MATERIALS
Any fabric; any two twisted threads; two blunt needles

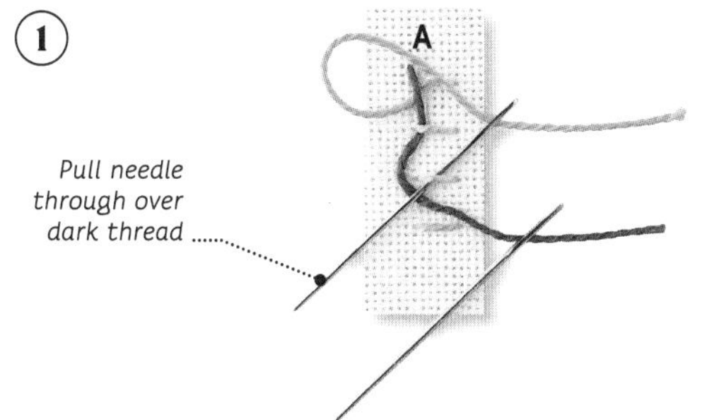

1
A
Pull needle through over dark thread

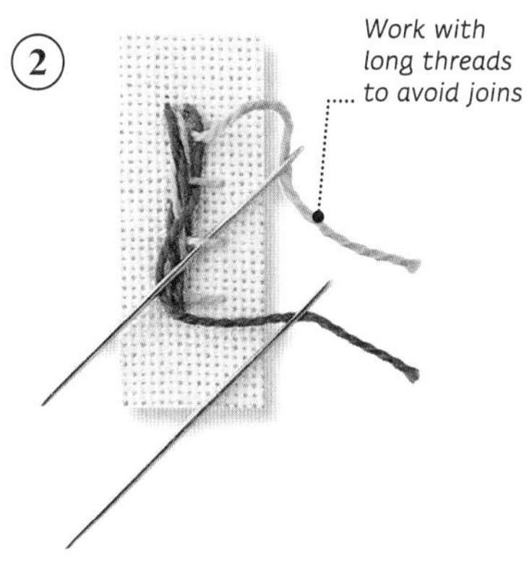

2
Work with long threads to avoid joins

1 Work a stack of straight stitches (see p.68, raised chain band step 1). Bring the dark thread up at **A**, pass the needle under the second stitch and take it to the right. Bring the light thread up at **A**. Slide the needle to the left below the first stitch and the dark thread, then take it under the third stitch and across the dark thread.

2 Continue weaving downwards, taking the two threads alternately under and over the straight stitches. Work the following rows in the same way, alternating the colour of the first stitch.

Stitch Variation

To work striped woven band stitch, start every twisted line with the same colour thread, to create solid blocks of alternate colours.

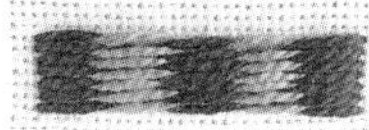

Portuguese Border

LEVEL
Advanced

USES
Raised borders

METHOD
Diagonal stitches woven over straight stitch foundations

MATERIALS
Any fabric; twisted thread in two colours; blunt needle

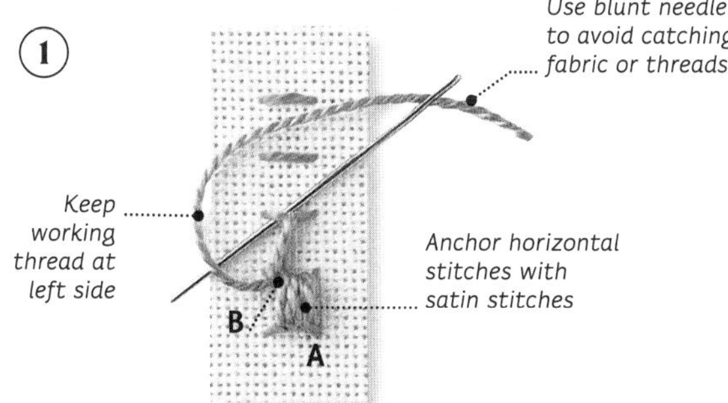

1
Use blunt needle to avoid catching fabric or threads
Keep working thread at left side
Anchor horizontal stitches with satin stitches
B
A

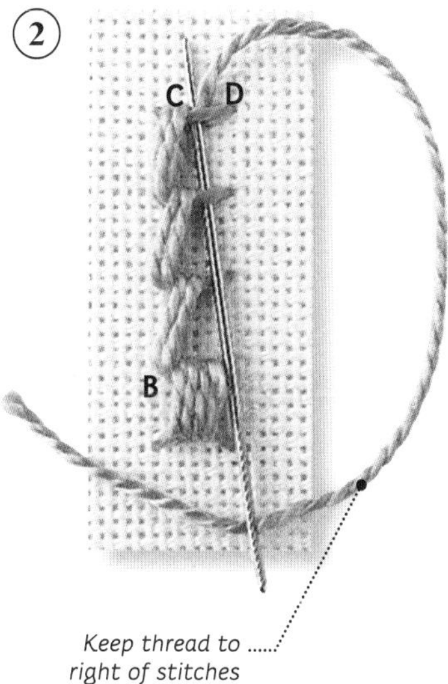

2
C
D
B
Keep thread to right of stitches

1 Work a stack of horizontal stitches (see p.68, raised chain band step 1). Bring the second thread up at **A** and make three satin stitches (see p.86) over the first two stitches. Come out at **B** and slide the needle downwards under the next two horizontal stitches, making a slanting stitch. Pass the needle under the third horizontal stitch again, to make a second stitch. Continue upwards, working pairs of slanting stitches.

2 At the top of the stack, take the needle down at **C** and out at **D**. Pass it upwards under the top two stitches. Continue as before, slanting the stitches in the opposite direction.

Filling Stitches

Powdered Filling and Isolated Stitches

These stand-alone detached stitches vary in size and shape from tiny dots and crosses through to stars, naturalistic flowers, and spiderwebs. Work them singly as accent stitches and highlights, space them regularly in rows to make geometric designs or sew them close together to create a textured surface.

Powdered (an old word for scattered) fillings are traditionally used to fill in an outlined shape, but you can also try using them in more unstructured, instinctive ways, sprinkled randomly across a surface and letting the design evolve as you embroider. Mindful stitching like this can be a calming way to both focus and relax.

Straight

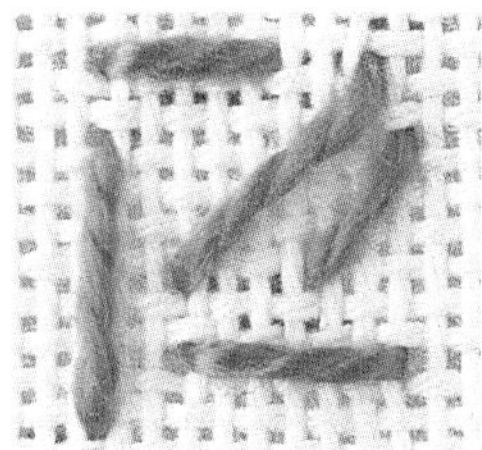

OTHER NAME
Stroke stitch

LEVEL
Easy

USES
Foliage; textured filling

METHOD
Randomly placed single stitches of varying length

MATERIALS
Any fabric; any thread

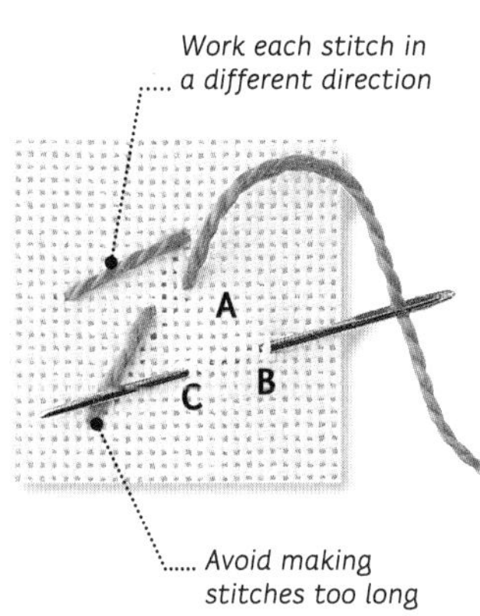

Work each stitch in a different direction
A
B
C
Avoid making stitches too long

Come up at **A**. Take the needle down to **B** and insert, then bring it out at **C**. Continue working straight stitches in a random pattern to fill the required area.

Arrowhead

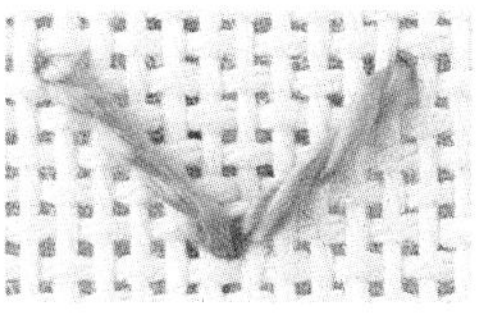

LEVEL
Easy

USES
Powdered filling; worked in vertical or horizontal rows as border stitch

METHOD
Two straight stitches worked at a right angle

MATERIALS
Any fabric; thick threads create raised effect

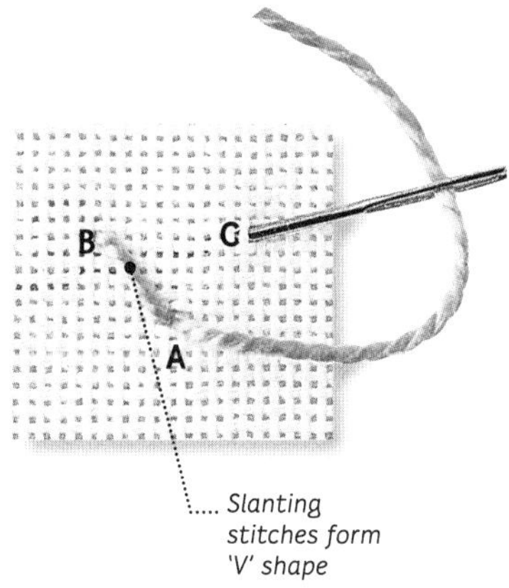

B
C
A
Slanting stitches form 'V' shape

Start at **A**. Make a diagonal straight stitch up to **B**, then come out again at **A**. Insert the needle at **C** to complete.

Dot

OTHER NAME
Backstitched seeding

LEVEL
Easy

USES
Powdered filling; worked in rows as outline

METHOD
Pairs of short, closely spaced back stitches

MATERIALS
Any fabric; pearl thread makes stitches stand out

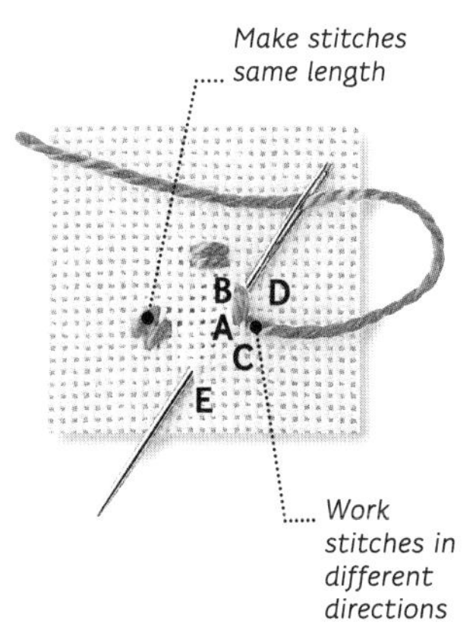

Make stitches same length
B
D
A
C
E
Work stitches in different directions

Come up at **A**. Insert the needle at **B** and bring it out at **C**. Insert at **D** to complete the second stitch, then bring the needle up at **E** to work the next pair of stitches.

St George Cross

OTHER NAME
Upright cross stitch

LEVEL
Easy

USES
Geometric or random fillings; isolated stitch

MATERIALS
Any fabric; thick threads create raised effect

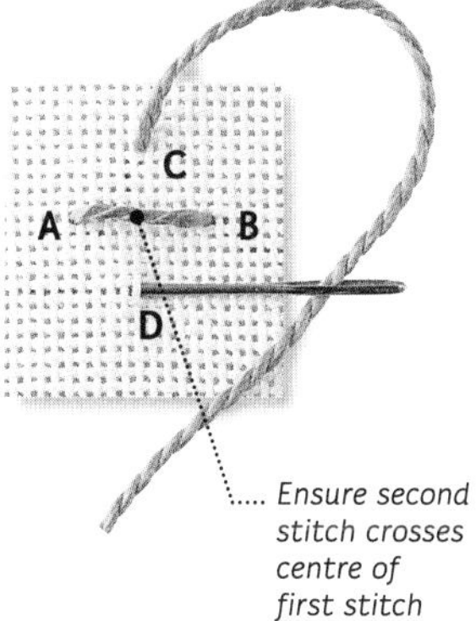

C
A
B
D
Ensure second stitch crosses centre of first stitch

Start at **A** and work a horizontal straight stitch across to **B**. Come out at **C**. Take the needle down over the first stitch and insert at **D** to complete the cross.

Ermine

LEVEL
Easy

USES
Scattered or regular filling; in rows as border; isolated stitch; in blackwork

METHOD
Wide cross stitch worked over upright straight stitch

MATERIALS
Evenweave fabric for a regular effect; any thread

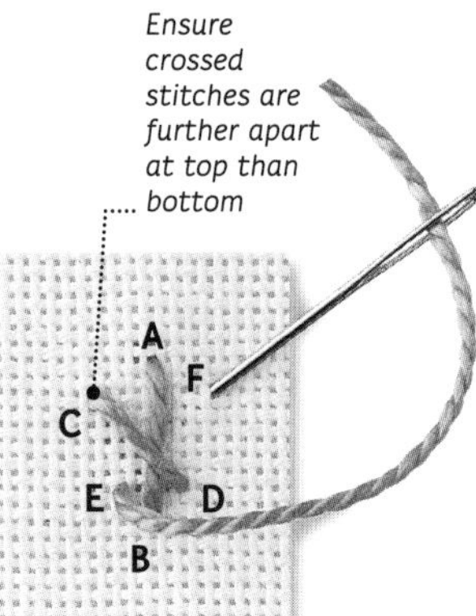

Ensure crossed stitches are further apart at top than bottom
A
F
C
E
D
B

Start at **A** and work a vertical straight stitch to **B**. Bring the needle out at **C** and insert at **D**. Come out at **E**. Take the needle across the two stitches and insert at **F** to complete.

Square Boss

OTHER NAME
Raised knot

LEVEL
Intermediate

USES
Light fillings; in rows as border; isolated stitch

METHOD
Cross stitch covered by back stitch square

MATERIALS
Any fabric; thick thread gives raised texture

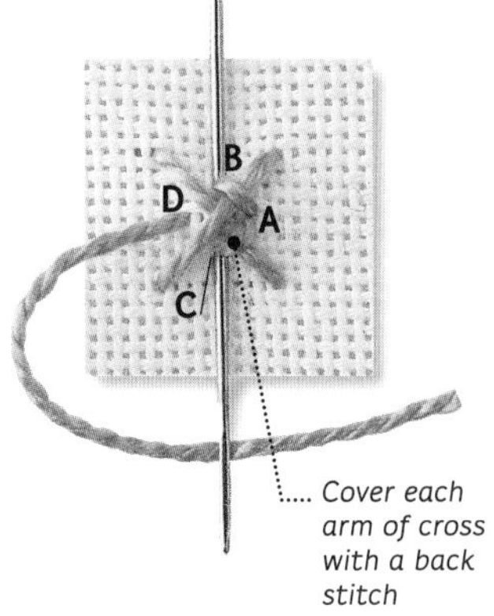

B
D
A
C
Cover each arm of cross with a back stitch

Make a cross stitch (see p.50). Bring the needle out at **A** and take it down at **B**. Come out at **C** and insert at **A**. Bring the needle out at **D** and insert at **C**. Work a back stitch from **B** to **D** to complete.

Star

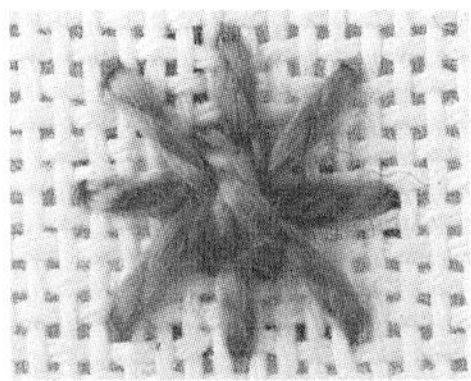

LEVEL
Intermediate

USES
Scattered as light filling; in rows as border; isolated stitch

METHOD
Elongated cross stitch worked over St George cross and cross stitches

MATERIALS
Any fabric; any thread

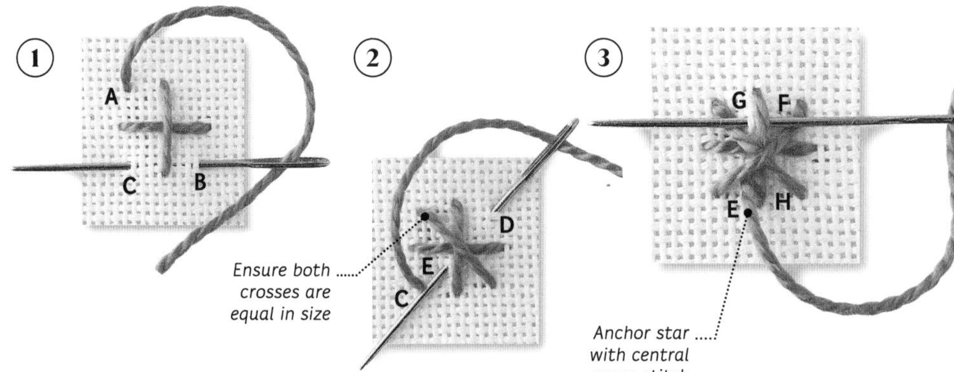

1
A
C
B
2
D
E
C
Ensure both crosses are equal in size
3
G
F
E
H
Anchor star with central cross stitch

1 Make a St George cross stitch (see p.73). Bring the needle out at **A**, and work a diagonal stitch down to **B**. Come out to the left of **B**, at **C**.

2 Take the needle diagonally up to **D** and insert. Come out near the centre of the stitch at **E**.

3 Insert the needle at **F**, then bring it out to the left at **G**. Take it down at **H** to complete the cross.

Technique Variation

For a decorative effect, stitch the small cross in the centre of the star (see step 3) using a different coloured thread.

Woven Star

LEVEL
Intermediate

USES
Powdered filling; isolated stitch

METHOD
Five interwoven straight stitches

MATERIALS
Any fabric; any thread

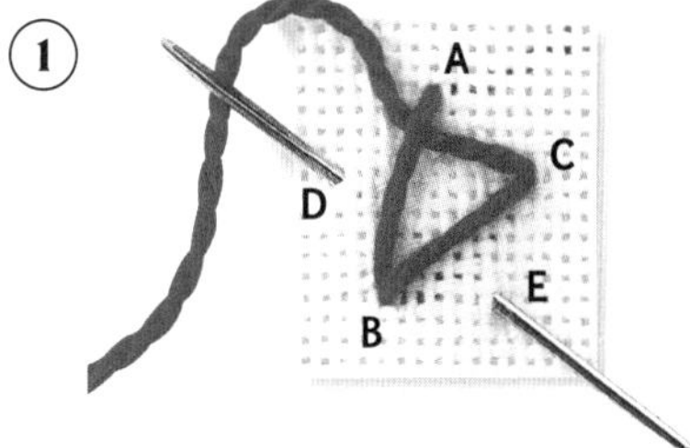
1
A
C
D
E
B

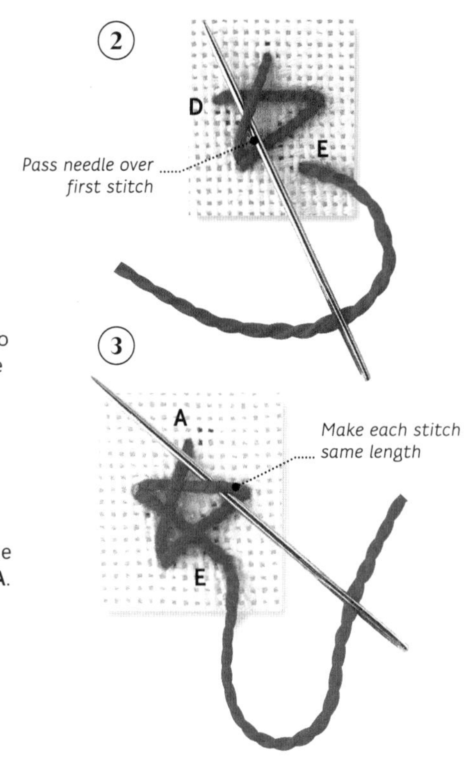
2
D
Pass needle over first stitch
E
3
A
Make each stitch same length
E

1 Start at **A** and work a diagonal stitch down to **B**. Come out at **C** and re-insert at **B**. Bring the needle up again at **C** and slide it under the first stitch. Insert at **D** and come out at **E**.

2 Take the needle over the first thread and under the second, then re-insert at **D**.

3 Come out again at **E**. Slide the needle over the first thread, under the second and insert at **A**.

Woven Cross

LEVEL
Intermediate

USES
Powdered filling; isolated stitch

METHOD
Four interwoven straight stitches

MATERIALS
Any fabric; any thick thread

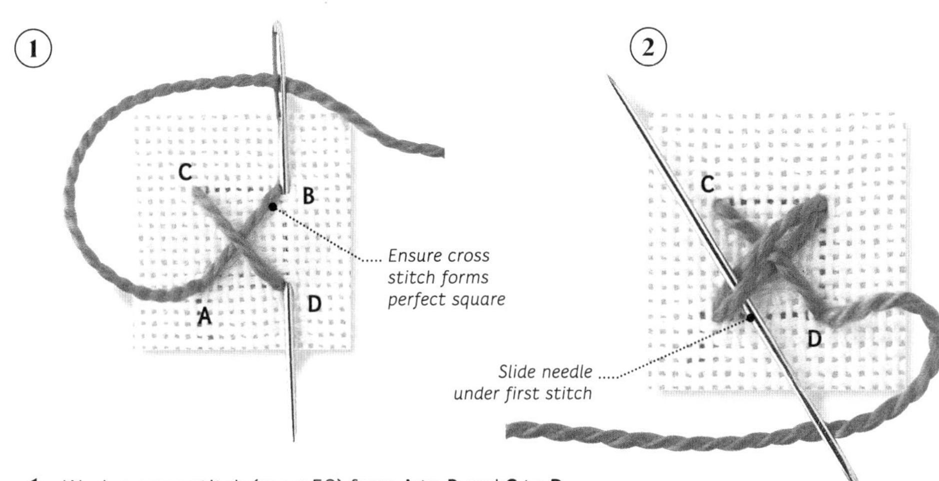
1
C
B
Ensure cross stitch forms perfect square
A
D
2
C
D
Slide needle under first stitch

1 Work a cross stitch (see p.50) from **A** to **B** and **C** to **D** Bring the needle back up at **A**, insert it again at **B** and come out at **D**.

2 Pass the needle under the first thread and over the second, then insert at **C** to complete the cross.

French Knot

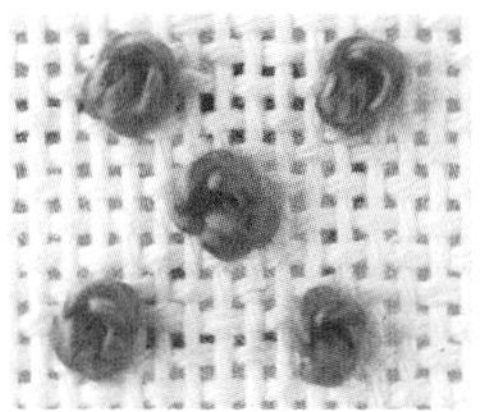

LEVEL
Intermediate

USES
Light or solid powdered filling; singly as raised highlight

METHOD
Twisted knotted stitch

MATERIALS
Any fabric; any twisted embroidery threads; small-eyed needle

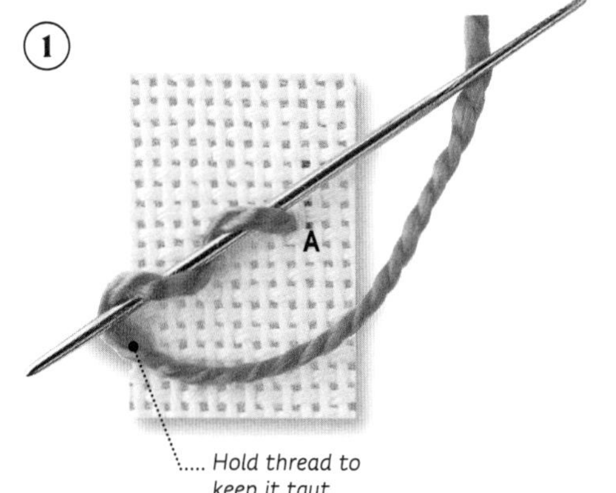

1
A
Hold thread to keep it taut

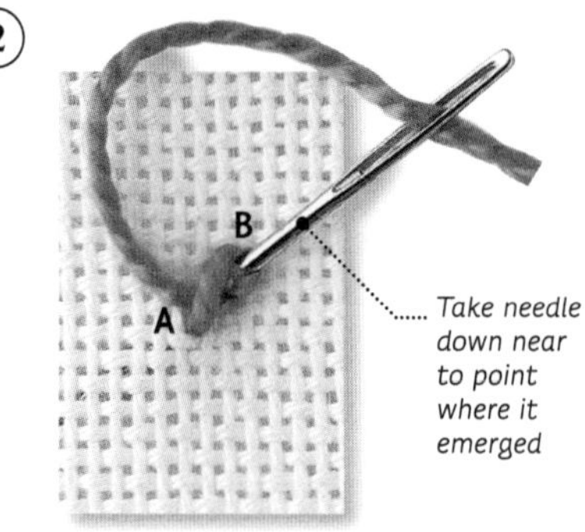

2
B
A
Take needle down near to point where it emerged

1 Start at **A**. Hold the thread taut and wrap it twice around the needle, then pull it gently to tighten the loops.

2 Maintaining the tension, insert the needle close to **A**, at **B**, pushing it down through the two loops to form a round knot.

Stitch Variation

To work pistil stitch, insert the needle a short distance from where it emerged, to form a long tail. Make eight stitches in a circle to create a flower centre or floral shape.

Bullion Knot

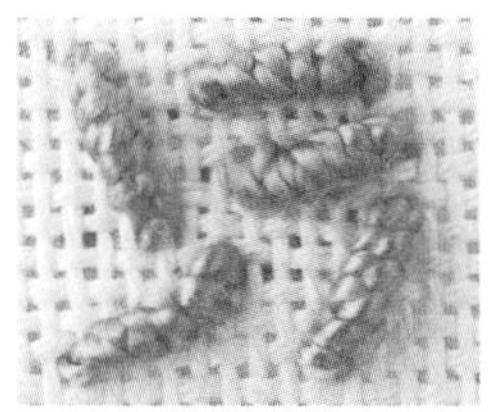

OTHER NAME
Caterpillar stitch

LEVEL
Intermediate

USES
Powdered filling; accent stitch; in rows as border

METHOD
Long twisted knot

MATERIALS
Any fabric; any twisted embroidery thread

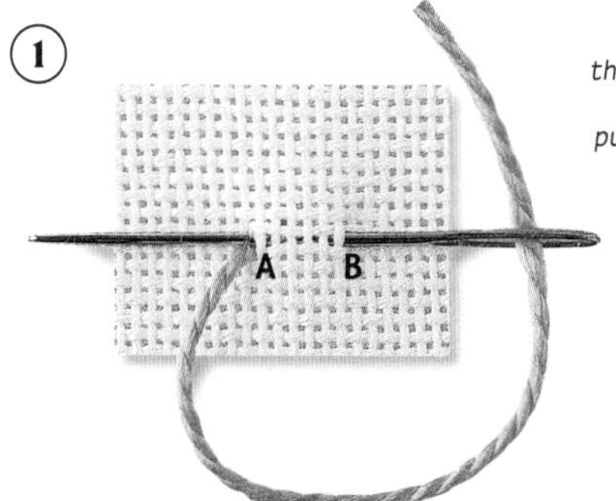

1
A
B

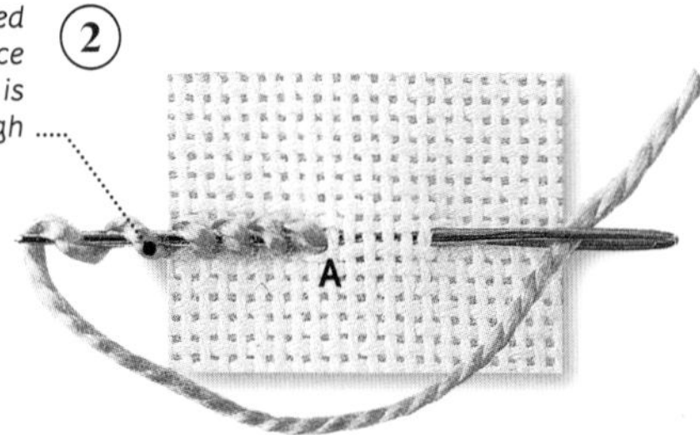

Hold coiled thread in place as needle is pulled through
2
A

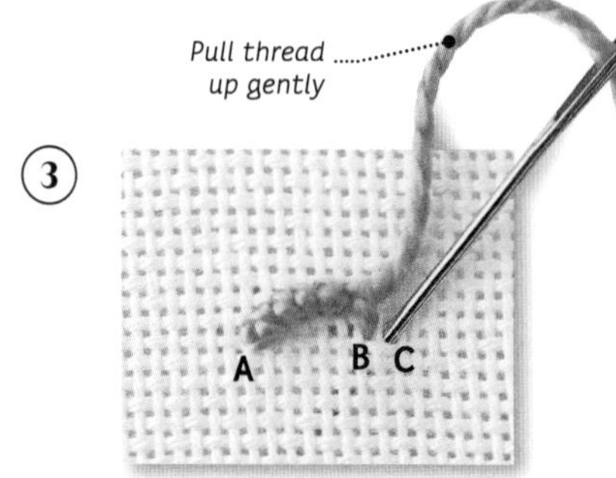

Pull thread up gently
3
A
B
C

1 Start at **A**. Take the needle down at **B** and bring the point back through at **A**.

2 Wrap the thread six times around the needle, holding the loops down with a finger. Using the other hand, pull the needle carefully through the fabric and the coiled thread.

3 Take the needle back down at **C** and pull the working thread up so that the loops lie flat.

Danish Knot

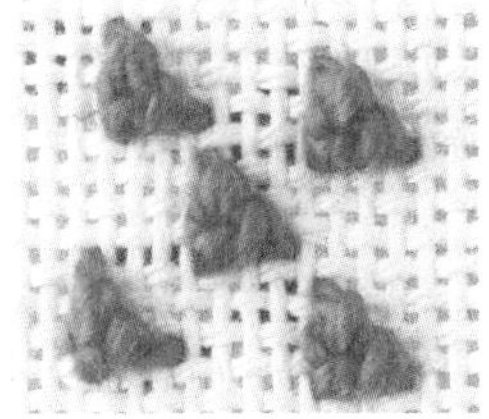

LEVEL
Intermediate

USES
Powdered filling; triangular accent stitch

METHOD
Looped knot worked over short diagonal stitch

MATERIALS
Any fabric; thick twisted thread

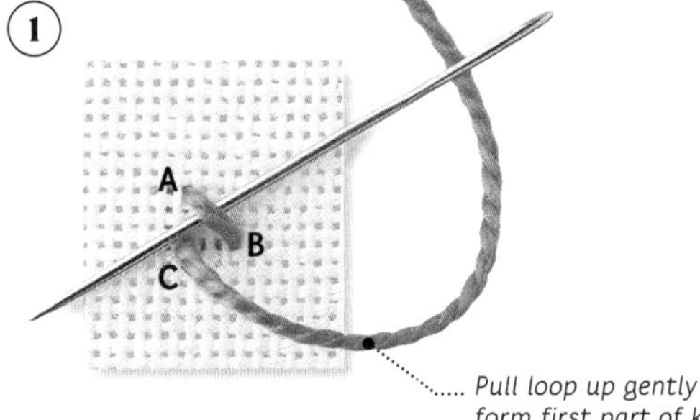

1
A
B
C
Pull loop up gently to form first part of knot

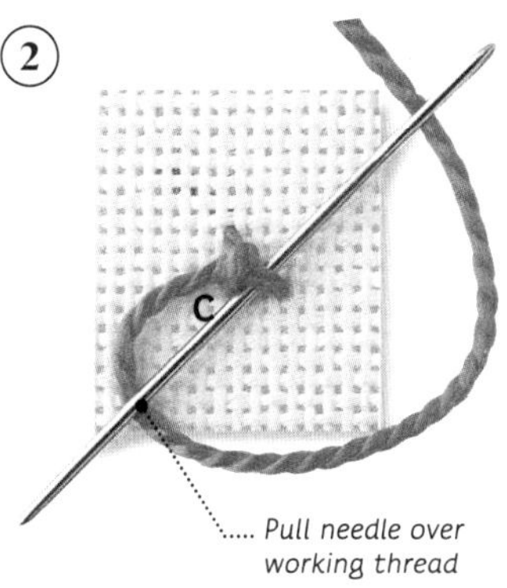

2
C
Pull needle over working thread

1 Start at **A** and work a short diagonal stitch down to **B**. Bring the needle out at **C** and slide it under the stitch from right to left.

2 Take the needle across to the right of the knot. Pass it under the diagonal stitch from right to left for a second time.

3 Insert the needle at **C** to complete the knot.

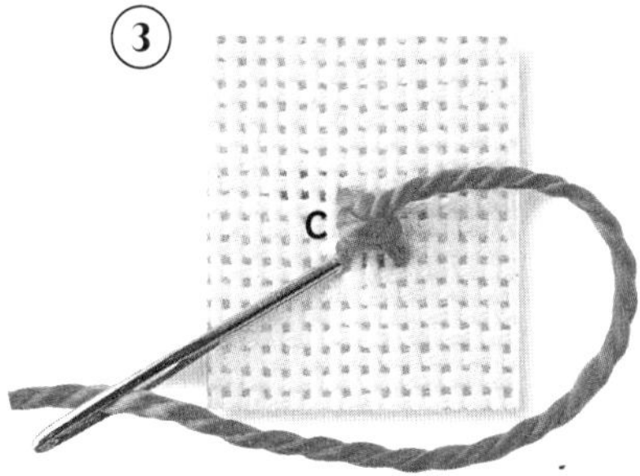

3
C

Four-legged Knot

OTHER NAME
Knot stitch

LEVEL
Intermediate

USES
Powdered filling; isolated stitch

METHOD
Upright cross with knotted centre

MATERIALS
Any fabric; any thick thread

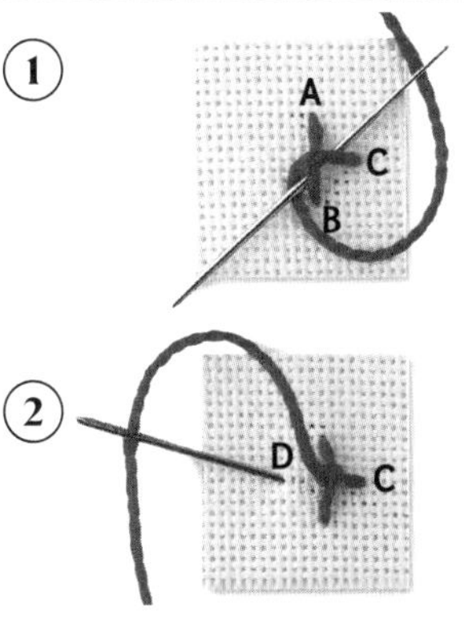

1
A
C
B
2
D
C

1 Start at **A** and work an upright stitch down to **B**. Come out at **C**. Loop the thread to the left, and slide the needle under the stitch.

2 Pull the thread gently to form a knot. Insert the needle at **D** to complete the stitch.

Sword

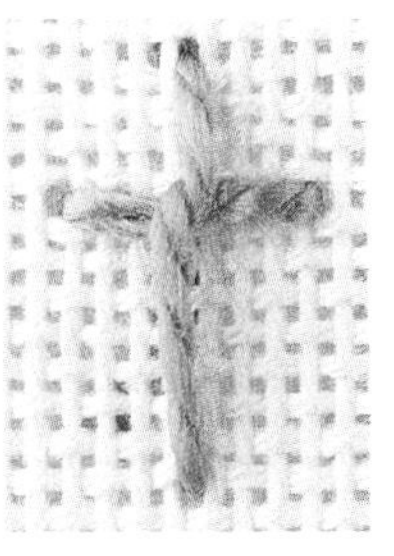

LEVEL
Easy

USES
Worked randomly as light filling; in rows as border

METHOD
Looped, elongated cross

MATERIALS
Any fabric; any thick thread

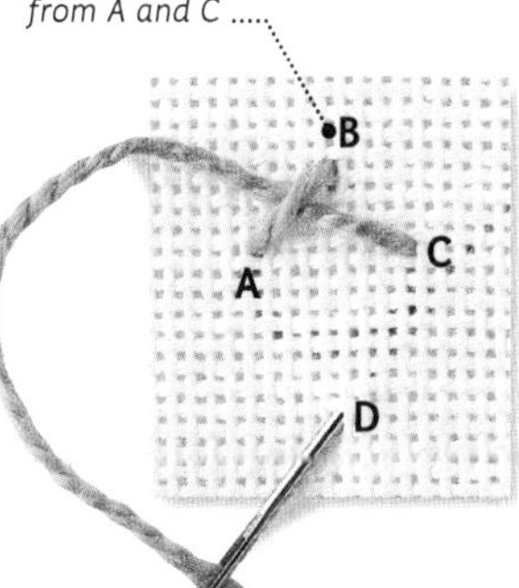

Ensure B is equidistant from A and C
B
A
C
D

Start at **A** and work a loose diagonal stitch up to **B**. Bring the needle out at **C** and slide it under the stitch from right to left. Take it down at **D**, pulling gently so that the two stitches form a cross.

Fly

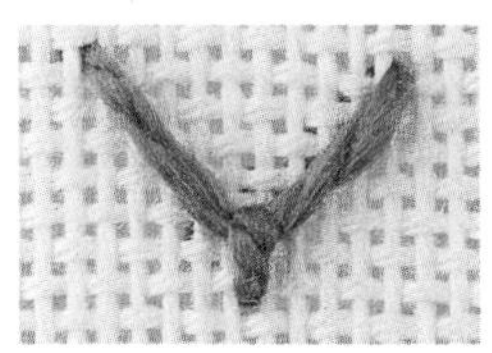

OTHER NAMES
Y-stitch; open loop stitch

LEVEL
Easy

USES
Light or heavy filling; worked in horizontal or vertical rows as border

METHOD
Tied loop stitch

MATERIALS
Any fabric; any thick thread

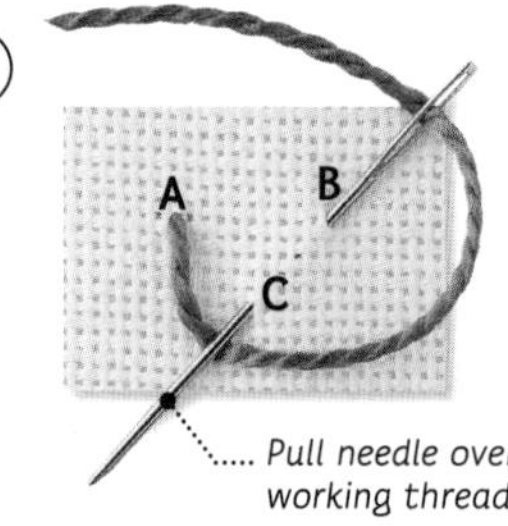
A
B
C
Pull needle over working thread

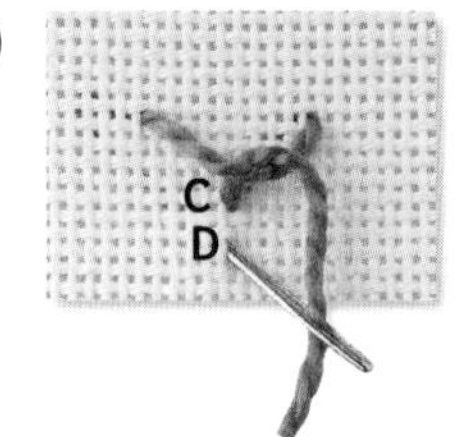
C
D

1 Start at **A** and work a loose horizontal stitch across to **B**. Bring the needle out at **C**.

2 Take the needle down at **D** to make a tie stitch (see p.20).

Sheaf Filling

LEVEL
Intermediate

USES
Powdered filling; in rows as border; isolated stitch

METHOD
Three upright straight stitches tied at the centre

MATERIALS
Any fabric; any thick thread

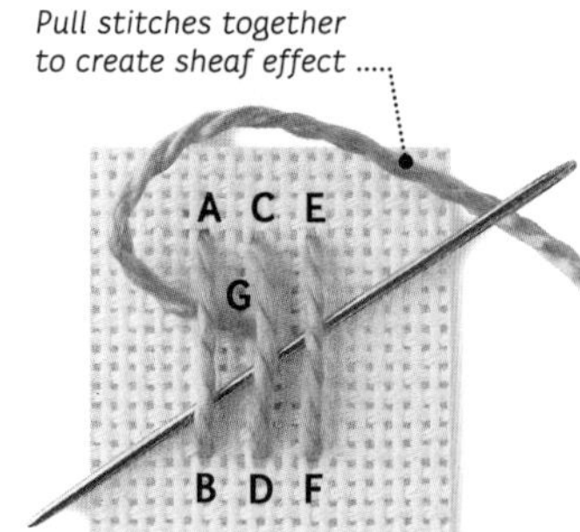
Pull stitches together to create sheaf effect
A C E
G
B D F

Make three parallel straight stitches from **A** to **B**, **C** to **D** and **E** to **F**. Come up at **G** and pass the needle to the left, under the first stitch. Take the needle across to the right and slide it back under the stitches. Take it to the right again and pull the thread up gently. Insert at **G** to complete.

Crown

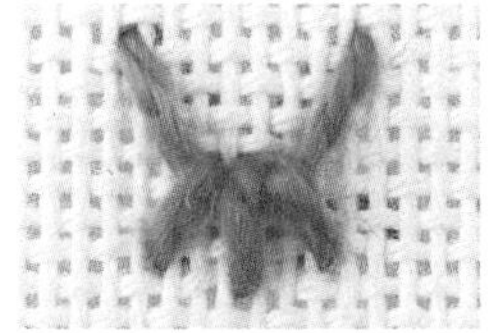

LEVEL
Intermediate

USES
Powdered filling; in rows as border; isolated stitch

METHOD
Looped stitch tied down with three straight stitches

MATERIALS
Any fabric; any thick thread

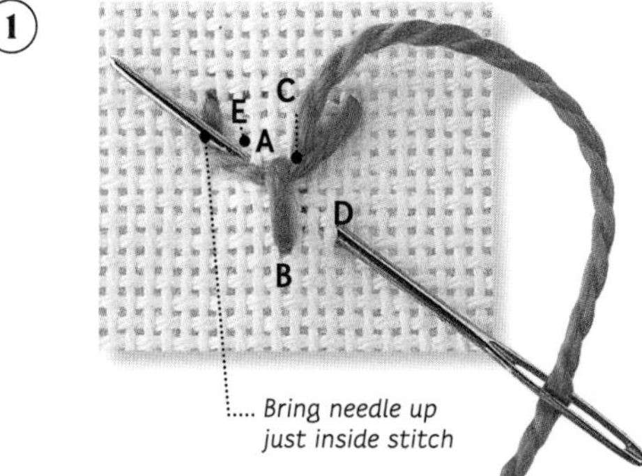
C
E
A
D
B
Bring needle up just inside stitch

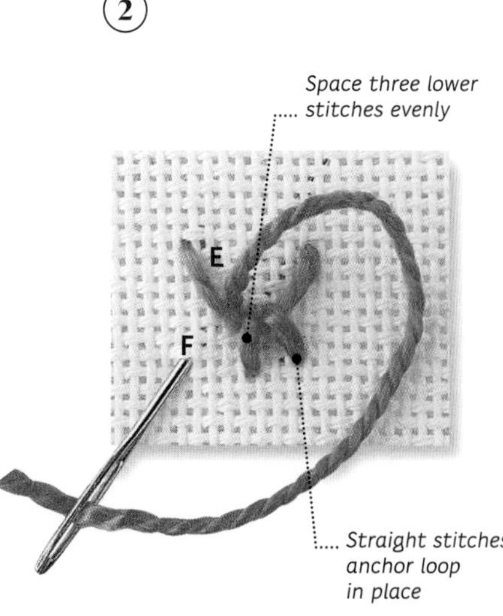
Space three lower stitches evenly
E
F
Straight stitches anchor loop in place

1 Work a loose horizontal straight stitch. Come out above the thread at **A** and insert the needle at **B**, pulling the loop downwards. Come out at **C**, take the needle over the thread and insert at **D**, then come out at **E**.

2 Take the needle down over the thread and insert at **F** to complete the stitch.

Sorbello

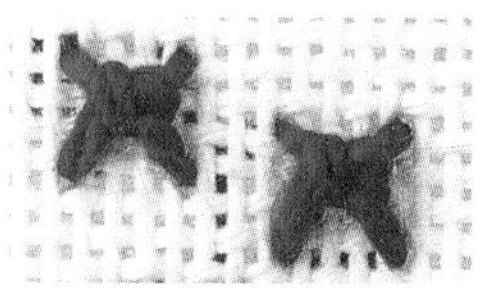

LEVEL
Intermediate

USES
In straight rows as filling; in rows as border; isolated stitch

METHOD
Heavy square knot

MATERIALS
Any fabric; twisted or pearl threads give a raised effect

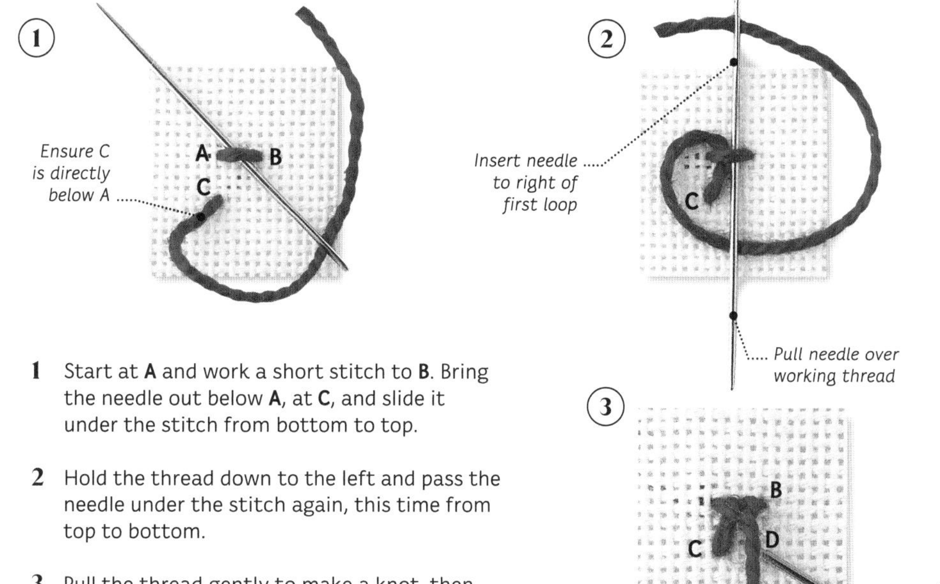
1
Ensure C is directly below A
A
B
C
2
Insert needle to right of first loop
C
Pull needle over working thread
3
B
C
D

1 Start at **A** and work a short stitch to **B**. Bring the needle out below **A**, at **C**, and slide it under the stitch from bottom to top.

2 Hold the thread down to the left and pass the needle under the stitch again, this time from top to bottom.

3 Pull the thread gently to make a knot, then insert the needle below **B** at **D** to complete the stitch.

Palestrina Knot

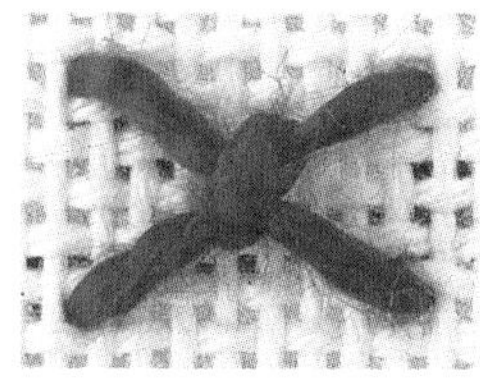

LEVEL
Intermediate

USES
Geometric filling; worked in rows as border; isolated stitch

METHOD
Rectangular looped knot

MATERIALS
Any fabric; any thick thread

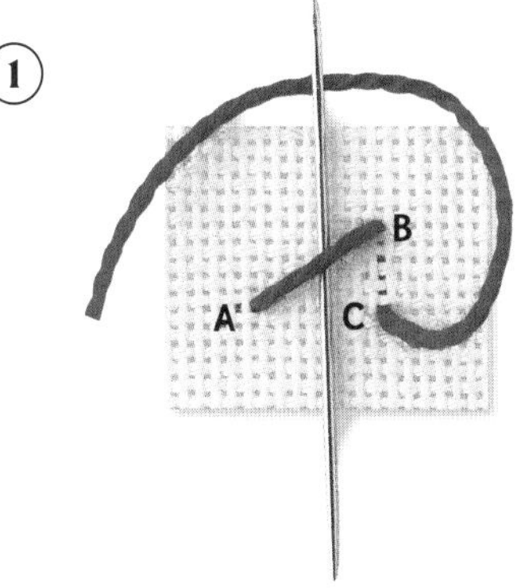
1
A
B
C

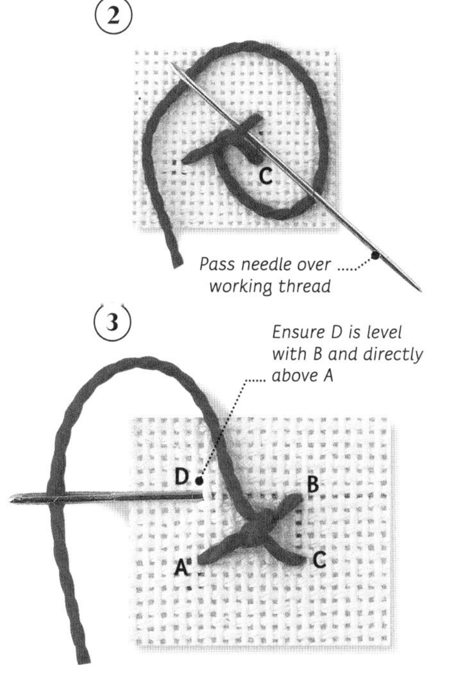
2
C
Pass needle over working thread
3
Ensure D is level with B and directly above A
D
B
A
C

1 Start at **A** and work a diagonal stitch to **B**. Bring the needle out level with **A**, at **C**, and slide it under the stitch from top to bottom.

2 Pass the needle under the diagonal stitch again, from top to bottom and to the right of the first loop.

3 Pull the thread gently to form a knot, then take the needle down diagonally opposite **C**, at **D**, to complete the stitch.

Link

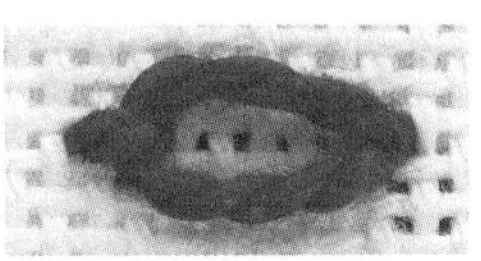

OTHER NAME
Detached chain stitch

LEVEL
Easy

USES
Scattered as light filling; leaves and flower petals

METHOD
Single looped stitch

MATERIALS
Any fabric; any thread

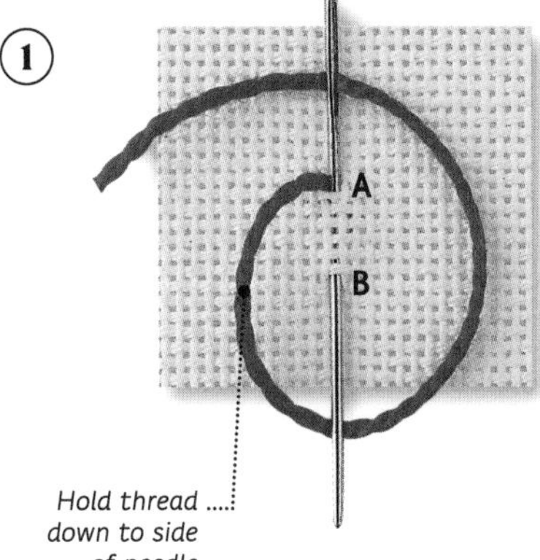

1
A
B
Hold thread down to side of needle

2

Tie stitch secures loop

B

C

1 Start at **A**. Make a loop and take the needle down at **A**. Come out at **B** and pull the needle through over the working thread.

2 Insert the needle directly below **B**, at **C**, making a tie stitch (see p.20) to complete.

Stitch Variation

Lazy daisy stitch is formed by making several link stitches in a circle, all starting at the centre. Each stitch represents a petal and the whole looks like a flower head.

Berry

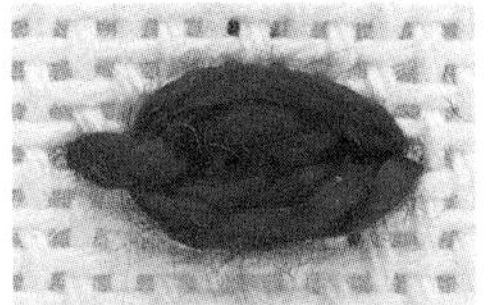

LEVEL
Intermediate

USES
Powdered filling; flowers and leaves

METHOD
Double link stitch

MATERIALS
Any fabric; any thread

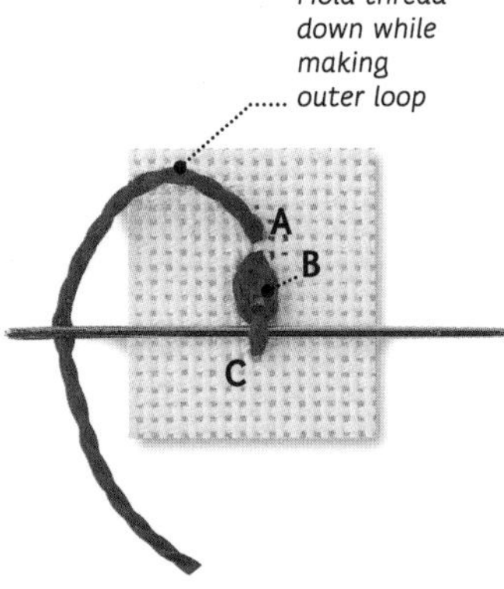

Hold thread down while making outer loop
A
B
C

Make a small link stitch (see above). Bring the needle out at **A** and slide it under the tie stitch between **B** and **C**. Take the needle back up and insert at **A** to complete the stitch.

Picot

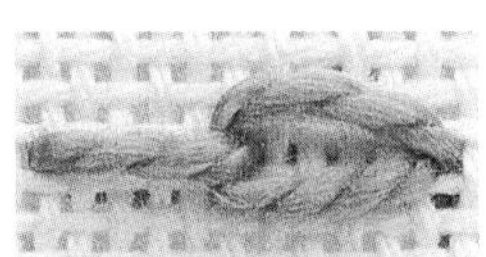

OTHER NAME
Long-tailed daisy stitch

LEVEL
Easy

USES
Powdered filling; in circles as floral motif

METHOD
Link variation with long tie stitch

MATERIALS
Any fabric; any thread

Work elongated tie stitch to form tail

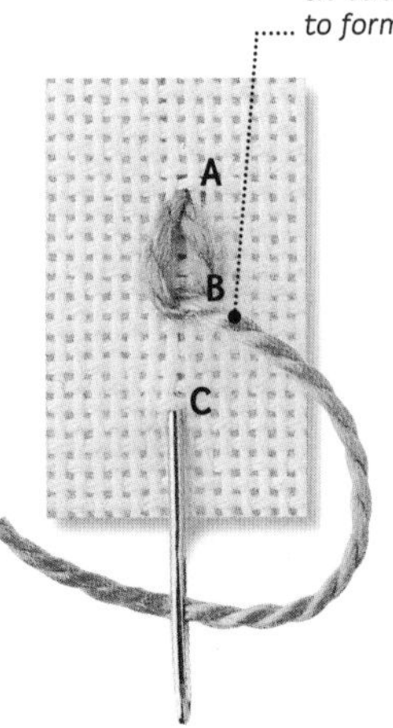

A
B
C

Start at **A** and follow step 1 of link stitch (see above). Take the needle down below **B**, at **C**, to make a long tie stitch.

Detached Wheatear

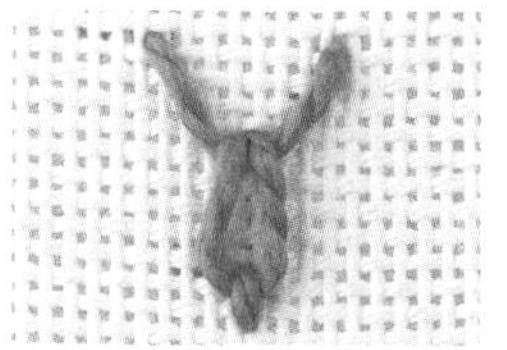

OTHER NAMES
Tete-de-boeuf stitch; ox-head stitch

LEVEL
Intermediate

USES
Powdered filling; isolated stitch

METHOD
Link stitch worked over loose straight stitch

MATERIALS
Any fabric; any thread

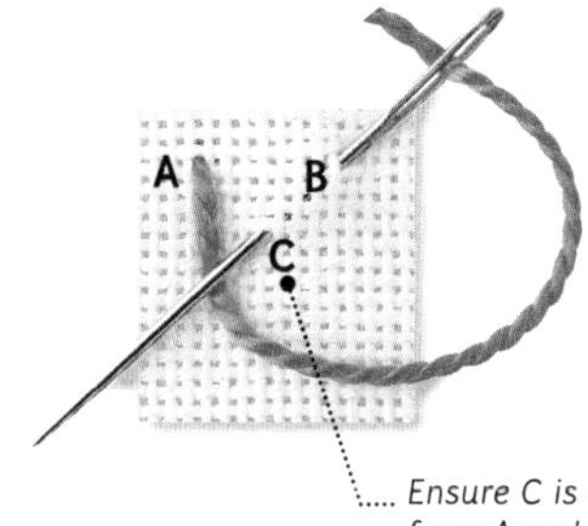
1
A
B
C
Ensure C is equidistant from A and B

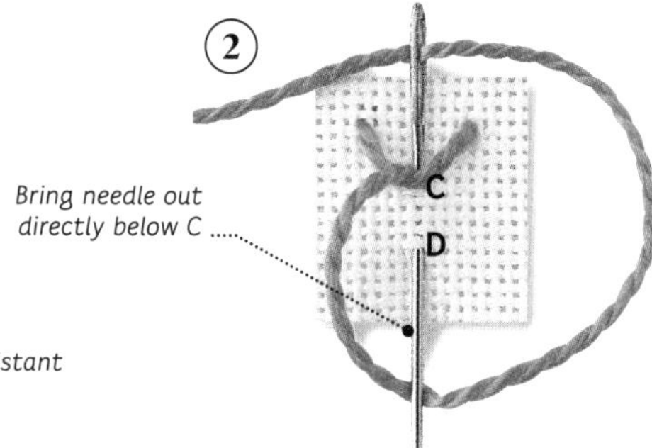
2
C
D
Bring needle out directly below C

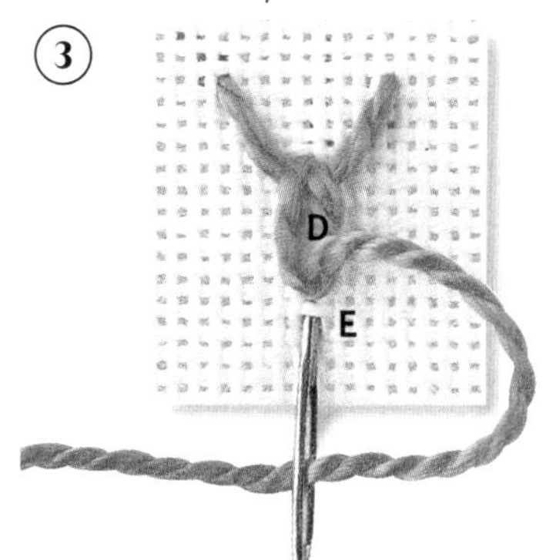
3
D
E

1 Start at **A**. Insert the needle at **B** and bring it out at **C**, passing over the working thread.

2 Make a loop and take the needle down at **C**. Come out at **D**, passing the needle over the working thread.

3 Take the needle down at **E** to form a short tie stitch (see p.20) to complete.

Tulip

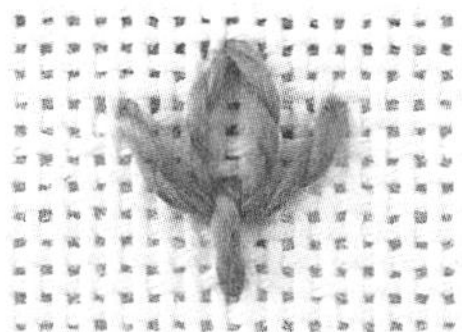

LEVEL
Intermediate

USES
In alternate rows as powdered filling; naturalistic flowers

METHOD
Straight stitch worked through link stitch

MATERIALS
Any fabric; any thread

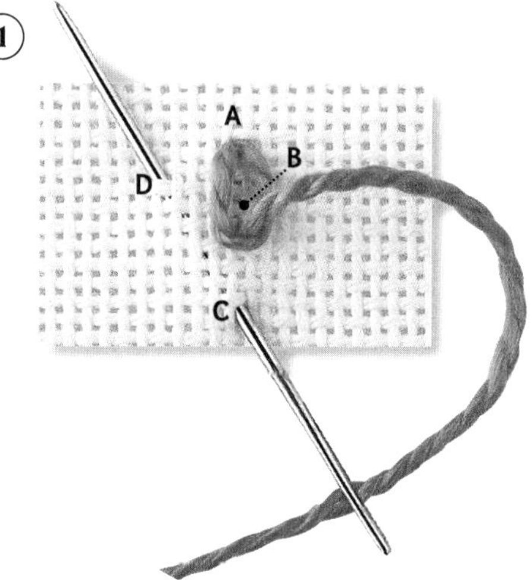
1
A
B
D
C

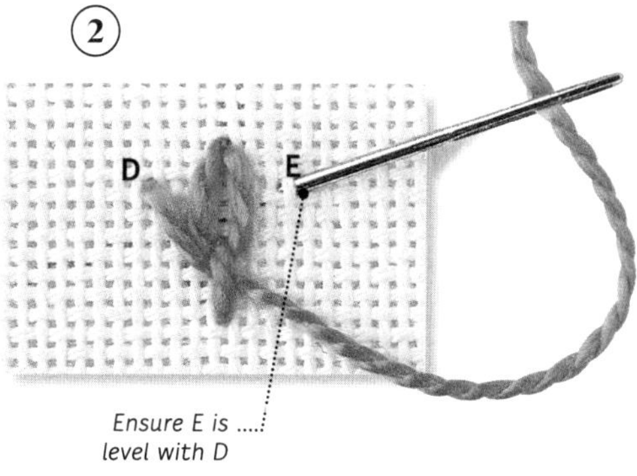
2
D
E
Ensure E is level with D

1 Start at **A** and work a picot stitch from **A** to **B** (see p.80). Take the needle down at **C** and bring it out to the left, at **D**.

2 Pass the needle under the tie stitch and insert it at **E** to complete the 'leaves'.

Technique Variation

Make a slanting straight stitch on either side of the picot stitch, instead of a single one passing beneath the tie stitch (see step 2 above). This creates the effect of two separate leaves at the base of the flower.

Woven Spider Web

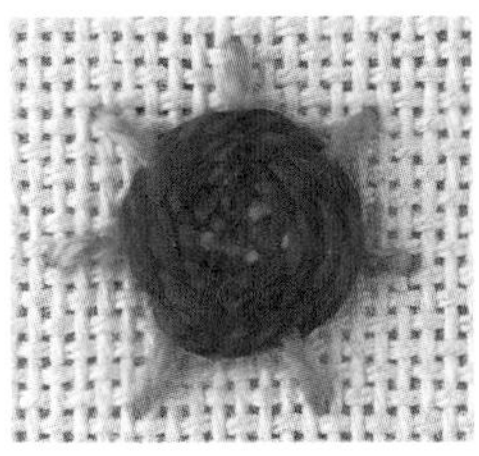

LEVEL
Intermediate

USES
Isolated stitch; large-scale powdered filling

METHOD
Solid circle woven on foundation of seven straight stitches

MATERIALS
Any fabric; any thread in two colours; blunt needle

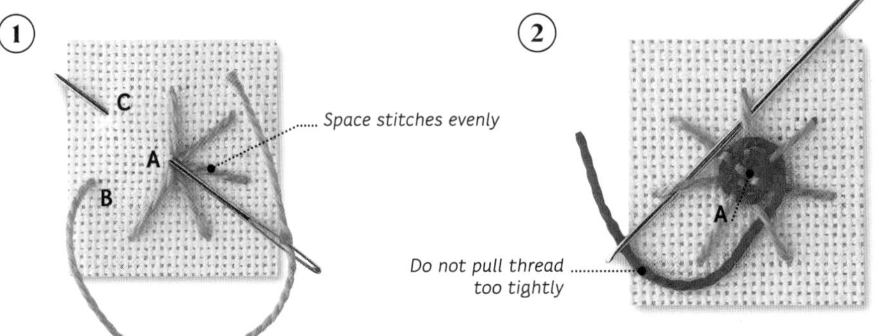
1
C
A
B
Space stitches evenly
2
A
Do not pull thread too tightly

1 Work a foundation of five straight stitches (see p.73), all radiating from **A**. Bring the needle up at **B** and take it back down at **A**. Come out at **C**, ready to work the final stitch.

2 Bring the second thread up at **A**. Working clockwise, weave it alternately over and under the straight stitches until only the tips are left uncovered. Take the needle to the back to finish.

Stitch Variation

To make a ribbon rose, use a length of narrow silk embroidery ribbon for the weaving in step 2 (see above). Allow it to twist slightly to create the raised petal effect.

Ribbed Web

OTHER NAME
Ribbed spider web

LEVEL
Intermediate

USES
Isolated stitch

METHOD
Back stitched spiral over large star stitch

MATERIALS
Any fabric; any thick thread in two colours; blunt needle

A
Work in anti-clockwise direction

Work a star stitch (see p.74) omitting the final cross. Come up at **A**. Slide the needle under the first two stitches to the left, then take it under the second and third stitches, making a back stitch (see p.40). Continue working round the star stitch until only the tips can be seen.

Buttonhole Wheel

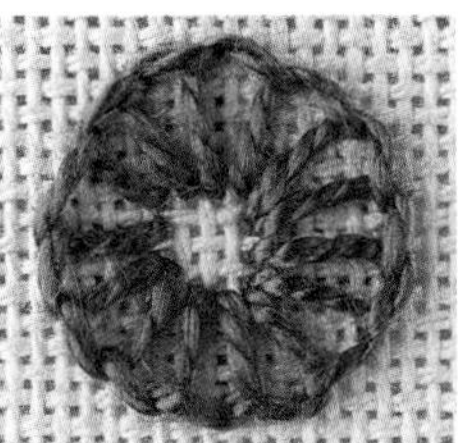

LEVEL
Intermediate

USES
Isolated stitch

METHOD
Buttonhole stitch worked within a ring

MATERIALS
Any fabric; any thread

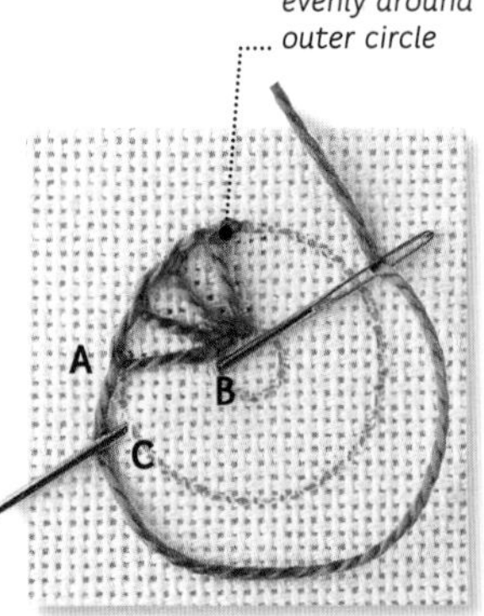
Space stitches evenly around outer circle
A
B
C

Mark two concentric circles. Come up at **A**, and insert the needle at **B** on the inner circle. Bring the needle out at **C**, passing it over the working thread. Continue stitching until the ring is complete.

Shisha

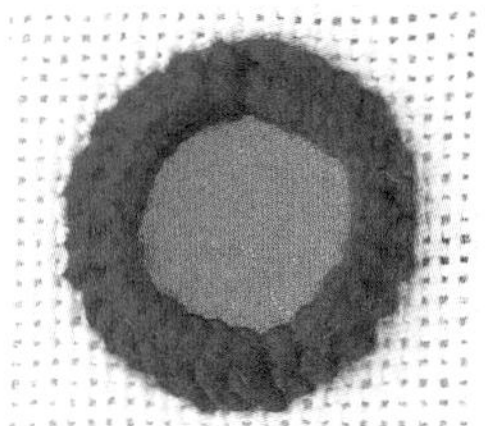

LEVEL
Advanced

USES
Indian embroidery; with couched gold threads

METHOD
Mirror disc attached to fabric with ring of twisted stitches

MATERIALS
Any fabric; any thick thread; shisha mirror; frame

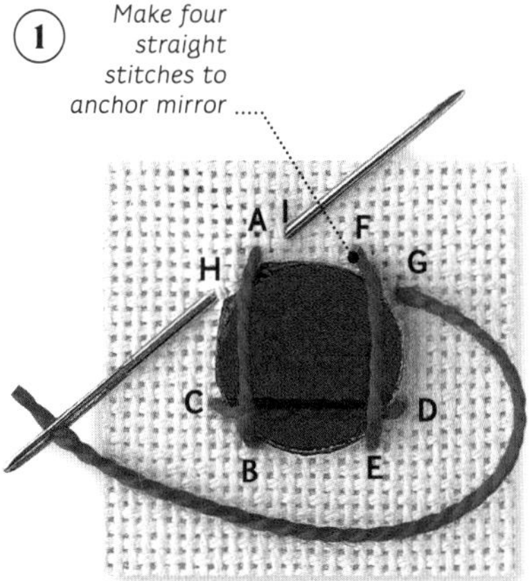
1
Make four straight stitches to anchor mirror
A
I
F
G
H
C
D
B
E

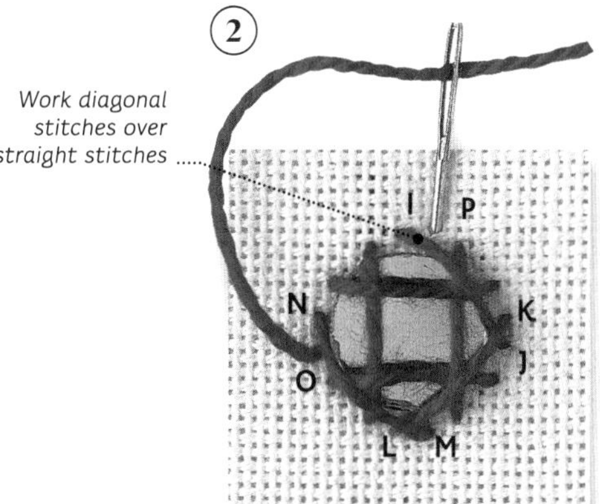
2
Work diagonal stitches over straight stitches
I
P
N
K
J
O
L
M

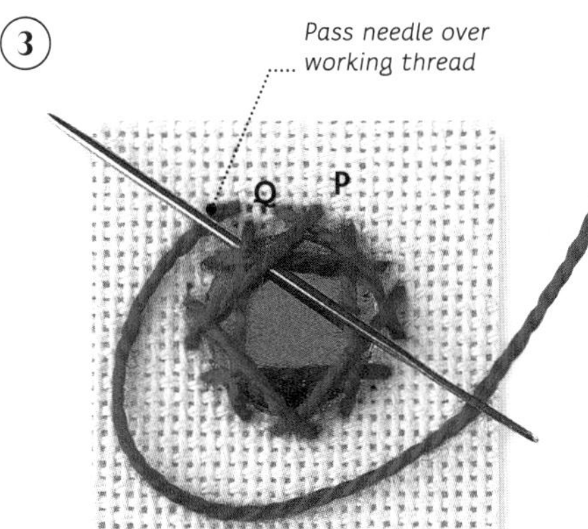
3
Pass needle over working thread
Q
P

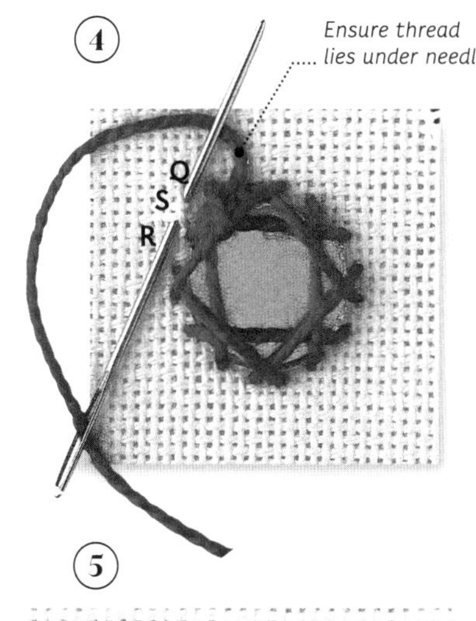
4
Ensure thread lies under needle
Q
S
R

5
S
Keep tension even when working twisted stitches

1 Place the mirror in position. Start at **A** and work a straight stitch down to **B**. Come out at **C** and insert at **D**. Come up at **E** and down at **F**, then come out at **G** and go down at **H**. Bring the needle up at **I**, ready to start the next four stitches.

2 Take the needle down to **J** to make a diagonal stitch. Bring it out at **K** and insert at **L**. Come out at **M**, down at **N**, out at **O**, then take the needle up to **P** and insert.

3 Bring the needle out at **Q**, just outside the straight stitches and pass it beneath the threads from right to left.

4 Insert the needle at **R** and bring it up at **S**, to make a small back stitch. Pull it through over the working thread.

5 Slide the needle back under the straight stitches and pull it through gently over the looped thread. Repeat steps 4 and 5 all the way around the mirror to complete.

Open and Solid Filling Stitches

These are the essential "colouring in" stitches, used to fill outlines and create areas of texture within an embroidery. Open fillings allow the background fabric to show through, whereas solid fillings cover it completely to give denser blocks of pattern.

Long and short stitch is used for needle painting – a contemporary name for the historic technique of silk shading – in which single strands of closely toning embroidery thread are built up like brush strokes to create an image. The stitches blend together to create subtly naturalistic shading, which is especially effective for depicting flowers, foliage, birds, and even portraits.

Damask

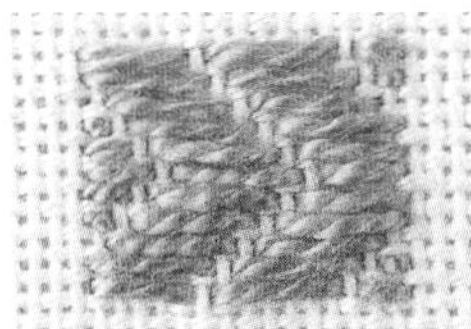

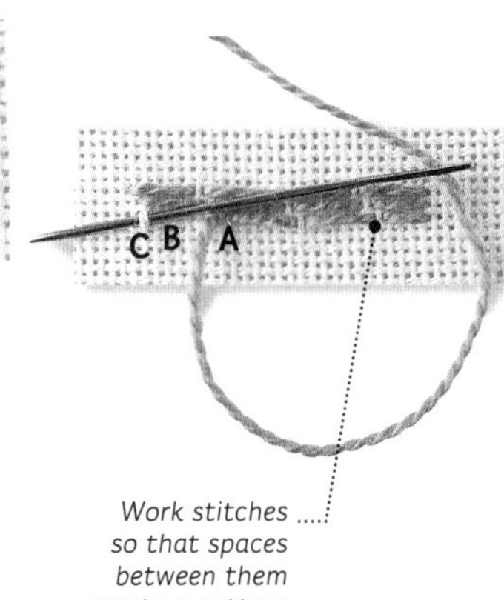
C B A

Work stitches so that spaces between them create a pattern

LEVEL
Easy

USES
Solid filling patterns; geometric bands

METHOD
Closely spaced rows of running stitch

MATERIALS
Evenweave fabric; any thread

Come up at **A**, to the right of the start of the stitch above. Insert the needle at **B**, to the right of the end of the stitch above. Bring the needle up one thread to the left, at **C**. Repeat, always following the previous line of stitching.

Double Damask

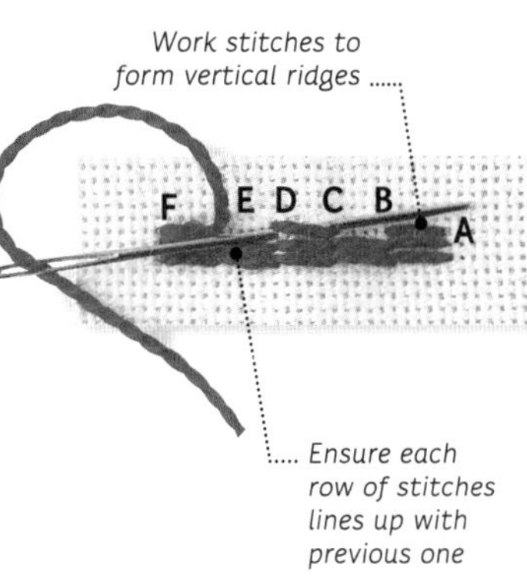
F E D C B A

Work stitches to form vertical ridges

Ensure each row of stitches lines up with previous one

LEVEL
Intermediate

USES
Solid filling stitch that appears the same at front and back

METHOD
Double running stitch in closely spaced rows

MATERIALS
Evenweave fabric; any thread

Work a row of evenly spaced running stitches (see p.39), from **A** to **B**, **C** to **D** and **E** to **F**. Fill in the spaces on the return journey; bring the needle back out at **E**, insert at **D** and come out at **C**. Work the following rows directly above.

Brick and Cross

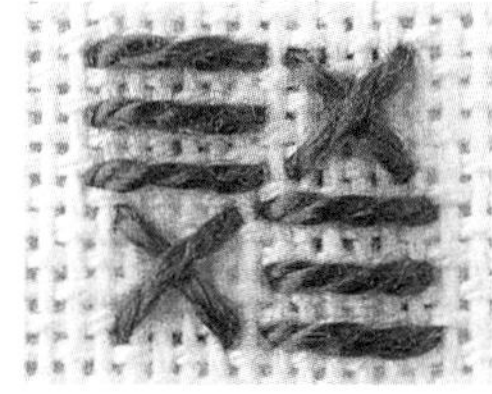

LEVEL
Intermediate

USES
Open geometric filling

METHOD
Alternate cross and groups of straight stitches, worked in vertical rows

MATERIALS
Evenweave fabric; any thread

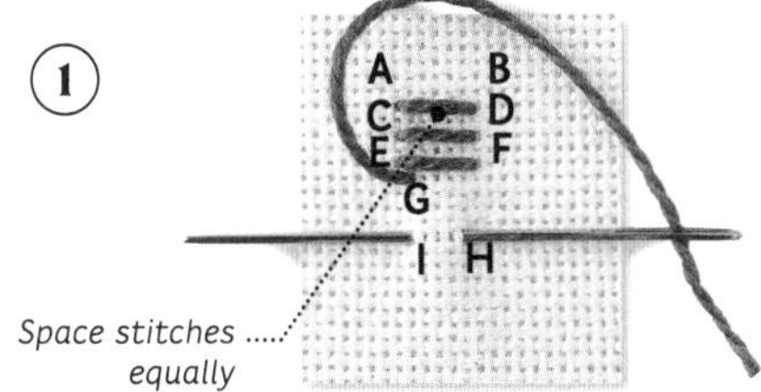
1
A B
C D
E F
G
I H

Space stitches equally

1 Make three parallel straight stitches from **A** to **B**, **C** to **D** and **E** to **F**. Bring the needle out at **G**. Work a diagonal stitch to **H**, then come out directly below **G**, at **I**.

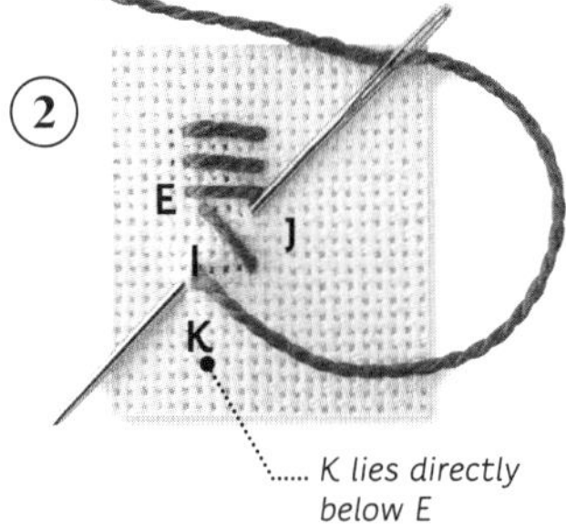
2
E
J
I
K

K lies directly below E

2 Insert the needle at **J** to complete the cross stitch. Bring the needle out to the left of **I**, at **K**.

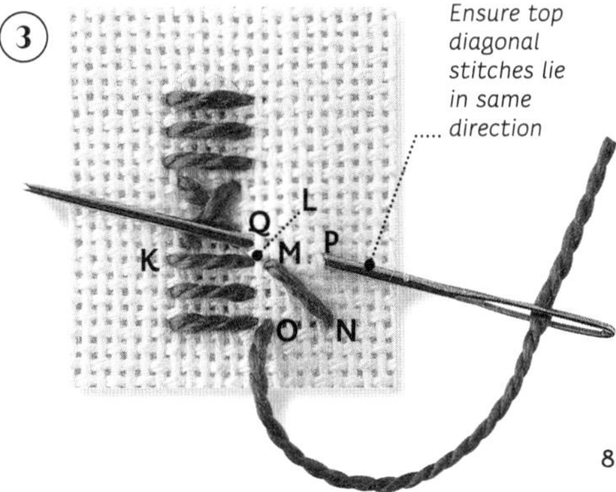
3
L
Q
K
M
P
O
N

Ensure top diagonal stitches lie in same direction

3 Insert at **L**, then make two more straight stitches. Come out level with **L**, at **M**, and insert at **N**. Bring the needle out at **O** and insert it at **P** to complete the second cross stitch. Come out at **Q** to begin the next three straight stitches.

Satin

OTHER NAME
Long stitch

LEVEL
Intermediate

USES
Solid filling; bands

METHOD
Closely worked straight stitches

MATERIALS
Any fabric; any thread – stranded silk or cotton gives lustrous finish

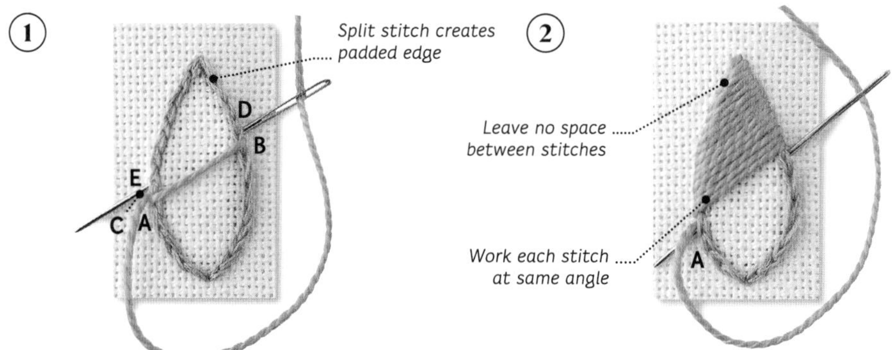

1
Split stitch creates padded edge
D
B
E
C A
2
Leave no space between stitches
Work each stitch at same angle
A

1 Outline the area to be covered with split stitch (see p.40). Start the satin stitch at the widest point of the shape. Work a diagonal stitch from **A** up to **B** and bring the needle out next to **A**, at **C**. Take it down next to **B**, at **D**. Come out at **E** ready for the next stitch.

2 Repeat, varying the stitch length until the top part of the shape is covered. Bring the needle out again just below **A** and work downwards to fill the rest of the shape.

Technique Variation

When working satin stitch over a geometric shape or as a border, work the stitches at a right angle to the outline. Start stitching at one end and work to the other.

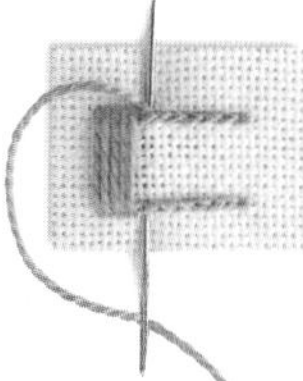

Surface Satin

LEVEL
Intermediate

USES
Solid filling; bands

METHOD
Closely worked straight stitches: uses less thread than satin stitch

MATERIALS
Any fabric; any thread – stranded silk or cotton for smooth surface; frame

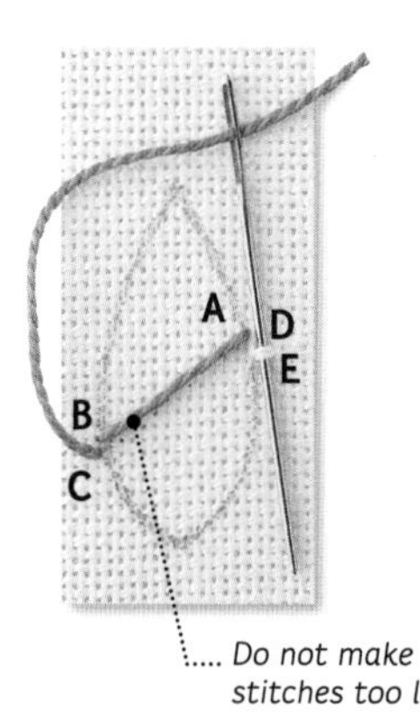

A
D
E
B
C
Do not make stitches too long

Mark the required shape. Work a diagonal stitch from **A** down to **B** and come up directly below, at **C**. Take the needle up to **D** and bring it out at **E**. Fill the lower part of the shape in this way. Come back up above **A** to work the remaining area.

Encroaching Satin

LEVEL
Intermediate

USES
Solid filling for larger areas

METHOD
Overlapping narrow rows of satin stitch

MATERIALS
Any fabric; any thread, in shades of the same colour; frame

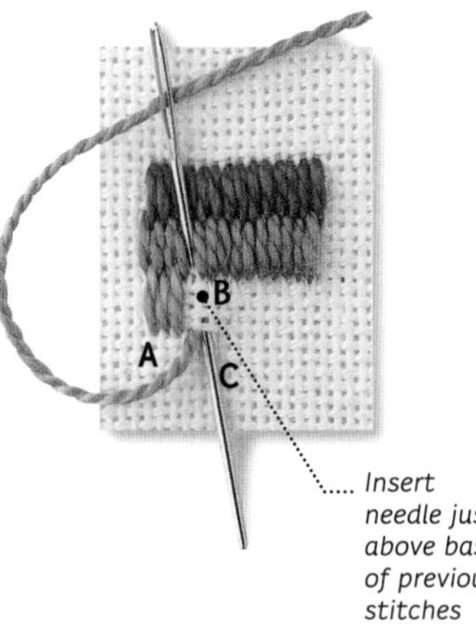

B
A
C
Insert needle just above base of previous stitches

Work a row of satin stitch (see above). On the following rows, bring the needle out at **A** and insert at **B**, between two stitches on the row above. Come up next to **A**, at **C**. Repeat to the row's end.

Long and Short

LEVEL
Advanced

USES
Shaded filling, giving three-dimensional effect

METHOD
Interlocking satin stitches

MATERIALS
Any fabric; any thread, in shades of the same colour; frame

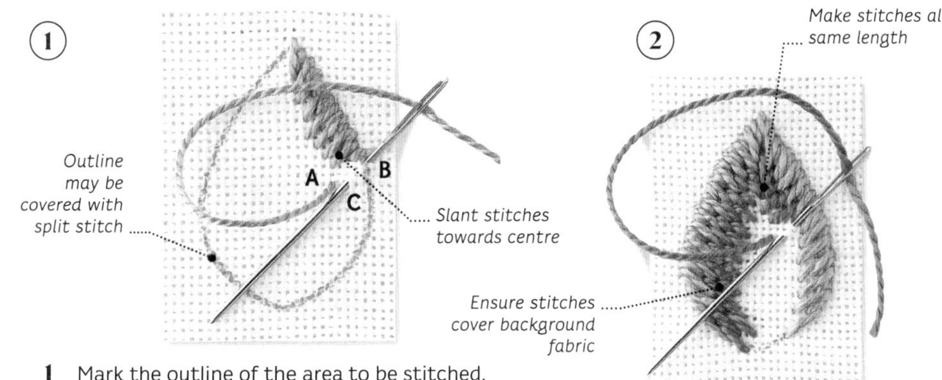
1
Outline may be covered with split stitch
A
B
C
Slant stitches towards centre
2
Make stitches all same length
Ensure stitches cover background fabric

1 Mark the outline of the area to be stitched. Work a row of alternate long and short satin stitches (see p.86) around the edge. Come up at **A** and take the needle down at **B** to make a long stitch. Bring it out at **C** to make a short stitch. Continue in this way to complete the first round.

2 Using a darker shade, work a row of long satin stitches which interlock with the first round. Fill in the centre with a third shade.

Technique Variation

When filling square or rectangular shapes, work the first row in alternate long and short stitches and subsequent rows in long stitches only, so they interlock as before.

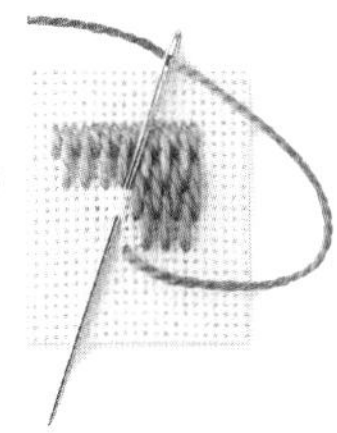

Buttonhole Filling

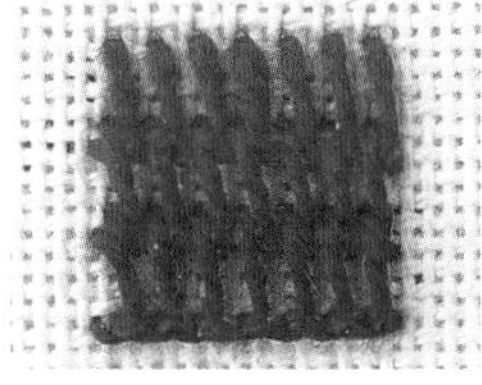

OTHER NAME
Buttonhole shading

LEVEL
Intermediate

USES
Shaded filling

METHOD
Overlapping rows of buttonhole stitch

MATERIALS
Any fabric; any thread, in shades of the same colour; frame

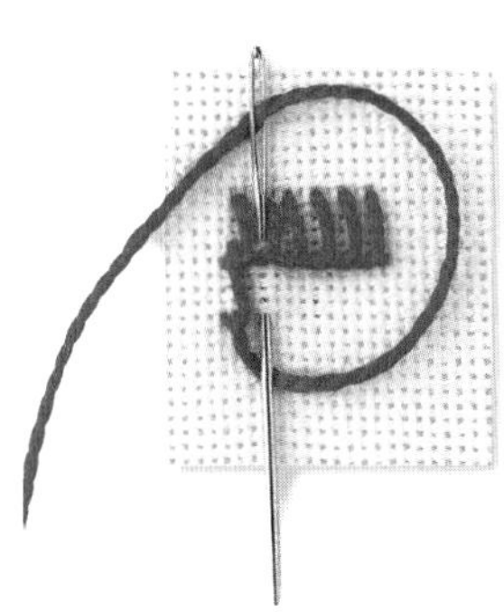

Work a row of buttonhole stitch (see p.58) using the lightest thread. With a darker tone, work the second row directly below, so that the upright stitches overlap the base of the previous row. Work subsequent rows in progressively darker tones to create the effect of shading.

Stem Filling

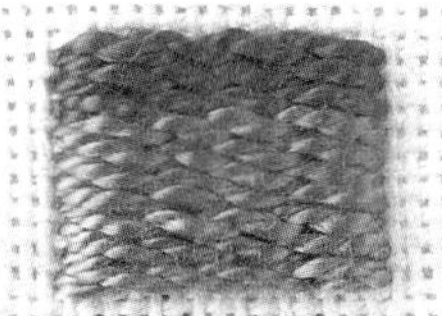

OTHER NAME
Stem stitch shading

LEVEL
Intermediate

USES
Shaded filling

METHOD
Closely spaced lines of stem stitch

MATERIALS
Any fabric; any thread, in shades of the same colour

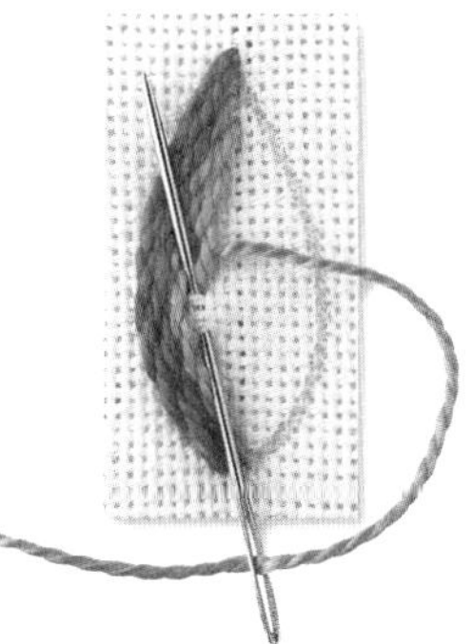

Mark the outline of the area to be stitched. Using the darkest thread, work two rows of stem stitch (see p.41) along one side of the outline. Work the next two rows in a lighter shade. Continue to fill the shape with rows of stem stitch, graduating the colour to create a shaded effect.

Leaf

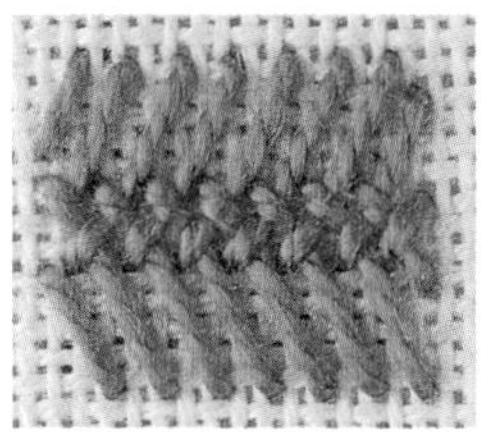

LEVEL
Intermediate

USES
Open filling for leaves, petals and wide borders

METHOD
Overlapping diagonal stitches worked upwards

MATERIALS
Any fabric; any thread; frame

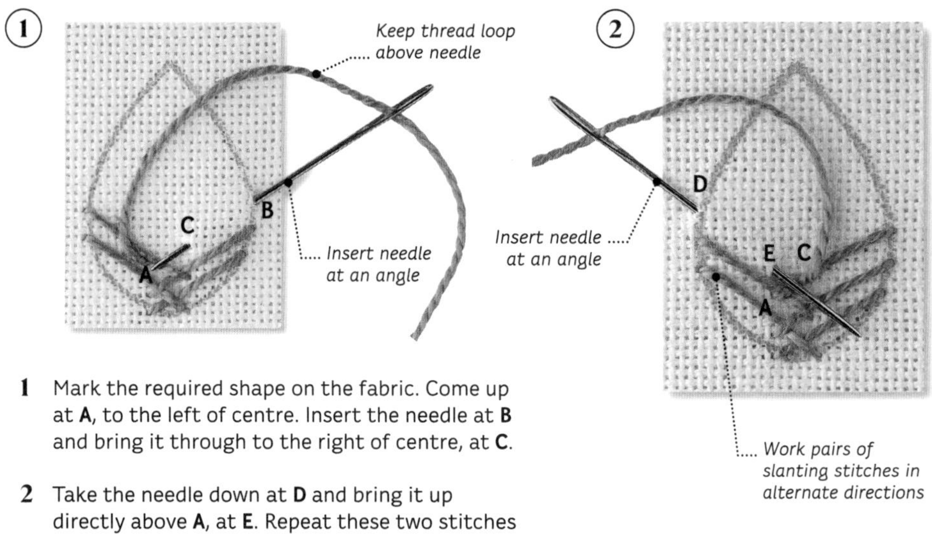
1
Keep thread loop above needle
C
B
A
Insert needle at an angle
2
D
Insert needle at an angle
E
C
A
Work pairs of slanting stitches in alternate directions

1 Mark the required shape on the fabric. Come up at **A**, to the left of centre. Insert the needle at **B** and bring it through to the right of centre, at **C**.

2 Take the needle down at **D** and bring it up directly above **A**, at **E**. Repeat these two stitches to fill the space, decreasing the length as the leaf tapers to a point. Work a narrow outline stitch (see pp.38–46) around the outside edge to complete.

Open Fishbone

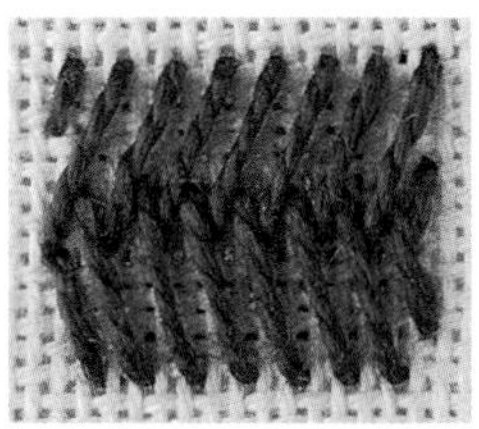

LEVEL
Easy

USES
Light filling for small leaf or petal shapes; open borders

METHOD
Alternate slanting stitches, worked downwards

MATERIALS
Any fabric; any thread; frame

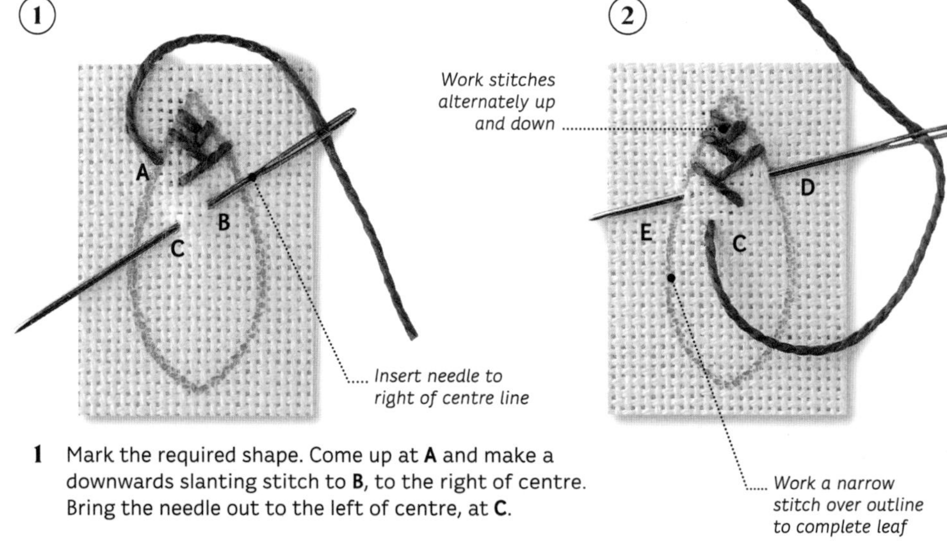
1
A
B
C
Insert needle to right of centre line
2
Work stitches alternately up and down
D
E
C
Work a narrow stitch over outline to complete leaf

1 Mark the required shape. Come up at **A** and make a downwards slanting stitch to **B**, to the right of centre. Bring the needle out to the left of centre, at **C**.

2 Take the needle up to the right and insert at **D**. Come out at **E**, ready to work the next downwards stitch. Repeat these two stitches to continue, altering the length as the outline widens or narrows.

Attached Fly

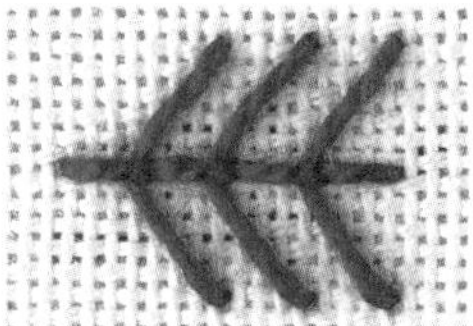

OTHER NAME
Fishbone

LEVEL
Easy

USES
Open filling for narrow leaf or geometric shapes; light borders

METHOD
Row of linked fly stitches worked downwards

MATERIALS
Any fabric; any thread; embroidery frame

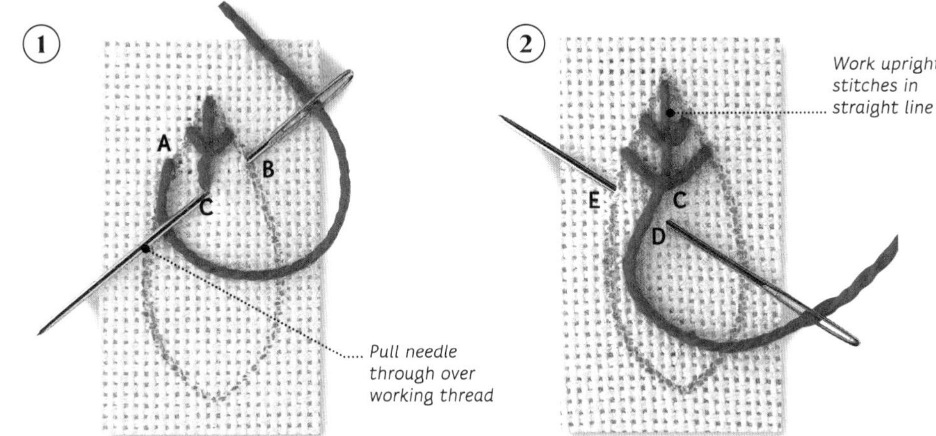

1
A
B
C
Pull needle through over working thread
2
Work upright stitches in straight line
E
C
D

1 Mark the outline of the area to be filled. Come out at **A** and insert the needle on the same level, at **B**. Bring it up in the centre at **C**.

2 Insert the needle directly below **C**, at **D**, to make a straight stitch, and bring it out at **E**. Repeat steps 1 and 2 to continue, varying the stitch length as required.

Stitch Variation

Close fly stitch is made by reducing the length of the straight stitches (see step 2).

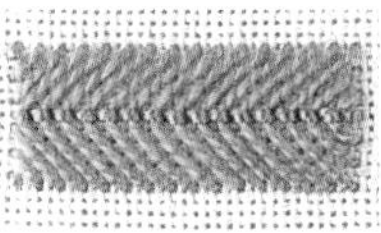

Cretan

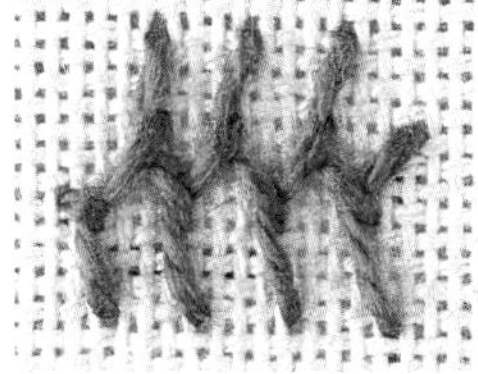

OTHER NAME
Cretan filling

LEVEL
Easy

USES
Open filling for leaf or geometric motif; borders

METHOD
Looped vertical stitch, worked downwards

MATERIALS
Any fabric; any thread; frame

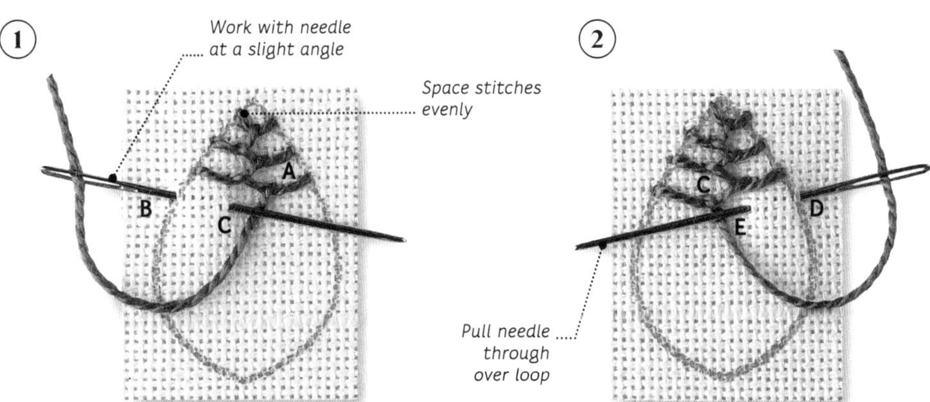

1
Work with needle at a slight angle
Space stitches evenly
A
B
C
2
C
D
E
Pull needle through over loop

1 Mark the shape to be filled. Come up to the right of centre at **A**, then take the needle across to **B** and insert. Come out to the left of centre at **C**. Pull the needle through over the working thread.

2 Take the needle down at **D** and come out at **E**. Repeat these two steps to fill the required area.

Stitch Variation

Close Cretan stitch is formed by working each new stitch immediately below the last, so no space is left between them.

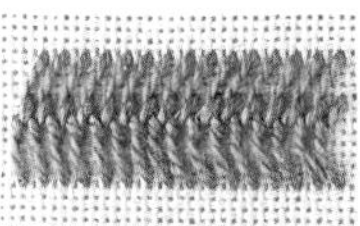

Romanian Couching

LEVEL
Intermediate

USES
Solid filling for large areas

METHOD
Closely spaced long couched stitches

MATERIALS
Any fabric; any thread – stranded cotton gives smooth surface; frame

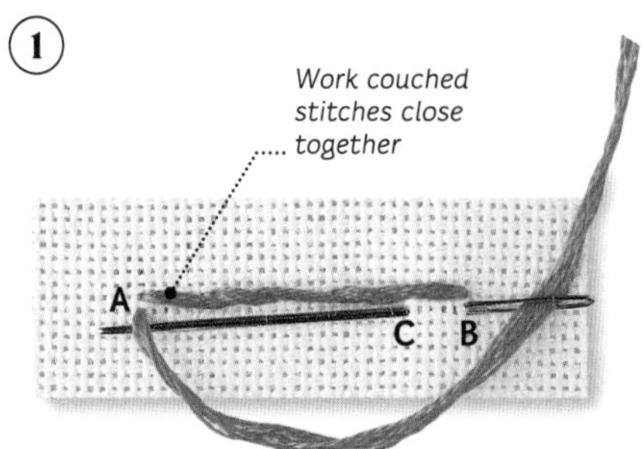

1
Work couched stitches close together
A
C
B

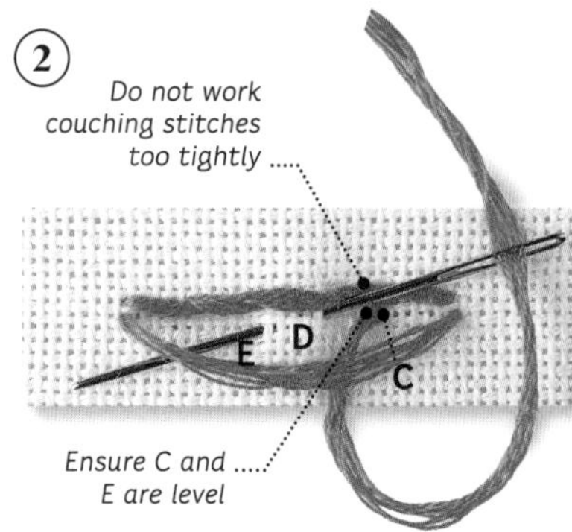

2
Do not work couching stitches too tightly
E
D
C
Ensure C and E are level

1 Come up at **A** and work a long horizontal stitch across to **B**. Bring the needle out level with **A**, at **C**.

2 Make a couching stitch: take the needle over the long stitch and insert at **D**. Draw the thread up gently to tighten. Come out at **E**, ready to make the next couching stitch.

Stitch Variation

Bokhara couching is worked in the same way, but the couching stitches are much shorter and made at a steep angle.

Spiral Couching

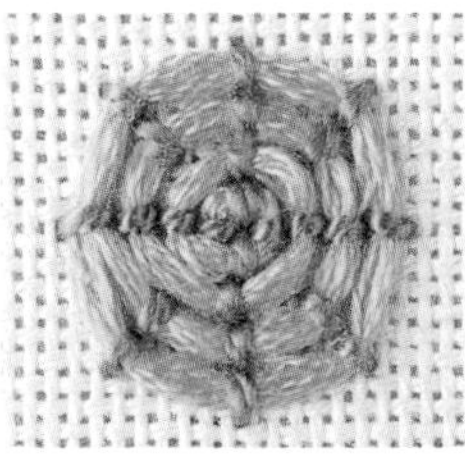

LEVEL
Intermediate

USES
Solid filling for circles; metal thread embroidery

METHOD
Laid threads worked within a circle

MATERIALS
Any fabric; thick or fragile threads; finer couching thread; frame

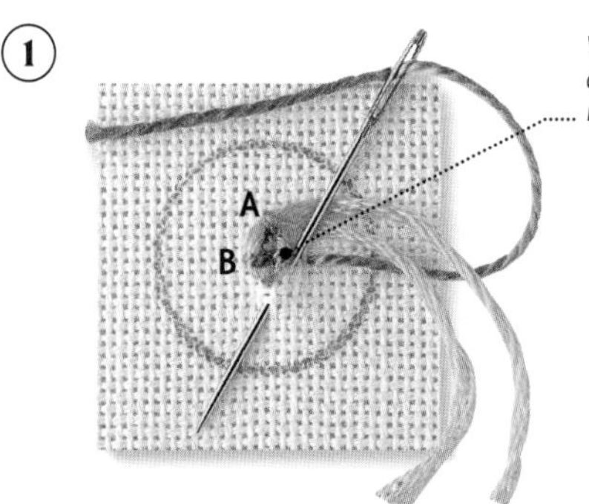

1
Work first round of couching stitches at right angles
A
B

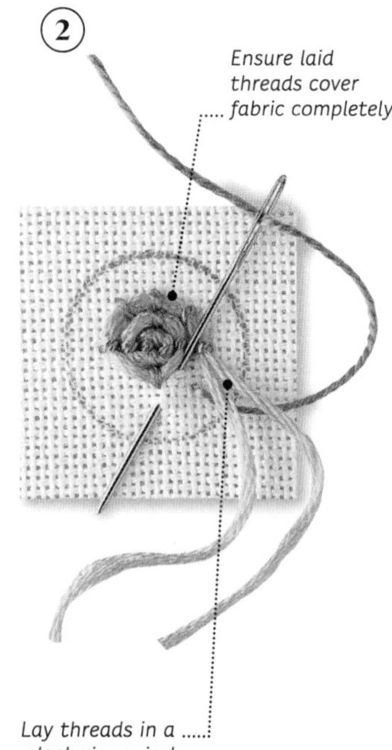

2
Ensure laid threads cover fabric completely
Lay threads in a clockwise spiral

1 Mark a circle and bring the couching thread up just above the centre, at **A**. Fold the laid thread in half, pass the needle through the loop and insert at **B** to make a couching stitch. Curve the threads to the right. Work three more stitches, to complete the round. Make another round of four couching stitches.

2 Continue couching the laid threads in a spiral, spacing the stitches further apart as it increases in diameter. Take the ends through to the back to finish.

Couched Filling

LEVEL
Intermediate

USES
Decorative open filling

METHOD
Straight stitch grid with cross stitch couching

MATERIALS
Any fabric; thread in two colours of the same or different thicknesses; frame

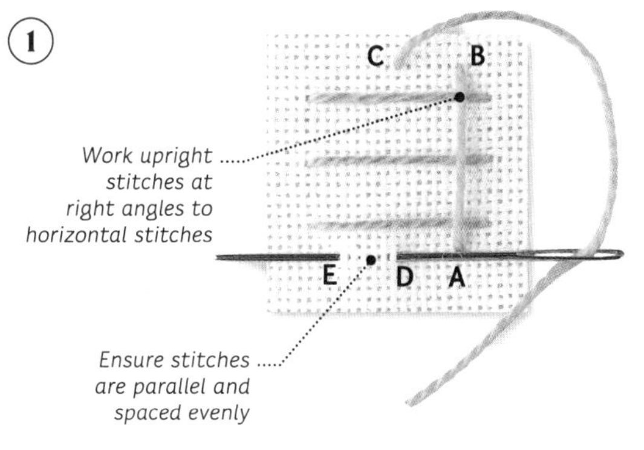

1
C
B
Work upright stitches at right angles to horizontal stitches
E
D
A
Ensure stitches are parallel and spaced evenly

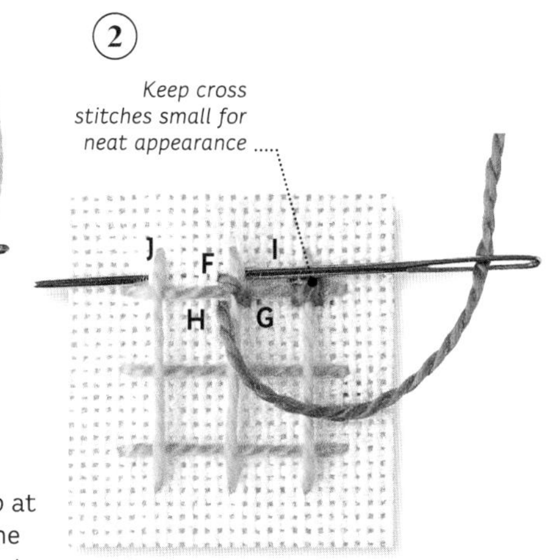

2
Keep cross stitches small for neat appearance
J
F
I
H
G

1 Using the first colour, make a foundation of horizontal straight stitches (see p.73). Come up at **A** to start working the vertical stitches. Take the needle down at **B**, then bring it out at **C**. Insert at **D** and come out at **E**, ready for the final stitch.

2 Work a cross stitch over each intersection of the straight stitches. Bring the second colour up at **F**. Take the needle down over the crossed threads and insert at **G**. Come up at **H** and insert at **I**, then come out at **J**, ready to make the next cross.

Laidwork

LEVEL
Advanced

USES
Decorative solid filling

METHOD
Surface satin stitch with trellis of couched straight stitches

MATERIALS
Any fabric; thread in three colours; frame

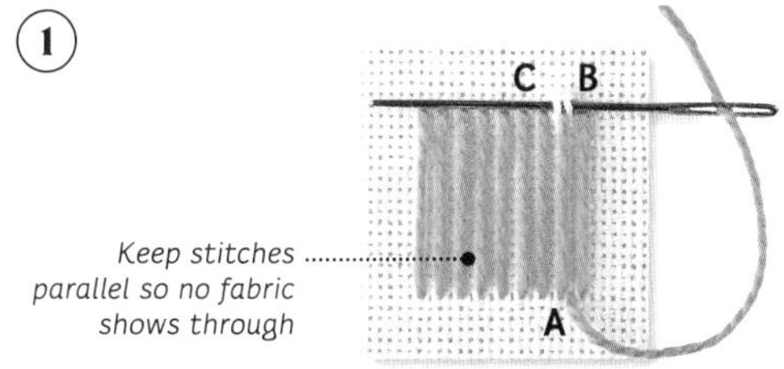

1
C
B
Keep stitches parallel so no fabric shows through
A

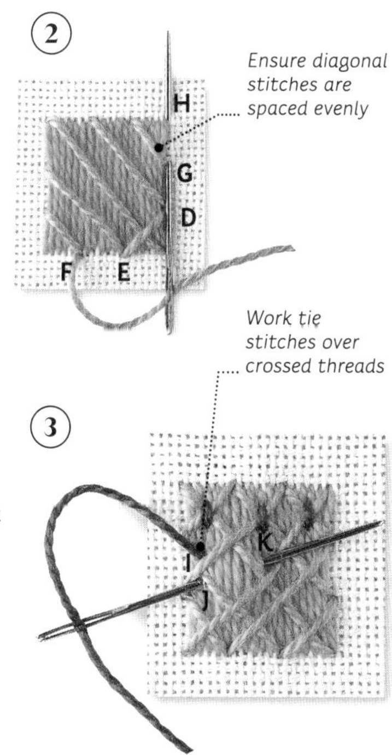

2
Ensure diagonal stitches are spaced evenly
H
G
D
F
E
Work tie stitches over crossed threads
3
K
I
J

1 Work a row of upright surface satin stitches (see p.86), leaving one stitch width between each. Bring the needle out at **A**, insert at **B** and come up at **C**. Repeat along the row to fill in the spaces.

2 Using the second thread, work a series of diagonal stitches across the foundation. Come up at **D** to start the second layer of stitches. Take the needle down at **E**, then bring it out at **F** and insert at **G**. Come out at **H**, ready to complete the trellis.

3 Work the short tie stitches (see p.20) in the third colour. Come up at **I**, take the needle down at **J** and bring it out again at **K**. Repeat at each intersection.

Back Stitch Trellis

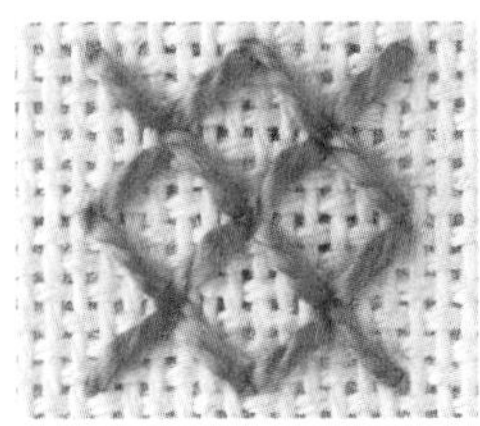

LEVEL
Intermediate

USES
Open geometric filling

METHOD
Intersecting diagonal rows of back stitch

MATERIALS
Any fabric – evenweave for a regular effect; any embroidery thread

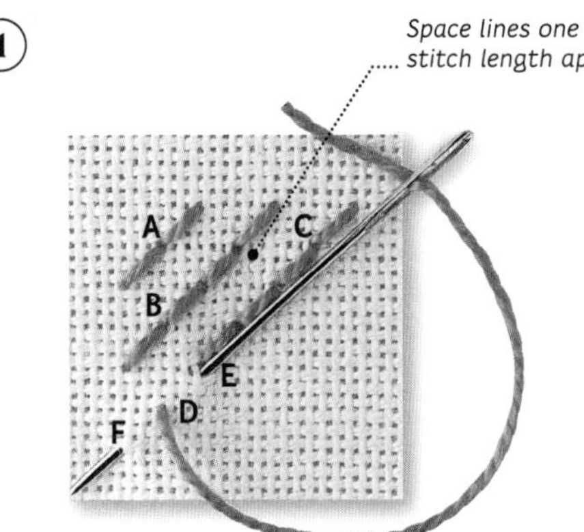
1
Space lines one stitch length apart
A
B
C
D
E
F

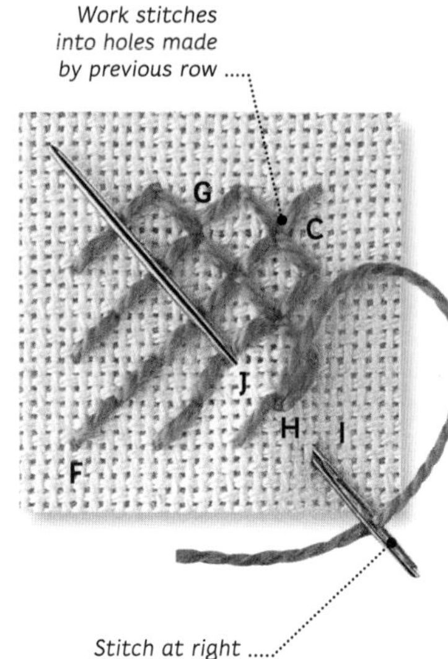
2
Work stitches into holes made by previous row
G
C
J
H
I
F
Stitch at right angles to previous row

1 Work a series of diagonal, parallel rows of back stitch (see p.40). Start the first row at **A**, the second at **B** and the third at **C**. Come out at **D**, insert the needle at **E** and bring it out at **F**. Continue until the required area is filled.

2 Work the next row in the opposite direction, starting at **C**, then **G**. Come out at **H**, insert at **I** and come up at **J**. Repeat to complete the trellis.

Japanese Darning

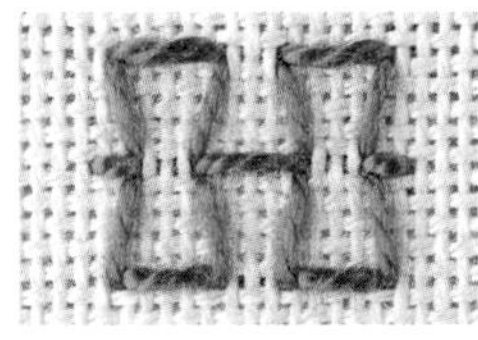

LEVEL
Intermediate

USES
Open geometric filling for larger areas

METHOD
Combination of running and straight stitches; Sashiko variation

MATERIALS
Any fabric – evenweave is easier to use; any embroidery thread

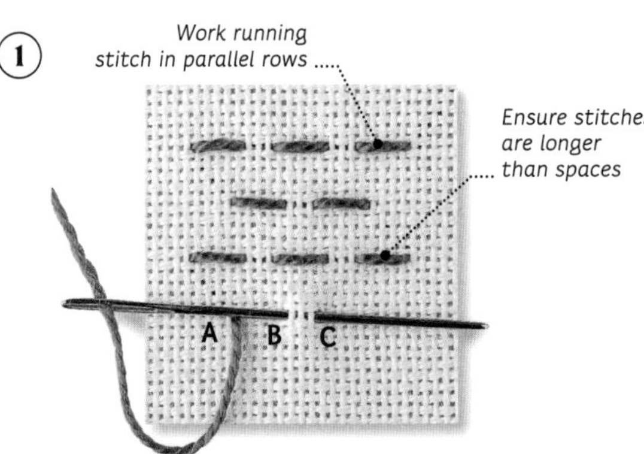
1
Work running stitch in parallel rows
Ensure stitches are longer than spaces
A
B
C

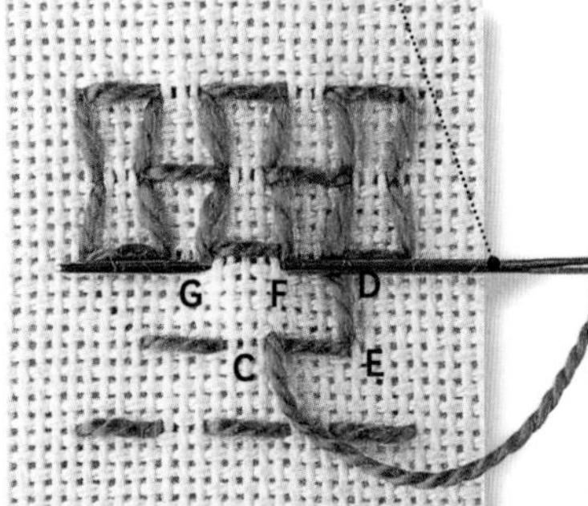
2
Work slanting stitches into holes made by running stitches
G
F
D
C
E

1 Work several horizontal rows of running stitch (see p.39), positioned so that the stitches in each row lie beneath the spaces in the row above. Come up at **A**, insert the needle at **B** and bring it out at **C**. Repeat to fill the required area.

2 Link the rows of running stitch with slanting stitches. Bring the needle out at **D** and take it down at **E**. Come up at **C**, go down at **F**, then up at **G**, ready to make the next stitch. Continue to the end of the row, before proceeding to the one below.

Cloud Filling

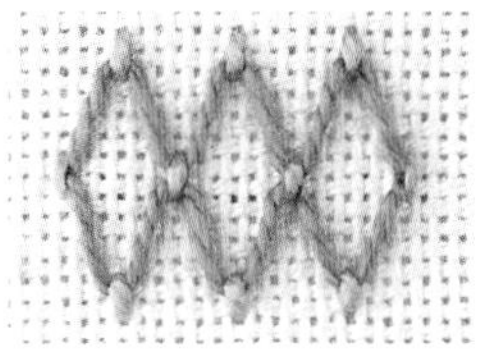

OTHER NAME
Mexican stitch

LEVEL
Intermediate

USES
Open filling; crewel work

METHOD
Interlaced rows of short upright stitches

MATERIALS
Any fabric – evenweave for regular effect; any thread in two colours; blunt needle

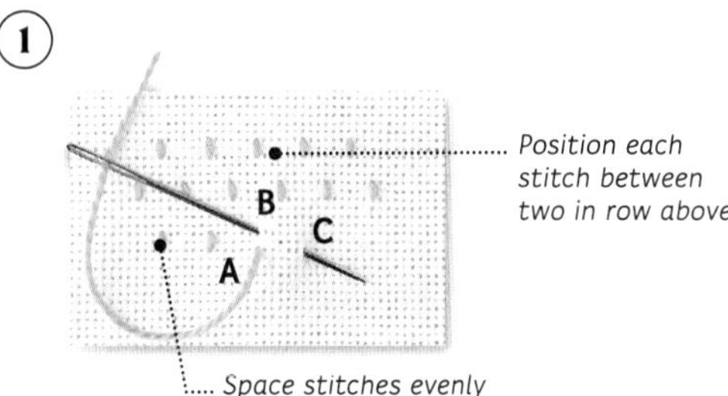

1
B
C
A
Position each stitch between two in row above
Space stitches evenly

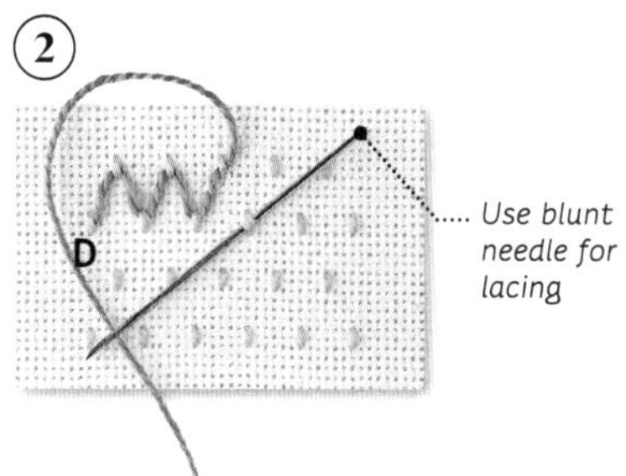

2
D
Use blunt needle for lacing

1 Work a foundation of short upright stitches, arranged in staggered rows. Come up at **A** and make a straight stitch to **B**, then bring the needle out at **C**. Repeat to fill the required area.

2 Bring the second thread up at **D**. Slide the needle under the first stitch in the top row from left to right. Pass it beneath the second stitch on the row below and continue lacing to the end.

3 Come up at **E**. Slide the needle under the first stitch on the third row, from right to left. Take it under the next stitch on the second row. Repeat to the end, then thread further rows in the same way.

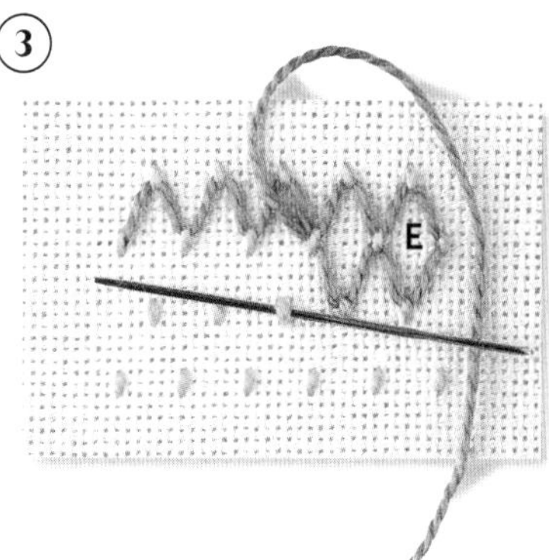

3
E

Wave Filling

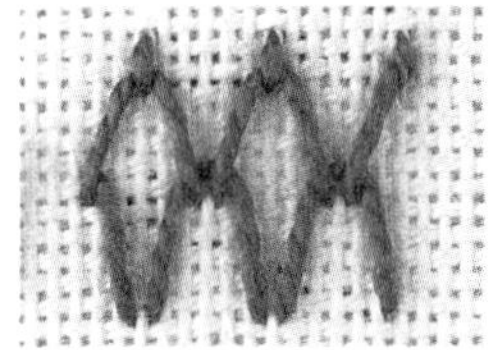

LEVEL
Intermediate

USES
Shaded or single colour open filling; crewel work

METHOD
Interlinked horizontal rows of looped stitches

MATERIALS
Any fabric; any thread in one or more colours; frame

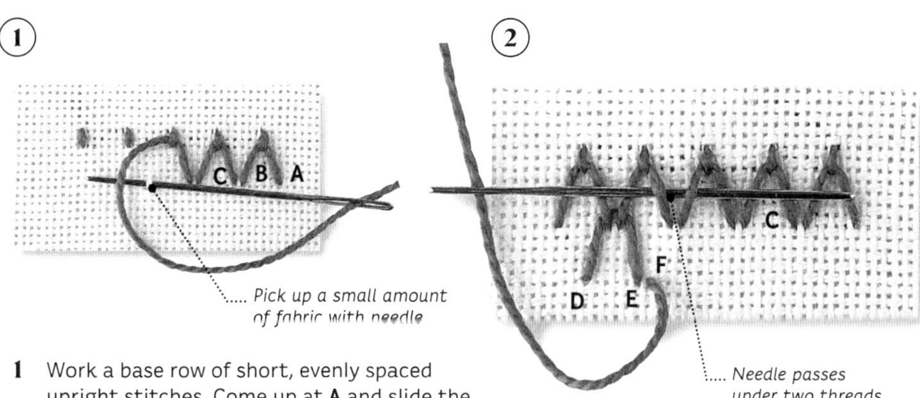

1
C
B
A
Pick up a small amount of fabric with needle
2
C
F
D
E
Needle passes under two threads

1 Work a base row of short, evenly spaced upright stitches. Come up at **A** and slide the needle under the first stitch. Take it back down to **B** and insert. Come out just to the left, at **C** and repeat to the end of the row.

2 Start the next row at **D**. Pass the needle under the next two stitches of the row above. Take it down and insert at **E**, then come out at **F**. Continue to the end of the row.

Technique Variation

Create a subtly shaded effect by stitching each successive row in a darker shade of the same colour.

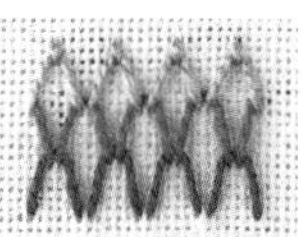

Openwork Stitches

Pulled Fabric Stitches

The three groups of openwork stitches are part of the wider family of needlework techniques known as whitework, which has long been used to create intricate patterns on household linen, and to embellish garments. These stitches are traditionally worked in white thread on white fabrics, but contemporary renderings in contrasting colours reveal their true diversity.

The decorative textures of pulled fabric, or pulled thread, embroidery are created by drawing together the warp and weft threads of an evenweave fabric with rows of tightly worked stitches. They appear in many embroidery traditions, from the delicate Jaali trellis work in Indian *Chikankari* embroidery to geometric Norwegian *Hardangersøm*, which is stitched onto linen.

Window Filling

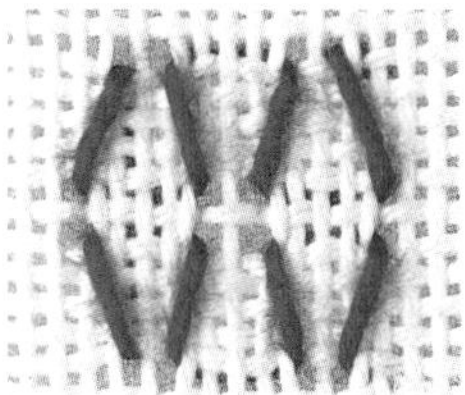

LEVEL
Easy

USES
Dense filling

METHOD
Diamond trellis with four small holes

MATERIALS
Evenweave fabric; any thread; blunt needle; frame

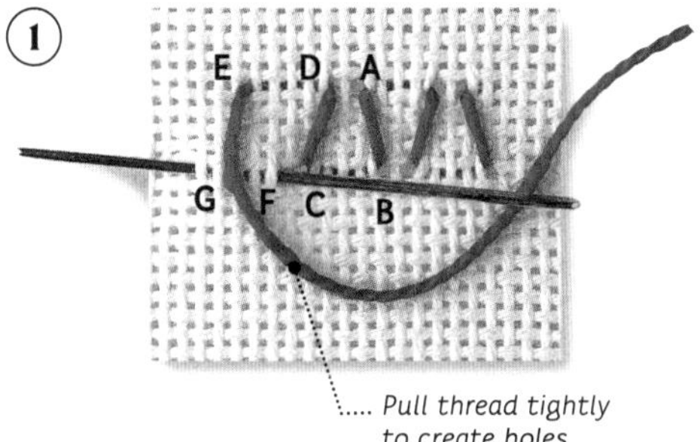
1
E D A
G F C B
Pull thread tightly to create holes

1 Come up at **A**. Work a diagonal stitch over five horizontal and two vertical threads, down to **B**. Come out five threads to the left, at **C**, then insert one thread to the left of **A**, at **D**. Bring the needle out five threads to the left, at **E** and go down one thread to the left of **C**, at **F**. Come out at **G** and continue to the end of the row.

2 Stitch the next row as a mirror image of the first. Come up at **H**, eleven threads below **E**, and insert one thread below **G**, at **I**. Repeat these two rows to continue.

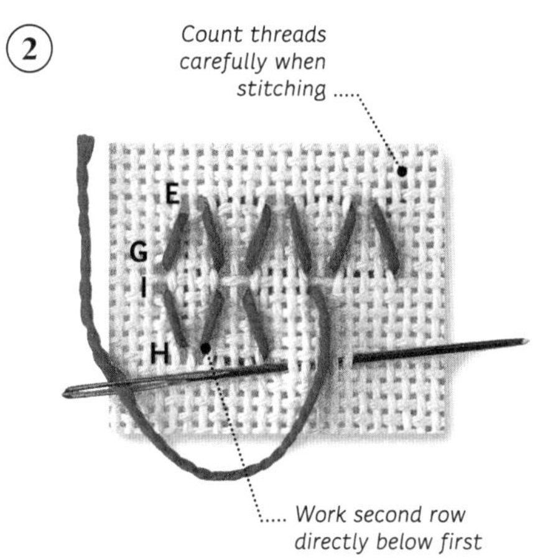
2
Count threads carefully when stitching
E
G
I
H
Work second row directly below first

Stitch Variation

Pulled wave filling, which has open holes, is worked in the same way, but no space is left between the stitches.

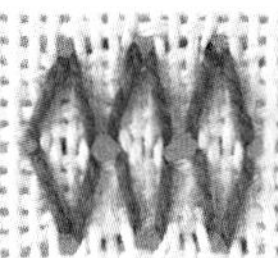

Three-sided

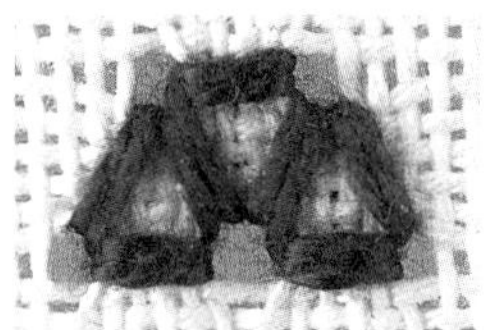

OTHER NAME
Straight line stitch

LEVEL
Easy

USES
Narrow borders

METHOD
Double back stitch worked in triangles

MATERIALS
Evenweave fabric; any thread; blunt needle; frame

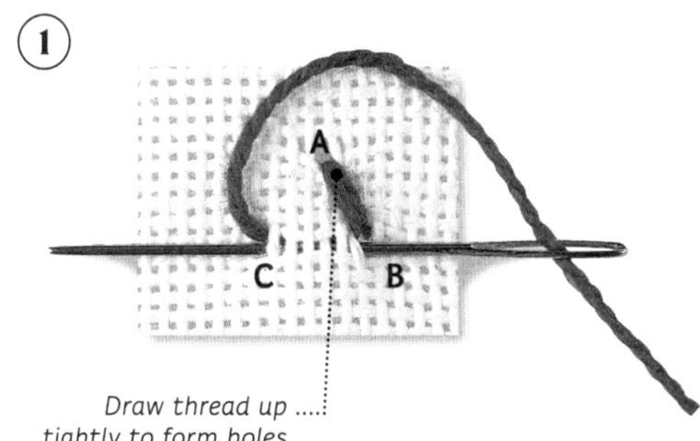
1
A
C B
Draw thread up tightly to form holes

1 Start at **A** and work a diagonal stitch over six horizontal and three vertical threads down to **B**. Come out again at **A** and re-insert at **B** to make a double back stitch. Come up six threads to the left of **B** at **C** and work another double back stitch.

2 Work another double back stitch up to **A** and come out six threads to the left, at **D**.

3 Take the needle down to **C** and make a double stitch. Repeat to the end of the row.

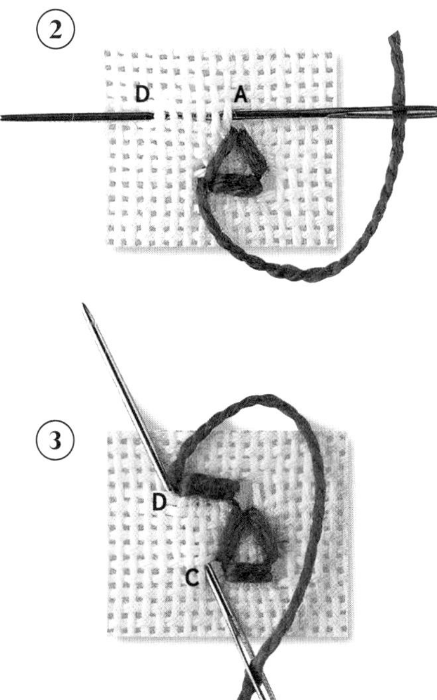
2
D A
3
D
C

Honeycomb Filling

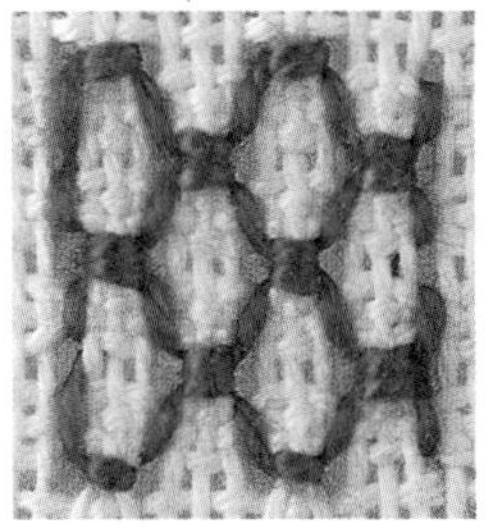

LEVEL
Intermediate

USES
Light filling with semi-open appearance

METHOD
Worked to form hexagonal lattice

MATERIALS
Evenweave fabric; any thread; blunt needle

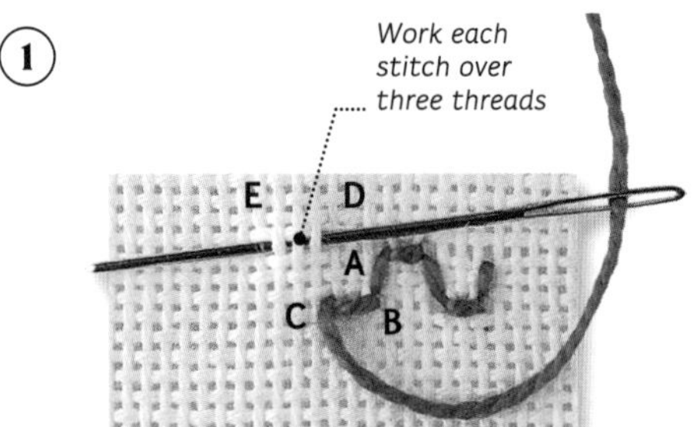
1
Work each stitch over three threads
E
D
A
C
B

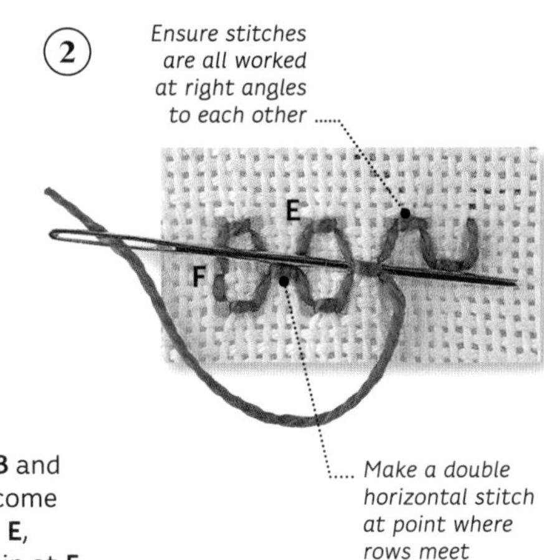
2
Ensure stitches are all worked at right angles to each other
E
F
Make a double horizontal stitch at point where rows meet

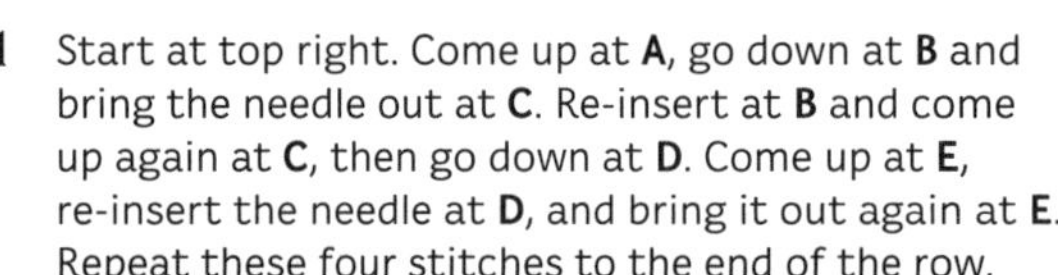

1 Start at top right. Come up at **A**, go down at **B** and bring the needle out at **C**. Re-insert at **B** and come up again at **C**, then go down at **D**. Come up at **E**, re-insert the needle at **D**, and bring it out again at **E**. Repeat these four stitches to the end of the row.

2 Work the second row as a mirror image of the first. Start at **F**, and turn the work upside-down if desired. Repeat these two rows to fill the required area.

Russian Filling

LEVEL
Advanced

USES
Dense filling with open holes

METHOD
Crossed diagonal stitches worked in two journeys

MATERIALS
Evenweave fabric; any thread; blunt needle

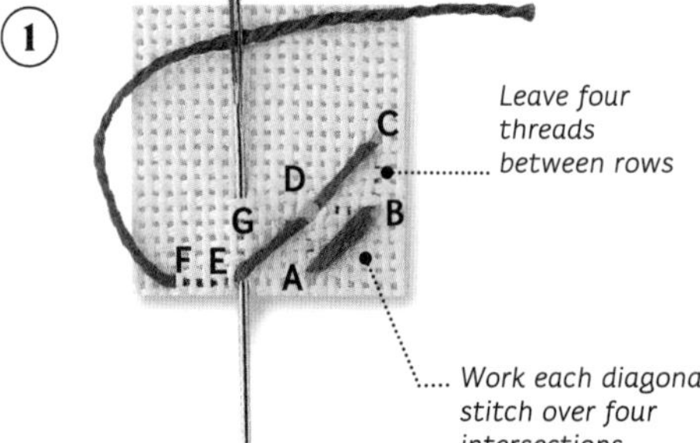
1
C
D
B
G
F E
A
Leave four threads between rows
Work each diagonal stitch over four intersections

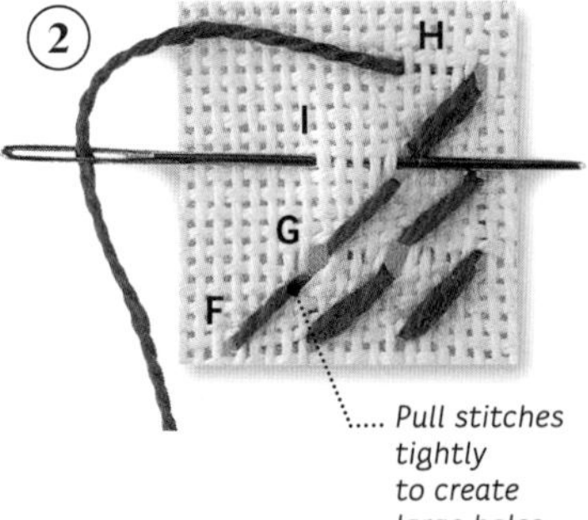
2
H
I
G
F
Pull stitches tightly to create large holes

1 Start at bottom right. Work a diagonal stitch from **A** to **B**. Come up at **C** and insert the needle at **D**. Bring it back up at **B**, down at **A**, then up again at **D** and down at **E**. Start the next row with a stitch from **F** to **G** and come up at **E**. Repeat these two rows until the top right corner of the area being filled is reached.

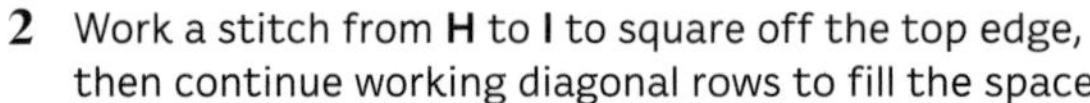

2 Work a stitch from **H** to **I** to square off the top edge, then continue working diagonal rows to fill the space.

3 The second journey, which completes the crosses, starts from **J** to **H**. Turn the work through 45 degrees to the left and stitch as before.

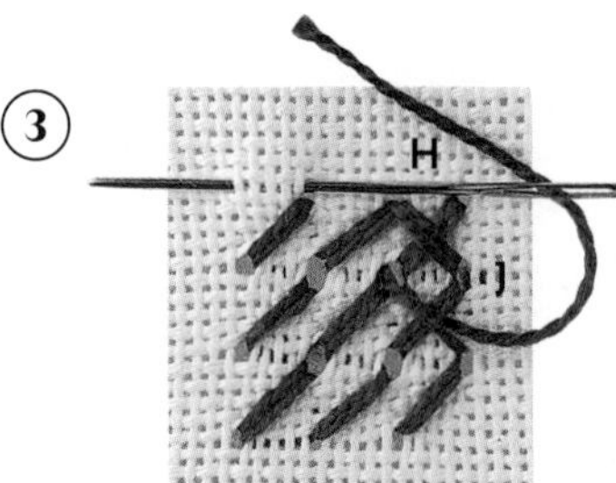
3
H
J

Diagonal Raised Band

LEVEL
Easy

USES
Ridged diagonal borders

METHOD
Diagonal row of tightly worked cross stitches

MATERIALS
Evenweave fabric; any thread; blunt needle; frame

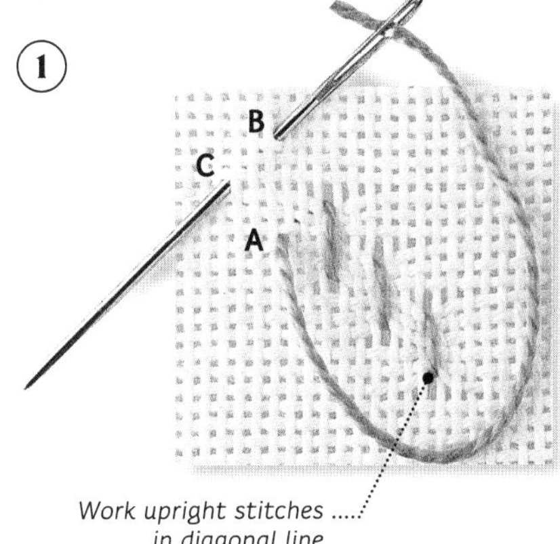
1
B
C
A
Work upright stitches in diagonal line

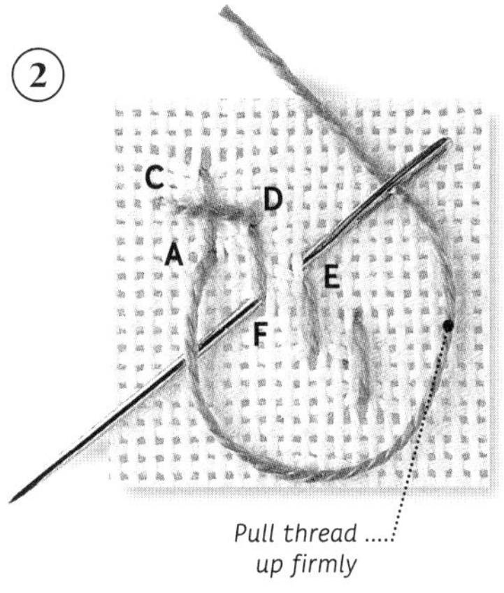
2
C
D
A
E
F
Pull thread up firmly

1 Work a row of upright stitches. Come out at **A**, take the needle up over six threads and insert it at **B**. Bring the needle out three intersections to the left, at **C**.

2 Insert the needle at **D** and bring it out again at **A**. Insert at **E** and come out at **F**, and continue to the end of the row.

Stitch Variation

Ridged filling is made by working diagonal raised band stitch in adjacent rows to make a solid pattern.

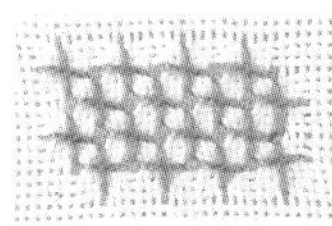

Punch

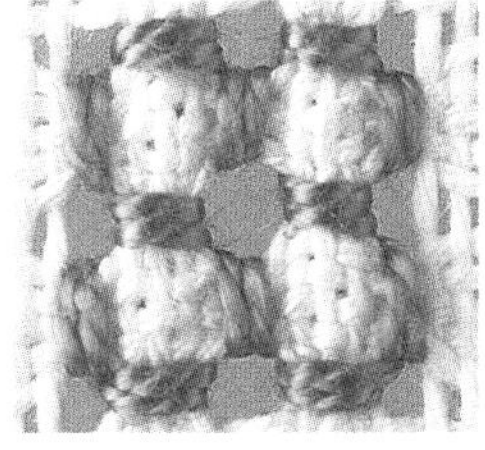

LEVEL
Easy

USES
Open filling with large holes

METHOD
Double back stitch worked in square grid

MATERIALS
Evenweave fabric; any thread; blunt needle; frame

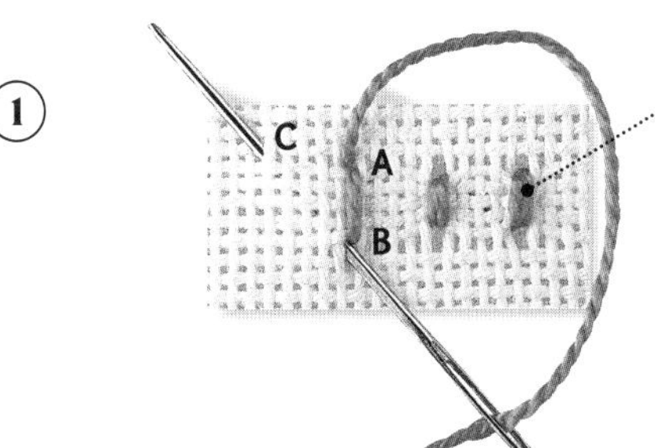
1
C
A
B
Work double stitches very tightly

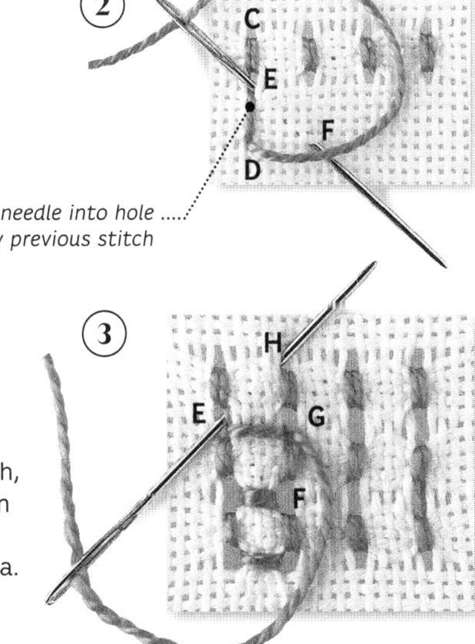
2
C
E
F
D
3
H
E
G
F
Insert needle into hole made by previous stitch

1 Come up at **A** and work an upright stitch over four threads to **B**. Make a second stitch in the same holes, then come out five intersections to the left, at **C**. Repeat to the end of the row.

2 Bring the needle out five threads below the final stitch, at **D**. Work a double back stitch between **D** and **E**, then come up five threads to the right, at **F**. Continue to the end of the row then repeat to fill the required area.

3 Work horizontal stitches between the upright rows. Come up at **G** and make a double back stitch to **E**. Bring the needle out at **H**, then continue working up and down the rows.

Cobbler Filling

LEVEL
Intermediate

USES
Light, open filling

METHOD
Straight stitches worked in vertical and horizontal rows to form pattern of detached squares

MATERIALS
Evenweave fabric; any thread; blunt needle; frame

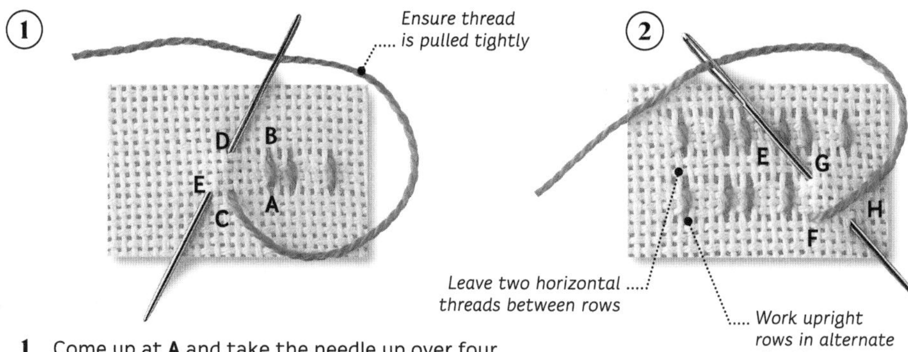

1
Ensure thread is pulled tightly
D
B
E
A
C
2
E
G
H
F
Leave two horizontal threads between rows
Work upright rows in alternate directions

1 Come up at **A** and take the needle up over four threads to **B**. Bring it out four threads to the left of **A** at **C**. Insert at **D** and come up two threads to the left of **C** at **E**. Repeat to the end of the row.

2 Work the following rows of upright stitches in line with the first. Bring the needle up six threads below the previous stitch, at **F**. Insert at **G** and come up at **H**.

3 Join the pairs of stitches to form squares. Bring the needle up at **D**, take it down at **B** and up at **C**. Insert at **A**, then continue working down and up the rows.

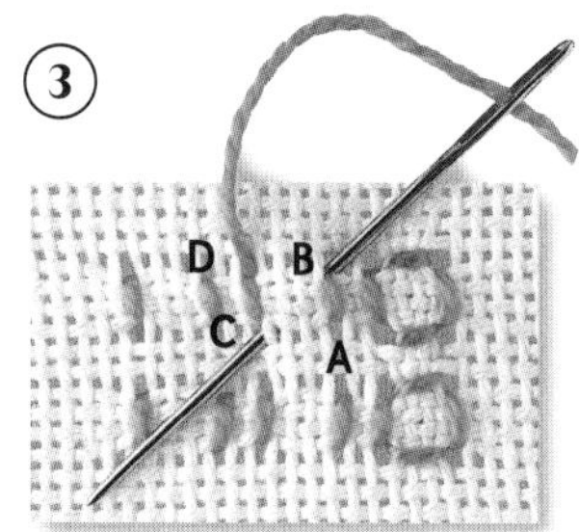

3
D
B
C
A

Step

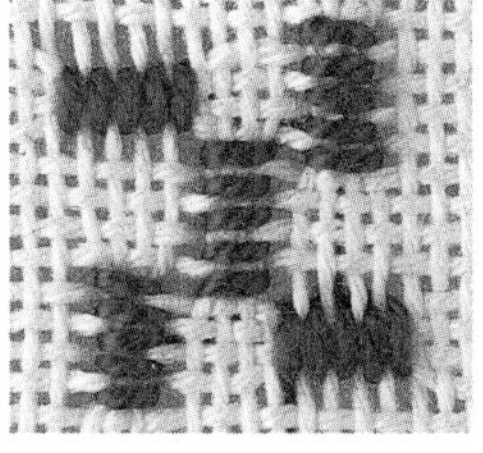

LEVEL
Intermediate

USES
Dense filling

METHOD
Diagonal rows made up of blocks of satin stitch set at alternate angles

MATERIALS
Evenweave fabric; any thread; blunt needle; frame

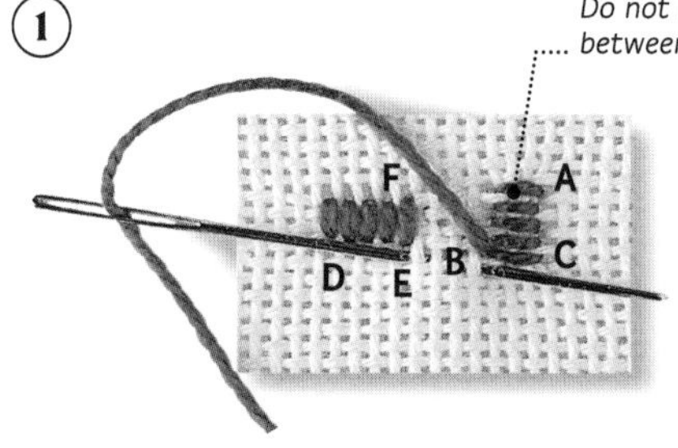

1
Do not leave any space between stitches
F
A
D
E
B
C

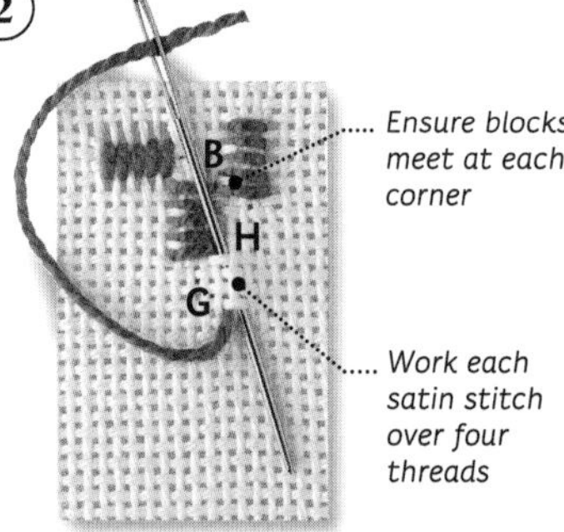

2
B
H
G
Ensure blocks meet at each corner
Work each satin stitch over four threads

1 Start at **A**. Work a block of five horizontal stitches over four threads, ending with **B** to **C**. Come up eight threads to the left of **B**, at **D**. Work five upright stitches over four threads, ending with **E** to **F**. Come out at **B**, insert at **E** and work four more horizontal stitches.

2 Come up eight threads below **B**, at **G**. Insert at **H**, work four more upright satin stitches.

3 Bring the needle out eight threads below **G**, at **I**. Work five stitches over four threads, ending at **J**. Come up at **G** to make a block of upright stitches. Continue making alternate blocks to fill the required area.

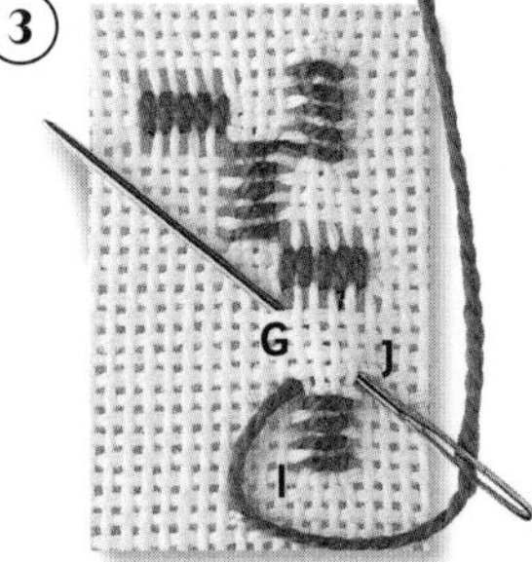

3
G
J
I

Mosaic Filling

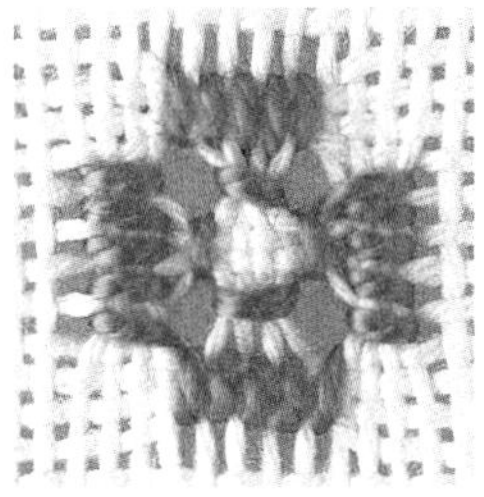

LEVEL
Advanced

USES
Dense chequered filling

METHOD
Block of satin stitch set in a square with back stitch centre

MATERIALS
Evenweave fabric; any thread; blunt needle; frame

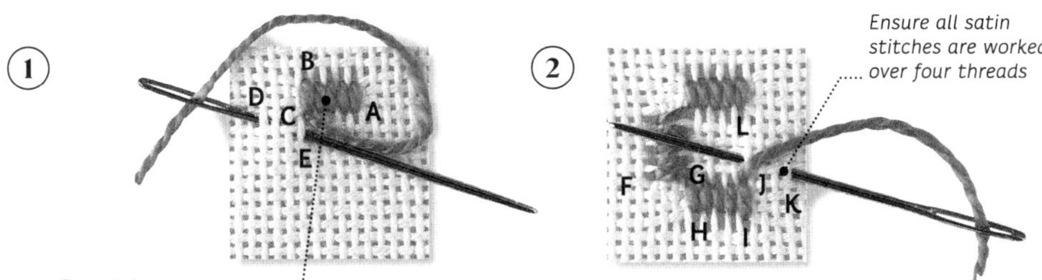
1
B
D
C
A
E
2
Ensure all satin stitches are worked over four threads
L
F
G
J
K
H
I

Do not leave any space between satin stitches

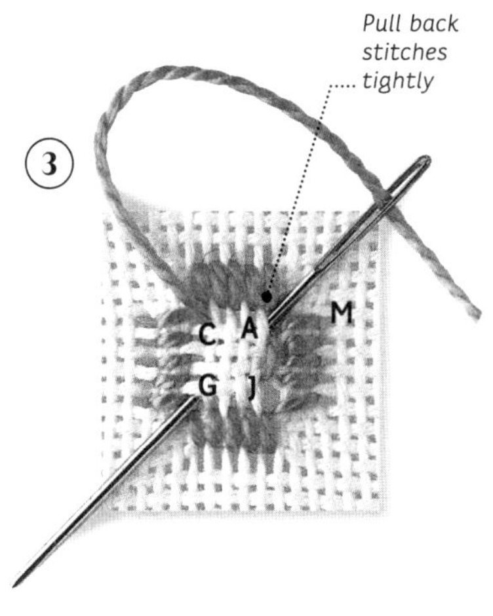
Pull back stitches tightly
3
C
A
M
G
J

1 Start at **A**. Work five satin stitches (see p.86) over four threads, finishing at **B**. Come out at **C**. Insert four threads to the left, at **D**, and come out at **E**.

2 Work four more horizontal stitches, finishing at **F**. Come up at **G** and insert the needle four threads below, at **H**. Work four more upright stitches, ending at **I**. Come up at **J**, insert at **K** and come out at **L**.

3 Work four more stitches, ending at **M**. Come back up at **A** and insert at **J**. Work three more back stitches from **C** to **A**, **G** to **C** and **J** to **G** to complete. Start the next stitch to the left (see Gallery p.31).

Diagonal Satin Filling

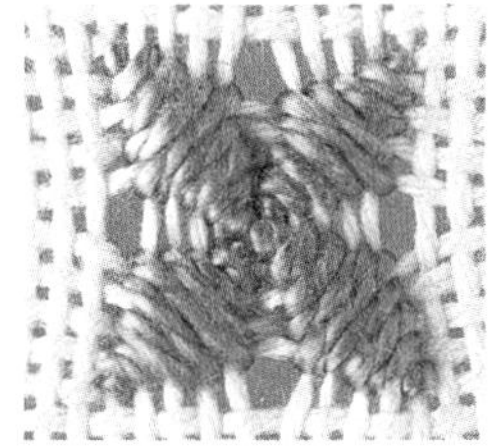

LEVEL
Intermediate

USES
Dense geometric filling

METHOD
Diagonal rows of satin stitch diamonds, worked in alternate directions

MATERIALS
Evenweave fabric; any thread; blunt needle; frame

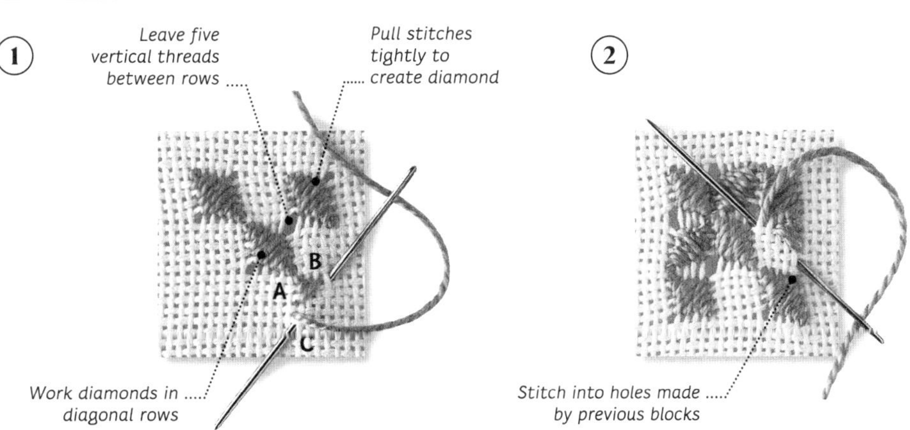
1
Leave five vertical threads between rows
Pull stitches tightly to create diamond
B
A
C
Work diamonds in diagonal rows
2
Stitch into holes made by previous blocks

1 Starting at top right, work a series of satin stitch (see p.86) diamonds to fill the required area. Come up at **A** and make a diagonal stitch over one intersection to **B**. Work four more stitches, increasing the length of each by one thread. Come up at **C** to work the longest stitch, then complete the diamond with four stitches which decrease in size.

2 Fill in the spaces with further rows of diamonds worked in the same way but in the opposite direction.

Back Stitch Rings

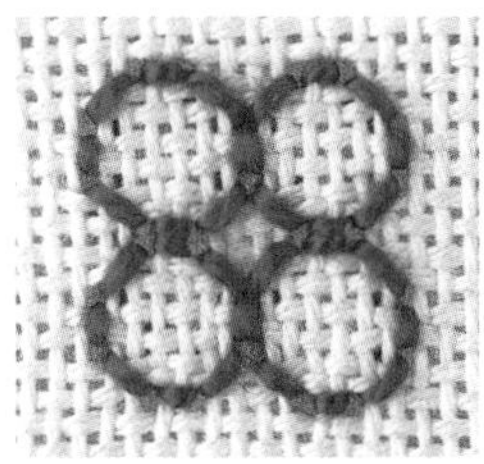

LEVEL
Intermediate

USES
Filling for large areas

METHOD
Intersecting rows of back stitch forming pattern of small circles

MATERIALS
Evenweave fabric; any thread; blunt needle; frame

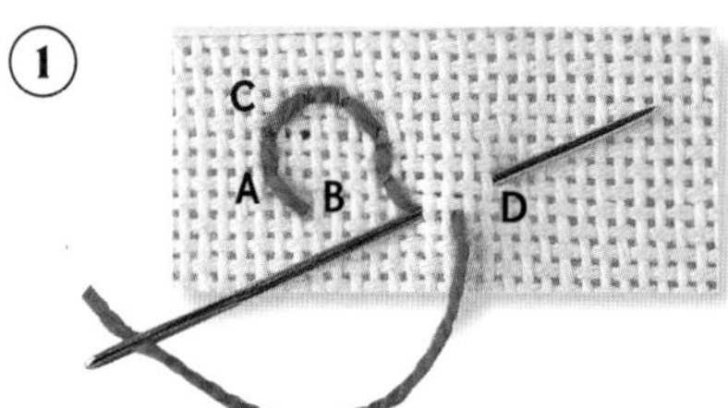
1
C
A
B
D

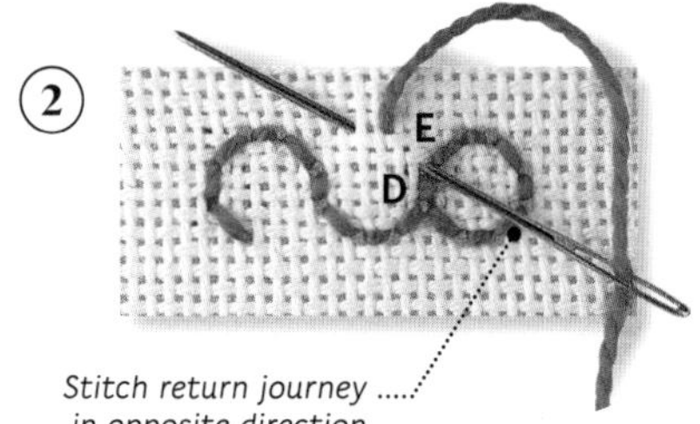
2
E
D
Stitch return journey in opposite direction

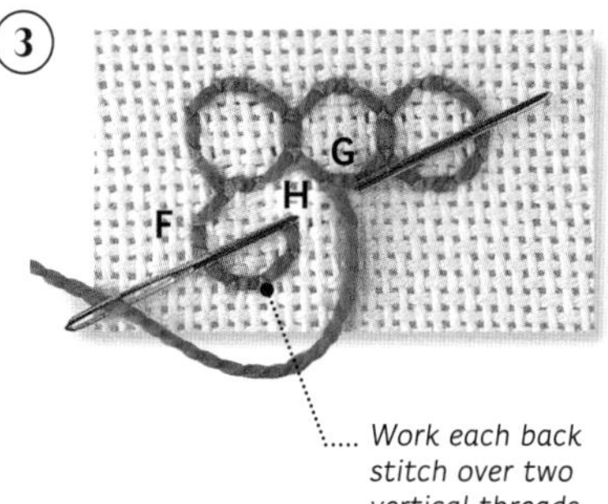
3
G
H
F
Work each back stitch over two vertical threads

1 Start at **A** and take the needle down over two intersections, at **B**. Come up two threads above **A**, at **C**, then continue working alternate straight and diagonal back stitches to form a row of semi-circles.

2 Work a full circle at the end of the row. The lines cross at the upright stitches; work a second back stitch between **E** and **D**, then continue stitching from right to left.

3 Come up at **F** to start the next row. Work from left to right, making a second horizontal stitch between **G** and **H**, and at each point where two rows meet.

Algerian Eye

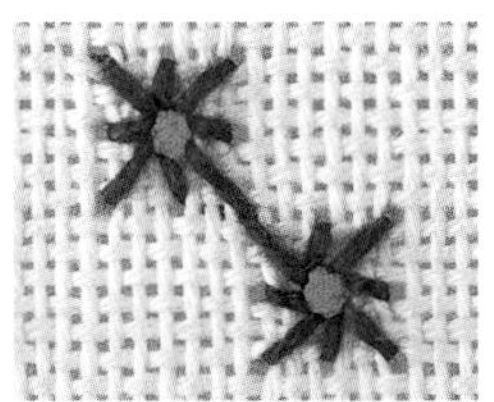

LEVEL
Intermediate

USES
Chequerboard filling for large areas

METHOD
Straight stitch stars worked in two journeys

MATERIALS
Evenweave fabric; any thread; blunt needle; frame

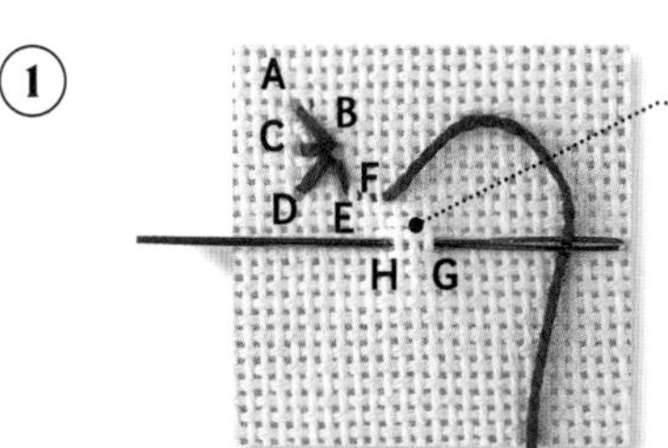
1
A
B
C
F
D
E
H
G
Work stitches over three vertical threads

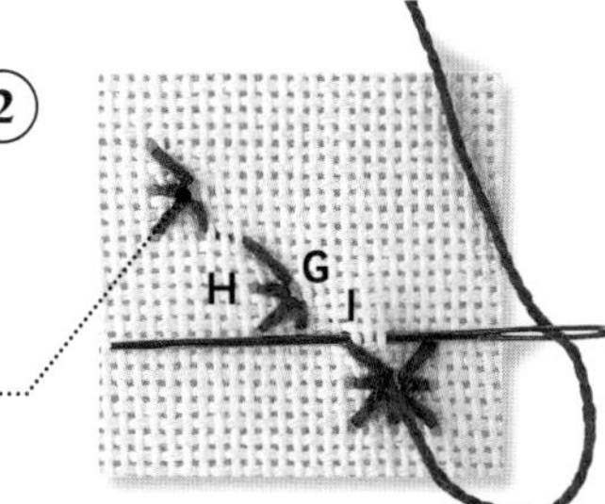
2
H
G
I
Pull stitches tightly to create centre holes

1 Start at **A** and take the needle down over three intersections, at **B**. Come up three threads to the left, at **C** and insert at **B**. Bring the needle up at **D**, down at **B**, up at **E** and down at **B**. Come out three threads to the right of **E**, at **F**. For the next half star, go down over three intersections, at **G**, and up at **H**.

2 Continue stitching downwards, working half stars to fill the required area. Complete the final star with four more straight stitches, finishing at **I**. Insert at **G** to continue the second journey.

3 Come up at **J**, six threads to the right of the top star, ready to work the next diagonal row of stars.

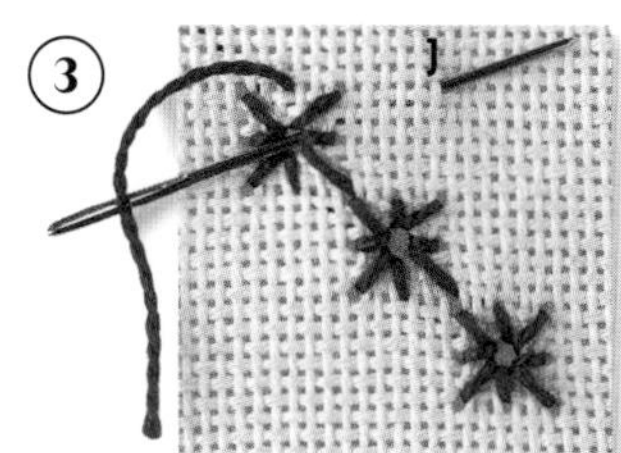
3
J

Outlined Diamond Eyelet

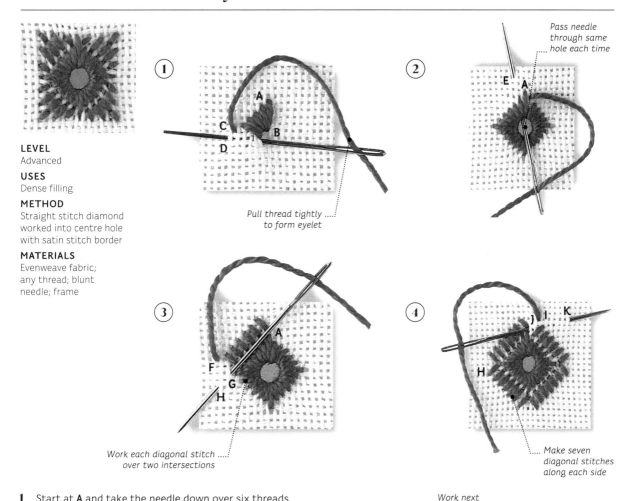

LEVEL
Advanced

USES
Dense filling

METHOD
Straight stitch diamond worked into centre hole with satin stitch border

MATERIALS
Evenweave fabric; any thread; blunt needle; frame

1

Pull thread tightly to form eyelet

2

Pass needle through same hole each time

3

Work each diagonal stitch over two intersections

4

Make seven diagonal stitches along each side

1 Start at **A** and take the needle down over six threads to **B**. Come up one intersection to the left of **A** and insert at **B**, then make four more clockwise diagonal stitches, ending with **C** to **B**. Come up at **D**, and work the remaining three quarters of the diamond in the same way.

2 When the diamond is complete, bring the needle up two intersections to the left of **A**, at **E**.

3 Insert the needle at **A**, then make a further six parallel straight stitches, ending with **F** to **G**. Come out two intersections down to the left, at **H**. Work similar rows of straight stitch along the other three sides.

4 Make the final stitch from **I** to **J**. Come up six threads to the right, at **K**, and repeat steps 1 to 3 to work the next diamond.

5 To work the next diamond to the left, come back up at **E** and take the needle down six threads to the left, at **L**.

Work next diamond in this space

5

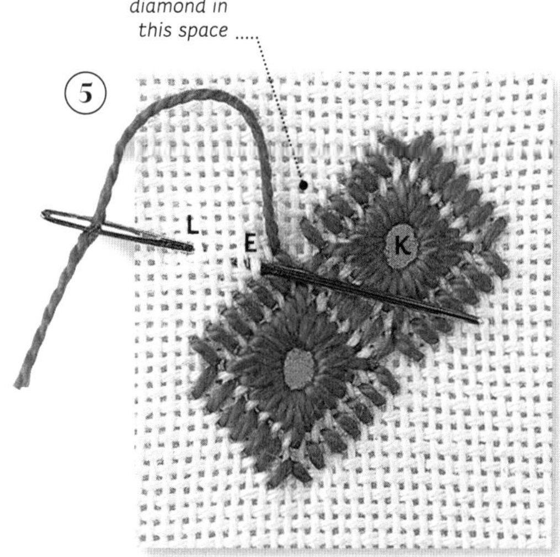
L
E
K

Drawn Thread and Insertion Stitches

These historic techniques combine decoration with utility, and both are still used on heirloom table linen and for garments, especially fine hand-stitched lingerie or baby clothes.

Drawn thread hems and borders developed as a way of creating an ornamental neatened edge, and are worked on evenweave fabric from which a number of threads have been withdrawn. The remaining threads are then bunched together with lines of tightly pulled stitches to form a regular pattern. Insertion stitches grew from an old way of seaming narrow widths of fabric into a set of intricate joining stitches which can be used on either plain or evenweave fabric.

Single Hem

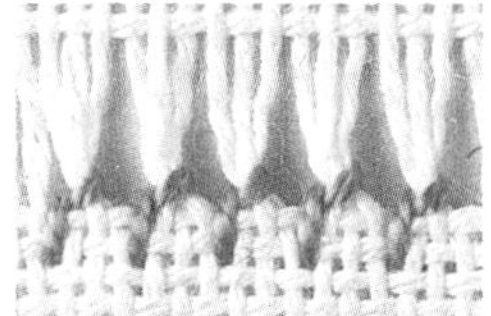

LEVEL
Easy

USES
Simple open border for hemmed edge

METHOD
Small groups of threads pulled into clusters along hem; worked on wrong side of fabric

MATERIALS
Evenweave fabric; any thread; blunt needle

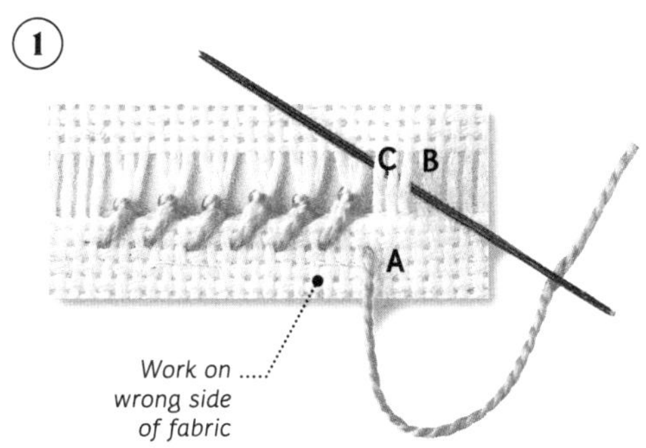
1
C
B
A
Work on wrong side of fabric

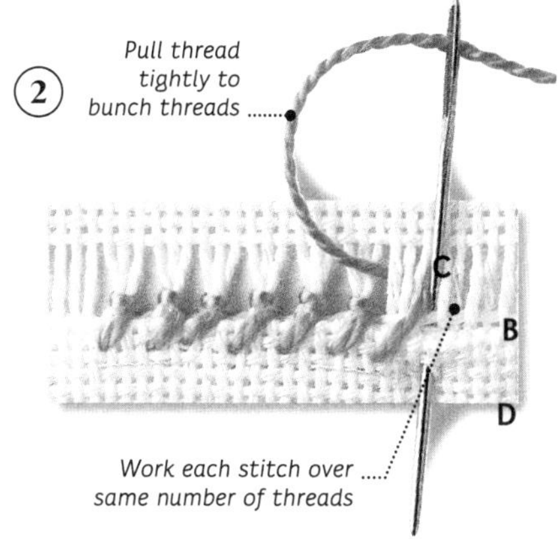
2
Pull thread tightly to bunch threads
C
B
D
Work each stitch over same number of threads

1 Draw out a few threads along the edge of the fabric (see p.20). Fold a double hem to the base of the threads and tack down. Come up at **A** and slide the needle under three threads to the right, from **B** to **C**.

2 Take the needle down at **B** and bring it out at **D**. Repeat these two steps to continue.

Stitch Variation

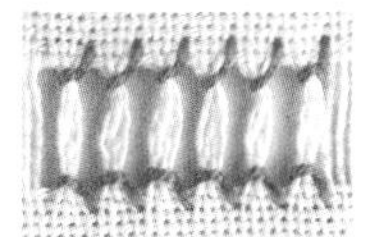

Ladder hem stitch is worked over a wider band of drawn threads. Work as for single hem stitch, then turn the fabric upside down and work a second row over the same groups of threads, making a series of bars.

Serpentine Hem

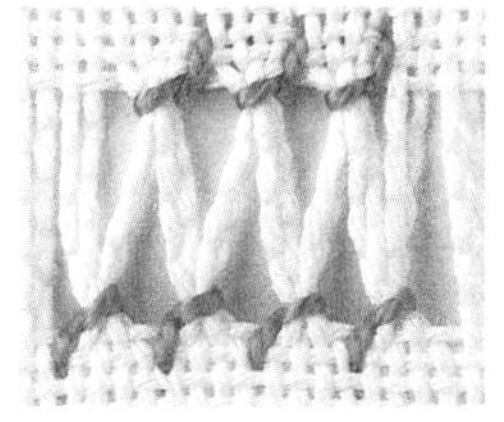

OTHER NAME
Trellis hem stitch

LEVEL
Easy

USES
Decorative edging

METHOD
Two staggered rows of hem stitch worked to create slanting bars

MATERIALS
Evenweave fabric; any thread; blunt needle

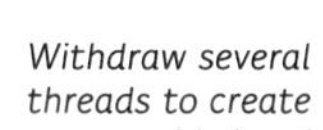
Withdraw several threads to create wide band

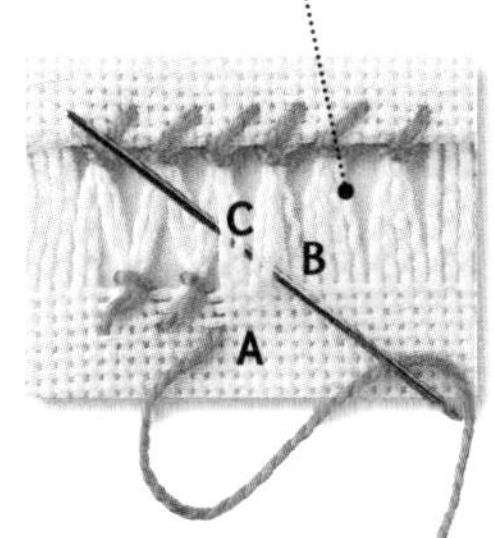
C
B
A

Work a row of hem stitch over groups of four threads (see above), then turn the fabric upside down. Come up at **A**. Pass the needle under two threads from each group, from **B** to **C**, and work a second row of hem stitch.

Antique Hem

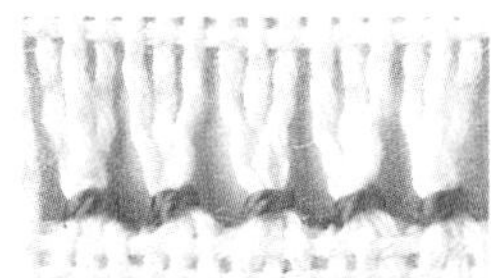

LEVEL
Easy

USES
Plain border for hem

METHOD
Hem stitch variation in which horizontal stitches only show on right side

MATERIALS
Evenweave fabric; any thread; blunt needle

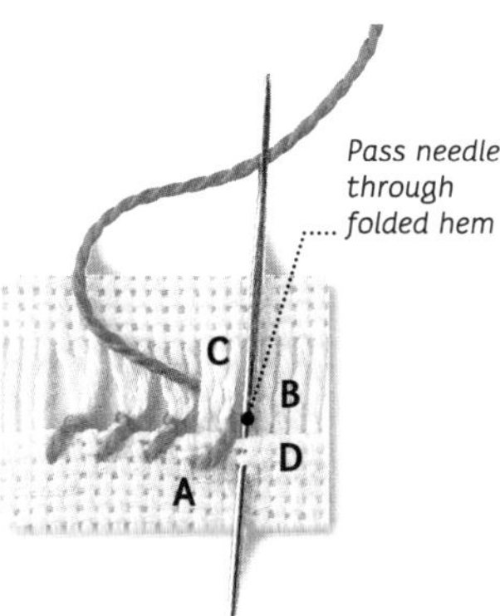
Pass needle through folded hem
C
B
D
A

Prepare the fabric as for single hem stitch (see above). With the wrong side facing, come up at **A**. Slide the needle under three threads to the right, from **B** to **C**. Insert the needle through the edge of the fold at **B** and come out at **D**. Pull up the thread; repeat this step to continue.

Italian Border

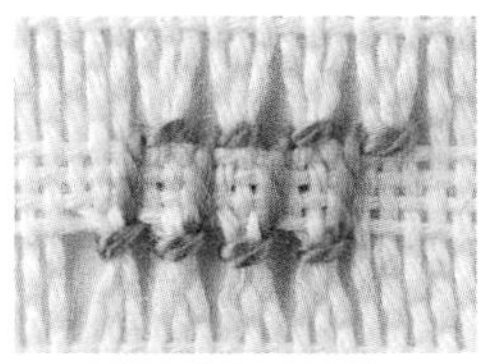

OTHER NAME
Italian hem stitch

LEVEL
Easy

USES
Open band; with hem stitch as decorative border

METHOD
Open border stitch, worked in two journeys

MATERIALS
Evenweave fabric; any thread; blunt needle

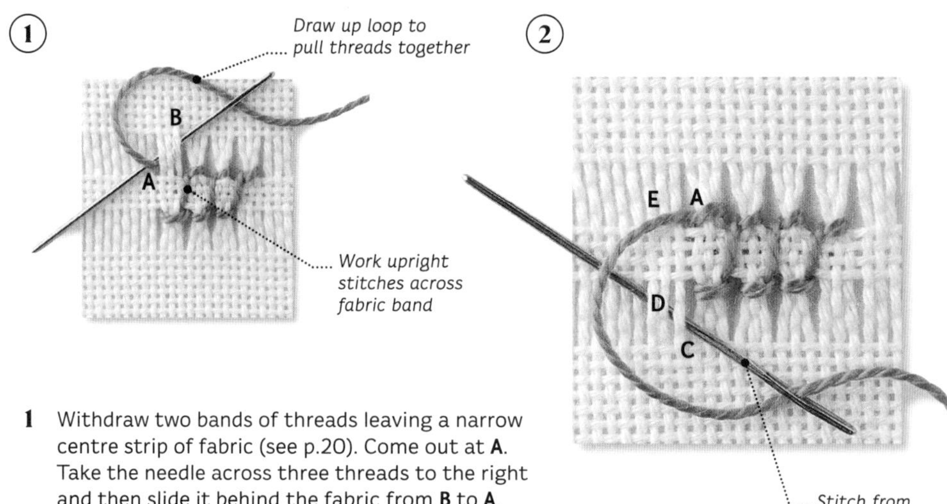
1
Draw up loop to pull threads together
B
A
Work upright stitches across fabric band
2
E
A
D
C
Stitch from right to left

1 Withdraw two bands of threads leaving a narrow centre strip of fabric (see p.20). Come out at **A**. Take the needle across three threads to the right and then slide it behind the fabric from **B** to **A**.

2 Take the needle down to **C**. Slide it behind three threads and come out at **D**. Go back down at **C** and come up at **E**, three threads to the left of **A**. Repeat steps 1 and 2 to continue.

Four-sided

LEVEL
Intermediate

USES
Open bands; can also be worked as pulled fabric stitch

METHOD
Pulled straight stitches, worked horizontally to form square pattern

MATERIALS
Evenweave fabric; any thread; blunt needle

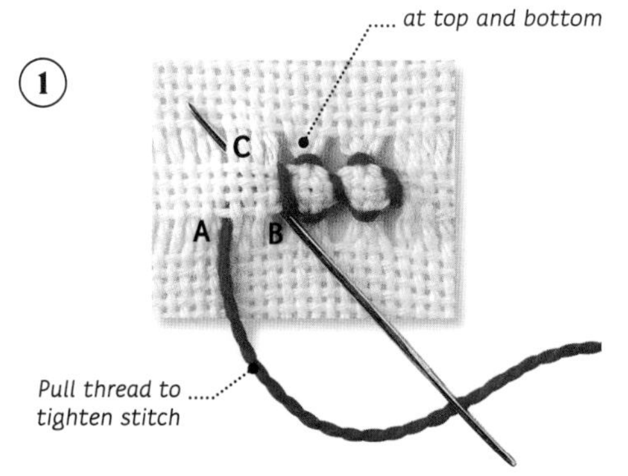
1
Work over same threads at top and bottom
C
A
B
Pull thread to tighten stitch

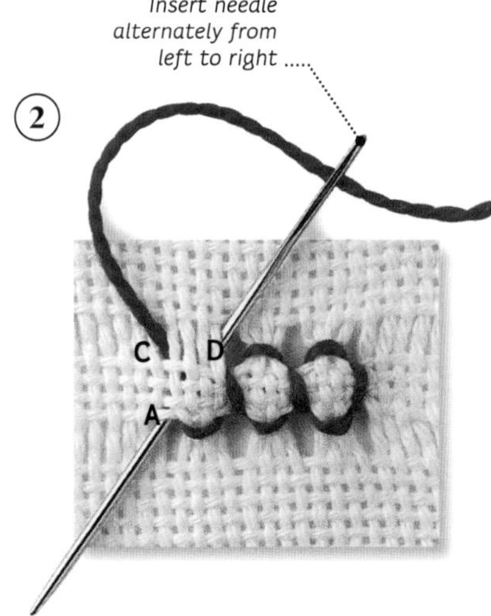
2
Insert needle alternately from left to right
C
D
A

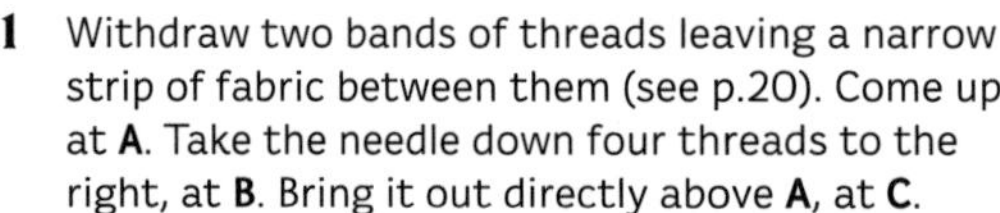

1 Withdraw two bands of threads leaving a narrow strip of fabric between them (see p.20). Come up at **A**. Take the needle down four threads to the right, at **B**. Bring it out directly above **A**, at **C**.

2 Take the needle down four threads to the right, at **D** and come up at **A**. Go down at **C** to make a vertical stitch and come up four threads to the left of **A**, ready to start the next stitch. Repeat these two steps to continue.

Chevron Border

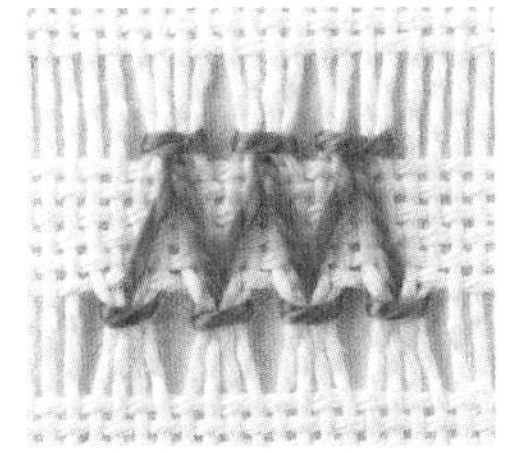

LEVEL
Intermediate

USES
Decorative open bands; with hem stitch as edging

METHOD
Chevron stitch variation; worked horizontally

MATERIALS
Evenweave fabric; any thread; blunt needle

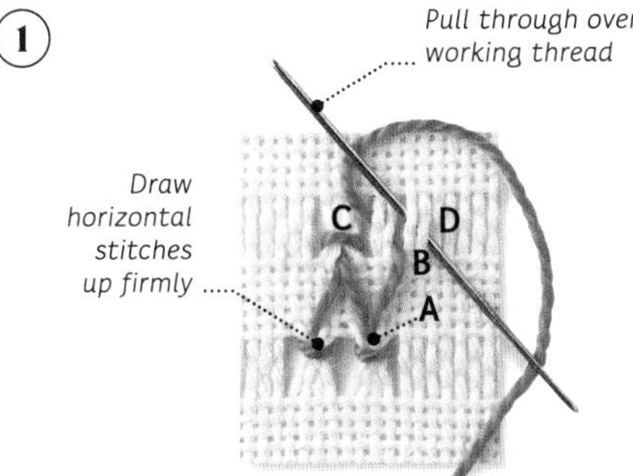
1
Pull through over working thread
Draw horizontal stitches up firmly
C
D
B
A

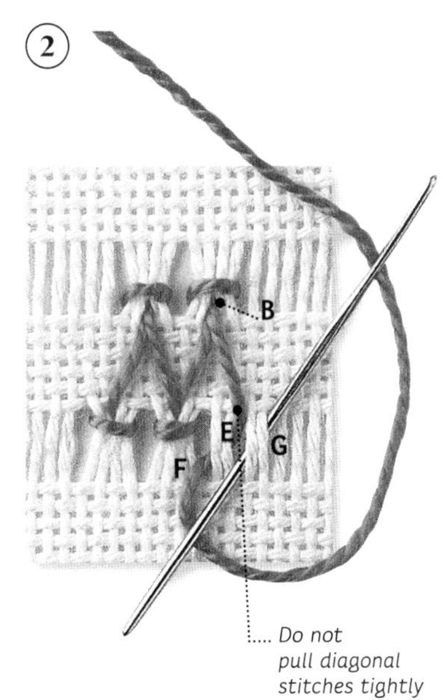
2
B
E
G
F
Do not pull diagonal stitches tightly

1 Prepare the fabric as for step 1 below. Come up at **A**. Take the needle diagonally up and slide it behind two threads from **B** to **C**. Take the needle across four threads to the right, and insert at **D**. Come up again at **B**.

2 Insert the needle at **E**. Slide it behind two threads to the left and come up at **F**. Take the needle across four threads and insert at **G**. Bring it out at **E** and pull through over the working thread. Repeat these two steps to the end of the row.

Diamond Border

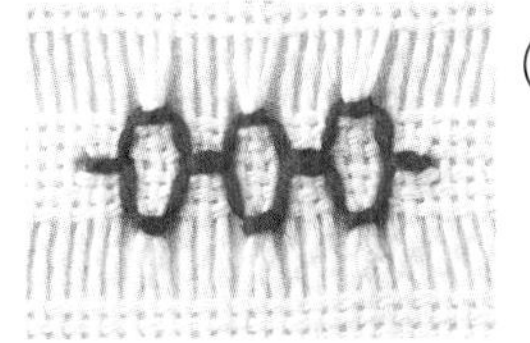

LEVEL
Intermediate

USES
Open border with hexagonal pattern

METHOD
Pulled straight stitches, worked in two journeys

MATERIALS
Evenweave fabric; any thread; blunt needle

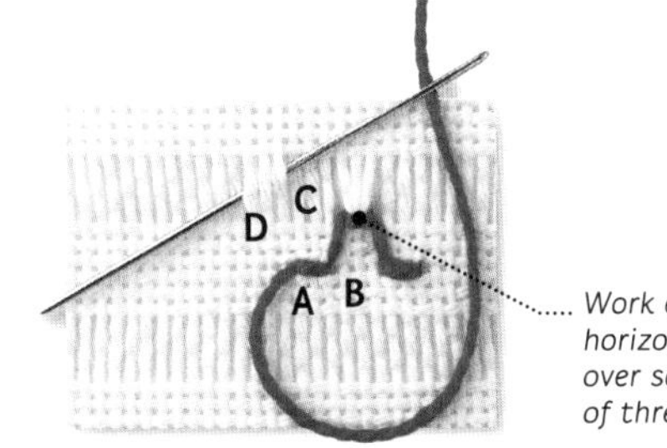
1
D
C
A
B
Work each horizontal stitch over same number of threads

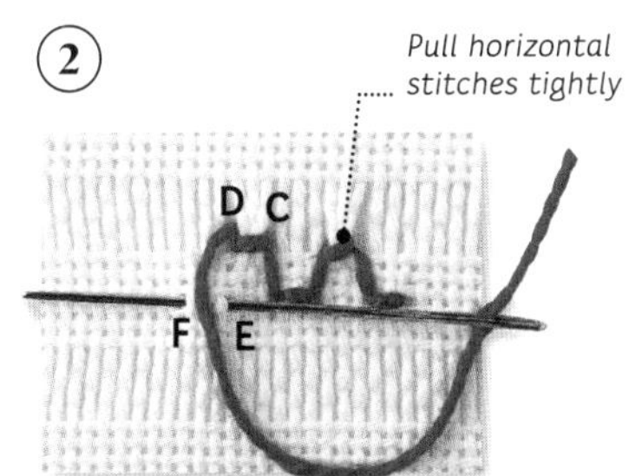
2
Pull horizontal stitches tightly
D
C
F
E

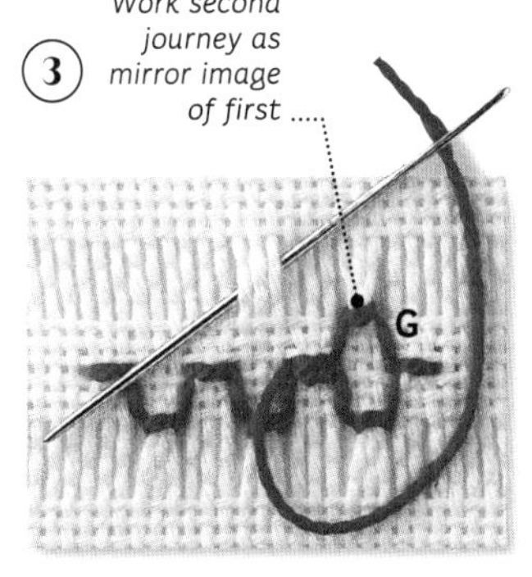
3
Work second journey as mirror image of first
G

1 Withdraw two bands of thread leaving a narrow strip of fabric between them (see p.20). Come up in the centre, at **A**. Take the needle down three threads to the right, at **B**, then bring it out at **A** again. Insert directly above, at **C** and slide the needle under three threads to the left, coming up at **D**.

2 Take the needle down at **C** and come back up at **D**. Insert it directly below, at **E** and come out on the same level, at **F**. Repeat steps 1 and 2 to the end of the row.

3 Turn the fabric the other way up to work the second journey. Come up at **G** and stitch as before.

Laced Insertion

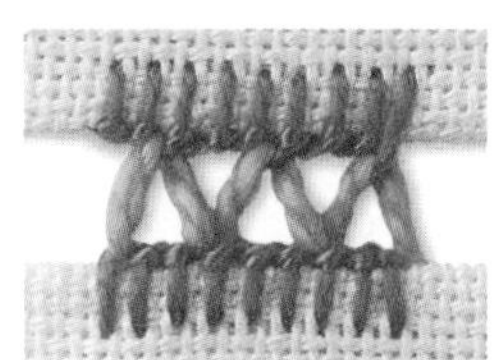

LEVEL
Easy

USES
Decorative joining stitch

METHOD
Two hems worked with Antwerp edging stitch, linked with interlacing

MATERIALS
Evenweave fabric; thick thread; blunt needle

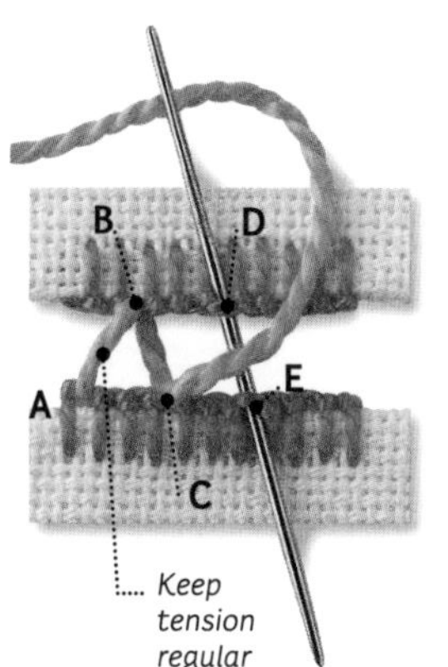
B
D
A
E
C
Keep tension regular

Work a row of Antwerp edging stitch (see p.112) along each hem. Mount the fabric on paper (see p.20). Come up at **A**. Pass the needle down over **B**. Slide it under **C**, from back to front. Take it over **D**, from front to back; repeat to the end of the seam.

Cretan Insertion

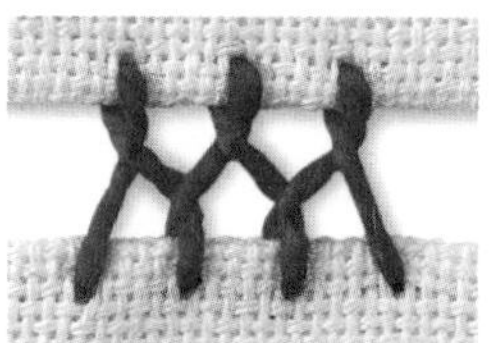

LEVEL
Easy

USES
Simple join for two straight edges

METHOD
Open Cretan stitch adapted as insertion

MATERIALS
Evenweave fabric; thick thread; blunt needle

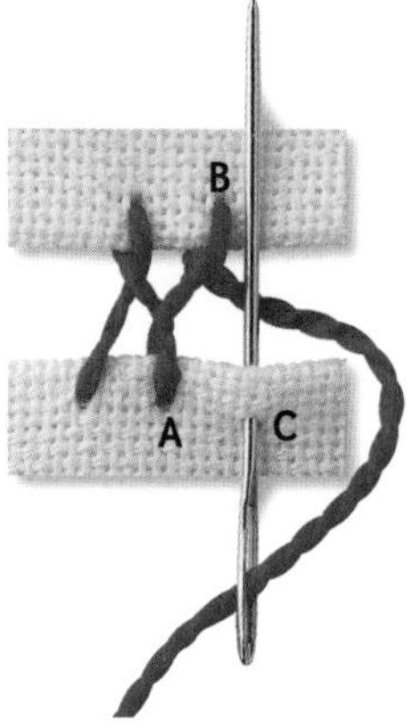
B
A
C

Mount the fabric on paper (see p.20). Take the needle through to the back at **A**, then insert it from the front at **B**. Bring it through behind the diagonal thread and take it down at **C**. Pull through over the working thread. Repeat to the end of the seam.

Bundle Stitch

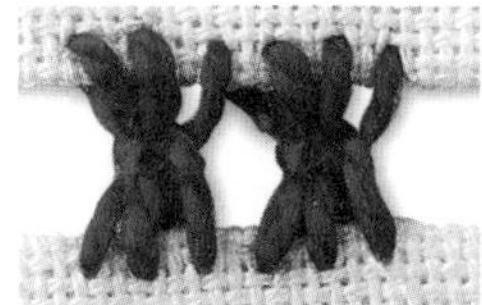

LEVEL
Intermediate

USES
Decorative method of joining two edges

METHOD
Groups of two stitches bound by a third, worked from top to bottom

MATERIALS
Evenweave fabric; any thread; blunt needle

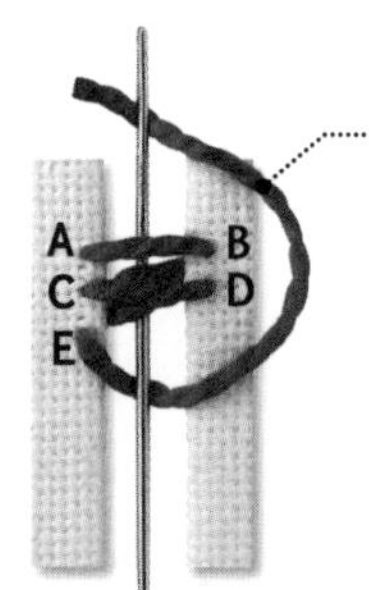
1
Loop thread from left to right
A
B
C
D
E

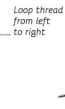

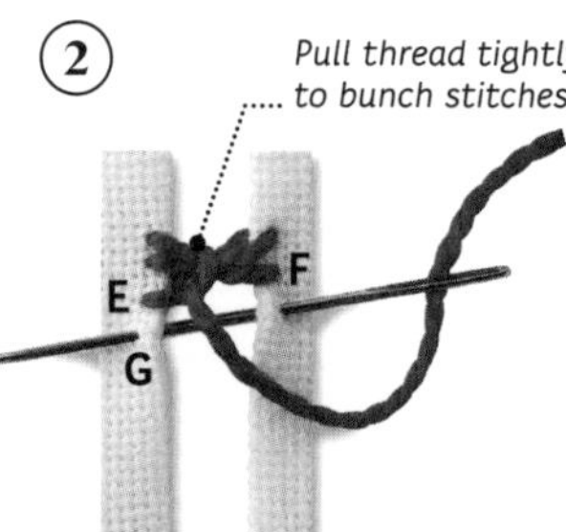
2
Pull thread tightly to bunch stitches
E
F
G

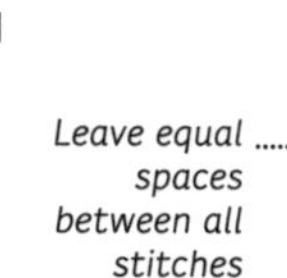

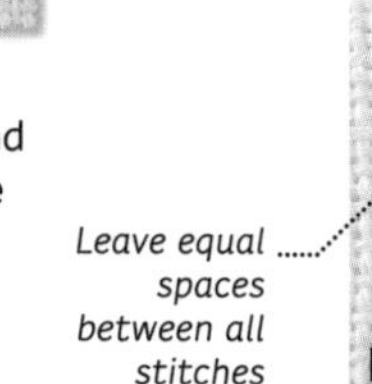

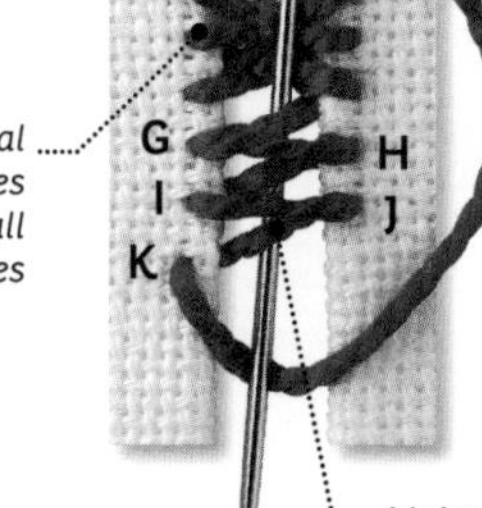
3
Leave equal spaces between all stitches
G
I
K
H
J
Maintain even tensio

1 Mount the fabric (see p.20). Start on the left, at **A** and work a straight stitch across to **B**, on the right. Make another stitch from **C** to **D**, then come out at **E**. Pass the needle behind all the threads, then pull through over the loop.

2 Insert the needle at **F**, then bring it out below **E** at **G**, ready to start the next group of stitches.

3 Insert at **H**, then make another stitch from **I** to **J**. Come out at **K**, take the needle behind the three diagonal and two horizontal threads, and pull through over the working thread. Repeat steps 1 to 3 to continue.

Knotted Insertion

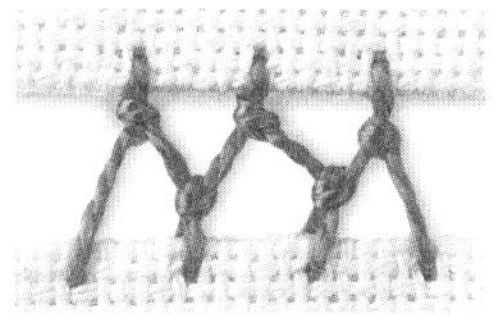

LEVEL
Advanced

USES
Decorative method of joining two edges

METHOD
Knotted joining stitch worked horizontally

MATERIALS
Evenweave fabric; thick thread; blunt needle

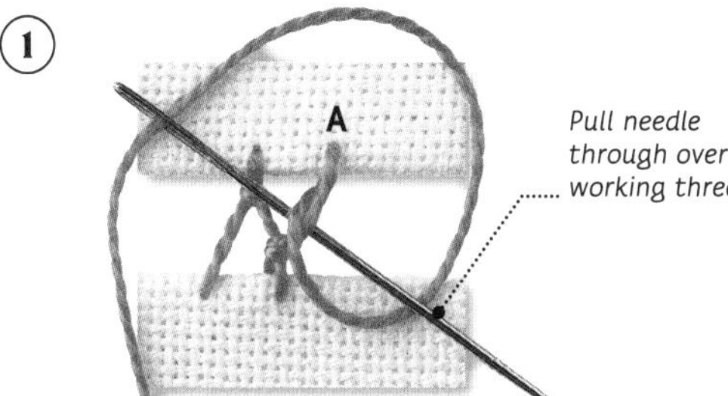
1
A
Pull needle through over working thread

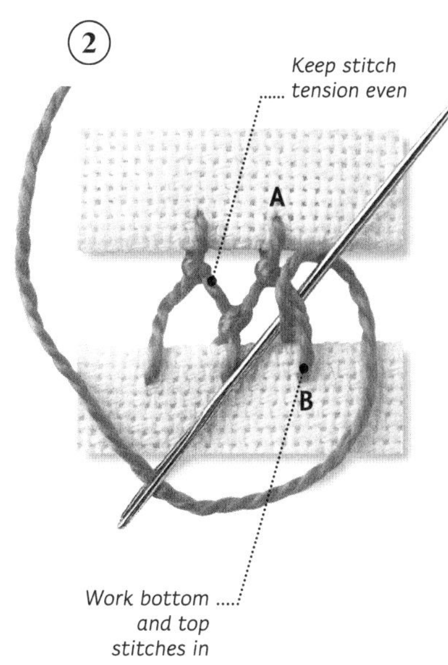
2
Keep stitch tension even
A
B
Work bottom and top stitches in same way

1 Mount the fabric on paper (see p.20). Take the needle down through the top hem at **A** and bring it out to the left of the diagonal stitch. Loop the working thread to the right and pass the needle under both threads. Pull the thread up tightly to form a knot.

2 Take the needle down to the bottom hem and insert at **B**. Bring it through to the left of the diagonal stitch and loop the thread to the right. Slide the needle under both threads and pull through tightly. Continue stitching alternately up and down to the end of the seam.

Buttonhole Insertion

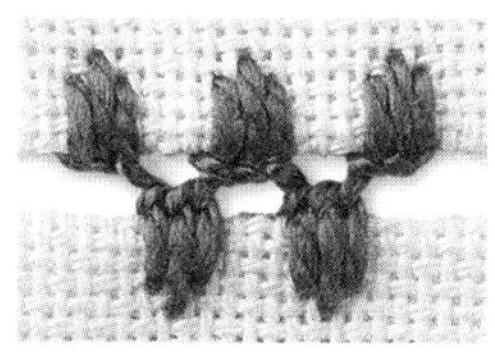

LEVEL
Advanced

USES
Decorative joining method

METHOD
Groups of three buttonhole stitches worked alternately from top to bottom

MATERIALS
Evenweave fabric; thick thread; blunt needle

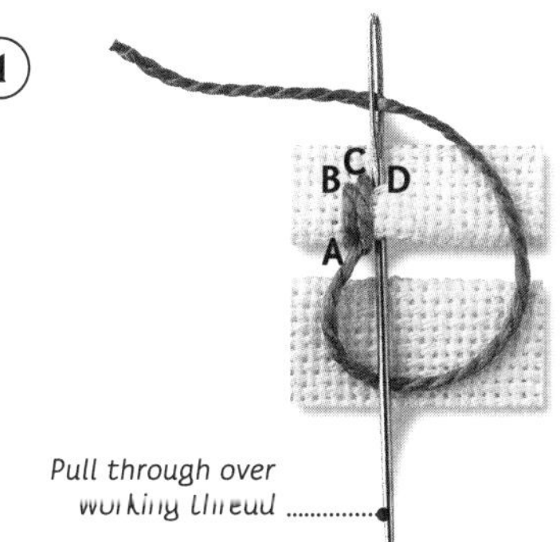
1
B
C
D
A
Pull through over working thread

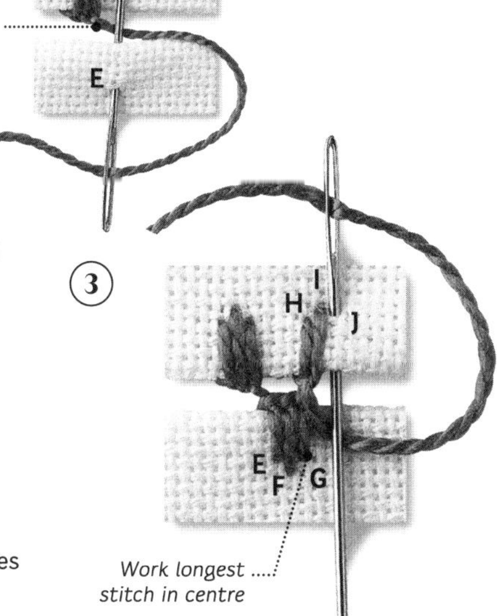
2
Make small diagonal stitch between two hems
D
E
3
H
I
J
E
F
G
Work longest stitch in centre

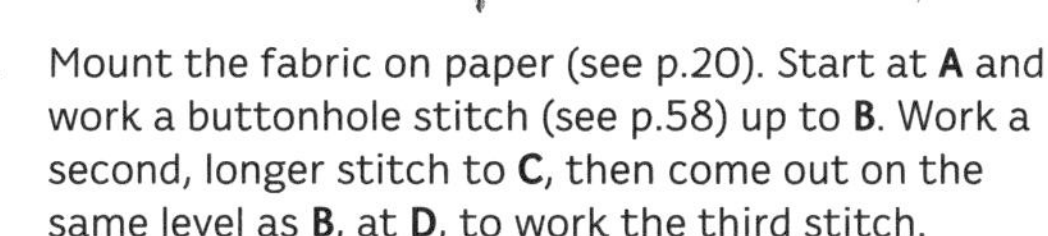

1 Mount the fabric on paper (see p.20). Start at **A** and work a buttonhole stitch (see p.58) up to **B**. Work a second, longer stitch to **C**, then come out on the same level as **B**, at **D**, to work the third stitch.

2 Take the needle down through the bottom hem, at **E** and pull it through over the working thread.

3 Work two more buttonhole stitches at **F** and **G**, varying the length as before, then take the needle back up to the top hem at **H**. Make two more stitches at **I** and **J**, then continue to the end of the seam.

Needleweaving Bars

OTHER NAME
Woven bars

LEVEL
Advanced

USES
Flat, heavy borders

METHOD
Weaving stitch, worked horizontally

MATERIALS
Evenweave fabric; any thread; blunt needle

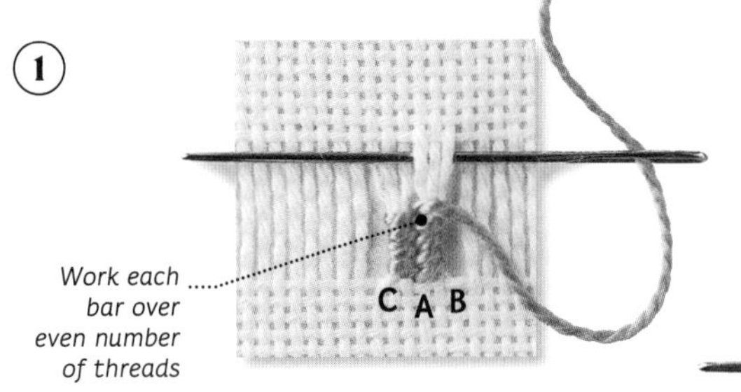
1
Work each bar over even number of threads
C A B

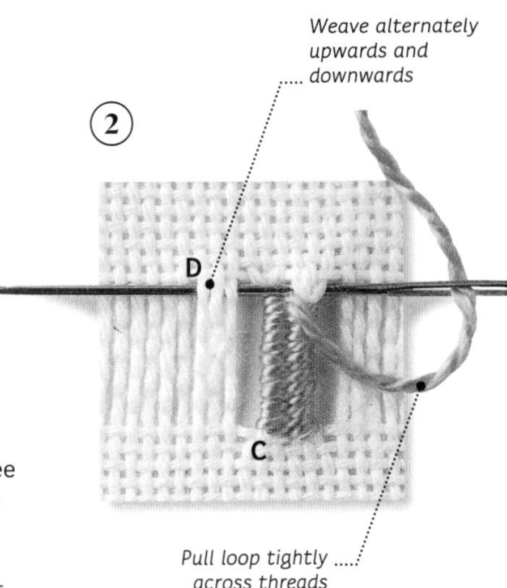
2
Weave alternately upwards and downwards
D
C
Pull loop tightly across threads

1 Withdraw a band of threads from the fabric (see p.20). Come up at **A** and take the needle across three threads to the right. Insert it at **B** and bring it back through at **A**. Insert over three threads to the left at **C**, then come back out in the centre, at **A**. Continue weaving upwards.

2 When the bar is complete, bring the needle out three threads to the left, at **D**. Work downwards as before, then continue weaving bars to the end of the row.

Zigzag Clusters

LEVEL
Advanced

USES
Heavy open borders

METHOD
Round, wrapped bars worked over foundation of drawn threads

MATERIALS
Evenweave fabric; any thread; blunt needle

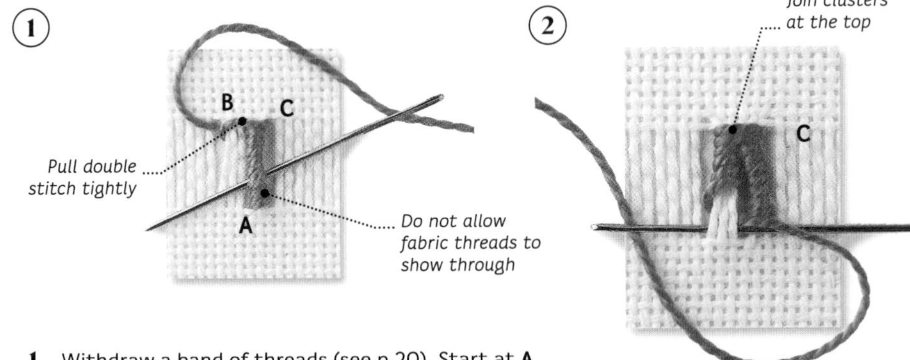
1
Pull double stitch tightly
B C
A
Do not allow fabric threads to show through
2
Join clusters at the top
C

1 Withdraw a band of threads (see p.20). Start at **A** and take the needle over three threads to the right. Come back up at **A**, then pass the needle in front of and behind the threads. Continue wrapping to the top, then come out three threads to the left, at **B**. Take the needle across six threads and insert at **C**, then come back up at **B**. Insert again at **C** and come up between the two groups of threads.

2 Take the needle back over three threads and continue wrapping to the bottom. Start the next and subsequent clusters three threads to the left.

Stitch Variation

Corded clusters are worked in the same way, but without the double linking stitches.

Cutwork and Edging Stitches

Cutwork eyelets – literally "little eyes" – of various shapes and sizes can be found alongside pulled fabric stitches, satin stitch, French knots, and other surface embroidery in many whitework techniques. Use them in Danish *Hedebo* or *Broderie Anglaise* (which, despite its name, originated in eastern Europe), as part of more complex *Richelieu* cutwork designs, or simply to decorate a garment.

Edging stitches give a fancy finish to a narrow folded hem, on either plain or evenweave fabric. They look particularly effective when worked in a thick, twisted thread as an alternative to machine-stitching around a skirt, cuff, or collar.

Antwerp Edging

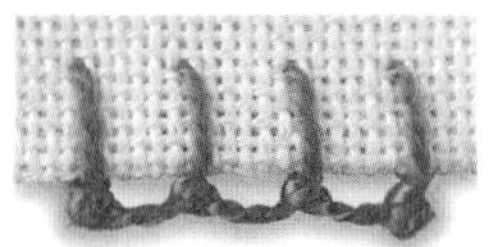

OTHER NAME
Knotted blanket stitch

LEVEL
Intermediate

USES
Decorative hems

METHOD
Blanket stitch variation, worked horizontally over edge of fabric

MATERIALS
Any fabric; thick twisted threads give best stitch definition

1

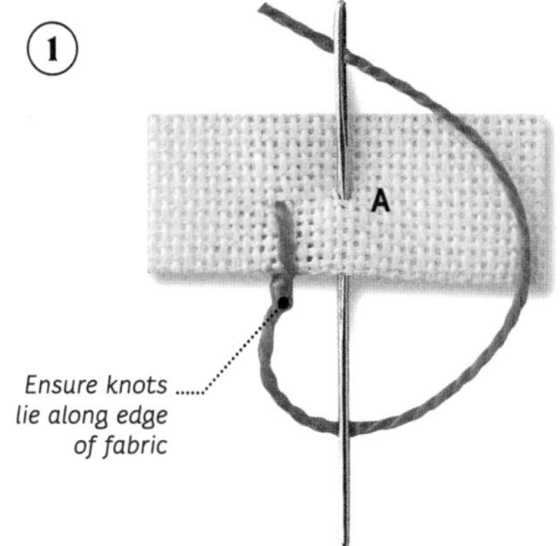
A
Ensure knots lie along edge of fabric

2

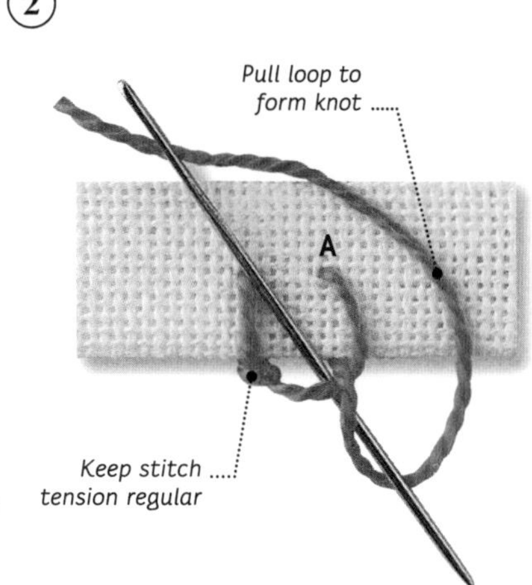
Pull loop to form knot
A
Keep stitch tension regular

1 Insert the needle at **A** and bring it out under the edge of the fabric. Pull through over the loop to make a blanket stitch (see p.58).

2 Take the needle back to the left and pass it behind the two threads. Draw up the working thread to form a knot. Repeat these two steps to continue along the edge.

Sailor Edging

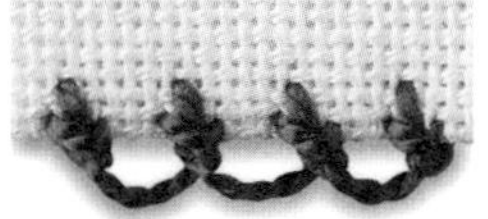

LEVEL
Intermediate

USES
Decorative hems

METHOD
Blanket stitch variation, worked downwards over edge of fabric

MATERIALS
Any fabric; any twisted thread

1

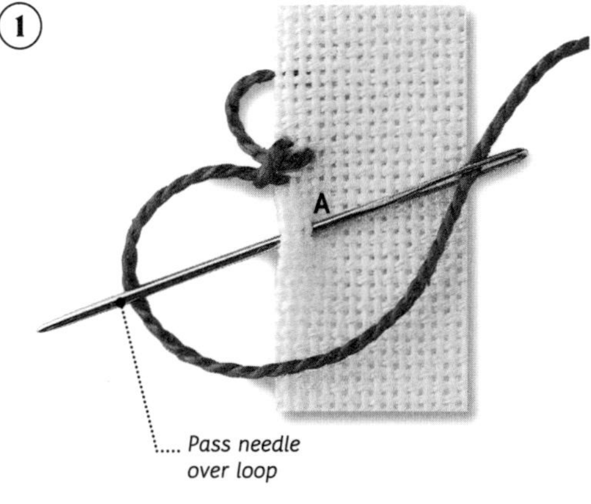
A
Pass needle over loop

2

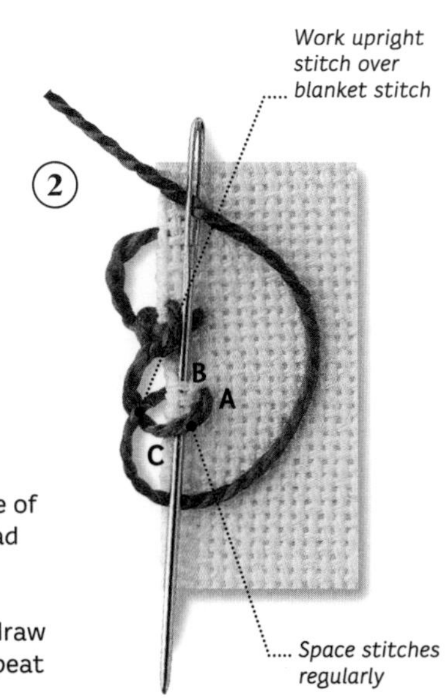
Work upright stitch over blanket stitch
B
A
C
Space stitches regularly

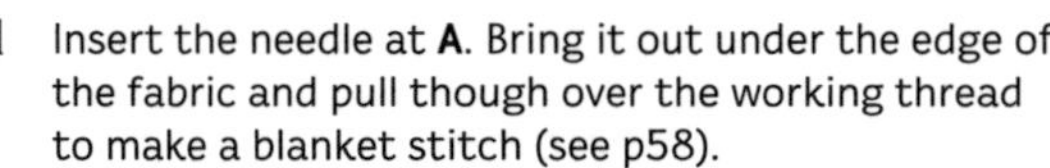

1 Insert the needle at **A**. Bring it out under the edge of the fabric and pull though over the working thread to make a blanket stitch (see p58).

2 Insert the needle at **B**. Bring it through at **C** and draw up the thread to make a short upright stitch. Repeat steps 1 and 2 to continue.

Looped Edge

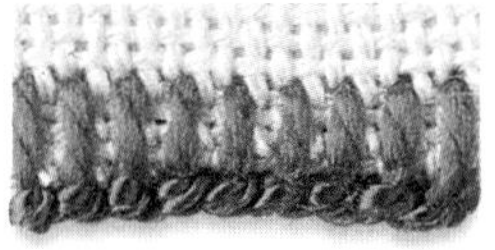

LEVEL
Intermediate

USES
Solid stitch for hems and neatening raw edges; foundation for laced insertion stitch

METHOD
Looped edging stitch, worked horizontally

MATERIALS
Any fabric; any thread depending on fabric

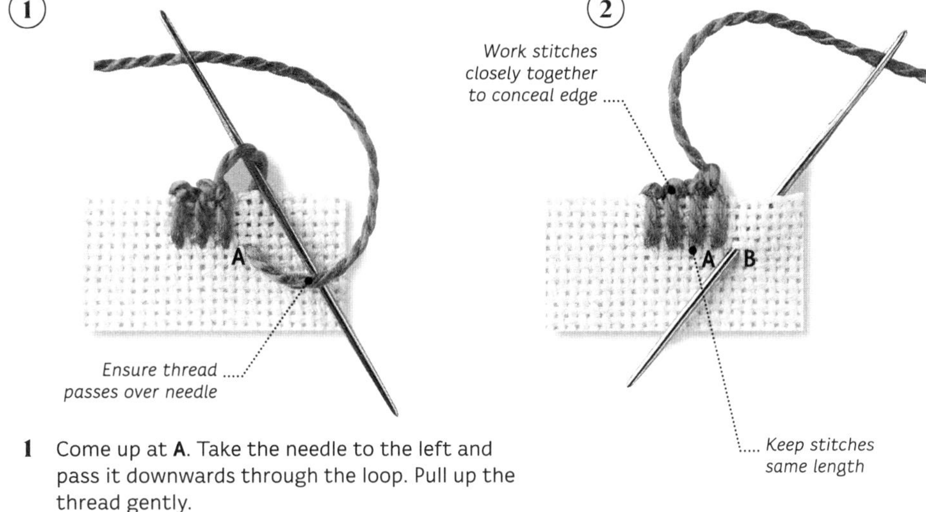

1
A
Ensure thread passes over needle
2
Work stitches closely together to conceal edge
A
B
Keep stitches same length

1 Come up at **A**. Take the needle to the left and pass it downwards through the loop. Pull up the thread gently.

2 Bring the needle out at **B**, ready to make the next stitch. Repeat these two steps to continue.

Half Chevron

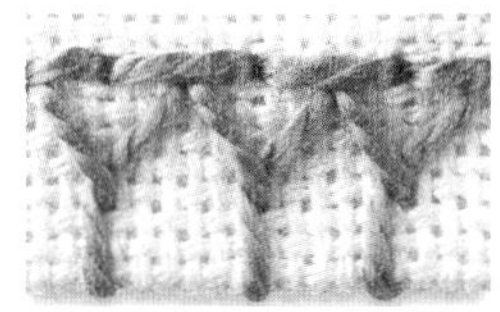

LEVEL
Intermediate

USES
To neaten folded edges and hems

METHOD
Chevron stitch variation, worked over edge of fabric

MATERIALS
Any fabric; any thread

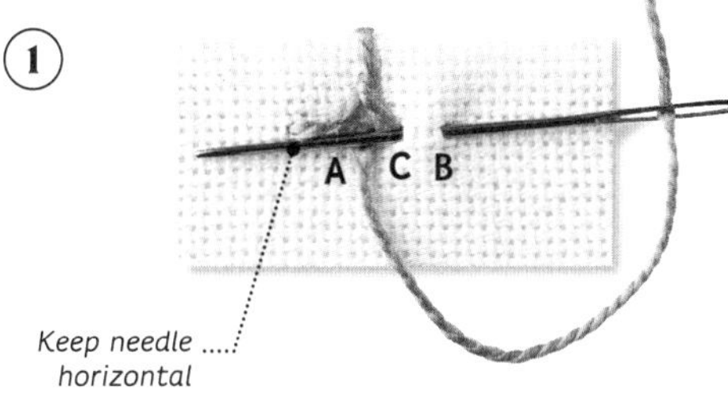

1
A
C
B
Keep needle horizontal

1 Come up at **A**, insert the needle at **B** and bring it out in the centre, at **C**.

2 Loop the thread from left to right. Take the needle behind the fabric and bring it through over the working thread, at **D**.

3 Insert the needle to the right of **B**, at **E**, then bring it through again at **B**. Repeat steps 1 to 3 to continue along the edge.

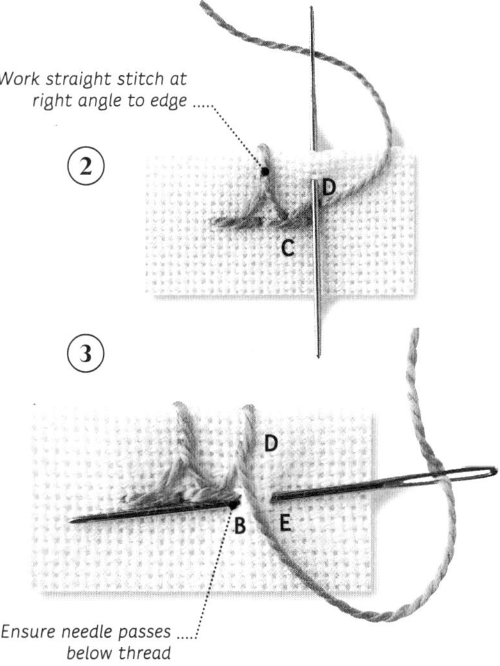

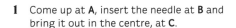

Work straight stitch at right angle to edge
2
D
C
3
D
B
E
Ensure needle passes below thread

Scalloped Edge

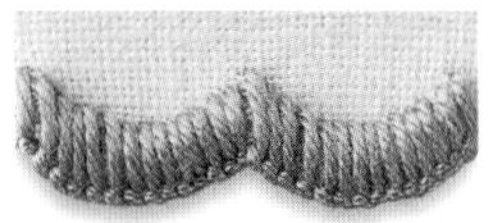

LEVEL
Intermediate

USES
Neatening curved and scalloped raw edges

METHOD
Buttonhole stitch worked over running stitch foundation

MATERIALS
Closely woven fabric; any fine thread; embroidery scissors

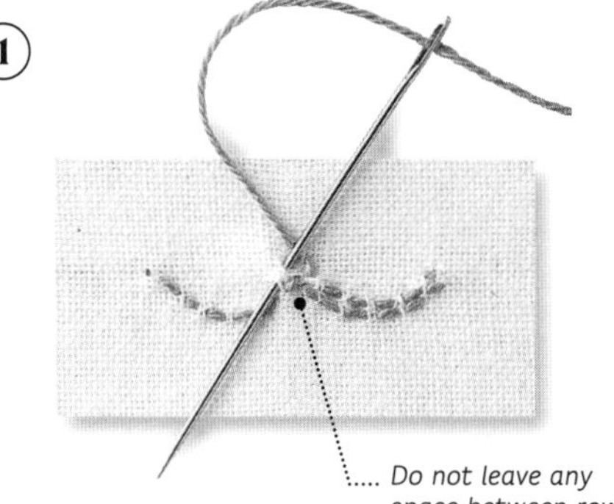
1
Do not leave any space between rows

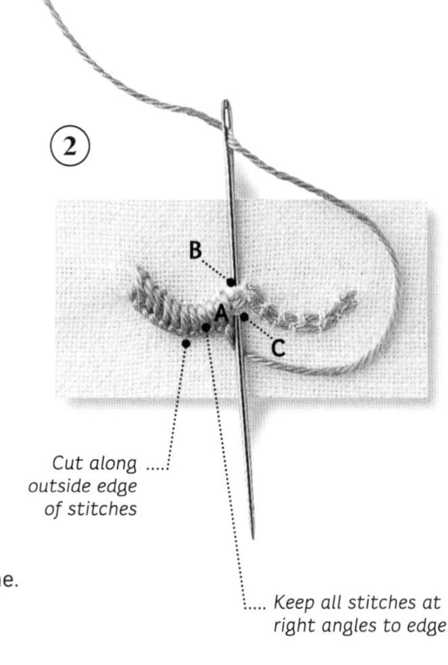
2
B
A
C
Cut along outside edge of stitches
Keep all stitches at right angles to edge

1 Sew two foundation rows of closely spaced running stitch (see p.39) along the outline of the edge to be worked.

2 Work a row of buttonhole stitch (see p.58) over the foundation, following the curve of the outline. Come up at **A**, insert at **B** and pull the needle through at **C**. Repeat to the end of the line. When the stitching is complete, trim away the surplus fabric using sharp embroidery scissors.

Ring Picot Edge

LEVEL
Advanced

USES
Decorative trim on buttonholed edges

METHOD
Buttonhole stitch worked over thread loop

MATERIALS
Closely woven fabric, any fine thread; embroidery scissors

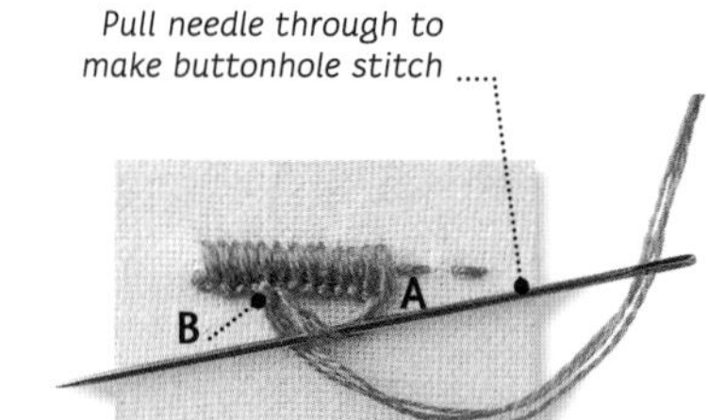
1
Pull needle through to make buttonhole stitch
A
B

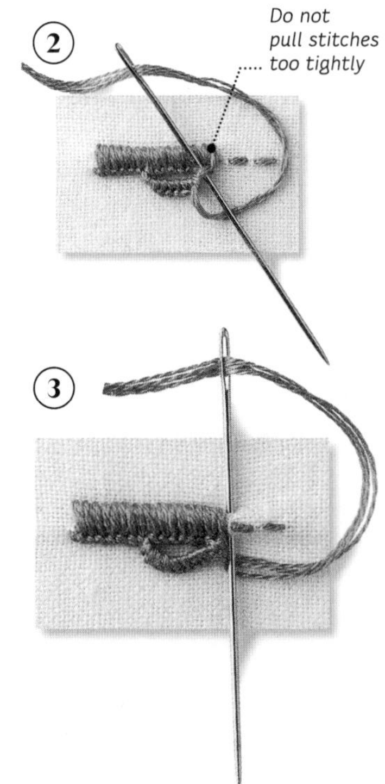
2
Do not pull stitches too tightly
3

1 Sew a line of closely spaced running stitch (see p.39) along the edge to be worked. Make a row of buttonhole stitch (see p.58) over it, finishing at the right edge of the picot, at **A**. Take the needle back to **B** and pass it under the horizontal thread to form the foundation loop. Slide the needle under the loop from right to left, over the working thread and gently pull through.

2 Work a series of buttonhole stitches to cover the foundation loop.

3 Continue working buttonhole stitch along the marked line. When complete, carefully trim away the surplus fabric using sharp embroidery scissors.

Buttonhole Eyelet

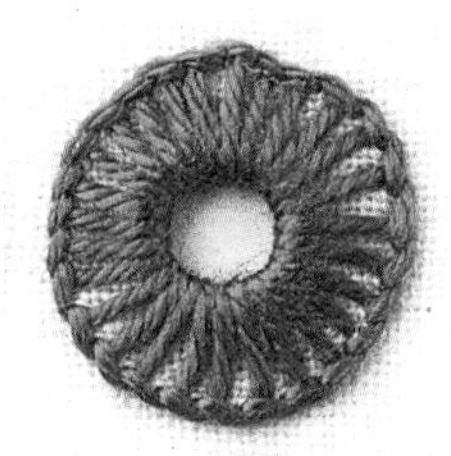

LEVEL
Advanced

USES
Circular holes; laced eyelets

METHOD
Buttonhole stitch worked in a ring around central opening

MATERIALS
Closely woven fabric; any fine thread; sharp scissors

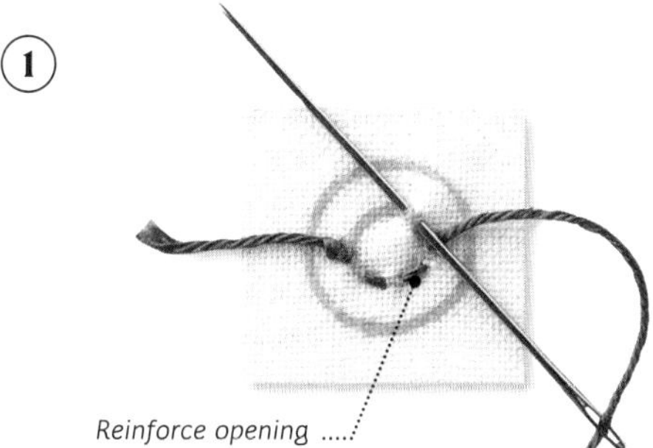
1
Reinforce opening with running stitch

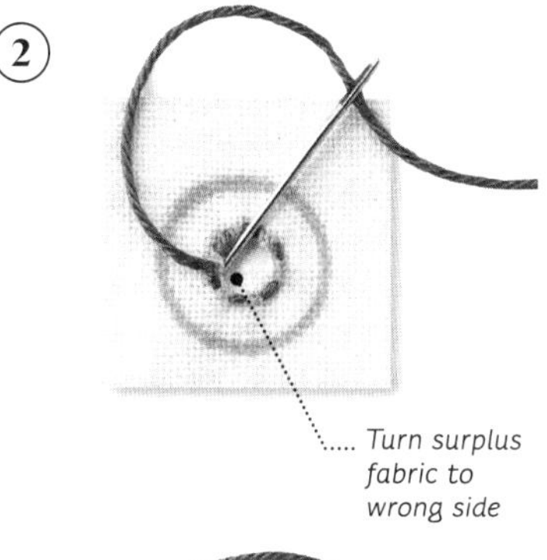
2
Turn surplus fabric to wrong side

1 Mark two concentric circles on the fabric. Outline the inner circle with a round of closely spaced running stitch (see p.39).

2 Clip the knot and make two cuts at right angles across the inner circle. Using the point of the needle, ease the fabric to the wrong side and finger press in place.

3 Come up at **A** on the outer circle and work a circle of buttonhole stitch (see p.58) into the centre. Trim any surplus fabric on the wrong side.

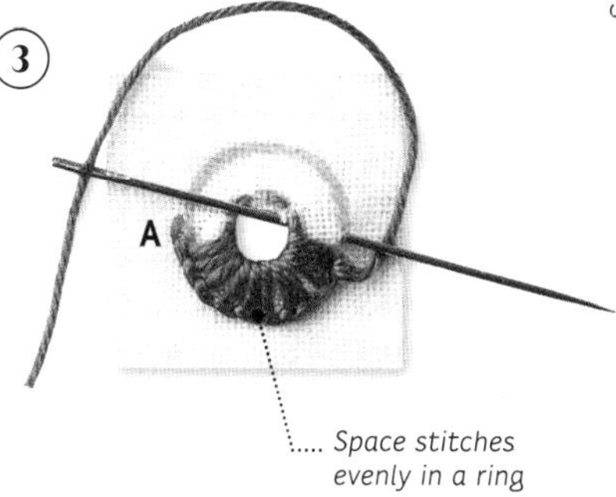
3
A
Space stitches evenly in a ring

Overcast Eyelet

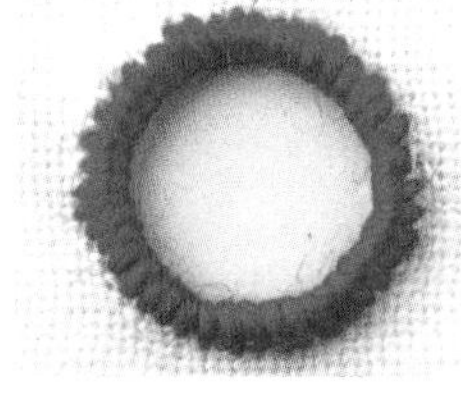

LEVEL
Advanced

USES
Broderie Anglaise; openwork

METHOD
Small open circle with bound edge

MATERIALS
Fine cotton or linen; any fine thread

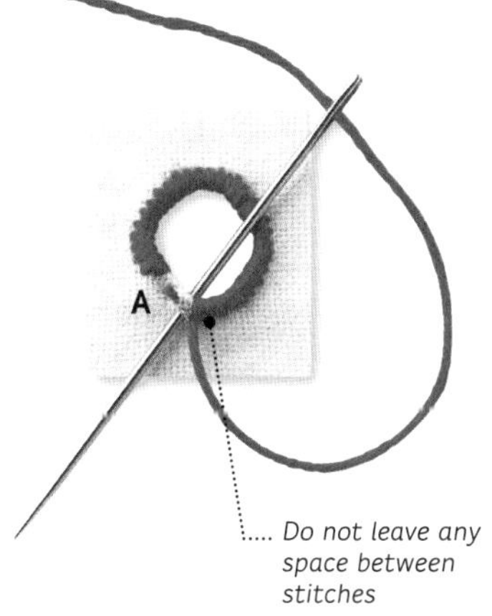
A
Do not leave any space between stitches

Draw a circle onto the fabric and prepare as for steps 1 and 2 above. Bring the needle up a short distance away from the folded edge, at **A** and work a ring of short stitches into the space.

Square Eyelet

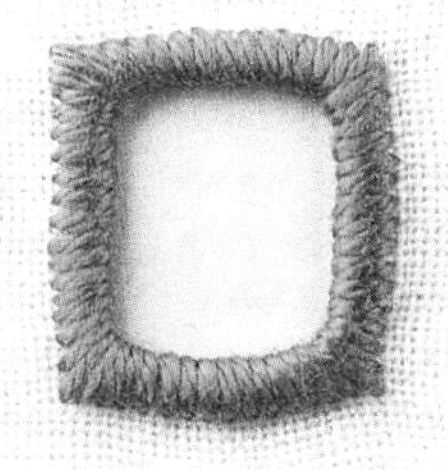

LEVEL
Advanced

USES
Broderie Anglaise; openwork

METHOD
Cut square with bound edge

MATERIALS
Any fine fabric; fine thread

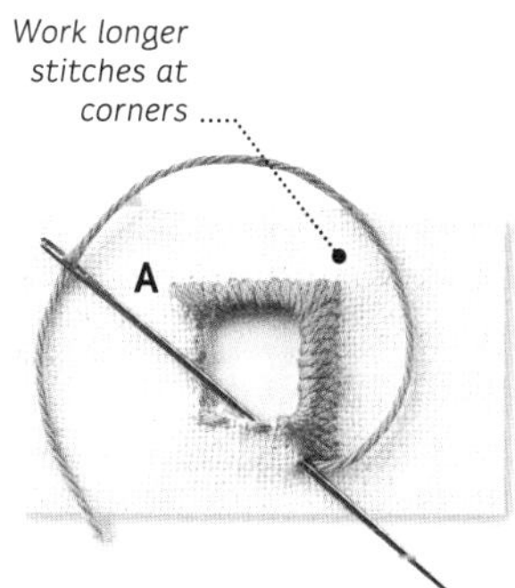
Work longer stitches at corners
A

Mark the outline and work a round of running stitch over it. Make two diagonal cuts across the square and finger press the surplus fabric to the wrong side. Come up at **A** and work a round of straight stitches into the opening, angling them at each corner.

Needlepoint Stitches

Straight Needlepoint Stitches

This first group of needlepoint stitches includes stripes, zigzags, and diamonds, which are used for fillings and backgrounds, in one or more colours. They are all made up of horizontal and vertical stitches, so they do not distort the square weave of the canvas and can therefore be stitched without a frame. Sew onto single canvas, using a yarn that is thick enough to conceal the background completely.

Bargello or Flame stitch is a technique in itself, which is becoming increasingly popular due to its repetitive, meditative way of working. There are many variations in which one sinuous line is repeated in shaded wools, producing an overall pattern that resembles the bold geometry and bright colours of sixties' Op Art.

Upright Gobelin

OTHER NAME
Straight Gobelin stitch

LEVEL
Easy

USES
Ridged fillings and backgrounds

METHOD
Horizontal rows of vertical straight stitches, worked alternately from right to left

MATERIALS
Single canvas; any thread

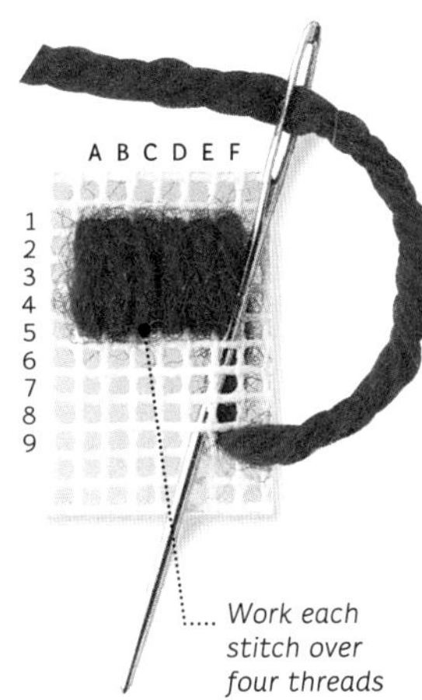
A B C D E F
1
2
3
4
5
6
7
8
9
Work each stitch over four threads

Starting at top left, make an upright stitch from **5A** to **1A** and repeat to the end of the line. Begin the next row at **9F** to **5F** and stitch towards the left. Repeat these two rows to fill the required area.

Gobelin Filling

LEVEL
Easy

USES
Twill effect backgrounds and shaded fillings

METHOD
Interlocking horizontal rows of upright stitches

MATERIALS
Single canvas; any thread

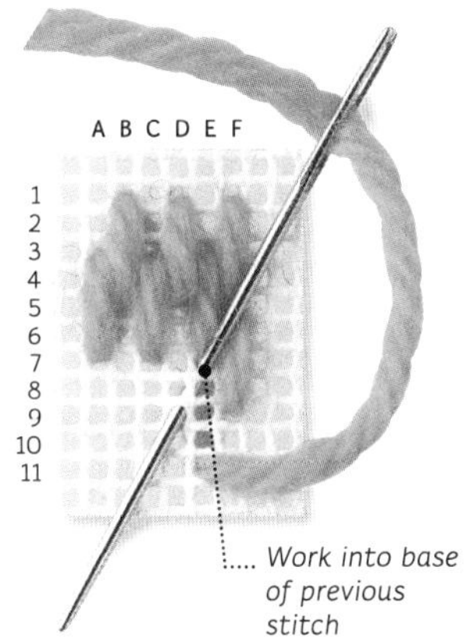
A B C D E F
1
2
3
4
5
6
7
8
9
10
11
Work into base of previous stitch

Start at top left. Work the first stitch from **7A** to **3A**, the second from **5B** to **1B** and repeat to the end of the line. Begin the next row at **9F** to **5F** and **11E** to **7E** and work towards the left; repeat these two rows to continue.

Parisian

LEVEL
Easy

USES
Textured fillings and large background areas

METHOD
Interlocking horizontal rows of alternate long and short upright stitches

MATERIALS
Single canvas; any thread

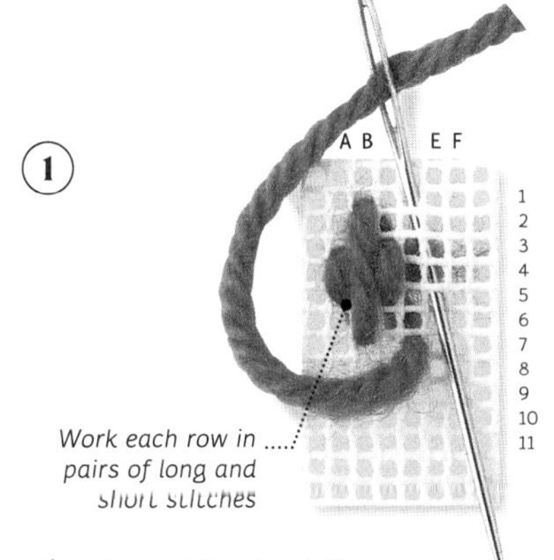
1
A B
E F
1
2
3
4
5
6
7
8
9
10
11
Work each row in pairs of long and short stitches

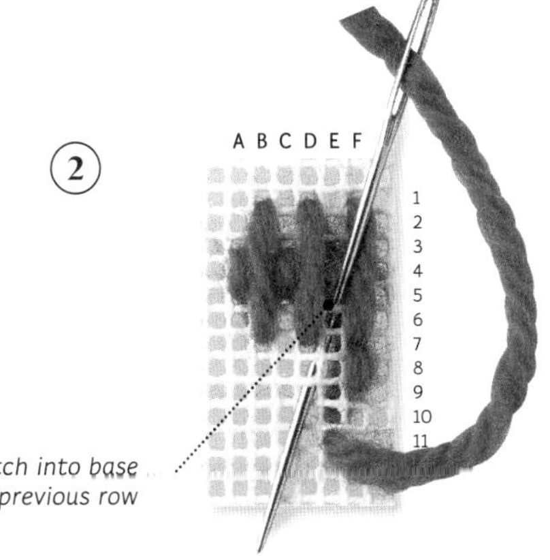
2
A B C D E F
1
2
3
4
5
6
7
8
9
10
11
Stitch into base of previous row

1. Start at the top left corner. Work a short stitch over two threads from **5A** to **3A** and a long stitch over six threads from **7B** to **1B**. Repeat these two stitches to the end of the line.

2. Begin the next row with a short stitch from **9F** to **7F** and a long stitch from **11E** to **5E**, then work alternate long and short stitches to the end of the row. Repeat these two steps to fill the required area.

Technique Variation

To create a secondary pattern within Parisian stitch, work all the long stitches in a dark yarn, then fill the spaces with short stitches in a contrasting colour.

Hungarian

LEVEL
Easy

USES
Textured fillings

METHOD
Horizontal rows of small interlocking diamonds

MATERIALS
Single canvas; any thread in one or two colours

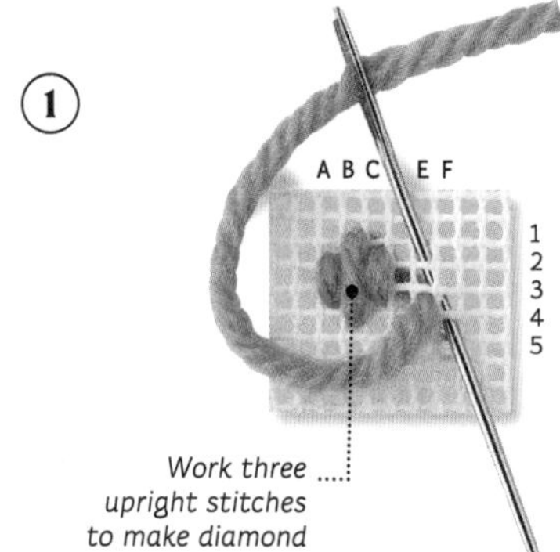

1
A B C E F
1
2
3
4
5
Work three upright stitches to make diamond

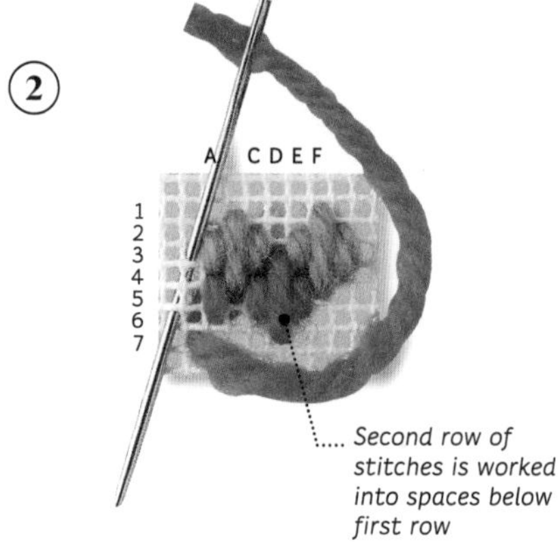

2
A C D E F
1
2
3
4
5
6
7
Second row of stitches is worked into spaces below first row

1 Starting at top left, make a short stitch over two threads from **4A** to **2A**. Work a long stitch from **5B** to **1B**, then another short stitch from **4C** to **2C**. Miss one space, then come up at **4E** to start the next diamond. Continue to the end of the line.

2 Using a contrasting colour, come up at **6E** to start the next row. Repeat the sequence of three stitches and one space, working from right to left.

Technique Variation

When Hungarian stitch is worked in just a single colour it produces a smooth, brocade-like texture which provides a good background for detailed tent stitch designs.

Hungarian Diamond

LEVEL
Easy

USES
Striped backgrounds and fillings

METHOD
Hungarian stitch variation on larger scale

MATERIALS
Single canvas; any thread

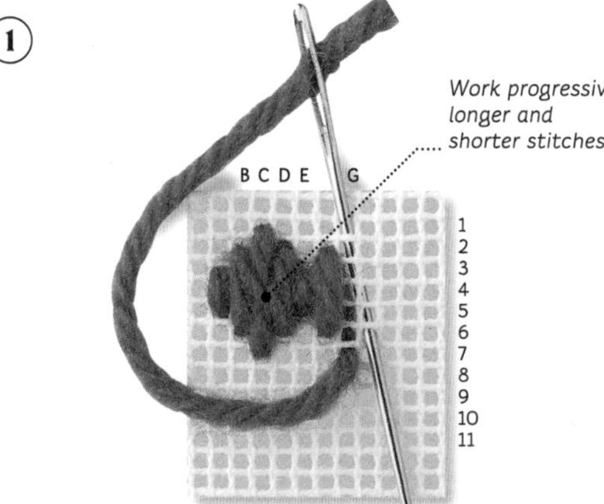

1
Work progressively longer and shorter stitches
B C D E G
1
2
3
4
5
6
7
8
9
10
11

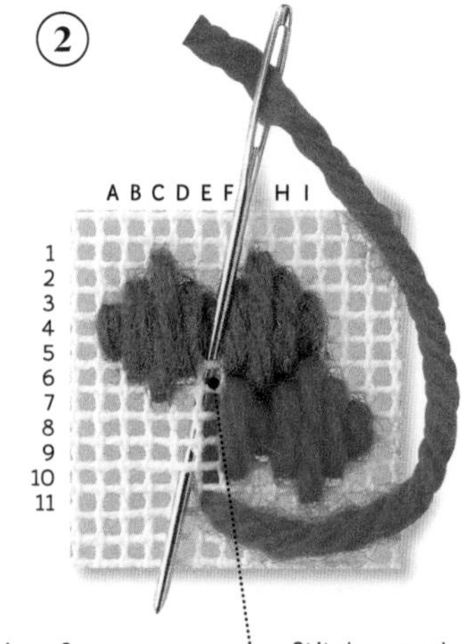

2
A B C D E F H I
1
2
3
4
5
6
7
8
9
10
11
Stitch second row in opposite direction, working into spaces left below first

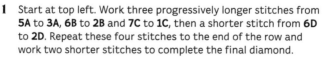

1 Start at top left. Work three progressively longer stitches from **5A** to **3A**, **6B** to **2B** and **7C** to **1C**, then a shorter stitch from **6D** to **2D**. Repeat these four stitches to the end of the row and work two shorter stitches to complete the final diamond.

2 Use a second colour for the next row. Start with a short stitch from **9K** to **7K** and continue as above, working from right to left. Repeat these two rows to fill the required area.

Single Twill

LEVEL
Easy

USES
Ridged fillings and woven effect backgrounds

METHOD
Diagonal rows of vertical straight stitches

MATERIALS
Single canvas; any thread

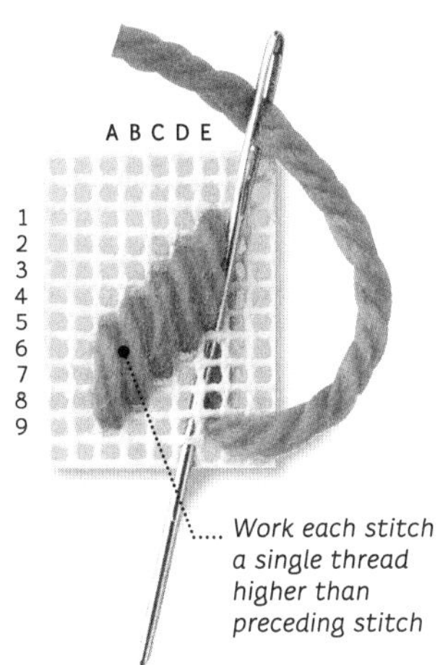
A B C D E
1
2
3
4
5
6
7
8
9
Work each stitch a single thread higher than preceding stitch

Start at the top left with a straight stitch from **9A** to **5A**. Work the next from **8B** to **4B** and continue stitching upwards. Start the next row at **9E** to **5E**, and continue working downwards. Repeat these two rows to continue.

Double Twill

LEVEL
Easy

USES
Textured fillings and backgrounds

METHOD
Alternate rows of long and short upright stitches, worked diagonally

MATERIALS
Single canvas; any thread

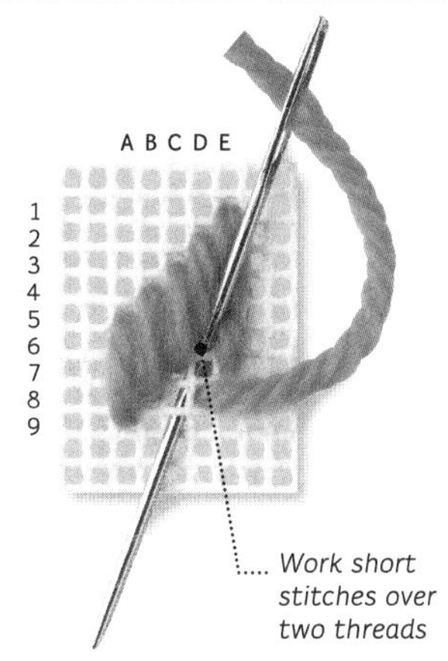
A B C D E
1
2
3
4
5
6
7
8
9
Work short stitches over two threads

Work the first row as for single twill stitch (see above). Start the second row with **7E** to **5E** and continue working short stitches downwards. Repeat these two rows to fill the required area.

Bargello

OTHER NAMES
Florentine stitch; flame stitch

LEVEL
Easy

USES
Large patterned areas

METHOD
Straight stitch worked in wide zigzag bands

MATERIALS
Single canvas; any yarn in a selection of toning and contrasting colours

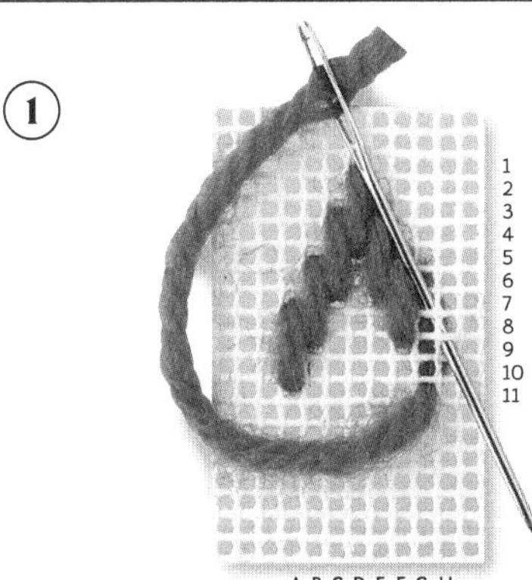
1
1
2
3
4
5
6
7
8
9
10
11
A B C D E F G H

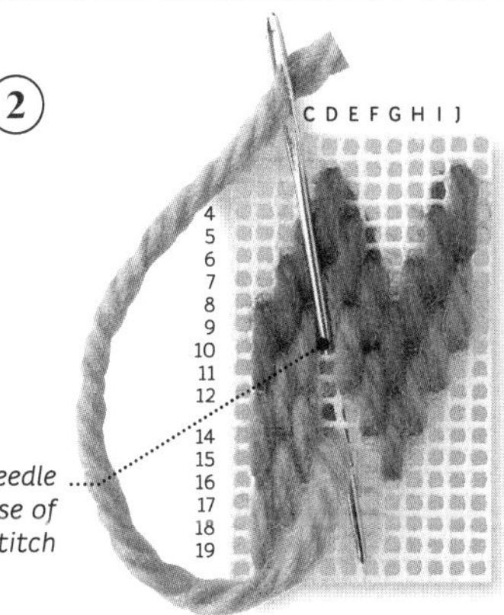
2
C D E F G H I J
4
5
6
7
8
9
10
11
12
14
15
16
17
18
19
Insert needle into base of previous stitch

1 Start at the left with a straight stitch from **11A** to **7A**. Make three stitches upwards from **9B** to **5B**, **7C** to **3C**, and **5D** to **1D**. Work the next three stitches downwards, leaving two threads between each, ending at **7G**. Come up at **9H** and repeat this sequence to the end of the row.

2 Stitch the next row in the same way, starting at **15A** and using a lighter shade of the same colour. The third row is worked in a paler yarn, starting at **19A**. Repeat these three rows to continue.

Technique Variation

To create a wider zigzag with a stepped effect, work blocks of two and three stitches in the centre of the diagonals. Add in a contrasting colour yarn to give more visual interest.

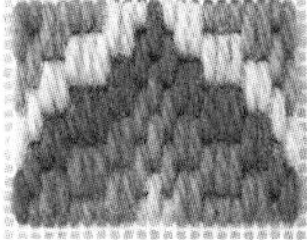

Chevron

LEVEL
Easy

USES
Backgrounds and fillings

METHOD
Alternate zigzag bands of long and short stitches

MATERIALS
Single canvas; any thread in one or two colours

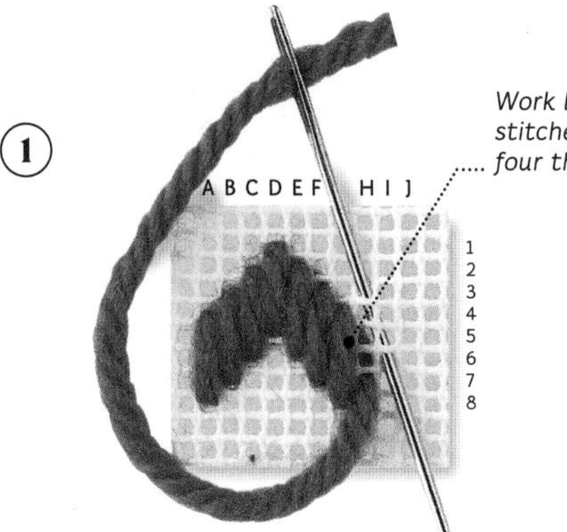
1
A B C D E F H I J
1
2
3
4
5
6
7
8
Work long stitches over four threads

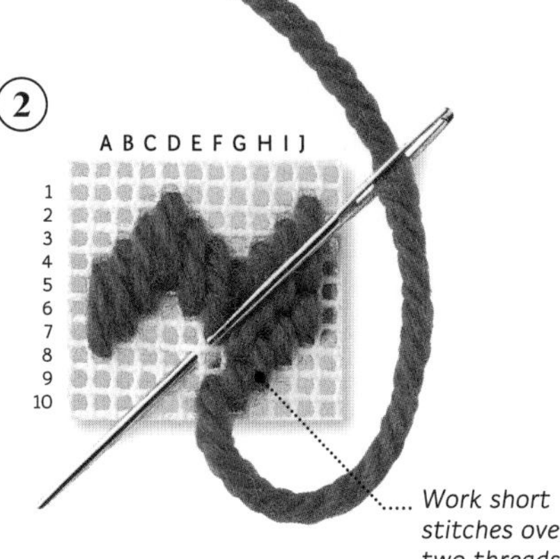
2
A B C D E F G H I J
1
2
3
4
5
6
7
8
9
10
Work short stitches over two threads

1 Start at the top left corner with a stitch from **8A** to **4A**. Work three more stitches upwards from **7B** to **3B**, **6C** to **2C**, and **5D** to **1D**, then two downwards stitches from **6E** to **2E** and **7F** to **3F**. Repeat this sequence to the end of the row.

2 Begin the next row with a short stitch from **7J** to **5J**. Continue stitching from right to left, working into the base of the previous row. Repeat these two rows to continue.

Technique Variation

Emphasize the zigzag pattern within chevron stitch by working alternate rows in different colour threads.

Hungarian Ground

LEVEL
Intermediate

USES
Geometric fillings

METHOD
Alternate straight stitch zigzags and diamonds

MATERIALS
Single canvas; any thread

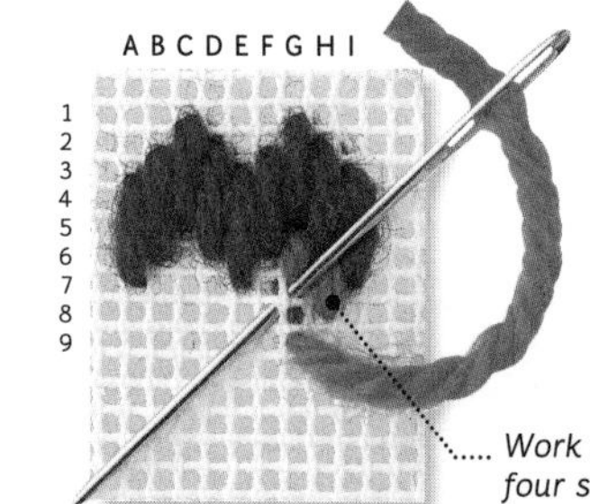
1
A B C D E F G H I
1
2
3
4
5
6
7
8
9
Work diamond block of four short stitches into space below chevron

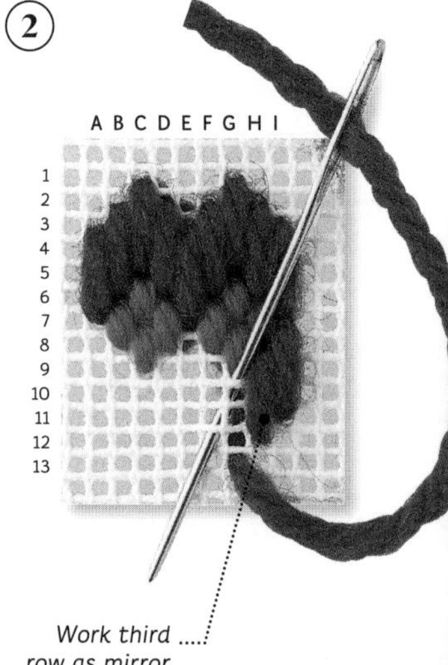
2
A B C D E F G H I
1
2
3
4
5
6
7
8
9
10
11
12
13
Work third row as mirror image of first

1 Start at the top left corner. Work three long stitches upwards from **7A** to **3A**, **6B** to **2B**, and **5C** to **1C** and one stitch downwards from **6D** to **2D**, then repeat this block to the end of the line. Using the second colour, make four short stitches from **8H** to **6H**, **7G** to **5G**, **9G** to **7G**, and **8F** to **6F**. Start the next diamond at **8D**.

2 With the first colour, work three stitches downwards from **11I** to **7I**, **12H** to **8H**, and **13G** to **9G**, then two stitches upwards from **12F** to **8F** and **11E** to **7E**. Repeat to the end of the row, then fill in the spaces with diamonds.

Straight Cushion

LEVEL
Easy

USES
Chequerboard fillings

METHOD
Alternate rows of diamonds worked in long and short straight stitches

MATERIALS
Single canvas; any thread or yarn in two colours

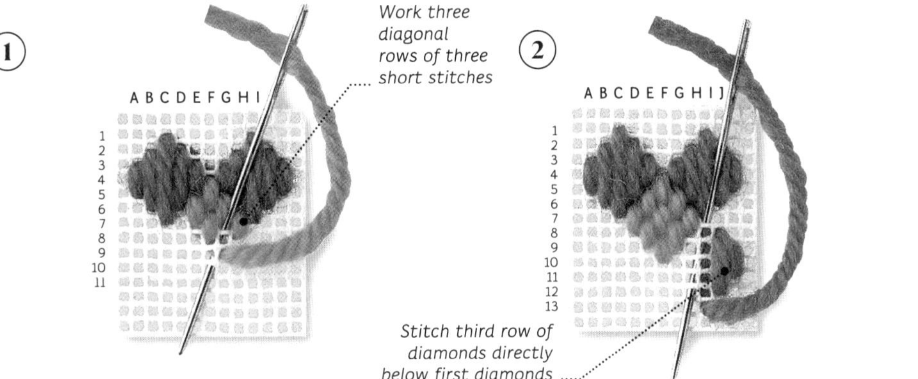

1
Work three diagonal rows of three short stitches
A B C D E F G H I
1 2 3 4 5 6 7 8 9 10 11
2
A B C D E F G H I J
1 2 3 4 5 6 7 8 9 10 11 12 13
Stitch third row of diamonds directly below first diamonds

1 Work the first row as step 1 of Scottish diamond stitch (see below) starting at **5A**. Using a second colour, work three rows of stitches, from **8H** to **6H**, **7G** to **5G**, **6F** to **4F**; **7E** to **5E**, **8F** to **6F**, **9G** to **7G** and **10F** to **8F**, **9E** to **7E**, and **8D** to **6D**.

2 Work the third row as the first, starting at **11K** and stitching from right to left. Continue working alternate rows of dark and light diamonds.

Technique Variation

Work straight cushion stitch in two shades of the same colour, instead of two contrasting yarns, to give a subtle brocade effect for fillings or large-scale backgrounds.

Scottish Diamond

LEVEL
Intermediate

USES
Textured fillings and backgrounds

METHOD
Straight stitch chevrons and diamonds worked in alternate rows

MATERIALS
Single canvas; any thread

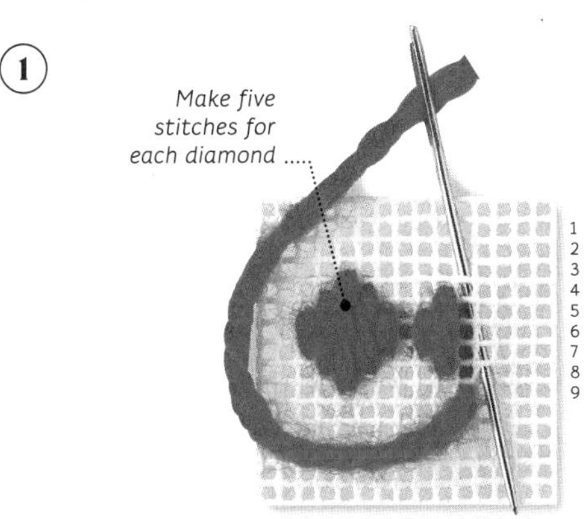

1
Make five stitches for each diamond
1 2 3 4 5 6 7 8 9
A B C D E F G H I J K L M

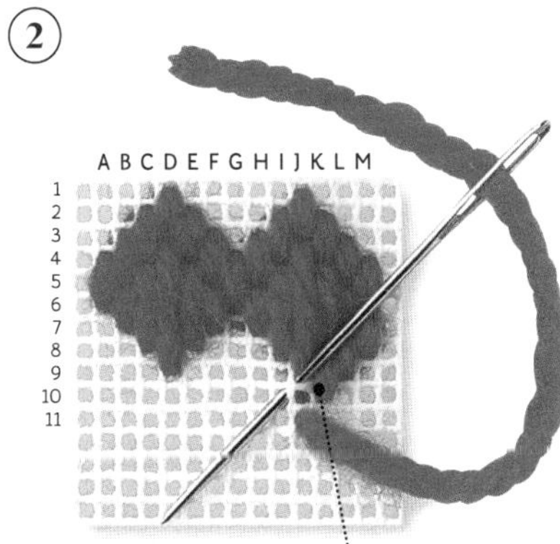

2
A B C D E F G H I J K L M
1 2 3 4 5 6 7 8 9 10 11
Work short stitches over two threads

1 Start at top left. Work five upright stitches in a diamond shape from **7B** to **5B**, **8C** to **4C**, **9D** to **3D**, **8E** to **4E**, and **7F** to **5F**. Repeat to the end of the line, leaving one space between each diamond.

2 Work a zigzag line above and below the diamonds. Start at **4A** to **6A**, then work three stitches upwards from **3B** to **5B**, **2C** to **4C**, and **1D** to **3D**, and two downwards from **2E** to **4E** and **3F** to **5F**. Repeat to the end of the row, then work a mirror image below, starting at **8M** to **6M**. Continue working alternate rows of diamonds and chevrons to fill the required area.

Diamond

LEVEL
Easy

USES
Fillings and backgrounds

METHOD
Large-scale variation of Hungarian stitch

MATERIALS
Single canvas; any thread in one or two colours

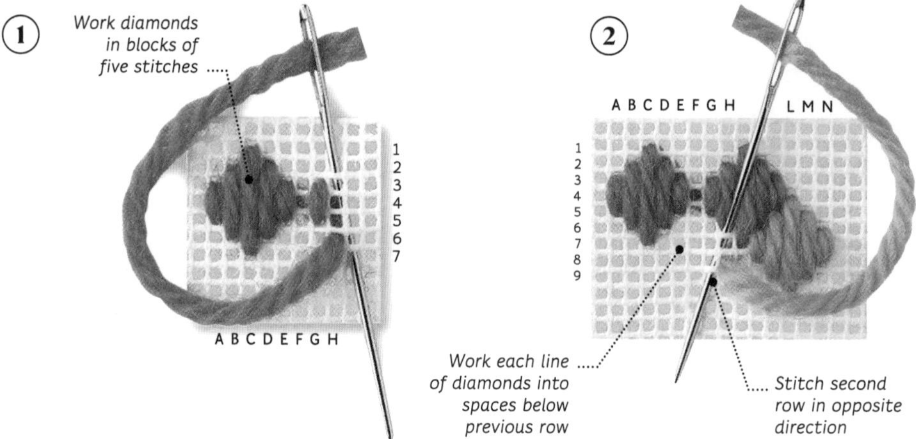
1
Work diamonds in blocks of five stitches
1 2 3 4 5 6 7
A B C D E F G H
2
A B C D E F G H L M N
1 2 3 4 5 6 7 8 9
Work each line of diamonds into spaces below previous row
Stitch second row in opposite direction

1 Start at top left. Work five upright stitches from **5A** to **3A**, **6B** to **2B**, **7C** to **1C**, **6D** to **2D** and **5E** to **3E**. Repeat to the end of the line, leaving one space between each block.

2 The second row is worked from right to left, using the same or a different colour. Start the first block at **8N** to **6N**, then repeat these two rows to continue.

Long Stitch Triangles

LEVEL
Easy

USES
Textured single-colour background or filling

METHOD
Two rows of interlocking straight stitch triangles, repeated horizontally

MATERIALS
Single canvas; any thread

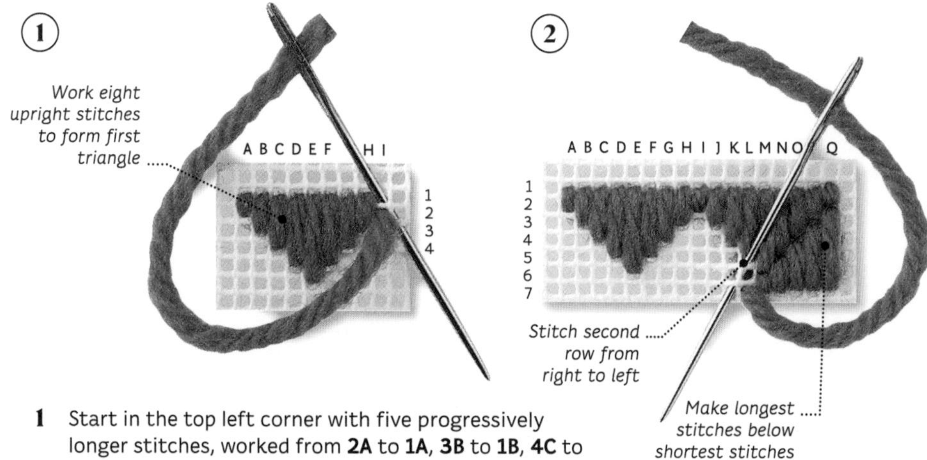
1
Work eight upright stitches to form first triangle
A B C D E F H I
1 2 3 4
2
A B C D E F G H I J K L M N O Q
1 2 3 4 5 6 7
Stitch second row from right to left
Make longest stitches below shortest stitches of previous row

1 Start in the top left corner with five progressively longer stitches, worked from **2A** to **1A**, **3B** to **1B**, **4C** to **1C**, **5D** to **1D** and **6E** to **1E**. Work three shorter stitches from **5F** to **1F**, **4G** to **1G** and **3H** to **1H**. Repeat this block to the end of the line.

2 Make a long stitch from **7Q** to **2Q**, then work four shorter stitches from **7P** to **3P**, **7O** to **4O**, **7N** to **5N** and **7M** to **6M**, and three longer stitches from **7L** to **5L**, **7K** to **4K** and **7J** to **3J**. Repeat these two rows to fill the required area.

Lozenge

LEVEL
Intermediate

USES
Harlequin filling or background for large areas

METHOD
Elongated diamonds, worked in interlocking diagonal rows

MATERIALS
Single canvas; two colours of any thread

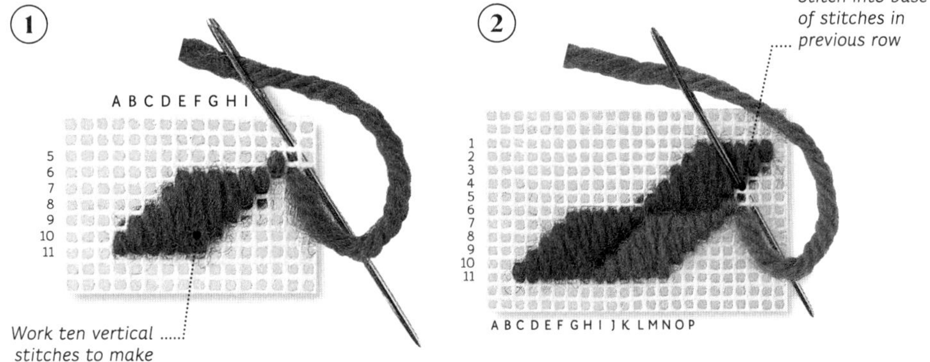
1
A B C D E F G H I
5
6
7
8
9
10
11
Work ten vertical stitches to make each diamond
2
Stitch into base of stitches in previous row
1
2
3
4
5
6
7
8
9
10
11
A B C D E F G H I J K L M N O P

1 Start at bottom left with five stitches from **11A** to **10A**, **11B** to **9B**, **11C** to **8C**, **11D** to **7D**, and **11E** to **6E**. Complete the diamond with five more stitches from **11F** to **6F**, **10G** to **6G**, **9H** to **6H**, **8I** to **6I**, and **7J** to **6J**. Begin the next diamond at **6K** to **5K** and contine working upwards.

2 Using a different colour, begin the second row at **11G** to **10G**. Work the third row in the first colour, starting at **11M** to **10M**. Fill in the required space above the stitches with further rows in alternate colours.

Straight Milanese

LEVEL
Intermediate

USES
Background or filling

METHOD
Interlocking rows of triangles worked vertically to create a wave pattern

MATERIALS
Single canvas; any thread in one or two colours

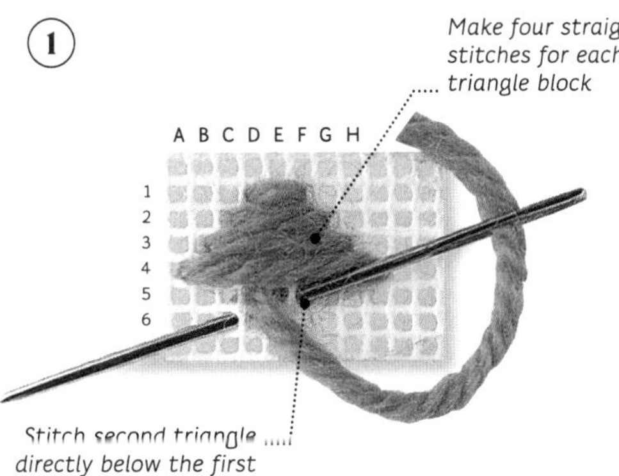
1
Make four straight stitches for each triangle block
A B C D E F G H
1
2
3
4
5
6
Stitch second triangle directly below the first

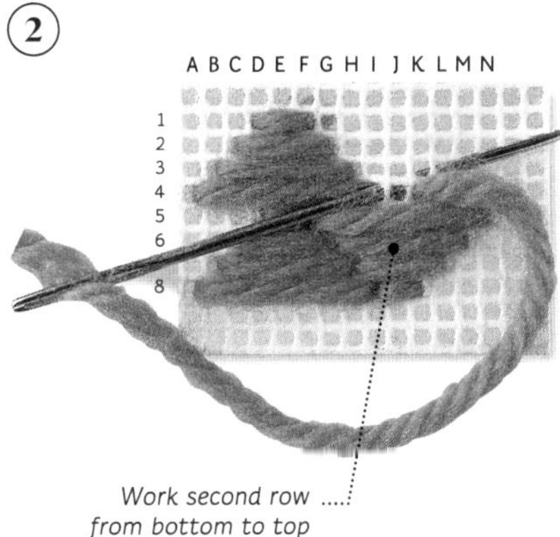
2
A B C D E F G H I J K L M N
1
2
3
4
5
6
8
Work second row from bottom to top

1 Start at top left. Work four horizontal stitches from **1D** to **1F**, **2C** to **2G**, **3B** to **3H** and **4A** to **4I**. Begin the next triangle at **5D** to **5F** and continue downwards to the end of the row.

2 Begin the next row with four stitches from **8K** to **8I**, **7L** to **7H**, **6M** to **6G**, and **5N** to **5F**. Continue working upwards, then repeat these two rows to fill the required area.

Technique Variation

For a more geometric effect, work alternate rows in contrasting or toning colours, to emphasize the triangular formation of straight milanese stitch.

Double Brick

OTHER NAME
Double Gobelin filling

LEVEL
Easy

USES
Single colour filling

METHOD
Interlocking rows of double straight stitches

MATERIALS
Single canvas; any thread

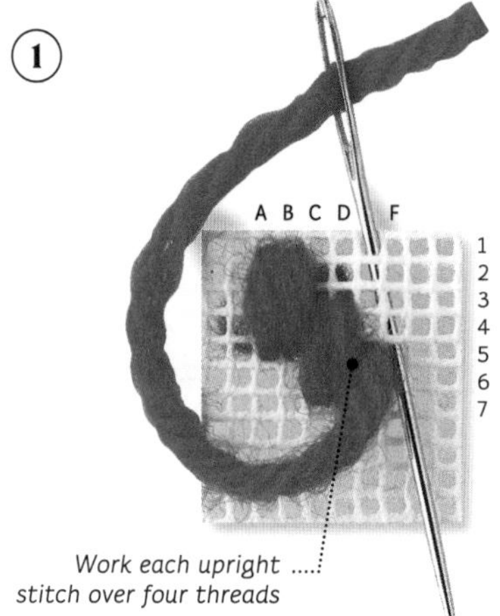

1
A B C D F
1
2
3
4
5
6
7
Work each upright stitch over four threads

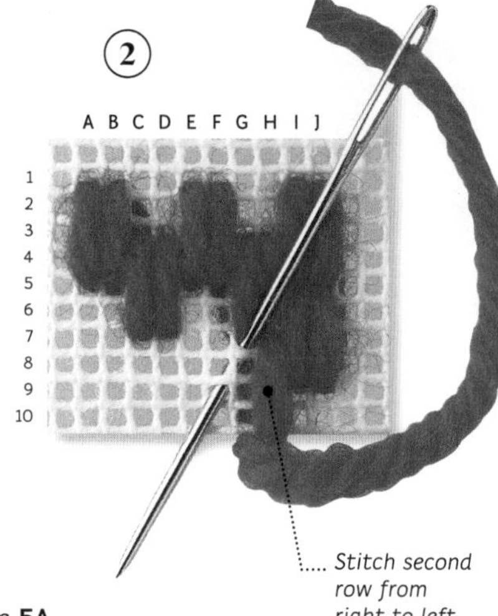

2
A B C D E F G H I J
1
2
3
4
5
6
7
8
9
10
Stitch second row from right to left

1 Start at top left. Work two parallel stitches from **5A** to **1A** and **5B** to **1B**, then two more from **7C** to **3C** and **7D** to **3D**. Come up at **5E** and continue working pairs of staggered straight stitches to the end of the row.

2 Work the second and subsequent rows in the same way, starting with a pair of stitches from **9J** to **5J** and **9I** to **5I**.

Brick Filling

LEVEL
Intermediate

USES
Small-scale fillings

METHOD
Pairs of horizontal straight stitches divided by vertical stitches

MATERIALS
Single canvas; any thread in two colours

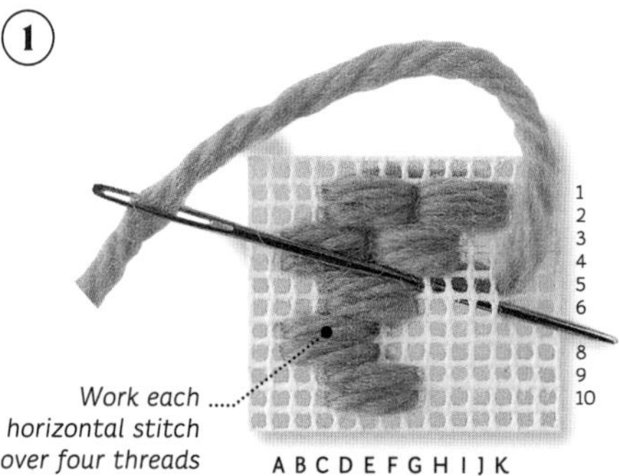

1
1
2
3
4
5
6
8
9
10
Work each horizontal stitch over four threads
A B C D E F G H I J K

2
Work each upright stitch over one thread
A B C D E F G H I J K L M N O
1
2
3
4
5
6
7
8
9
10
Avoid catching long stitches with needle

1 Starting at bottom left, work two horizontal stitches from **10G** to **10C** and **9G** to **9C**, then a second staggered pair from **8E** to **8A** and **7E** to **7A**. Continue upwards, then work the second row downwards in the same way, starting at **1K** to **1G**. Repeat these two rows to fill the required area.

2 Using a contrasting thread, work short upright stitches at the points where pairs of stitches meet, starting with **1G** to **2G**.

Technique Variation

Working the vertical stitches (see step 2, above) in the same thread as the horizontal stitches produces a more textured surface with a quilted appearance.

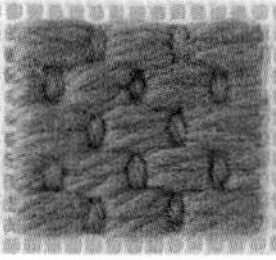

Long and Short Brick

OTHER NAMES
Brick stitch

LEVEL
Intermediate

USES
Fillings and backgrounds

METHOD
Alternate pairs of long and short stitches

MATERIALS
Single canvas; one or two colours of any thread

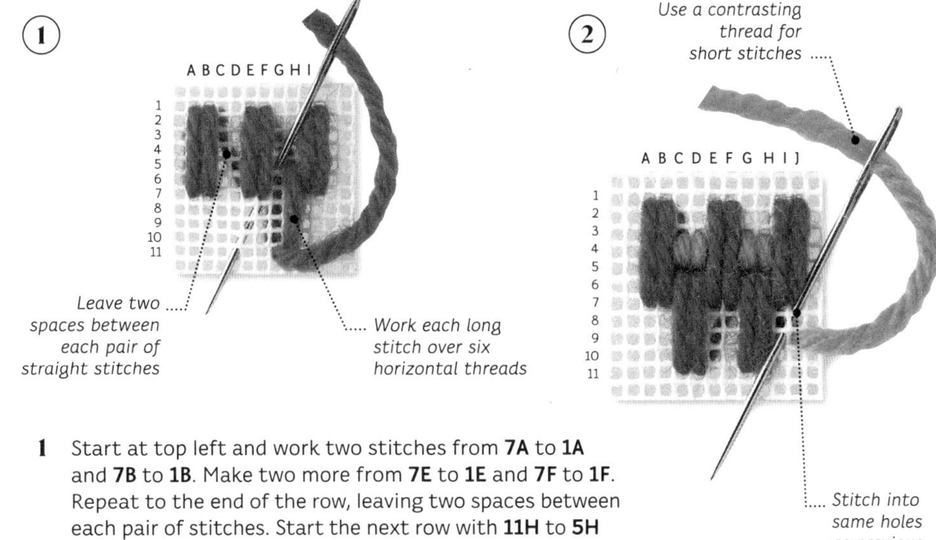
1
A B C D E F G H I
1 2 3 4 5 6 7 8 9 10 11
Leave two spaces between each pair of straight stitches
Work each long stitch over six horizontal threads
2
Use a contrasting thread for short stitches
A B C D E F G H I J
1 2 3 4 5 6 7 8 9 10 11
Stitch into same holes as previous stitches

1 Start at top left and work two stitches from **7A** to **1A** and **7B** to **1B**. Make two more from **7E** to **1E** and **7F** to **1F**. Repeat to the end of the row, leaving two spaces between each pair of stitches. Start the next row with **11H** to **5H** and **11G** to **5G** and continue working from right to left.

2 Fill in the spaces with pairs of short stitches, starting with **5C** to **3C** and **5D** to **3D**. Repeat these two steps to continue.

Basket Filling

LEVEL
Intermediate

USES
Large-scale woven-look filling or background

METHOD
Straight stitch worked in alternate vertical and horizontal blocks

MATERIALS
Single canvas; any thread

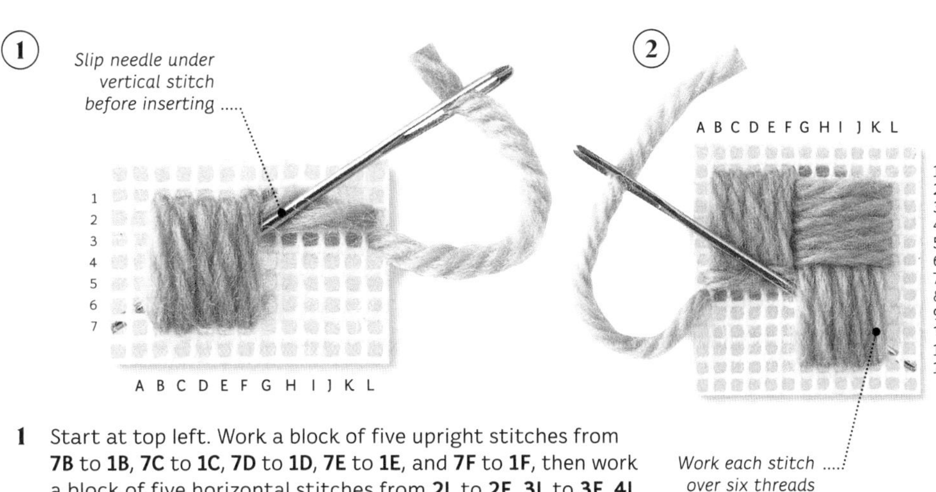
1
Slip needle under vertical stitch before inserting
1 2 3 4 5 6 7
A B C D E F G H I J K L
2
A B C D E F G H I J K L
1 2 3 4 5 6 7 8 9 10 11 12
Work each stitch over six threads

1 Start at top left. Work a block of five upright stitches from **7B** to **1B**, **7C** to **1C**, **7D** to **1D**, **7E** to **1E**, and **7F** to **1F**, then work a block of five horizontal stitches from **2L** to **2F**, **3L** to **3F**, **4L** to **4F**, **5L** to **5F**, and **6L** to **6F**. Repeat to the end of the line.

2 Work five upright stitches below the horizontal block, starting with **12K** to **6K** and ending with **12G** to **6G**. Work a horizontal block under the upright block, starting at **7A** to **7F** and ending with **12A** to **12F**. Repeat to the end of the line, then repeat these two rows to continue.

Diagonal Needlepoint Stitches

This section starts with tent stitch and its variations, which are the most frequently used of all needlepoint stitches. Like others in the group, they are worked at a slant across the thread intersections. This tends to pull the canvas out of shape, even when it is mounted in a frame, so the finished piece should be stretched and blocked back into shape (see p.21).

Needlepoint tapestry is worked in tent stitch only, creating a smooth surface that resembles a hand-woven tapestry. There are many kits available, but it is creatively satisfying to transfer your own original design onto canvas with waterproof markers.

Half Cross

LEVEL
Easy

USES
Charts; printed canvases

METHOD
Small slanting stitches

MATERIALS
Double canvas; thick yarn

TIP
Turn work upside-down for return journey to stitch rows in same direction

A B C D F
1
2
3
4

Start at top left. Stitch over one intersection, from **2A** to **1B** and **2B** to **1C**, then repeat to the end of the line. Begin the next row with **2F** to **3E** and **2E** to **3D**. Repeat these two rows to continue.

Basketweave Tent

OTHER NAMES
Continental stitch; diagonal tent stitch

LEVEL
Intermediate

USES
Backgrounds and fillings

METHOD
Tent stitch worked in diagonal rows

MATERIALS
Single canvas; any thread

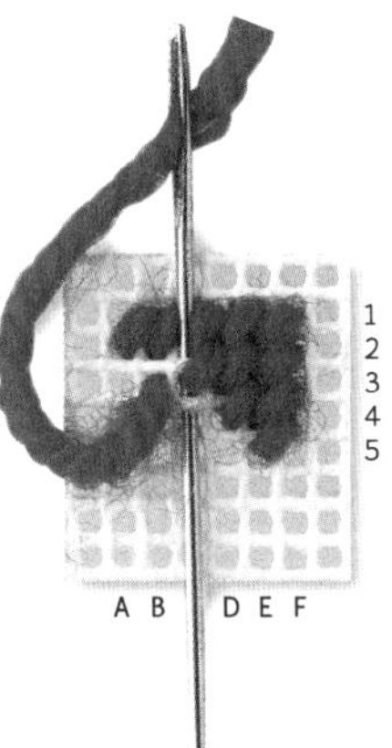
1
2
3
4
5
A B D E F

Starting at top right, make a stitch from **2E** to **1F**. Work the next row upwards from **3E** to **2F** and **2D** to **1E** and the third downwards from **2C** to **1D**, **3D** to **2E**, and **4E** to **3F**. Begin the following row with **5E** to **4F**: continue working up, then down.

Tent

OTHER NAME
Petit point

LEVEL
Easy

USES
Backgrounds; detailed charted or printed patterns

METHOD
Worked horizontally

MATERIALS
Single canvas; any thread

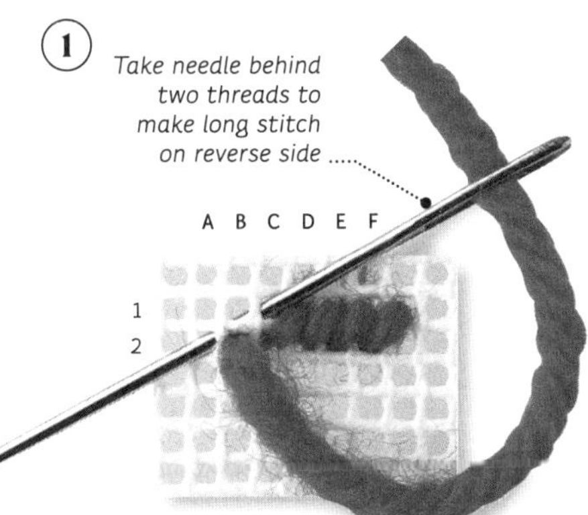
1
Take needle behind two threads to make long stitch on reverse side
A B C D E F
1
2
2
Work each stitch in same direction
A B C D E F G
1
2
3
Keep needle at an angle

1 Start at top right and sew a diagonal stitch from **2F** to **1G**. Work the second stitch from **2E** to **1F** and repeat to the end of the row.

2 Turn the canvas the other way up and repeat step 1 or work the second row from left to right, starting with **2B** to **3A**. Repeat these two rows.

Stitch Variation

Trammed tent stitch is sewn over long straight stitches worked through the small holes on a double canvas. This gives a ridged effect and because it is hardwearing, this stitch is often used for seat covers.

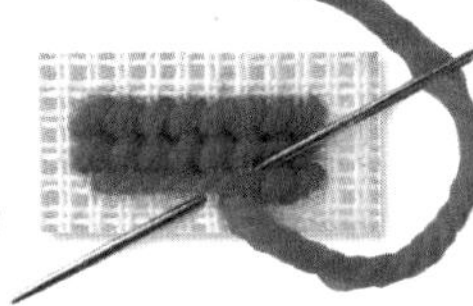

Gobelin

OTHER NAMES
Oblique Gobelin; gros point

LEVEL
Easy

USES
Backgrounds and fillings

METHOD
Long diagonal stitches worked in horizontal rows

MATERIALS
Single canvas, any thread

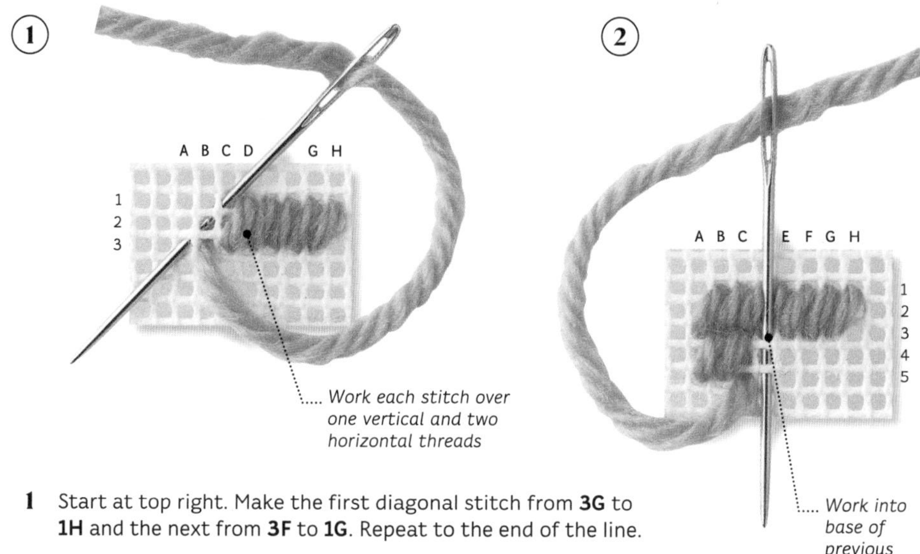
1
A B C D
G H
1
2
3
Work each stitch over one vertical and two horizontal threads
2
A B C
E F G H
1
2
3
4
5
Work into base of previous stitch

1 Start at top right. Make the first diagonal stitch from **3G** to **1H** and the next from **3F** to **1G**. Repeat to the end of the line.

2 Begin the return journey with two stitches from **5A** to **3B** and **5B** to **3C**, and continue to the end of the row. Repeat these two rows to fill the required area.

Encroaching Gobelin

LEVEL
Easy

USES
Backgrounds; filling for plain or shaded areas

METHOD
Overlapping rows of diagonal stitches, worked horizontally

MATERIALS
Single canvas; any yarn

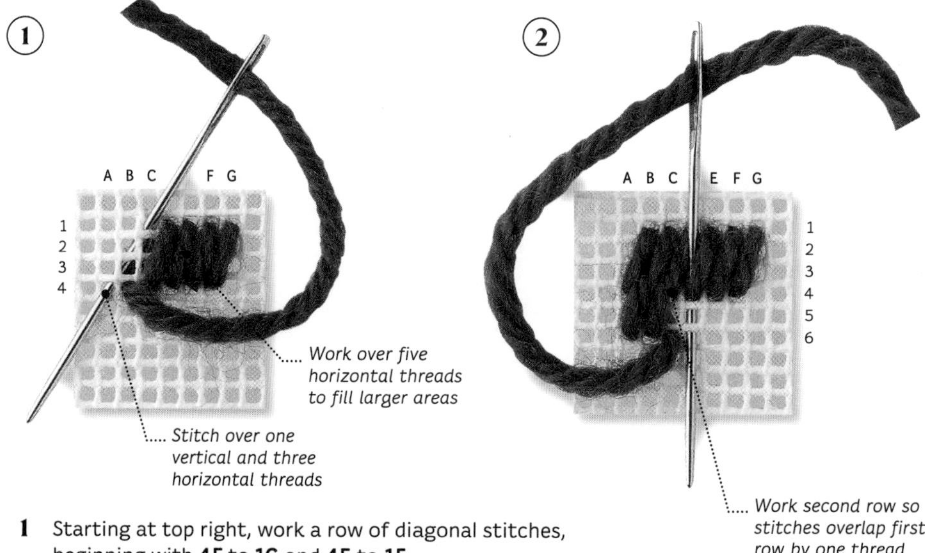
1
A B C
F G
1
2
3
4
Work over five horizontal threads to fill larger areas
Stitch over one vertical and three horizontal threads
2
A B C
E F G
1
2
3
4
5
6
Work second row so stitches overlap first row by one thread

1 Starting at top right, work a row of diagonal stitches, beginning with **4F** to **1G** and **4E** to **1F.**

2 Work the first stitch of the next row from **6A** to **3B** and the second from **6B** to **3C**. Continue to the end of the line and repeat these two steps to continue.

Reversed Sloping Gobelin

LEVEL
Easy

USES
Plain or shaded fillings and backgrounds

METHOD
Vertical rows of diagonal straight stitches worked alternately down and up

MATERIALS
Any canvas; any thread

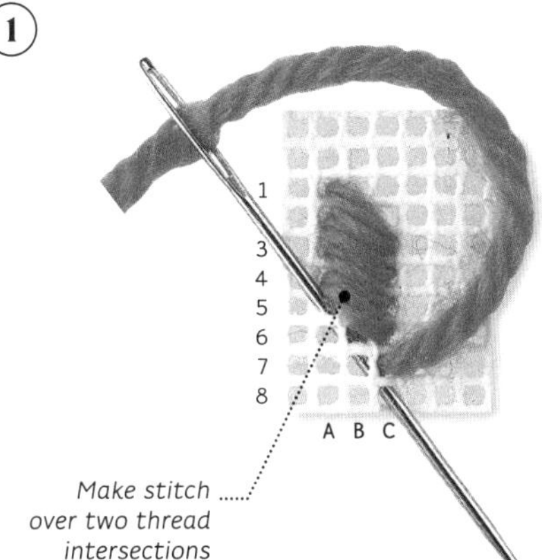
1
1
3
4
5
6
7
8
A B C
Make stitch over two thread intersections

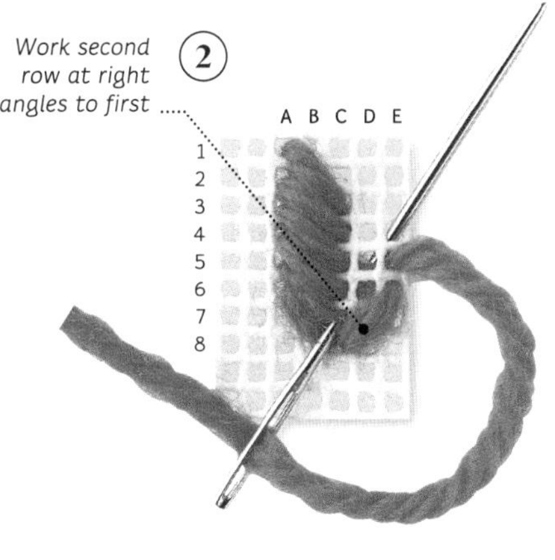
2
Work second row at right angles to first
A B C D E
1
2
3
4
5
6
7
8

1 Start at top left and work a diagonal stitch from **3C** to **1A**. Work the next stitch from **4C** to **2A** and repeat downwards to the end of the line.

2 Begin the next line with a stitch in the opposite direction from **6E** to **8C**, then continue working upwards. Repeat these two rows.

Technique Variation

To produce a shaded effect, work the stitches in the lower part of the stitched area with a selection of progressively darker tones of the main colour.

Canvas Stem

LEVEL
Intermediate

USES
Textured background, filling or chevron border

METHOD
Two upright rows of diagonal stitches, set in a V-shape, and divided by lines of back stitch

MATERIALS
Double canvas; two colours of any yarn

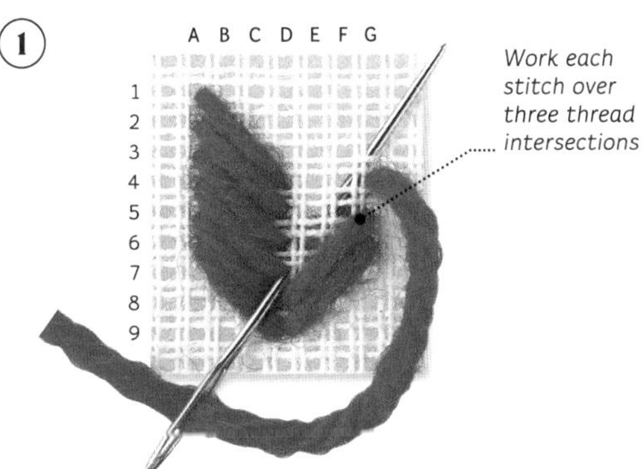
1
A B C D E F G
1
2
3
4
5
6
7
8
9
Work each stitch over three thread intersections

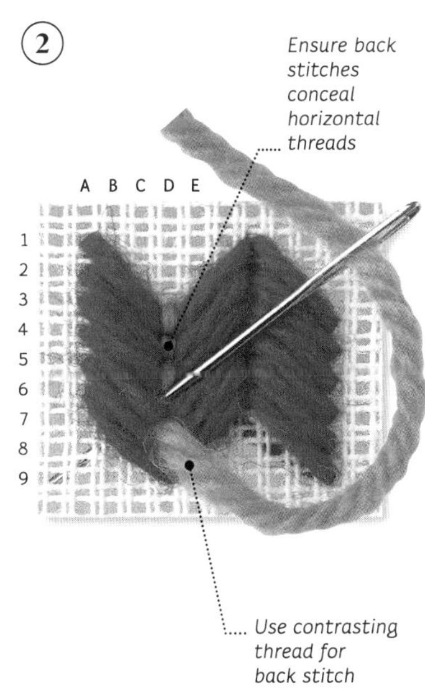
2
Ensure back stitches conceal horizontal threads
A B C D E
1
2
3
4
5
6
7
8
9
Use contrasting thread for back stitch

1 Starting at top left, make a diagonal stitch from **4D** to **1A**. Work the second stitch directly below, from **5D** to **2A**, and continue stitching downwards. Begin the next row at **6G** to **9D**. Make another stitch from **5G** to **8D** and continue working upwards. Repeat these two rows to cover the required area.

2 Make two back stitches from **4D** to **3D** and **5D** to **4D** and continue downwards. Work further rows of back stitch into the holes between the lines of diagonal stitches.

Florence

OTHER NAME
Diagonal mosaic stitch

LEVEL
Easy

USES
Plain or striped fillings

METHOD
Alternate long and short slanting stitches, worked diagonally

MATERIALS
Any canvas; any thread

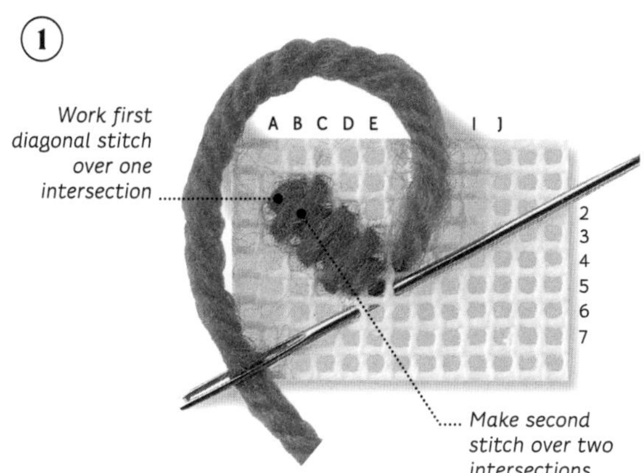

1
Work first diagonal stitch over one intersection
A B C D E
I J
2
3
4
5
6
7
Make second stitch over two intersections

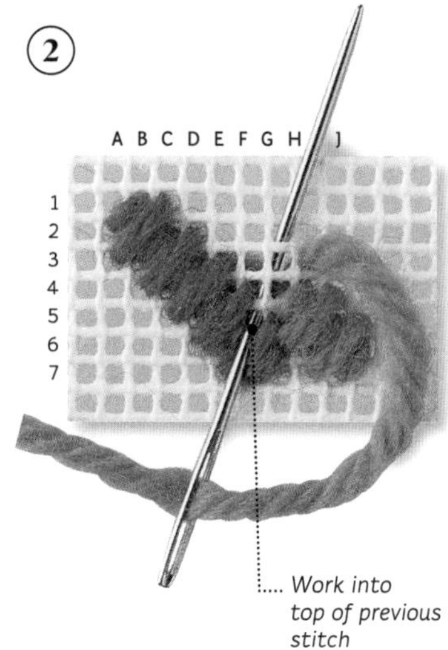

2
A B C D E F G H
J
1
2
3
4
5
6
7
Work into top of previous stitch

1 Start at top left. Make a short stitch from **1B** to **2A**, followed by a longer stitch from **1C** to **3A**. Continue working alternate long and short stitches downwards to the bottom edge of the area being filled.

2 The next row is worked upwards using the same or a different colour yarn. Begin with a short stitch from **6J** to **7I** and a long one from **5J** to **7H** and repeat to the end of the row. Repeat these two steps to continue.

Cashmere

LEVEL
Easy

USES
Textured plain or striped backgrounds and fillings

METHOD
Groups of three diagonal stitches worked vertically

MATERIALS
Any canvas; any thread

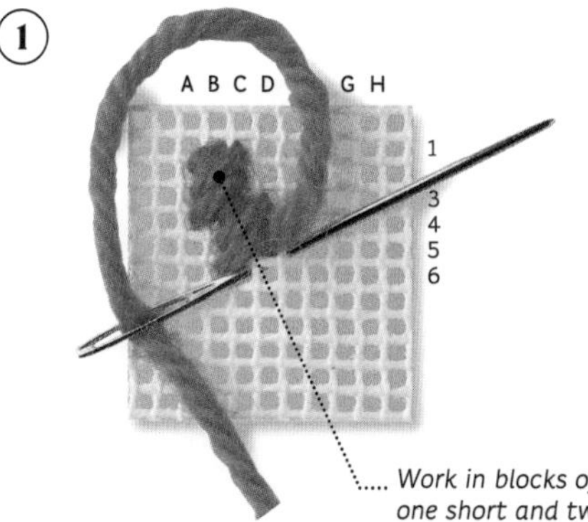

1
A B C D
G H
1
3
4
5
6

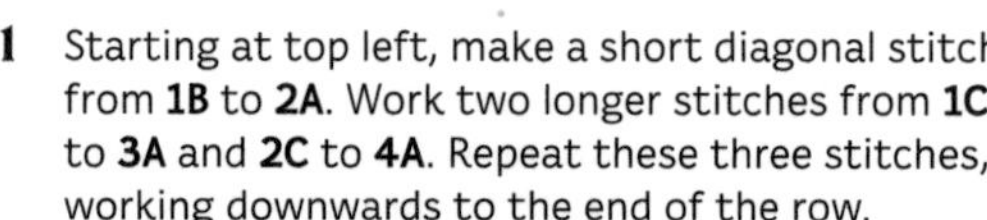

Work in blocks of one short and two long stitches

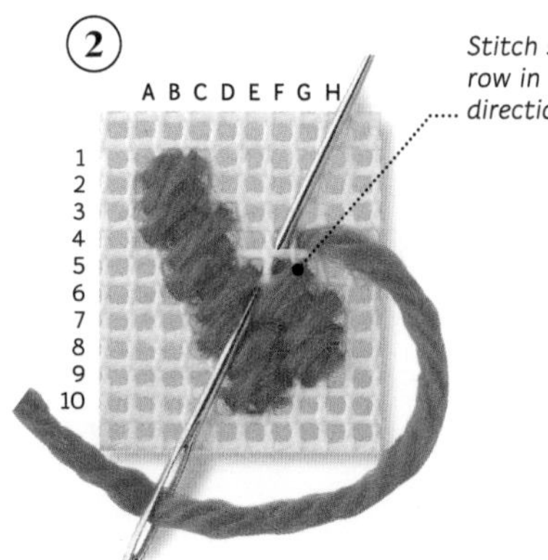

2
A B C D E F G H
1
2
3
4
5
6
7
8
9
10
Stitch second row in opposite direction

1 Starting at top left, make a short diagonal stitch from **1B** to **2A**. Work two longer stitches from **1C** to **3A** and **2C** to **4A**. Repeat these three stitches, working downwards to the end of the row.

2 The next row is worked upwards. Make a short stitch from **8H** to **9G** and the next two long stitches from **7H** to **9F** and **6H** to **8F**. Repeat steps 1 and 2 to fill the required area.

Technique Variation

Work alternate rows in a second colour to create a pattern of ridged diagonal stripes.

Diagonal

LEVEL
Easy

USES
Plain or striped filling or background for large areas

METHOD
Graduated straight stitches worked in diagonal rows

MATERIALS
Any canvas; one or two colours of any thread

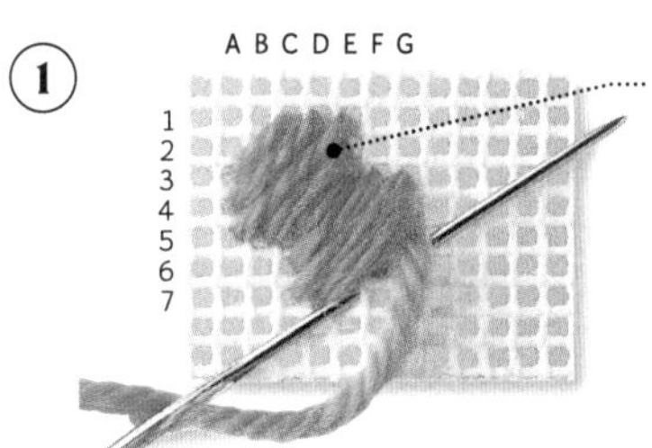

1
A B C D E F G
1 2 3 4 5 6 7
Work in blocks of four stitches

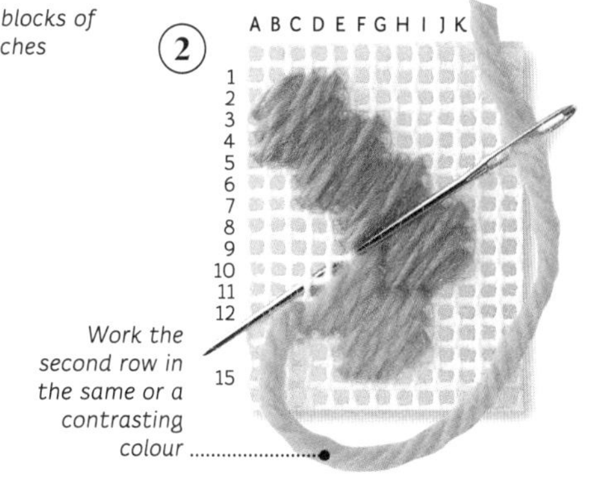

2
A B C D E F G H I J K
1 2 3 4 5 6 7 8 9 10 11 12 15
Work the second row in the same or a contrasting colour

1 Start at the top left corner. Each row is made up of blocks of four stitches, beginning with **1C** to **3A**, **1D** to **4A**, **1E** to **5A**, and **2E** to **5B**. Work the first stitch of the next block from **3E** to **5C** and continue working downwards.

2 The next row is worked upwards in the same way. Make the first block from **13I** to **15G**, **12I** to **15F**, **11I** to **15E**, and **11H** to **14E**. Repeat these two rows to continue and fill in the spaces with additional diagonal stitches (see p.19).

Technique Variation

For a more unusual effect, use one colour to sew the diagonal stitch, then work rows of contrasting back stitch (see p.40) between the lines. This will conceal any canvas that may show through and creates the illusion of a set of diagonal laid threads couched by zigzag lines of back stitch.

Byzantine

LEVEL
Step stitch

LEVEL
Easy

USES
Large scale fillings and backgrounds

METHOD
Diagonal straight stitches, worked in zigzag lines

MATERIALS
Any canvas; any thread

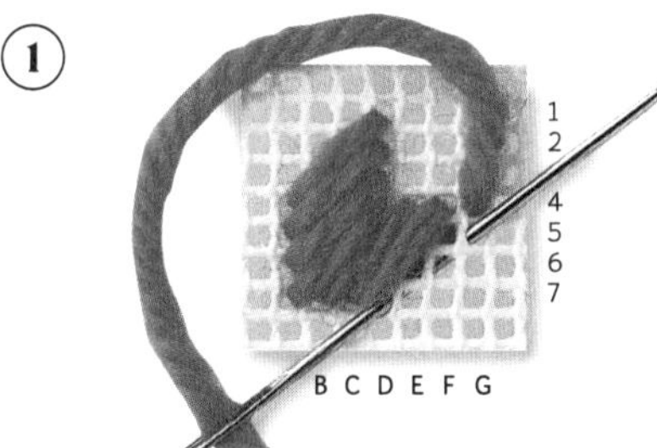

1
1 2 4 5 6 7
B C D E F G

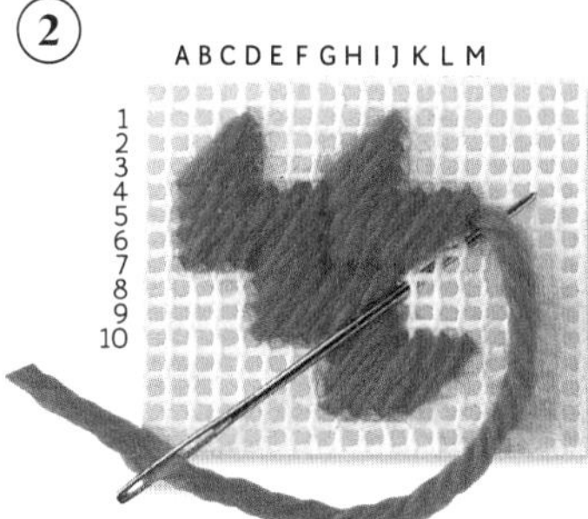

2
A B C D E F G H I J K L M
1 2 3 4 5 6 7 8 9 10

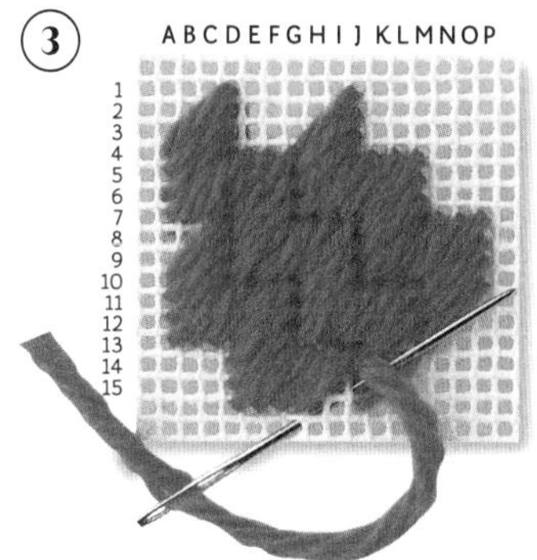

3
A B C D E F G H I J K L M N O P
1 2 3 4 5 6 7 8 9 10 11 12 13 14 15

1 Start at top left. Each zigzag is made up of repeated blocks of six diagonal stitches. Work the first four stitches downwards from **1D** to **4A**, **2D** to **5A**, **3D** to **6A**, and **4D** to **7A**. The next two stitches are worked to the right, from **4E** to **7B** and **4F** to **7C**. Start the next block at **4G**.

2 Work the second row level with and to the right of the first, starting at **1J** to **4G**. Make further rows to the right to fill the area required.

3 Complete any space at the bottom left corner with extra zigzags, starting at **10A** to **7D**, then work short stitches to fill the gaps (see p.19).

Jacquard

LEVEL
Intermediate

USES
Zigzag filling for large areas

METHOD
Stepped rows of alternate diagonal and tent stitch

MATERIALS
Single canvas; one or two colours of any threads

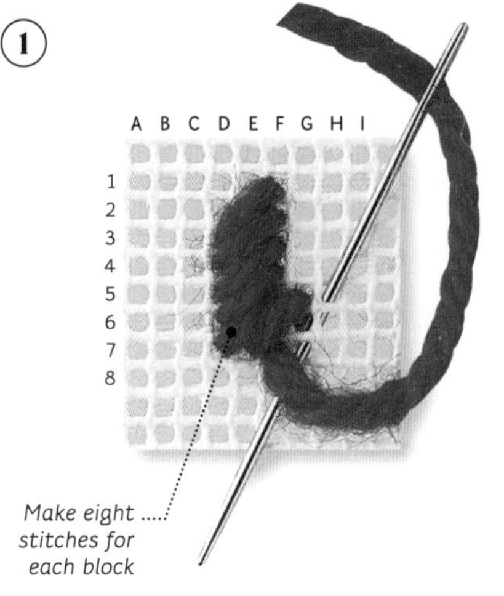
1
A B C D E F G H I
1 2 3 4 5 6 7 8
Make eight stitches for each block

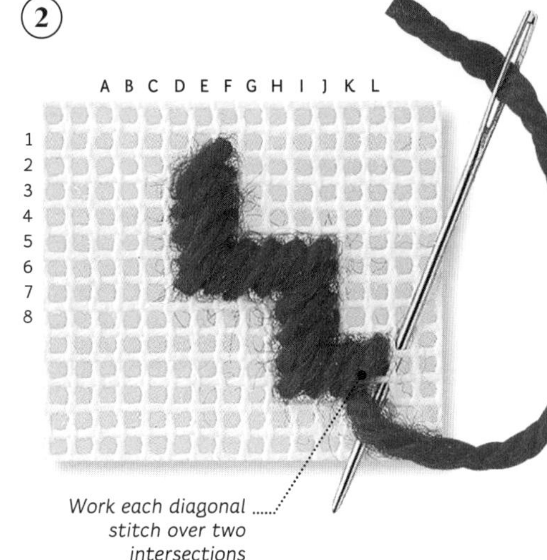
2
A B C D E F G H I J K L
1 2 3 4 5 6 7 8
Work each diagonal stitch over two intersections

3
A B C D E F G H I J K L M N
1 2 3 4 5 6 7 8
Work tent stitch over one intersection

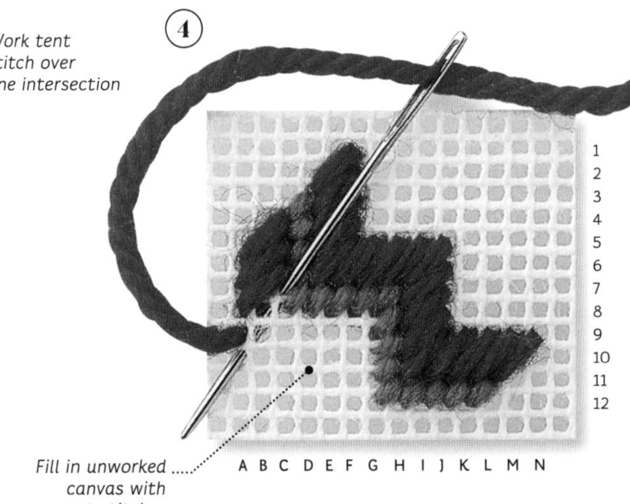
4
1 2 3 4 5 6 7 8 9 10 11 12
A B C D E F G H I J K L M N
Fill in unworked canvas with part stitches

1 Start at top left. Work a block of five diagonal stitches downwards from **3D** to **1F, 4D** to **2F, 5D** to **3F, 6D** to **4F**, and **7D** to **5F**, and three to the right from **7E** to **5G, 7F** to **5H**, and **7G** to **5I**.

2 Repeat this block to the bottom right corner of the area to be filled.

3 Using the second colour, work a block of five tent stitches downwards from **4C** to **3D, 5C** to **4D,** and **6C** to **5D, 7C** to **6D**, and **8C** to **7D** and three to the right from **8D** to **7E, 8E** to **7F, 8F** to **7G**. Repeat this block to the end of the row.

4 Repeat step 1, starting with **6A** to **4C**, then continue working these two rows in alternate colours to fill the space.

Technique Variation

Work this stitch in one single colour to create a brocade-like background. Lustrous threads give a smooth, shiny surface that will add to the woven effect.

Moorish

LEVEL
Intermediate

USES
Large-scale filling with zigzag pattern

METHOD
Alternate rows of graduated diagonal stitches and tent stitch

MATERIALS
Any canvas; any thread in one or two colours

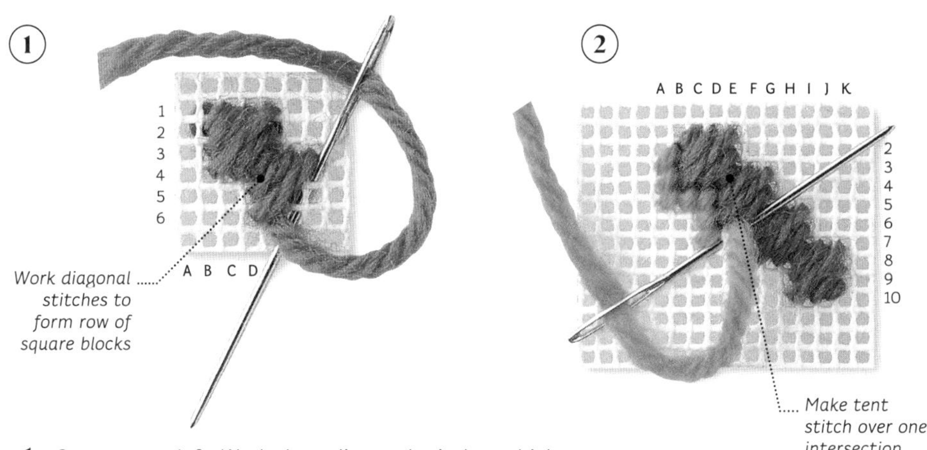
1
1
2
3
4
5
6
A B C D
Work diagonal stitches to form row of square blocks
2
A B C D E F G H I J K
2
3
4
5
6
7
8
9
10
Make tent stitch over one intersection

1 Start at top left. Work three diagonal stitches which increase in length from **2B** to **1C**, **3B** to **1D**, and **4A** to **1E**, then a shorter stitch from **4C** to **2E**. Repeat these four stitches to continue the row.

2 Using the second thread, work a stepped line of tent stitch to the left of the first row. Start with **2B** to **3A**, **3B** to **4A, 4B** to **5A** and **4C** to **5B**, then repeat these four stitches. Repeat steps 1 and 2 to continue, working each successive row into the spaces left by the row before.

Milanese

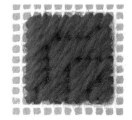

LEVEL
Intermediate

USES
Brocade-like background or filling for larger areas

METHOD
Diagonal rows of alternate long and short back stitch forming triangular pattern

MATERIALS
Any canvas; any thread

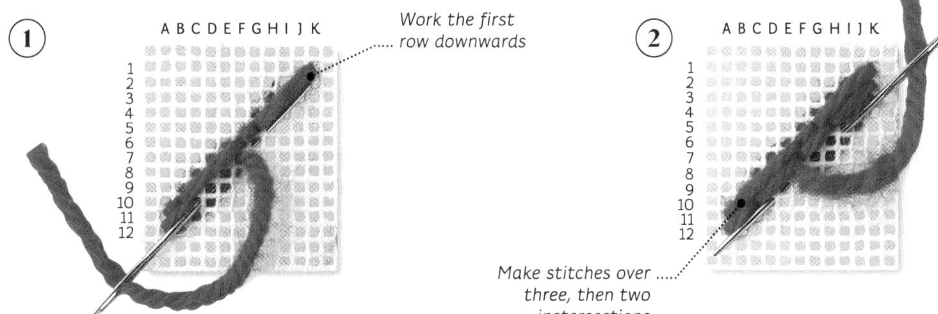
1
A B C D E F G H I J K
1
2
3
4
5
6
7
8
9
10
11
12
Work the first row downwards
2
A B C D E F G H I J K
1
2
3
4
5
6
7
8
9
10
11
12
Make stitches over three, then two instersections

1 Start at top right. Work a long stitch from **5G** to **1K** and a short stitch from **6F** to **5G**, then repeat these two stitches to the end of the line. Start the next row with a short stitch from **10C** to **12A** and a long stitch from **7F** to **10C**, and repeat these two stitches, working upwards.

2 Start the third row with **5I** to **3K** and **8F** to **5I**, and repeat these two stitches, working downwards.

3 Work the fourth row upwards, starting with **10E** to **14A** and **9F** to **10E**. Repeat these four rows to continue.

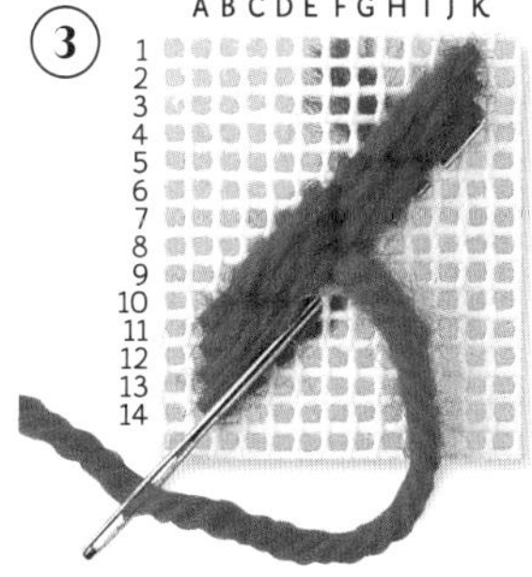
3
A B C D E F G H I J K
1
2
3
4
5
6
7
8
9
10
11
12
13
14

Mosaic

LEVEL
Easy

USES
Fine textured backgrounds

METHOD
Long and short diagonal stitches worked in horizontal rows to form square pattern

MATERIALS
Any canvas, any thread

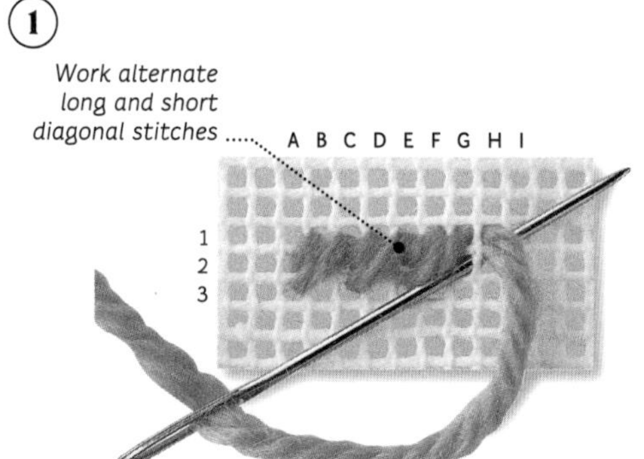
1
Work alternate long and short diagonal stitches
A B C D E F G H I
1
2
3

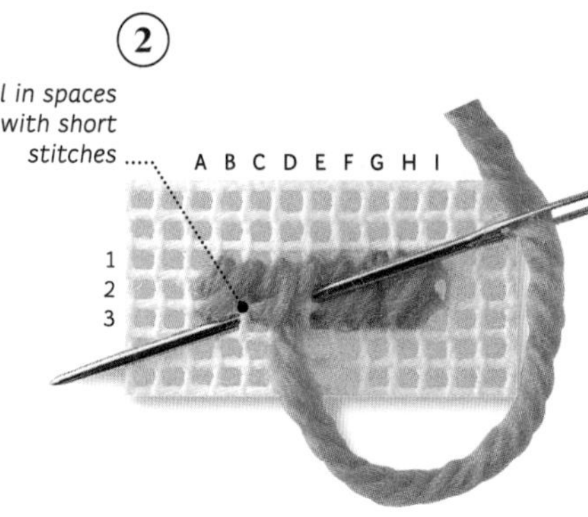
2
Fill in spaces with short stitches
A B C D E F G H I
1
2
3

1 Start at top left with two diagonal stitches from **1B** to **2A** and **1C** to **3A**. Repeat these two stitches to the end of the line.

2 Work the second row in the opposite direction. Make a short stitch from **3H** to **2I** to complete the first square, then continue working towards the left. Repeat these two rows to fill the required area.

Technique Variation

Change the visual effect by working the squares in two or more toning or contrasting colours to make a chequerboard pattern, ideal for filling smaller areas.

Cushion

LEVEL
Easy

USES
Filling or background with regular pattern of squares

METHOD
Graduated diagonal stitches worked in squares

MATERIALS
Any canvas; any thread

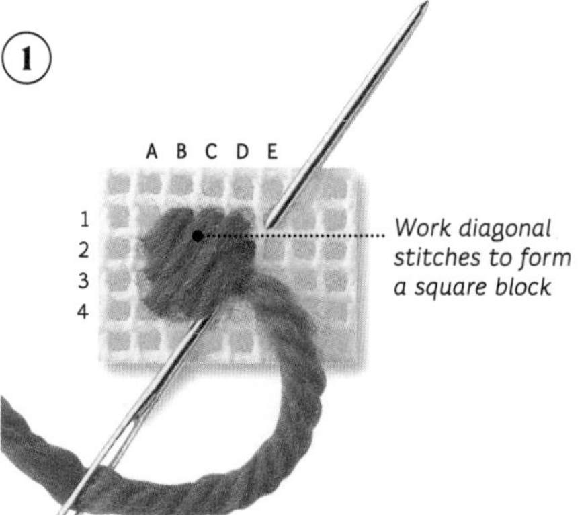
1
A B C D E
1
2
3
4
Work diagonal stitches to form a square block

2
A B C D E F G H I J
1
2
3
4
5

1 Starting at the top left corner, work five stitches from **1B** to **2A, 1C** to **3A, 1D** to **4A, 2D** to **4B** and **3D** to **4C**. Start the next block at **1E** to **2D** and continue to the end of the row.

2 Work the second row in the opposite direction, starting at **5G** to **4H**. Repeat steps 1 and 2 until the required space is filled.

Technique Variation

To prevent the canvas distorting, the square blocks can be worked in alternate directions using one or two colours.

Scottish

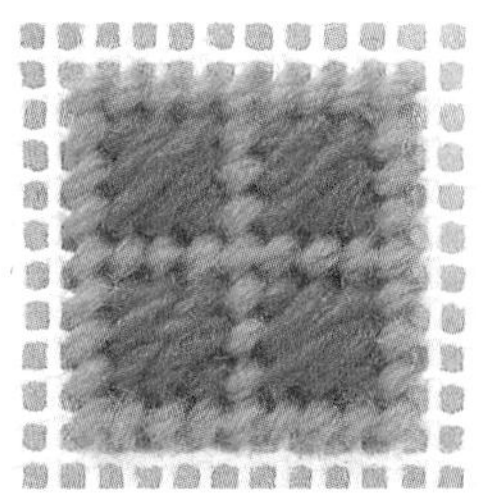

LEVEL
Intermediate

USES
Filling for large areas

METHOD
Cushion stitches framed with a grid of tent stitch

MATERIALS
Any canvas; any thread

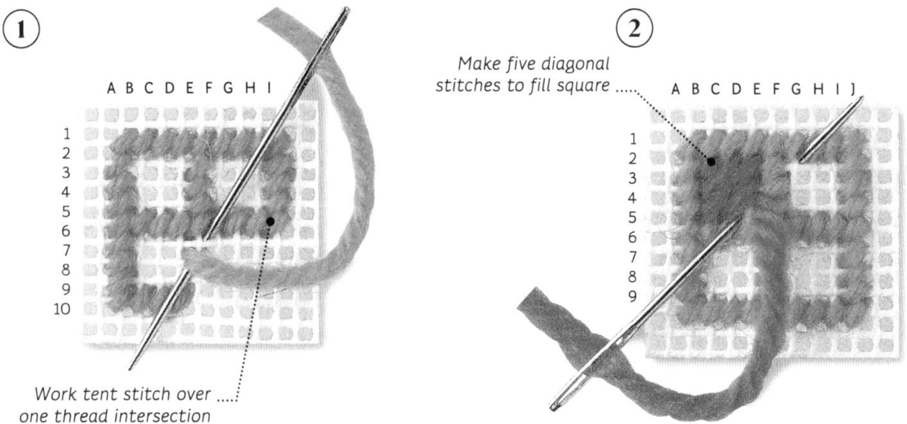
1
A B C D E F G H I
1 2 3 4 5 6 7 8 9 10
Work tent stitch over one thread intersection
2
Make five diagonal stitches to fill square
A B C D E F G H I J
1 2 3 4 5 6 7 8 9

1 Starting at top left, work the tent stitch frame (see p.129). Make a grid of horizontal and vertical rows, leaving a square of three canvas threads between the lines.

2 Fill the squares with cushion stitch (see p.136), using a second colour. Work the first block from **2C** to **3B**, **2D** to **4B**, **2E** to **5B, 3E** to **5C** and **4E** to **5D**, then come up at **2G** to start the next square.

Chequer

LEVEL
Intermediate

USES
Textured fillings

METHOD
Alternate large cushion stitches and square tent stitch blocks

MATERIALS
Any canvas; any thread in one or two colours

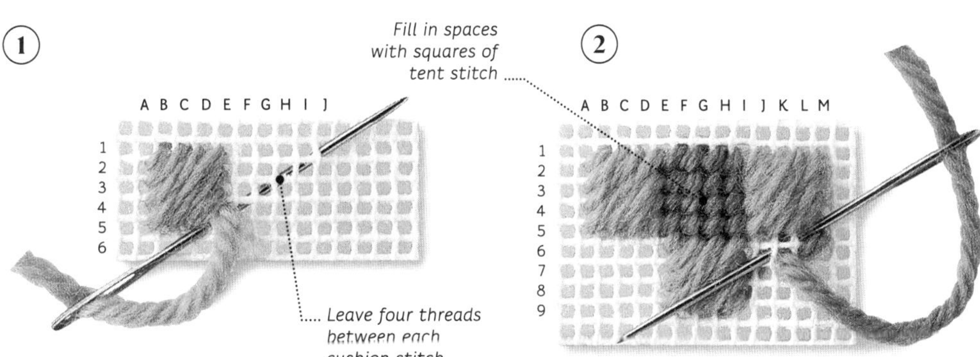
1
A B C D E F G H I J
1 2 3 4 5 6
Leave four threads between each cushion stitch
Fill in spaces with squares of tent stitch
2
A B C D E F G H I J K L M
1 2 3 4 5 6 7 8 9

1 Start at top left with the first cushion stitch. Make seven diagonal stitches from **1B** to **2A**, **1C** to **3A**, **1D** to **4A**, **1E** to **5A**, **2E** to **5B**, **3E** to **5C**, and **4E** to **5D**. Begin the next block with **1J** to **2I** and start the next row at **6E** to **5F**.

2 Using a second colour, work squares of tent stitch (see p.129) in the spaces between the cushion stitches. Starting with **2H** to **1I**, work four stitches, then work another three rows directly below. Repeat to fill all the unworked squares.

Cross and Star Needlepoint Stitches

These are the most complex and interesting stitches to work, all a combination of horizontal, vertical, and diagonal stitches. The various crosses feature two or more straight stitches that are worked one over the other, while the individual stitches that make up the stars radiate from a central point.

The heavier cross variations are worked on double canvas to give better coverage; the other stitches use single canvas. Whichever background is being used, the chosen thread should be thick enough to cover the canvas completely: mix woollen yarn and pearl threads to create multi-coloured patterns and textured effects.

Cross

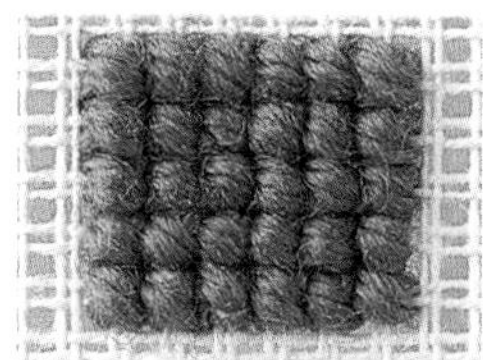

OTHER NAME
Berlin stitch

LEVEL
Easy

USES
Charted and printed designs; backgrounds

METHOD
Individual cross stitches, worked horizontally

MATERIALS
Double canvas; any thread or yarn

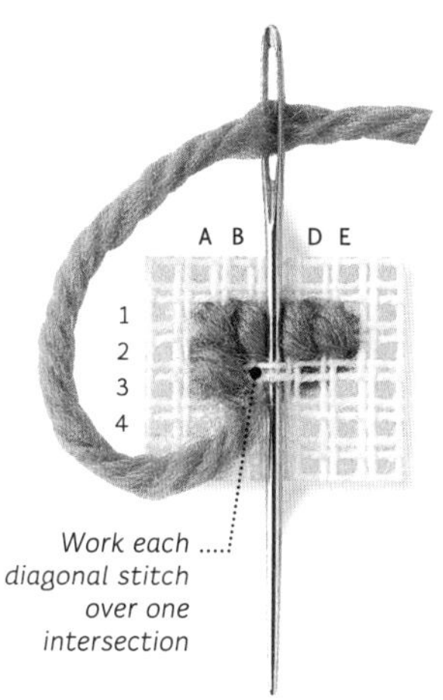
A B D E
1
2
3
4

Work each diagonal stitch over one intersection

Start at top right with two stitches from **1E** to **2D** and **1D** to **2E**. Begin the next cross at **1D** to **2C** and continue to the left. Work the first cross of the next row at **3A** to **2B** and **3B** to **2A**, then continue to the right. Repeat these two rows.

Diagonal Cross

LEVEL
Easy

USES
Backgrounds and fillings

METHOD
Single cross stitches, worked in diagonal rows

MATERIALS
Single canvas; any thread

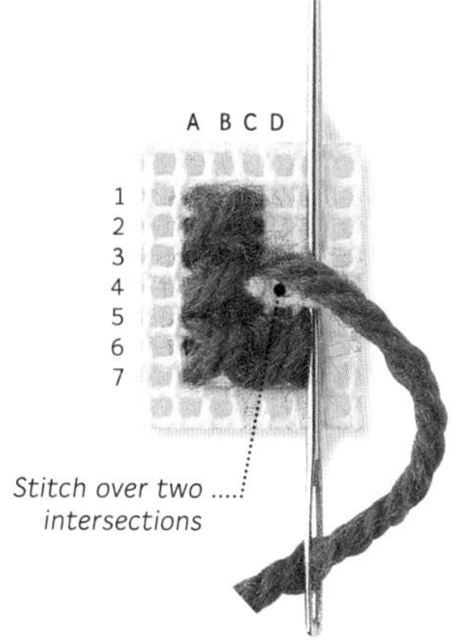
A B C D
1
2
3
4
5
6
7

Stitch over two intersections

Start at bottom left. Work three crosses from **5A** to **7C** and **5C** to **7A**; **7E** to **5C** and **7C** to **5E**; **5C** to **3A** and **5A** to **3C**. Begin the next row at **1A** to **3C** and **1C** to **3A**, and start the second cross at **3C** to **5E**. Repeat these two rows.

Double Cross

LEVEL
Intermediate

USES
Two-coloured backgrounds

METHOD
Spaced cross stitches with overlapping rows of elongated crosses

MATERIALS
Double canvas; thin and thick thread in two colours

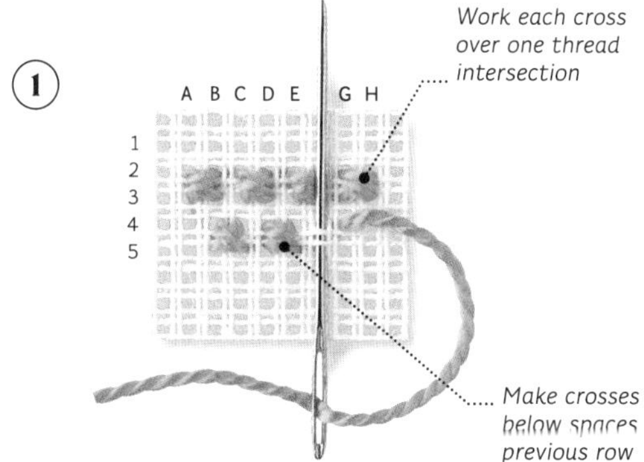
1
A B C D E G H
1
2
3
4
5

Work each cross over one thread intersection

Make crosses below spaces in previous row

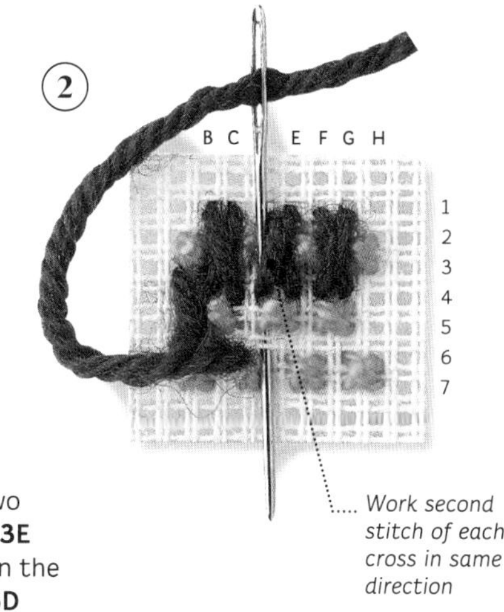
2
B C E F G H
1
2
3
4
5
6
7

Work second stitch of each cross in same direction

1 Start at top right, using the fine thread. Make two crosses from **2H** to **3G** and **2G** to **3H**, then **2F** to **3E** and **2E** to **3F** and continue towards the left. Begin the next row with **4C** to **5B** and **4B** to **5C** and **4E** to **5D** and **4D** to **5E**. Repeat these two rows.

2 Fill in the spaces with rows of long crosses in the thick thread, worked in alternate directions. Start with **4F** to **1G** and **4G** to **1F** and work towards the left. Begin the next row with a cross from **6A** to **3B** and **6B** to **3A** and continue towards the right.

Upright Cross

OTHER NAMES
Straight cross

LEVEL
Easy

USES
Fine textured backgrounds

METHOD
Crosses worked singly in interlocking diagonal rows

MATERIALS
Any canvas; any thread

Start at top left with two crosses from **3B** to **1B** and **2A** to **2C**, and **4C** to **2C** and **3B** to **3D**; continue downwards. Start the next row with **7D** to **5D** and **6C** to **6E**, **6C** to **4C** and **5B** to **5D** and continue upwards. Repeat these two rows to fill the required area.

Diamond Cross

LEVEL
Intermediate

USES
Raised backgrounds and textured fillings

METHOD
Cross stitches worked over larger upright cross stitches

MATERIALS
Single canvas; any thread

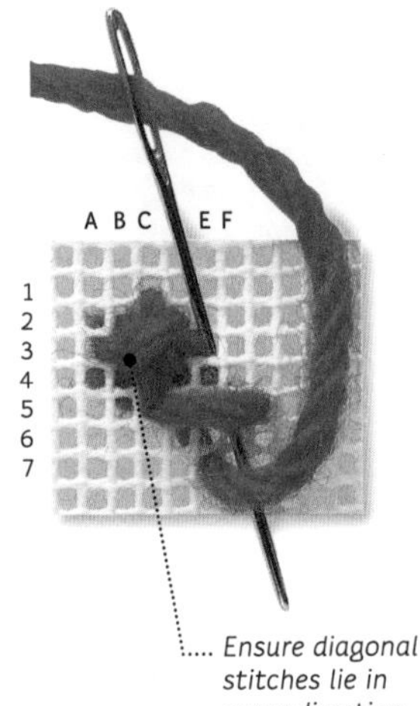
A B C E F
1
2
3
4
5
6
7
Ensure diagonal stitches lie in same direction

Start at top left. Work an upright cross from **3E** to **3A** and **5C** to **1C** covered by a cross from **4D** to **2B** and **4B** to **2D**. Begin the next stitch at **5G** to **5C**, then continue working in diagonal rows.

Smyrna Cross

OTHER NAMES
Leviathan stitch

LEVEL
Easy

USES
Raised backgrounds

METHOD
Upright cross worked over cross stitch

MATERIALS
Single canvas; any thread

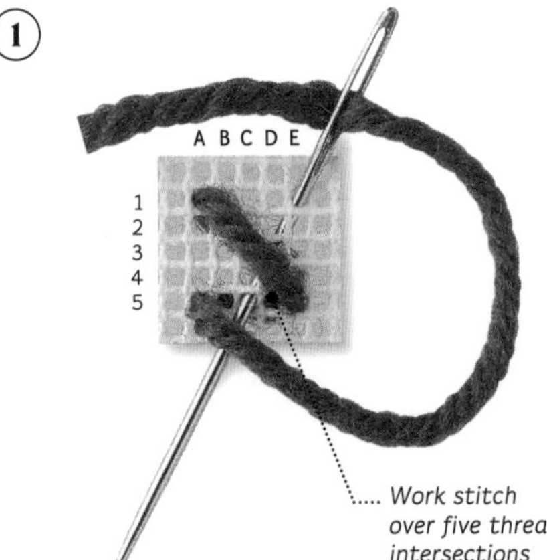
1
A B C D E
1
2
3
4
5
Work stitch over five thread intersections

2
Always work stitches in same order
A B C D
1
2
3
4
5

1 Start at top left with a diagonal stitch from **1A** to **5E** crossed by a second stitch from **5A** to **1E**. Bring the needle out at **5C**.

2 Make an upright stitch to **1C** and a horizontal stitch from **3A** to **3E**. Bring the needle out at **1E** to begin the next stitch, then continue working in horizontal rows.

Technique Variation

Work alternate crosses in toning or contrasting colours to create an all-over chequer pattern, for a colourful background.

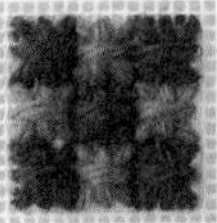

Double Leviathan

LEVEL
Intermediate

USES
Highly textured filling

METHOD
Smyrna cross variation

MATERIALS
Single canvas; any yarn or thread - lustrous pearl cotton gives good result

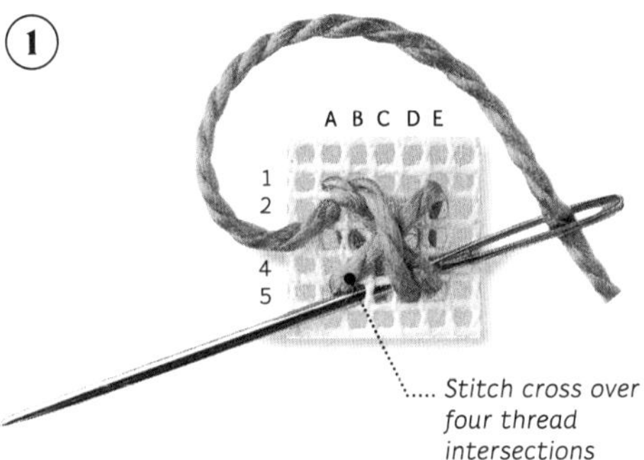

①
A B C D E
1
2
4
5
Stitch cross over four thread intersections

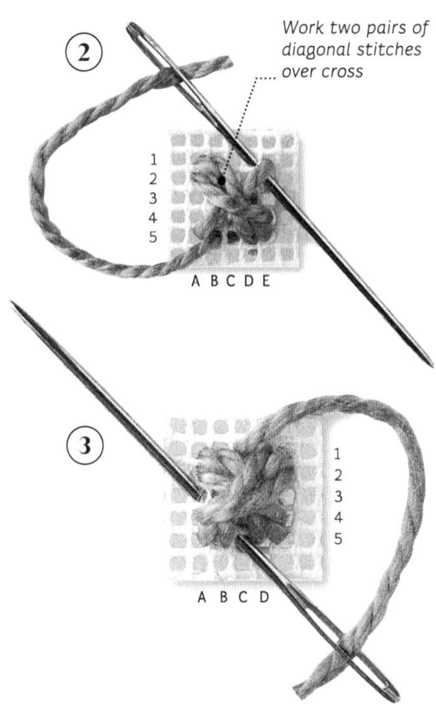

②
Work two pairs of diagonal stitches over cross
1
2
3
4
5
A B C D E
③
1
2
3
4
5
A B C D

1 Start at top left with a cross stitch from **1A** to **5E** and **1E** to **5A**. Work two diagonal stitches from **5D** to **1B** and **2A** to **4E** and bring the needle out at **5B**.

2 Make a diagonal stitch to **1D** and come up at **2E**.

3 Insert the needle at **4A**, then finish with an upright cross from **1C** to **5C** and **3A** to **3E**. Start the next stitch at **5A** and continue in horizontal rows.

Diagonal Tweed

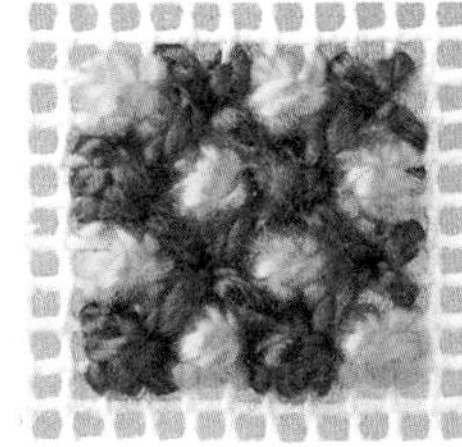

LEVEL
Intermediate

USES
Two-colour filling with raised surface

METHOD
Smyrna crosses alternated with large crosses covered by small upright crosses

MATERIALS
Single canvas; two colours of any thread

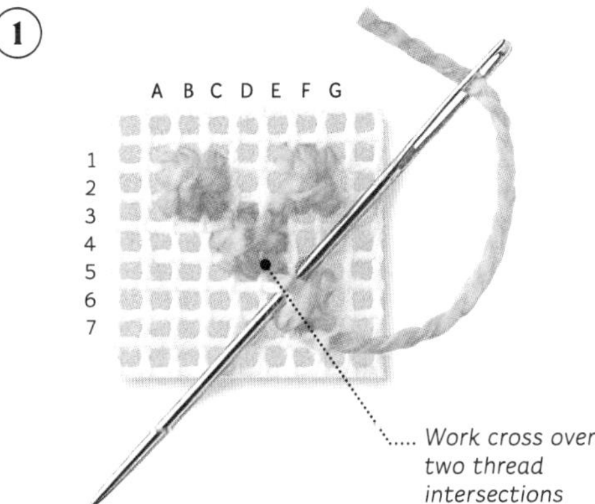

①
A B C D E F G
1
2
3
4
5
6
7
Work cross over two thread intersections

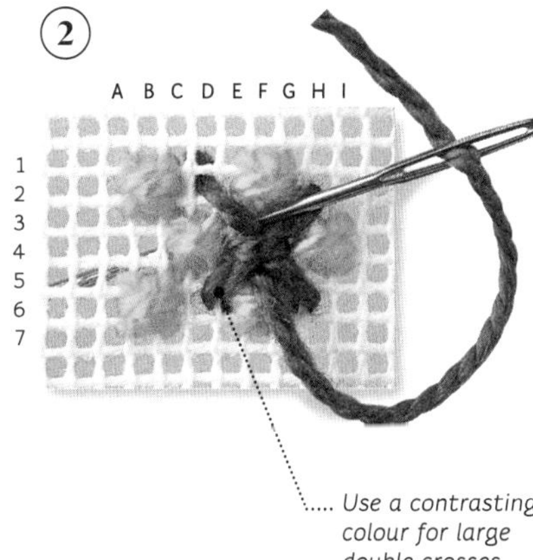

②
A B C D E F G H I
1
2
3
4
5
6
7
Use a contrasting colour for large double crosses

1 Starting at top left, work a series of small Smyrna cross stitches (see left). Leave two threads between each stitch and work the crosses in subsequent rows beneath these gaps.

2 Using the second thread, work a cross stitch from **6H** to **2D** and **6D** to **2H**. Make a horizontal stitch from **4E** to **4G**, then an upright stitch from **6F** to **3F**. Start the next large cross at **6D** and repeat along the row.

Broad Cross

LEVEL
Intermediate

USES
Basketweave filling for large areas

METHOD
Large square crosses worked in horizontal rows

MATERIALS
Single canvas; any thread

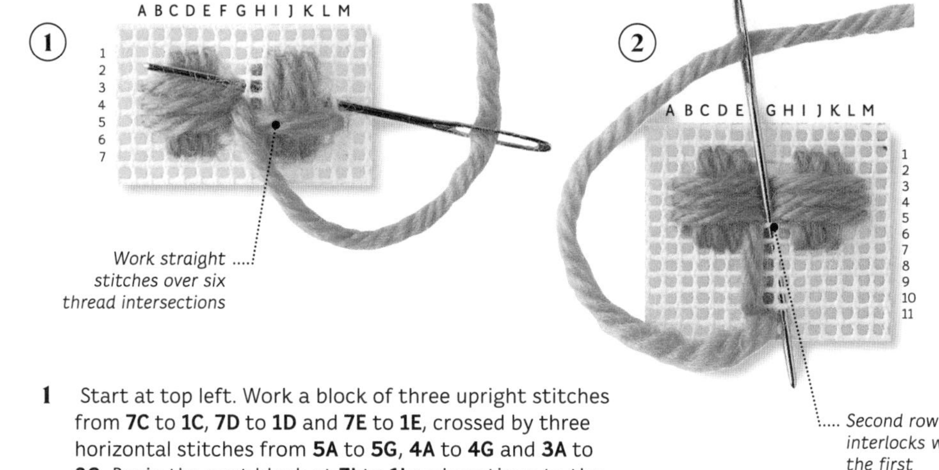

1
A B C D E F G H I J K L M
1
2
3
4
5
6
7
2
A B C D E G H I J K L M
1
2
3
4
5
6
7
8
9
10
11

Work straight stitches over six thread intersections

Second row interlocks with the first

1 Start at top left. Work a block of three upright stitches from **7C** to **1C**, **7D** to **1D** and **7E** to **1E**, crossed by three horizontal stitches from **5A** to **5G**, **4A** to **4G** and **3A** to **3G**. Begin the next block at **7I** to **1I** and continue to the end of the row.

2 The second row fits into the spaces between the crosses; begin the first block at **11F** and work subsequent rows in the same way, alternately from right to left.

Cross-corner Cushion

LEVEL
Intermediate

USES
Filling for large areas

METHOD
Cushion stitch variation with two layers of stitches, forming a diagonal pattern

MATERIALS
Single canvas; any thread – twisted embroidery cotton gives good results

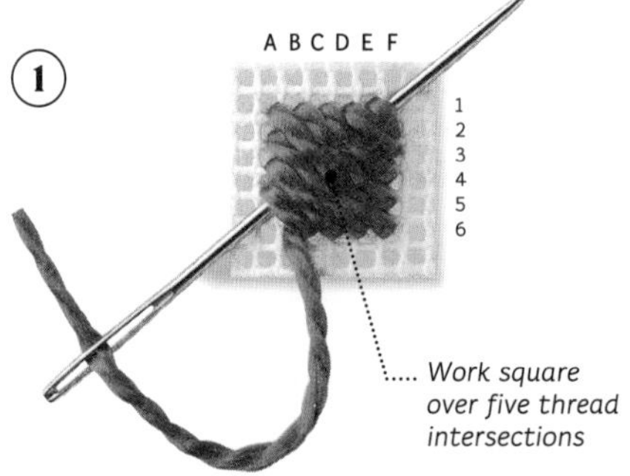

1
A B C D E F
1
2
3
4
5
6

Work square over five thread intersections

Work second layer of stitches at right angles to first

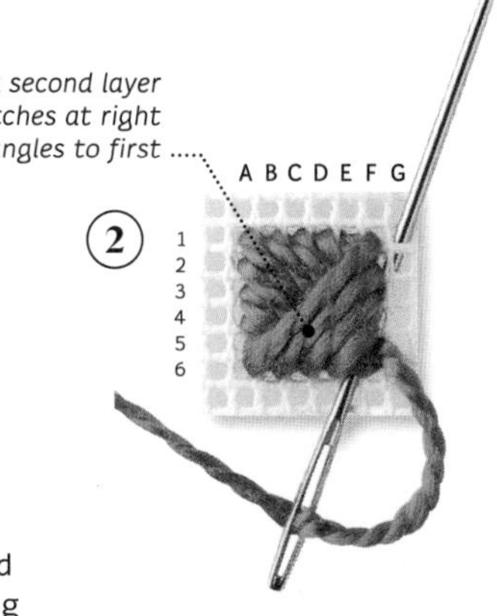

2
A B C D E F G
1
2
3
4
5
6

1 Start at top left with a square of nine graduated diagonal stitches starting at **2F** to **1E** and ending with **6B** to **5A**.

2 Work five more stitches in the opposite direction, from **1F** to **6A**, **2F** to **6B**, **3F** to **6C**, **4F** to **6D**, and **5F** to **6E**.

3 Repeat steps 1 and 2 along the row, reversing every other square. Work the next and subsequent rows as a mirror image of the one above.

3
A B C D E F G H I J K
1
2
3
4
5
6

Brighton

LEVEL
Intermediate

USES
Dense fillings and backgrounds

METHOD
Straight stitch hexagons, interspersed with contrasting upright crosses

MATERIALS
Single canvas; two colours of any thread

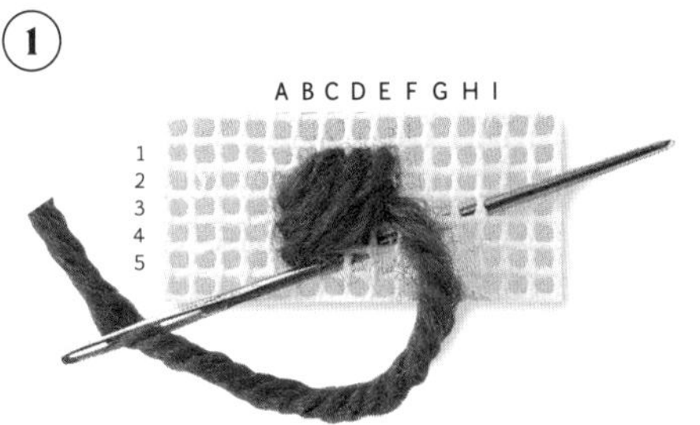
1
A B C D E F G H I
1
2
3
4
5

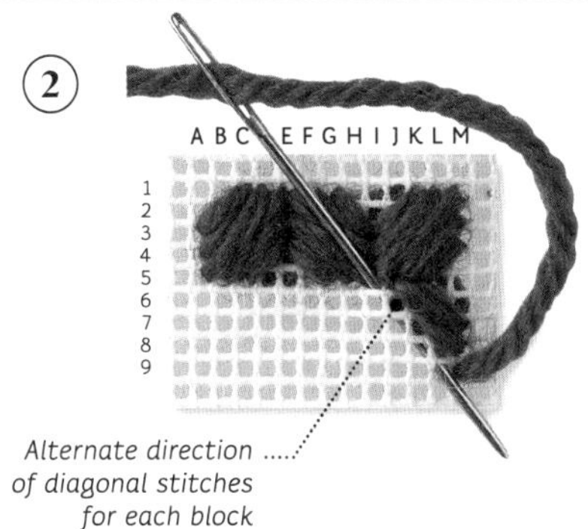
2
1
2
3
4
5
6
7
8
9

Alternate direction of diagonal stitches for each block

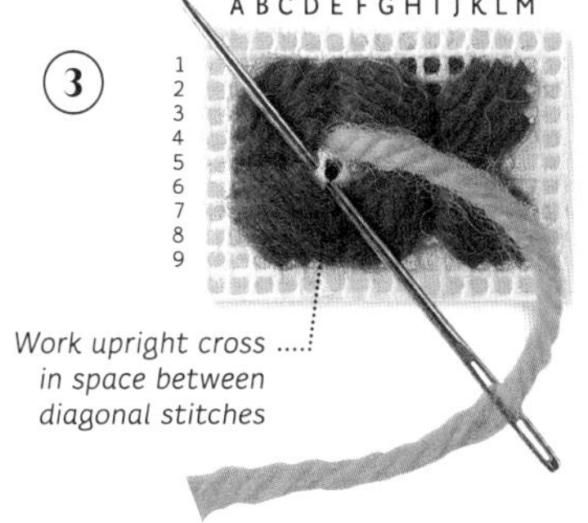
3
A B C D E F G H I J K L M
1
2
3
4
5
6
7
8
9

Work upright cross in space between diagonal stitches

1 Starting at top left, make a hexagonal block of five diagonal stitches from **1C** to **3A**, **1D** to **4A**, **1E** to **5A**, **2E** to **5B**, and **3E** to **5C**.

2 Reverse the direction for the second hexagon, starting at **3I** to **1G**. Repeat these two blocks to the end of the line. Work each subsequent row as a mirror image of the one above.

3 Using a contrasting thread, work an upright cross from **4E** to **6E** and **5D** to **5F**. Repeat to fill each space.

Rice

OTHER NAME
William and Mary stitch

LEVEL
Intermediate

USES
Solid lattice filling

METHOD
Back stitch square worked over large cross stitch

MATERIALS
Single canvas; one thick and one fine thread

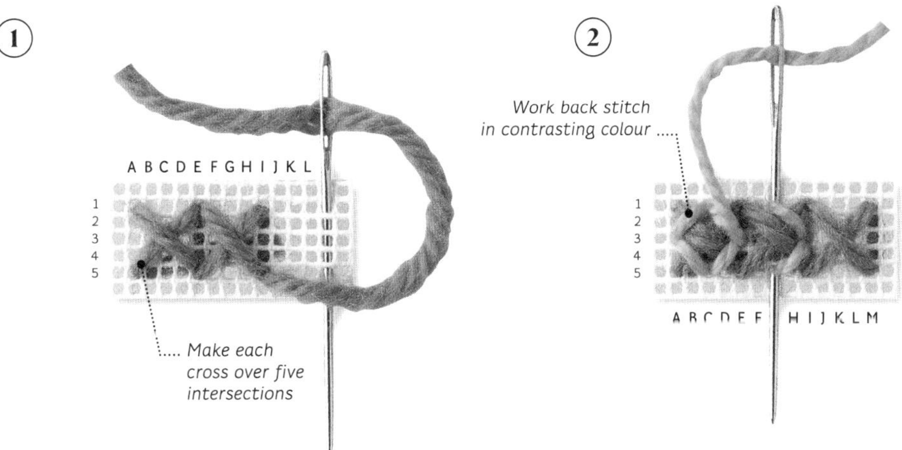
1
A B C D E F G H I J K L
1
2
3
4
5
2
1
2
3
4
5

Make each cross over five intersections

Work back stitch in contrasting colour

1 Start at top left. Using the thick thread, make a large cross stitch from **5A** to **1E** and **5E** to **1A**. Begin the next cross at **5E** to **1I** and continue along the row.

2 With the fine thread, work four back stitches over the first cross from **3E** to **5C**, **1C** to **3E**, **3A** to **1C**, and **5C** to **3A**. Repeat for each cross, starting the next back stitch square at **3I** to **5G**. Work the following rows in the same way, directly below the first.

Plaited Gobelin

LEVEL
Easy

USES
Woven effect backgrounds; filling for large areas

METHOD
Gobelin variation, worked in overlapping rows

MATERIALS
Double canvas; tapestry yarn or other thick thread

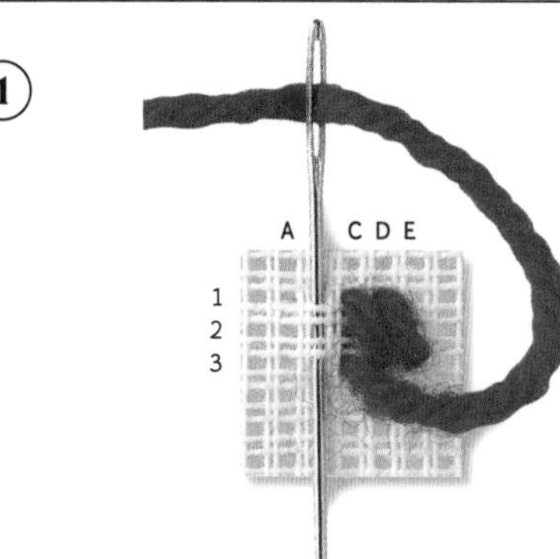

1
A C D E
1
2
3

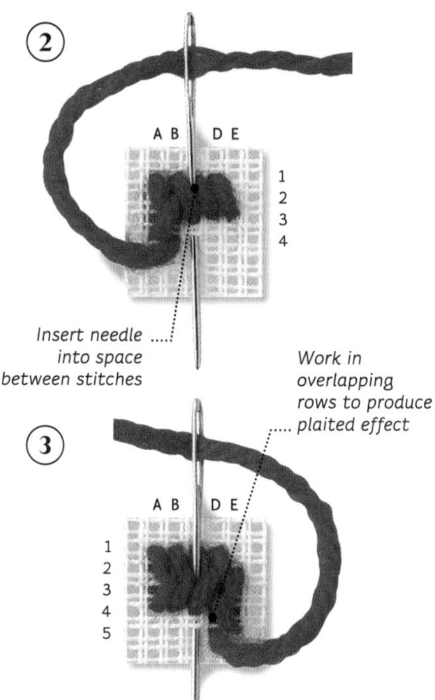

2
A B D E
1
2
3
4
Insert needle into space between stitches
Work in overlapping rows to produce plaited effect
3
A B D E
1
2
3
4
5

1 Start at the top right corner with a diagonal stitch from **3E** to **1D**. Work the next from **3D** to **1C** and continue stitching towards the left.

2 Begin the next row at **4A** to **2B** and repeat this stitch to the end of the row.

3 Work the third row as the first, starting at **5E** to **3D**. Continue working alternately to the left, then right.

Greek

LEVEL
Easy

USES
In single rows as outline; textured filling

METHOD
Herringbone variation, worked in horizontal rows

MATERIALS
Double canvas; any thick thread

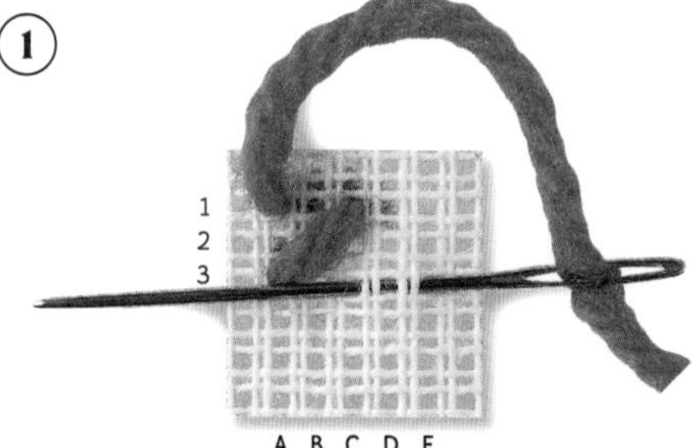

1
1
2
3
A B C D E

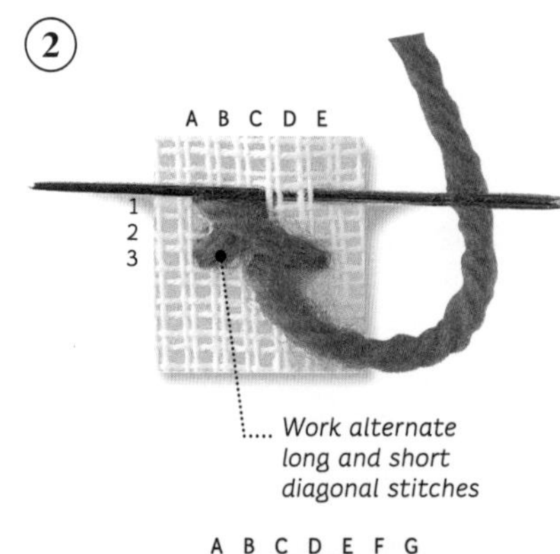

2
A B C D E
1
2
3
Work alternate long and short diagonal stitches

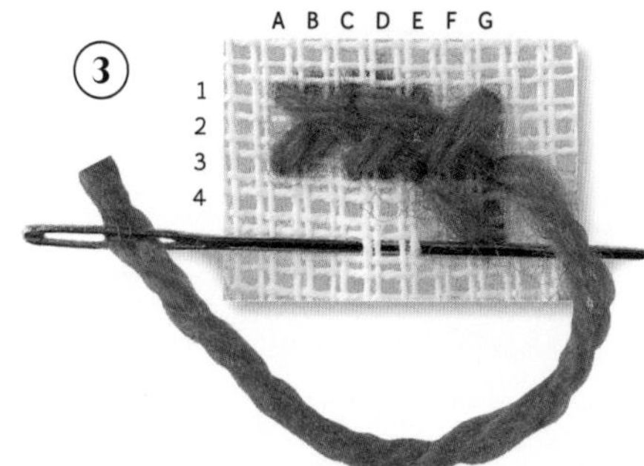

3
A B C D E F G
1
2
3
4

1 Start at top left. Make a short stitch from **1C** to **3A**, then a long stitch from **1A** to **3E**. Come up at **3C**.

2 Make a short stitch to **1E**, then continue working alternate long and short stitches to the end of the line.

3 Work the second row in the opposite direction starting with **5G** to **3E** and **3G** to **5C**. Repeat these two rows to continue.

Plait

LEVEL
Easy

USES
Solid ridged backgrounds; in single row as outline

METHOD
Rows of overlapping straight stitches

MATERIALS
Double canvas; any thick thread

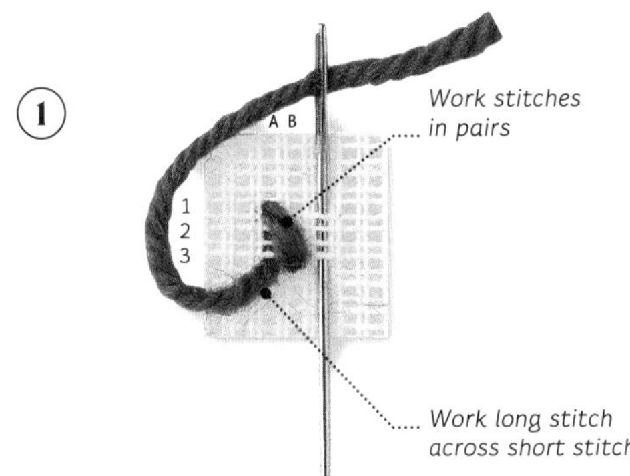
1
A B
Work stitches in pairs
1
2
3
Work long stitch across short stitch

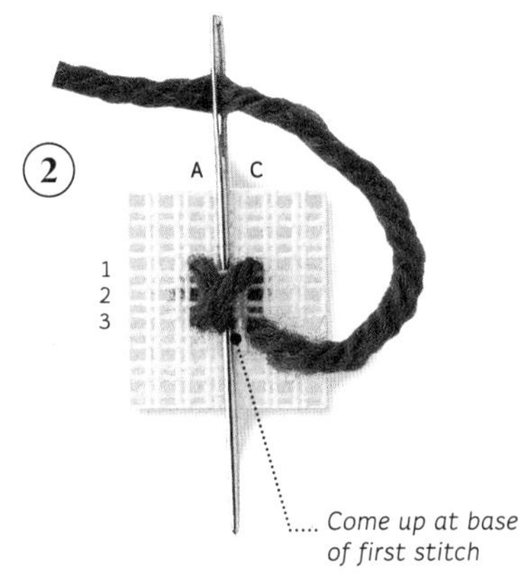
2
A C
1
2
3
Come up at base of first stitch

1 Start at top left with a diagonal stitch from **3B** to **1A**, crossed by a longer stitch from **3A** to **1C**. Come out at **3C** to start the next pair of stitches.

2 Work a short stitch up to **1B** and come out at **3B**. Continue working pairs of stitches to the end of the line, then stitch the second and subsequent rows directly below the first.

Technique Variation

Plait stitch can also be worked in vertical rows, depending on the effect required and the shape of the area to be filled.

Fishbone

LEVEL
Intermediate

USES
Textured chevron filling for large areas

METHOD
Diagonal stitches worked in alternate directions in vertical rows

MATERIALS
Double canvas; tapestry yarn or other thick thread

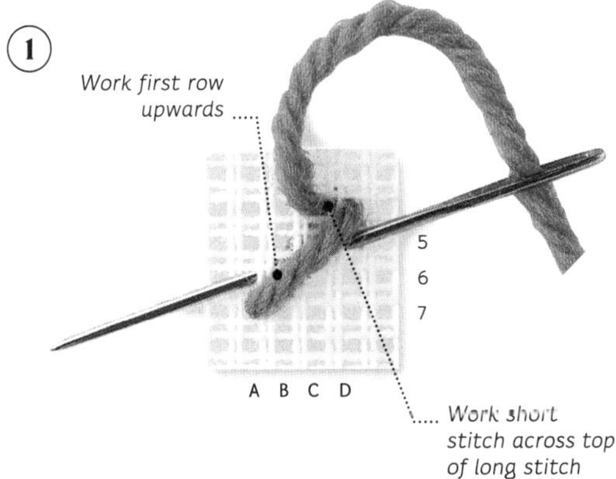
1
Work first row upwards
5
6
7
A B C D
Work short stitch across top of long stitch

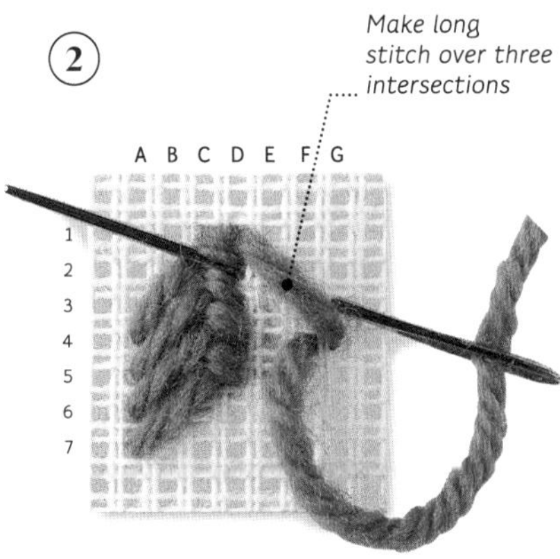
2
Make long stitch over three intersections
A B C D E F G
1
2
3
4
5
6
7

1 Start at bottom left. Make a long diagonal stitch from **7A** to **4D** and a short stitch from **4C** to **5D**. Come up at **6A** and repeat these two stitches to the end of the row.

2 Work the second row downwards. Make the first two stitches from **1D** to **4G** and **4F** to **3G**, then come up at **2D**. Repeat steps 1 and 2 to fill the required area.

Technique Variation

Repeat step 1 only to vary the surface of the stitch and work the rows in alternate light and dark colours to make a pattern of bold ridged vertical stripes.

Fern

LEVEL
Easy

USES
Ridged fillings and backgrounds

METHOD
Pairs of overlapping diagonal stitches worked in vertical rows

MATERIALS
Double canvas; any thick thread or yarn

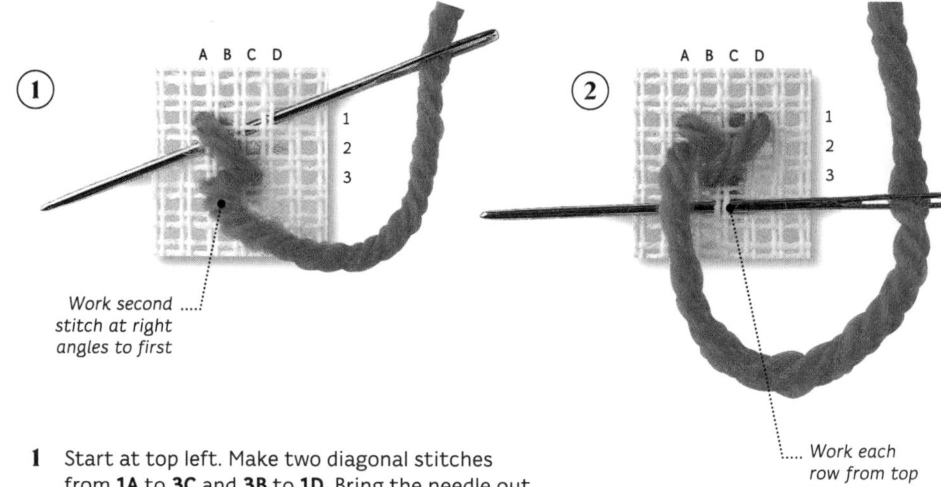

1
A B C D
1
2
3
Work second stitch at right angles to first
2
A B C D
1
2
3
Work each row from top to bottom

1 Start at top left. Make two diagonal stitches from **1A** to **3C** and **3B** to **1D**. Bring the needle out at **2A** ready to start the next stitches.

2 Work the next pair of stitches directly below the first, from **2A** to **4C** and **4B** to **2D**. Continue working downwards to the end of the row. Start the next row at **1D**.

Fir

OTHER NAME
Leaf stitch

LEVEL
Intermediate

USES
Filling for large areas

METHOD
Interlocking rows of hexagonal blocks

MATERIALS
Any canvas; any thread

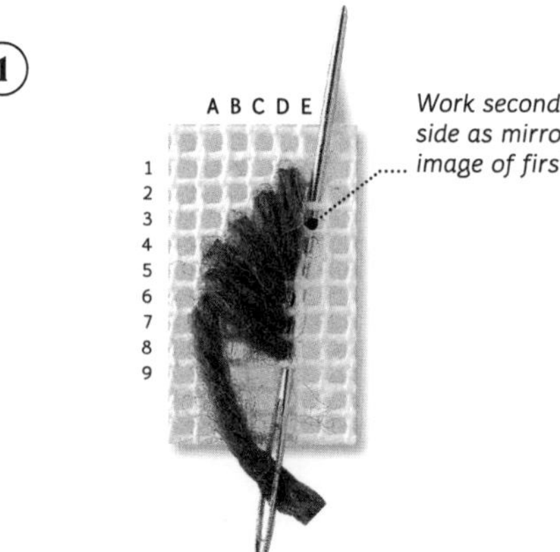

1
A B C D E
1
2
3
4
5
6
7
8
9
Work second side as mirror image of first

2
A B C D E F G H I J
1
2
3
4
5
6
7
8
9
Make eleven straight stitches for each block

1 Start at top left with an upright stitch from **1D** to **5D**. Work three slanting stitches from **2C** to **5D**, **3B** to **6D**, and **4A** to **7D**. Make two more stitches directly below, from **5A** to **8D** and **7A** to **9D**. Come up at **2E**.

2 Make six stitches to mirror step 1 from **2E** to **5D**, to **7G** to **9D**. Start the second block with **1J** to **5J** and continue working to the right. Stitch the next row into the spaces below the first.

Technique Variation

Work an upright stitch from **5D** to **9D** to vary the leaf shape and stitch the rows in two contrasting colours to create a striped filling.

Rhodes

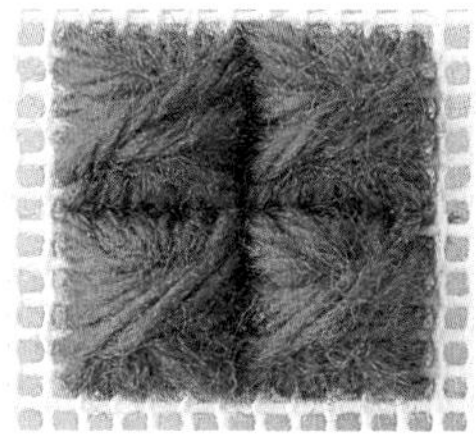

LEVEL
Intermediate

USES
3-dimensional fillings or background

METHOD
Raised square stitch worked in straight row

MATERIALS
Single canvas; any thread

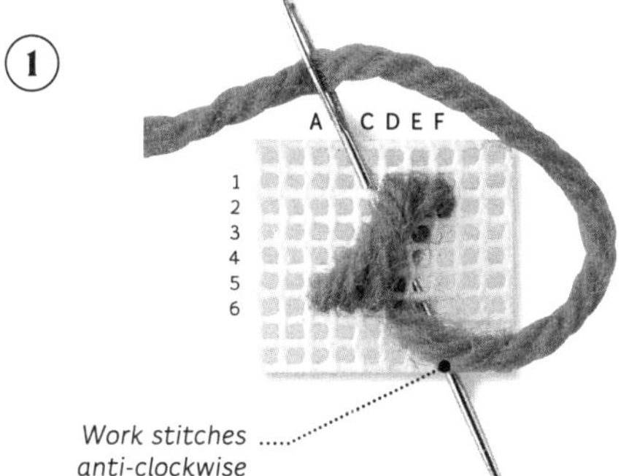
1
A C D E F
1
2
3
4
5
6
Work stitches anti-clockwise

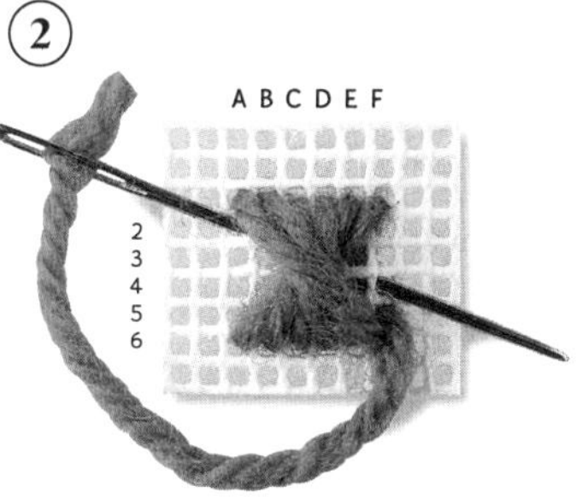
2
A B C D E F
2
3
4
5
6

1 Start at top left and work four diagonal stitches from **6A** to **1F**, **6B** to **1E**, **6C** to **1D** and **6D** to **1C**. Come up at **6E**.

2 Work another two stitches from **6E** to **1B**, and **6F** to **1A**. Insert the needle at **1B**, then come up at **4F**.

3 Make three more stitches to complete the square from **4F** to **3A**, **3F** to **4A**, and **2F** to **5A**. Come up at **6F**, ready to make the next block. Work the following rows directly below.

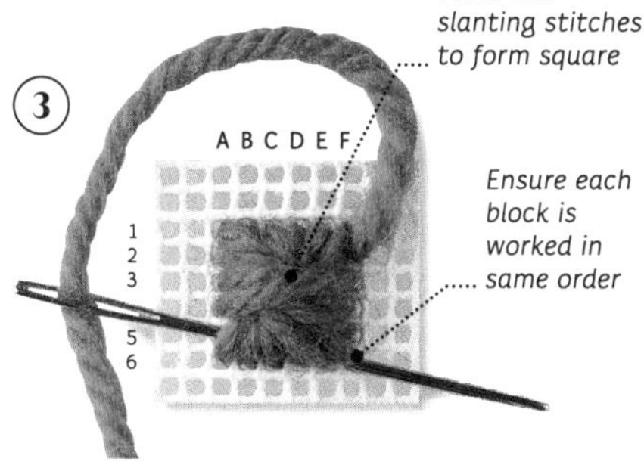
3
Make ten slanting stitches to form square
A B C D E F
1
2
3
5
6
Ensure each block is worked in same order

Half Rhodes

LEVEL
Intermediate

USES
Striped raised filling for large areas or backgrounds

METHOD
Rhodes stitch variation worked in diagonal rows

MATERIALS
Single canvas; any thread in one or two colours

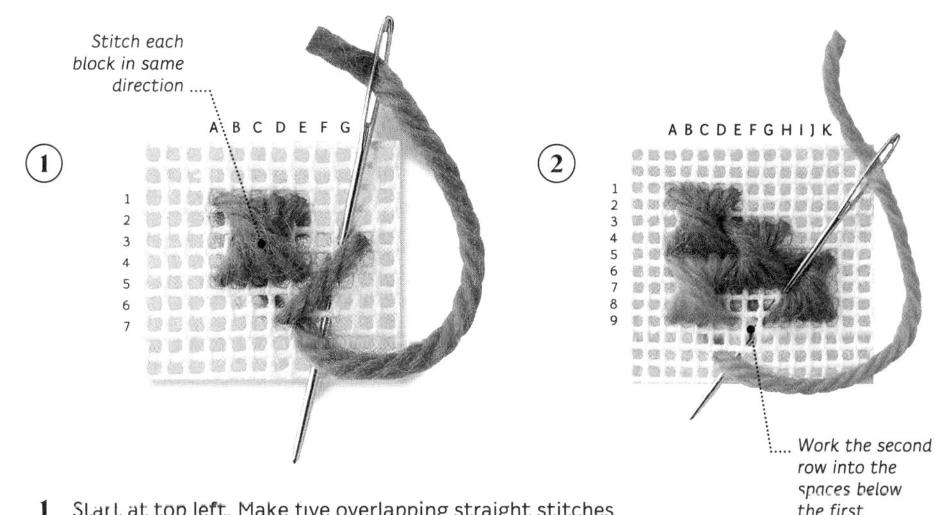
Stitch each block in same direction
1
A B C D E F G
1
2
3
4
5
6
7
2
A B C D E F G H I J K
1
2
3
4
5
6
7
8
9
Work the second row into the spaces below the first

1 Start at top left. Make five overlapping straight stitches from **5A** to **1E**, **5B** to **1D**, **5C** to **1C**, **5D** to **1B**, and **5E** to **1A**. Come up at **7D** to make the next block, then continue working downwards to the right.

2 Stitch the second row in a different colour, starting at **9A** to **5E**. Work the next and subsequent rows directly below the first.

Star

OTHER NAME
Algerian eye stitch

LEVEL
Intermediate

USES
Fine textured filling

METHOD
Straight stitch stars worked in horizontal rows

MATERIALS
Single canvas; thick thread

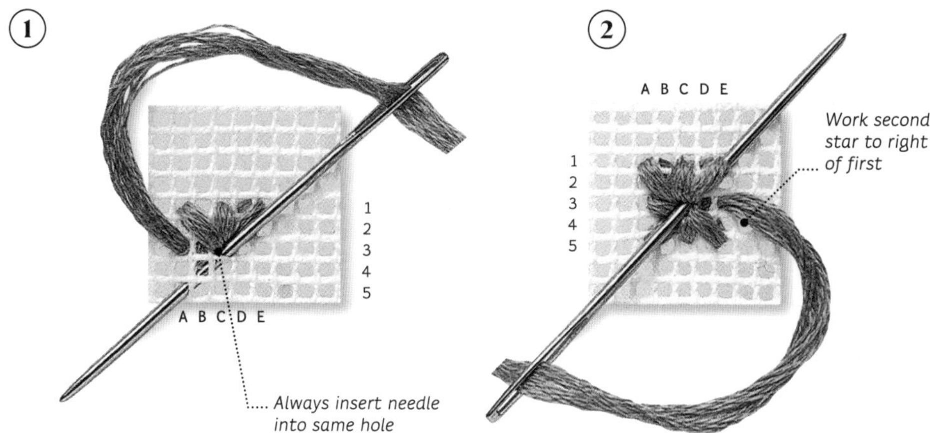

1
A B C D E
1 2 3 4 5
Always insert needle into same hole
2
A B C D E
1 2 3 4 5
Work second star to right of first

1 Start at top left with four straight stitches from **1E** to **3C**, **1C** to **3C**, **1A** to **3C**, and **3A** to **3C**.

2 Work four more stitches to complete the star, from **5A** to **3C**, **5C** to **3C**, **5E** to **3C**, and **3E** to **3C**. Begin the next star at **1E** and repeat steps 1 and 2 to continue. Work the next row directly below.

Eye

LEVEL
Intermediate

USES
Large scale filling

METHOD
Square blocks of straight stitch with open centres, outlined with back stitch

MATERIALS
Single canvas; thick thread; embroidery scissors

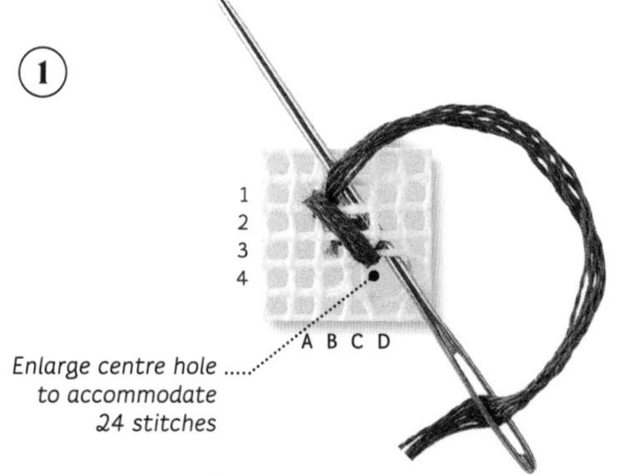

1
1 2 3 4
A B C D
Enlarge centre hole to accommodate 24 stitches

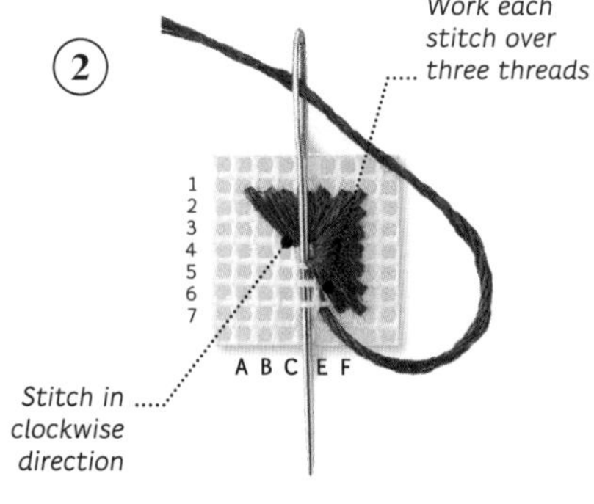

2
1 2 3 4 5 6 7
A B C E F
Work each stitch over three threads
Stitch in clockwise direction

1 Enlarge the hole at **4D** by carefully twisting the scissor point between the canvas threads. Work two straight stitches from **1A** to **4D** and **1B** to **4D**.

2 Make eleven more stitches into **4D**, starting from **1C**, **1D**, **1E**, **1F**, **1G**, **2G**, **3G**, **4G**, **5G**, **6G**, and **7G**. Work the second half as a mirror image of the first, then start the next block at **1G**. Finish off by outlining each square with back stitch (see p.40), worked over one thread.

Technique Variation

The back stitch outline can be worked in a contrasting colour to create a square grid pattern across the canvas.

Diamond Eye

LEVEL
Advanced

USES
Geometric background or filling for large areas

METHOD
Straight stitch diamonds with open centres, outlined in back stitch

MATERIALS
Single canvas; thick thread

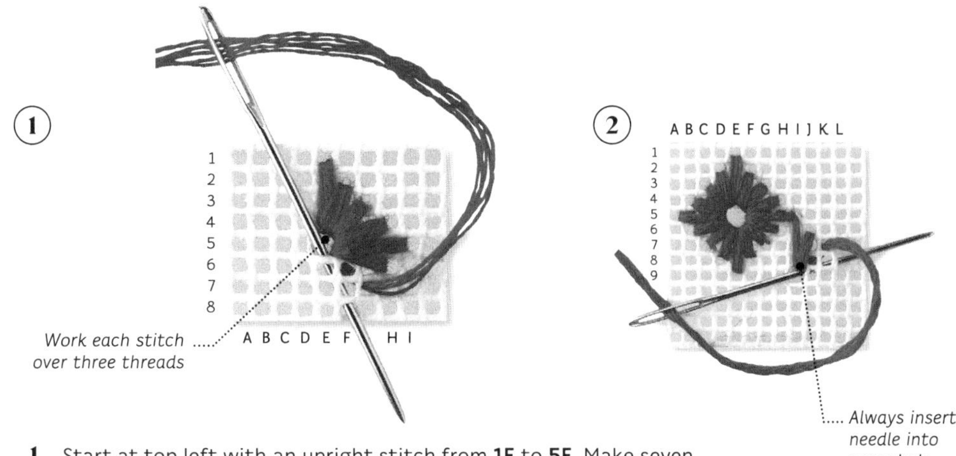

1
1 2 3 4 5 6 7 8
A B C D E F H I
Work each stitch over three threads
2
A B C D E F G H I J K L
1 2 3 4 5 6 7 8 9
Always insert needle into same hole

1 Start at top left with an upright stitch from **1E** to **5E**. Make seven more stitches into the same hole from **2F**, **3G**, **4H**, **5I**, **6H**, **7G**, **8F**, and **9E**, then work the second half of the diamond as a mirror image of the first.

2 Work the next block in the same way, starting with **5I** to **9I**, and stitch the next row directly below the first. When the area is complete, outline each diamond with back stitch (see p.40) worked over one thread, to conceal any canvas that may show through.

Fan

OTHER NAME
Ray stitch

LEVEL
Easy

USES
Fine textured filling

METHOD
Blocks of radiating stitches, worked in horizontal rows

MATERIALS
Single canvas; thick thread

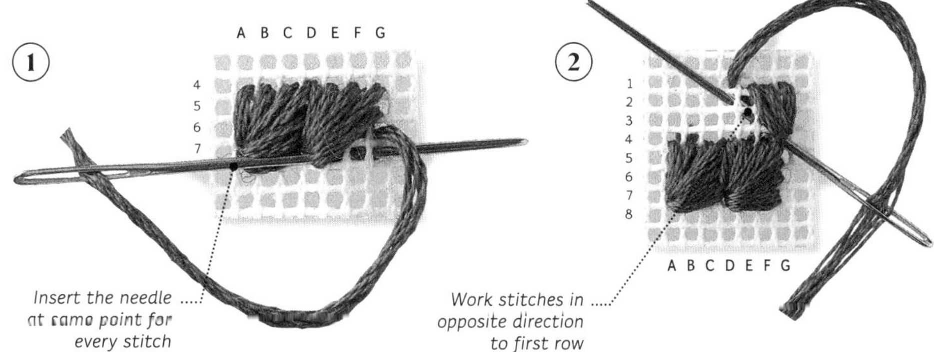

1
A B C D E F G
4 5 6 7
Insert the needle at same point for every stitch
2
1 2 3 4 5 6 7 8
A B C D E F G
Work stitches in opposite direction to first row

1 Starting at bottom left, make an upright stitch from **4A** to **7A**. Work six more stitches into the same hole, from **4B**, **4C**, **4D**, **5D**, **6D**, and **7D**, to form a square. Start the next block at **4D** to **7D** and continue working towards the right.

2 Work the next row directly above the first and stitch in the opposite direction, starting at **1G** to **4G**. Repeat steps 1 and 2 to continue.

Looped and Tied Needlepoint Stitches

Use these elaborate and complex stitches whenever unusual textures with a tactile element are required for backgrounds, or as part of a stitch sampler. They should all be worked in a frame on single canvas in a yarn that covers the background threads.

The tied and twisted stitches consist of long, straight stitches held down with shorter stitches to produce a dense, ridged surface. Looped Rya and Turkey stitch (named after the country where it originated) were traditionally used for creating entire rugs, but on a smaller scale are ideal for stitching raised areas within a design. The pile can be trimmed to give a plush or contoured finish to naturalistic animals, plants, and trees.

Rya

LEVEL
Advanced

USES
Looped or cut pile stitch for carpet-like texture

METHOD
Looped stitch worked over knitting needle in horizontal rows

MATERIALS
Single canvas; thick thread; knitting needle

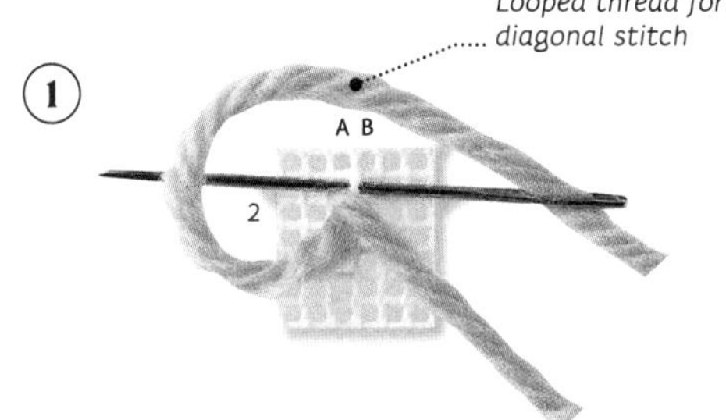

1
Looped thread forms diagonal stitch
A B
2

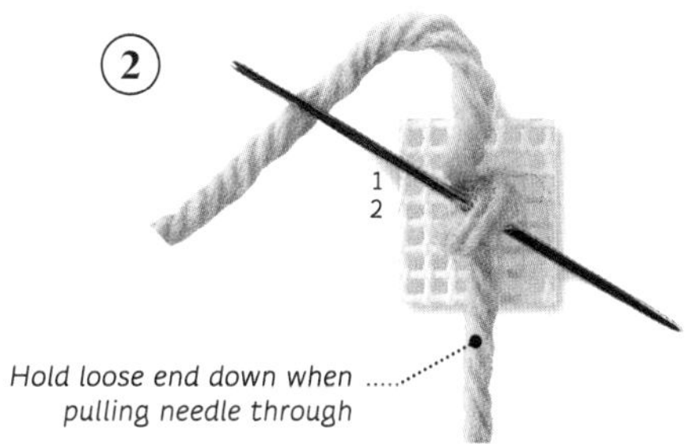

2
1
2
Hold loose end down when pulling needle through

1 Start at bottom left. Take the needle down at **1A** and bring it through at **2A**, leaving a short tail. Insert at **1B** and come back out at **1A**.

2 Pass the needle back under the diagonal loop and pull both ends tightly. Hold the knitting needle below the stitches and take the thread over and under it to form a loop.

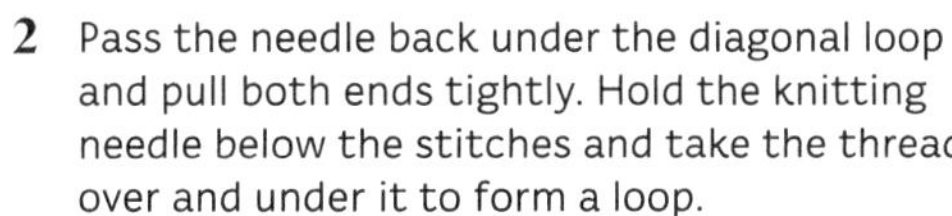

3 Repeat steps 1 and 2 to continue, starting the second stitch at **1B**. Work the next and subsequent rows directly above the first. Trim the pile if a tufted effect is required.

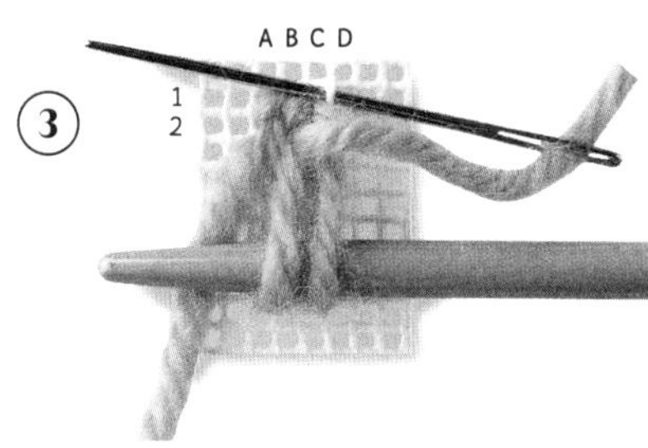

3
A B C D
1
2

Turkey

OTHER NAME
Ghiordes knot stitch

LEVEL
Advanced

USES
Tufted filling; background

METHOD
Looped stitch, with cut pile

MATERIALS
Single or rug canvas; thick thread or yarn

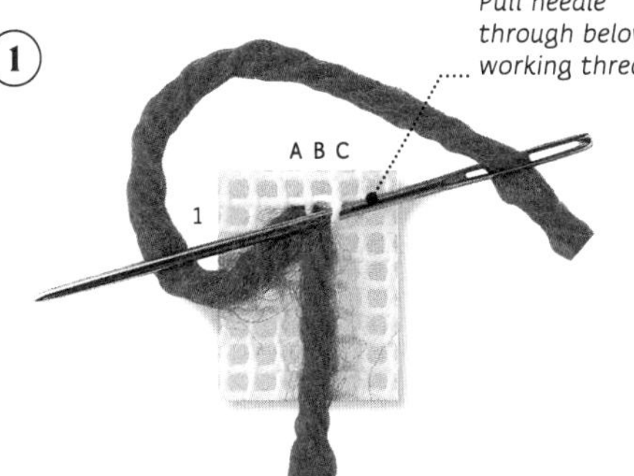

1
Pull needle through below working thread
A B C
1

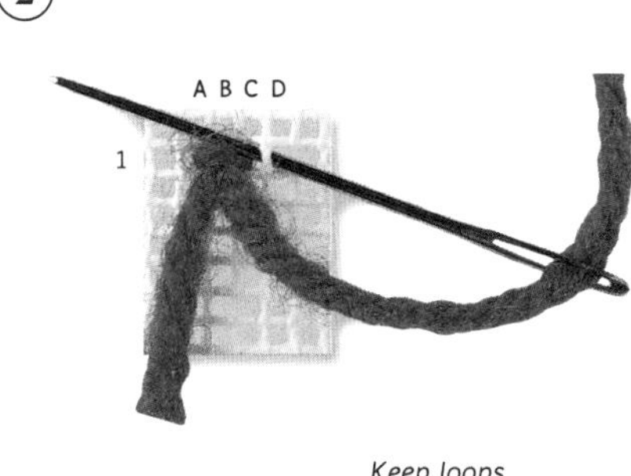

2
A B C D
1

1 Start at bottom left. Insert the needle at **1B** and bring it out at **1A**. Take it down at **1C** and come out again at **1B**.

2 Repeat step 1, starting at **1D**. Leave a loop of thread between the stitches.

3 Continue working towards the right, ensuring the loops are the same length. Work each following row one space above. When the stitching is complete, cut and trim the loops to create a pile.

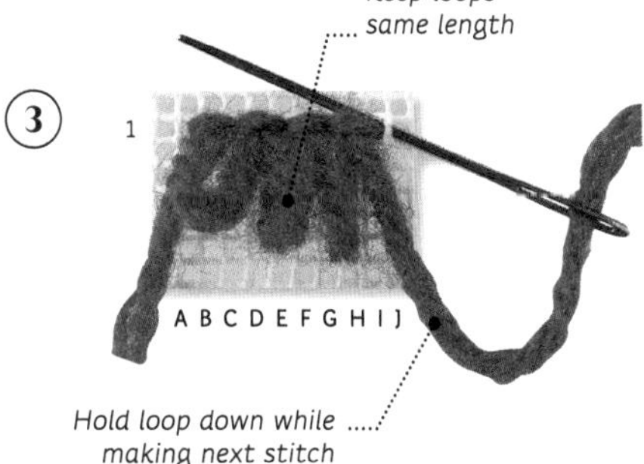

3
Keep loops same length
1
A B C D E F G H I J
Hold loop down while making next stitch

Houndstooth

LEVEL
Advanced

USES
Raised geometric filling

METHOD
Looped stitches worked over diagonal stitch, with upright cross infill

MATERIALS
Single canvas; thick and fine threads in two colours

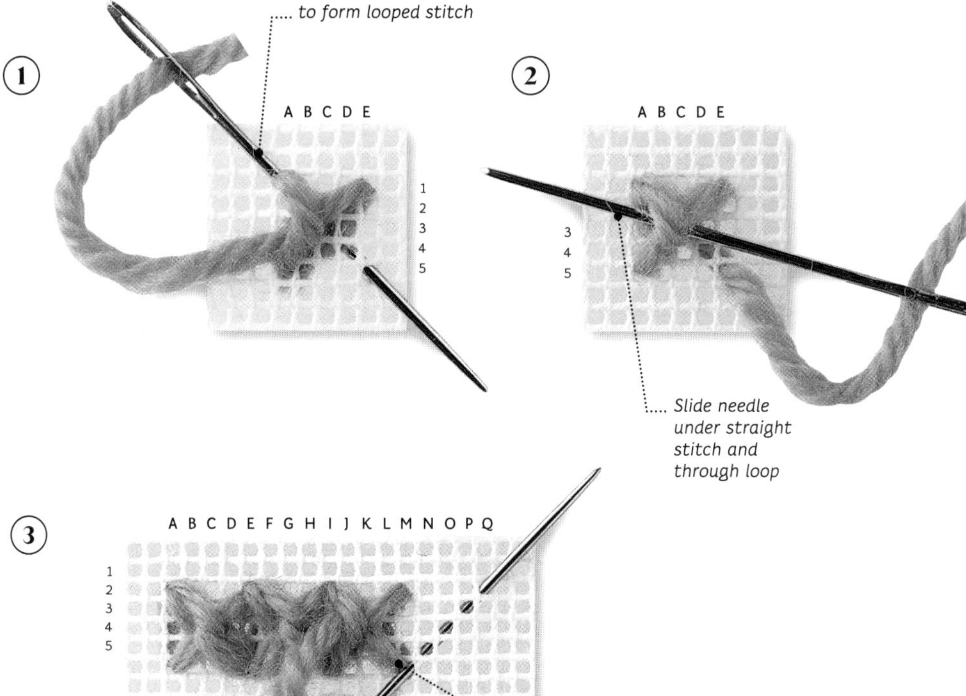
1
Re-insert needle at 1A to form looped stitch
A B C D E
1
2
3
4
5
2
A B C D E
3
4
5
Slide needle under straight stitch and through loop
3
A B C D E F G H I J K L M N O P Q
1
2
3
4
5
Work stitches in horizontal row

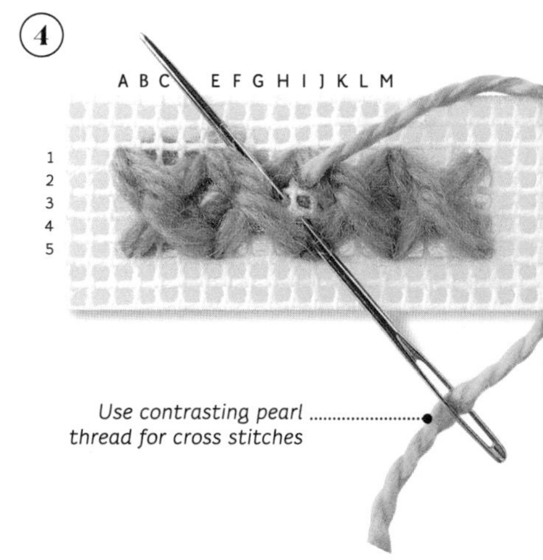
4
A B C E F G H I J K L M
1
2
3
4
5
Use contrasting pearl thread for cross stitches

1 Start at top left. Make a diagonal stitch from **5A** to **1E**. Bring the needle out at **1A**, then slide it under the stitch from left to right. Take the needle back down at **1A** and come up at **5E**.

2 Pass the needle under the diagonal stitch and through the centre of the looped stitch from right to left. Take it down again at **5E** to form a second looped stitch.

3 Repeat steps 1 to 3 to the end of the row, starting the next stitch at **1I**. Work the next and subsequent rows directly below the first.

4 Using a finer thread in a different colour, work a series of small upright crosses (see p.140) to fill in the spaces between the stitches. Make two straight stitches from **2I** to **4I** and **3H** to **3J**, and continue along the row.

Knitting

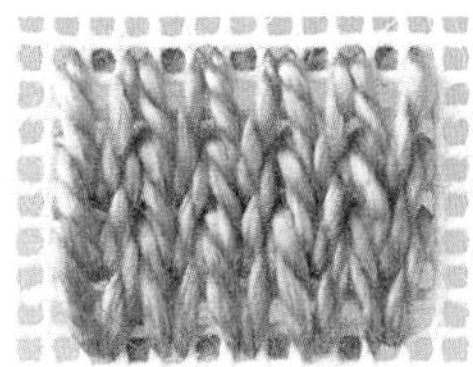

LEVEL
Easy

USES
Filling resembling knitted stocking stitch

METHOD
Overlapping diagonal stitches worked vertically in alternate directions

MATERIALS
Single canvas; any thread

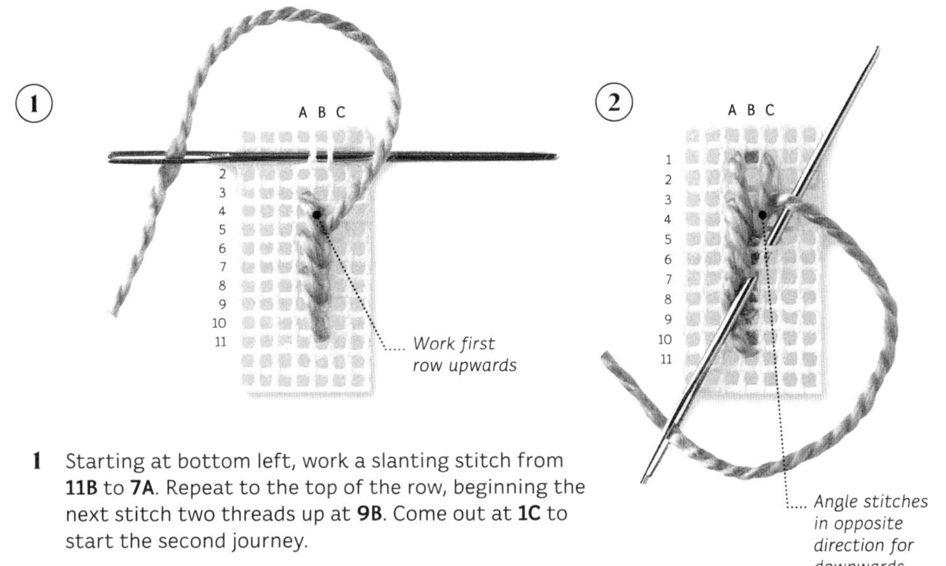
1
A B C
2
3
4
5
6
7
8
9
10
11
Work first row upwards
2
A B C
1
2
3
4
5
6
7
8
9
10
11
Angle stitches in opposite direction for downwards journey

1 Starting at bottom left, work a slanting stitch from **11B** to **7A**. Repeat to the top of the row, beginning the next stitch two threads up at **9B**. Come out at **1C** to start the second journey.

2 Work the second row downwards in the same way, starting with stitches from **1C** to **5B** and **3C** to **7B**. Repeat these two steps to fill the required area.

Old Wheatsheaf

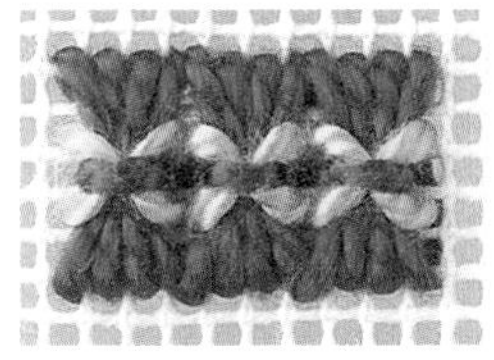

LEVEL
Advanced

USES
In single row as border; filling for large areas

METHOD
Sheaf filling variation with contrast interlacing

MATERIALS
Single canvas; any thread in two contrasting colours

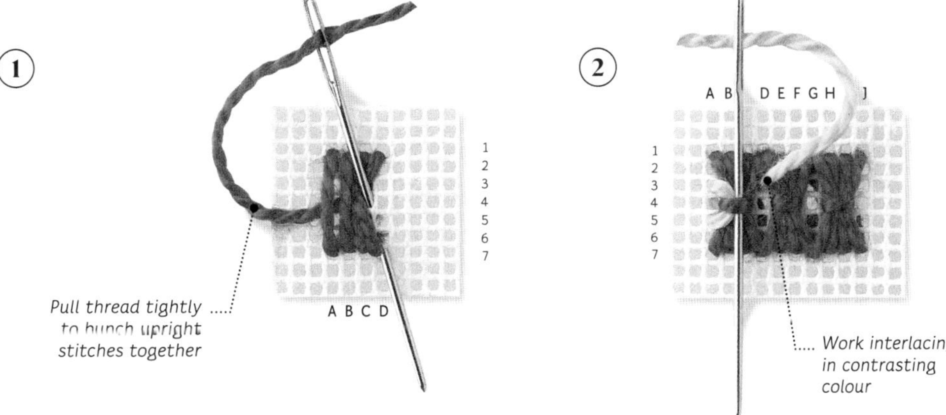
1
1
2
3
4
5
6
7
A B C D
Pull thread tightly to bunch upright stitches together
2
A B D E F G H J
1
2
3
4
5
6
7
Work interlacing in contrasting colour

1 Start at top left. Work four upright stitches from **7A** to **1A**, **7B** to **1B**, **7C** to **1C**, and **7D** to **1D**. Bring the needle up behind the stitches at **4B** and insert it at **4C** to make a tie stitch (see p.20). Start the next sheaf at **7D** to **1D**. Work the following rows directly below the first.

2 Using the second thread, bring the needle up at **3A**. Slide it downwards under the tie stitch, and insert at **5A**. Come up at **3D**, pass the needle under the tie stitch again, and take it down at **5D**. Lace each sheaf in the same way.

Tied Gobelin

OTHER NAME
Knotted stitch

LEVEL
Intermediate

USES
Filling with ridged texture

METHOD
Horizontal rows of interlocking tied diagonal stitches

MATERIALS
Single canvas; any thread

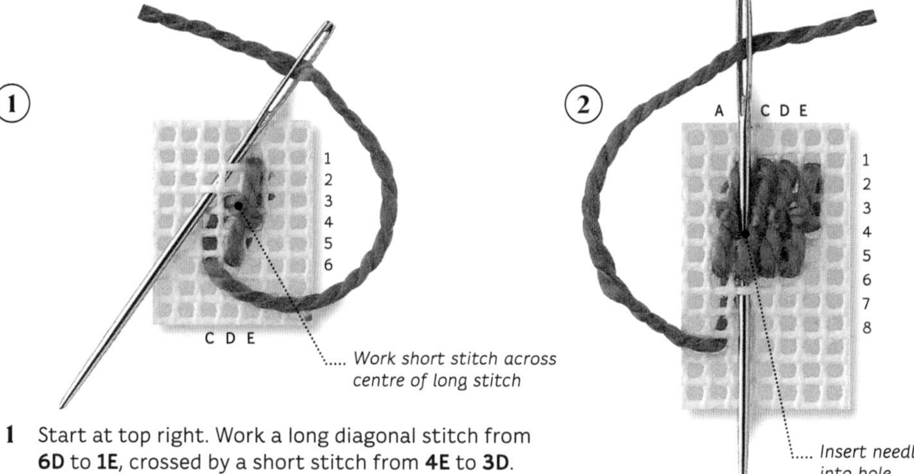

1
C D E
1 2 3 4 5 6
Work short stitch across centre of long stitch
2
A C D E
1 2 3 4 5 6 7 8
Insert needle into hole at base of tie stitch

1 Start at top right. Work a long diagonal stitch from **6D** to **1E**, crossed by a short stitch from **4E** to **3D**. Make the next pair of stitches from **6C** to **1D** and **3C** to **4D**, and continue working to the left.

2 The next row is stitched in the opposite direction. Work the first two stitches from **9A** to **4B** and **7B** to **6A** and repeat to the end of the row. Repeat these two rows to fill the required area.

French

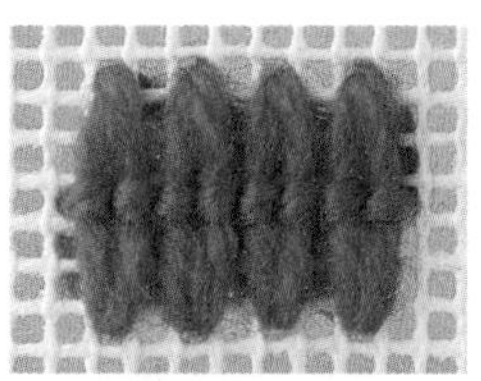

LEVEL
Intermediate

USES
Textured, ridged filling or background

METHOD
Pairs of tied upright stitches worked in horizontal rows

MATERIALS
Single canvas; any thread

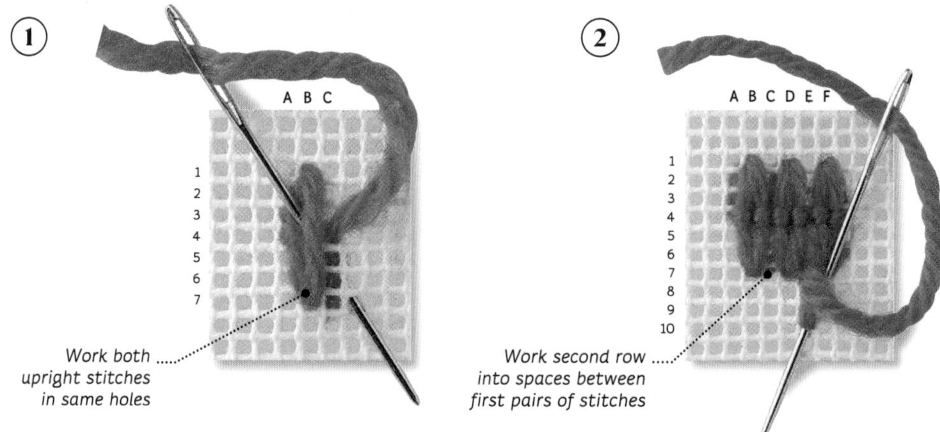

1
A B C
1 2 3 4 5 6 7
Work both upright stitches in same holes
2
A B C D E F
1 2 3 4 5 6 7 8 9 10
Work second row into spaces between first pairs of stitches

1 Start at top left. Make an upright stitch from **7B** to **1B** held down by a tie stitch (see p.20) from **4B** to **4A**. Work a second upright stitch from **7B** to **1B** and anchor it with a tie stitch from **4C** to **4B**. Continue making pairs of tied stitches to the end of the row.

2 Work the next row in the opposite direction, starting with an upright stitch from **10E** to **4E** and a tie stitch from **7E** to **7F**. Repeat these two rows to continue.

Pineapple

LEVEL
Advanced

USES
Two-coloured geometric filling for large areas

METHOD
Tied cross stitches worked over upright Gobelin stitch

MATERIALS
Single canvas; any thread in two colours

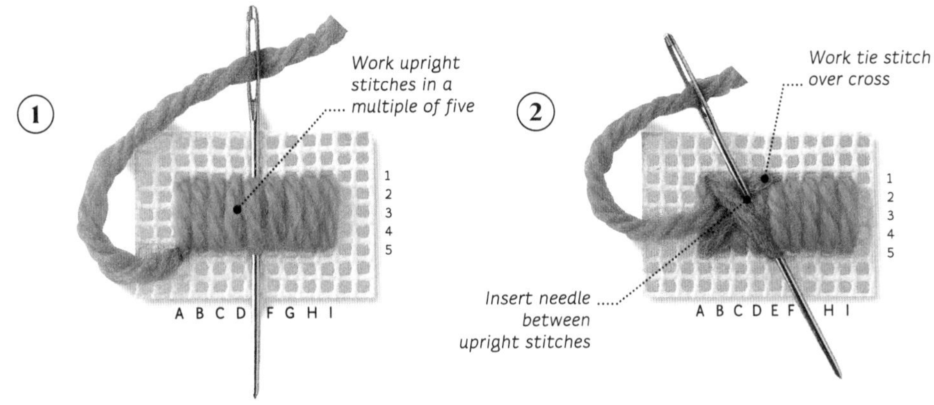

1
Work upright stitches in a multiple of five
A B C D F G H I
1 2 3 4 5
2
Work tie stitch over cross
Insert needle between upright stitches
A B C D E F H I
1 2 3 4 5

1 Start at top left and work a row of upright Gobelin stitch (see p.119) starting at **5A** to **1A**. Using the second thread, make a diagonal stitch from **5A** to **1E** and come out at **5E**.

2 Insert the needle at **1A** to complete the cross, then make a horizontal tie stitch (see p.20) from **3B** to **3D**. Continue working crosses along the row, then work subsequent rows directly below.

Arrow

LEVEL
Intermediate

USES
Textured filling; in single rows as a border

METHOD
Angled variation of sheaf filling, worked in rows

MATERIALS
Single canvas; any thread

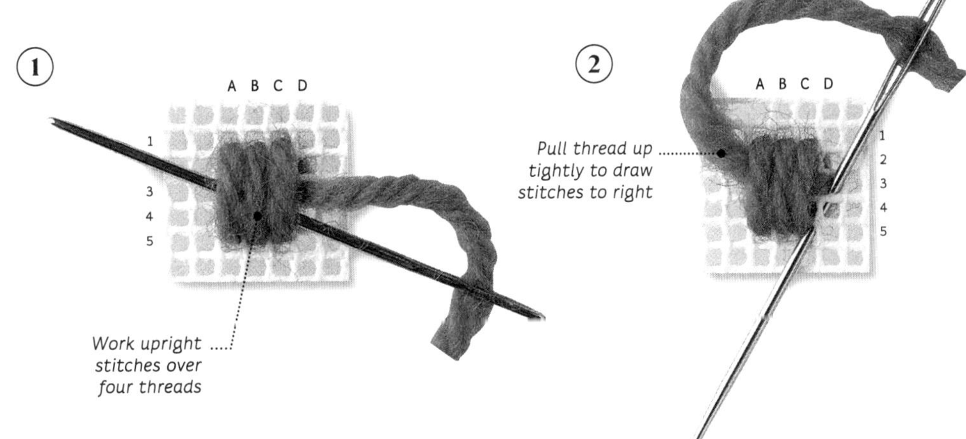

1
A B C D
1 3 4 5
Work upright stitches over four threads
2
A B C D
1 2 3 4 5
Pull thread up tightly to draw stitches to right

1 Starting in the top left corner, work three upright stitches from **5A** to **1A**, **5B** to **1B**, and **5C** to **1C**. Bring the needle out at **3D** and slide it under the three stitches from right to left.

2 Take the needle back down at **3D** and bring it out at **5C**, ready to make the next upright stitch. Repeat steps 1 and 2 to continue, and work the following rows directly below the first.

Index

D

E

F

G

H

I

J

K

L

M

N

O

P

Q

R

Author's acknowledgments

No writer works in isolation, and this book came about through the joint skills of the art and editorial teams at both Dorling Kindersley and C&B Packaging.

I am indebted to Samantha Gray, who first suggested my name to the publishers. Nigel Duffield, Mary Lindsay, Sarah Hall, and Cathy Shilling at DK have given me every encouragement, along with their invaluable guidance and enthusiasm, from the outset.

Managing editor Kate Yeates has been my mainstay: her dedication and constant good humour have helped me through to the end of the project. Special thanks also to Roger Bristow and Helen Collins at C&B Packaging for their invaluable creative input, to Sam Lloyd for patiently photographing all the many stitch samples and to Heather Dewhurst for editing my text so meticulously.

Thanks especially to Zara Anvari and Amy Slack, who have guided me through this updated edition.

This edition is dedicated to my son, Alex Haydn-Williams.

Publisher's acknowledgments

For their work on the first edition, DK would like to thank DMC Creative World Ltd for supplying the materials and equipment used to create the step-by-step examples and finished stitch samples. For their work on previous editions, DK would also like to thank Mary Lindsay, Sarah Hall, Michelle Thomas, Jason Little, Stephanie Jackson, Jonathan Metcalf, Nigel Duffield, as well as Nicola Munro, Cathy Shilling, Christopher Gordon, Andy Crawford, Steve Gorton for additional assistance. Thanks also to the team at C&B Packaging Ltd: Kate Yeates, Heather Dewhurst, Roger Bristow, Helen Collins, Suzanne Metcalfe-Megginson, Bill Mason, and Sampson Lloyd.

For their work on the 2022 edition, DK would like to thank Andrew Pinder for his illustration work, Ruth Jenkinson for additional photography, and Francesco Piscitelli for proofreading. Thanks also to Evelin Kasikov for her beautiful hand-stitched jacket design.

Picture credits

The publisher would like to thank the following for their kind permission to reproduce their photographs:

(Key: a-above; b-below/bottom; c-centre; f-far; l-left; r-right; t-top)

8 © The Metropolitan Museum of Art: Purchase, Mrs. Jackson Burke Gift, 1979 (br). Powerhouse Museum / Museum of Applied Arts & Sciences: Collection: Museum of Applied Arts and Sciences. Gift of Robert Swieca, 2011. Photographer Marinco Kojdanovski (t). 9 Alamy Stock Photo: CMA / BOT (clb)

All other images © Dorling Kindersley

DK
Penguin
Random
House

DK UK
Project Editor Amy Slack
Senior Designer Glenda Fisher
Design Assistant Eloise Grohs
Production Editor David Almond
Production Controller Luca Bazzoli
Jacket Designer Evelin Kasikov
Jacket Editor Jasmin Lennie
Senior Acquisitions Editor Zara Anvari
Design Manager Marianne Markham
Art Director Maxine Pedliham
Publisher Katie Cowan

DK India
Editor Ankita Gupta
Art Editors Mohd Zishan, Bhagyashree Nayak
DTP Designer Rajdeep Singh
Managing Editor Soma B. Chowdhury
Managing Art Editor Ivy Sengupta
Pre-production Manager Sunil Sharma
Editorial Head Glenda Fernandes
Design Head Malavika Talukder

This edition published in 2022
First published in Great Britain in 1999 by
Dorling Kindersley Limited
DK, One Embassy Gardens, 8 Viaduct Gardens,
London, SW11 7BW

The authorised representative in the EEA is
Dorling Kindersley Verlag GmbH. Arnulfstr. 124,
80636 Munich, Germany

10 9 8 7 6 5 4 3 2 1
001–333474–Oct/2022

A CIP catalogue record for this book
is available from the British Library.
ISBN: 978-0-2415-9325-7

Printed and bound in Slovakia

For the curious
www.dk.com

MIX
Paper from
responsible sources
FSC
www.fsc.org
FSC™ C018179